REWRITING THE GERMAN PAST ——

REWRITING THE GERMAN PAST

History and Identity in the New Germany

Edited by
REINHARD ALTER
and PETER MONTEATH

HUMANITIES PRESS
NEW JERSEY

This collection first published in 1997 by
Humanities Press International, Inc.
165 First Avenue, Atlantic Highlands, New Jersey 07716

This collection © 1997 by Humanities Press International, Inc.

Library of Congress Cataloging-in-Publication Data
Rewriting the German past : history and identity in the new Germany /
    edited by Peter Monteath and Reinhard Alter.
        p.   cm.
    Includes bibliographical references and index.
    ISBN 0-391-04025-1. — ISBN 0-391-04026-X (pbk.)
    1. Germany—History—Unification, 1990.   2. Germany—Ethnic
relations.   3. Political culture—Germany.   4. Germany (East)—
Politics and government—1982–1990.   I. Monteath, Peter.
II. Alter, Reinhard.
DD290.29.R48   1997
943.087′9—dc21   96-49082
                                                                    CIP

Printed in the United States of America

10   9   8   7   6   5   4   3   2   1

CONTENTS ─────────────

ACKNOWLEDGMENTS —

In 1992 the editors of this volume invited scholars from Europe, the United States, and Australia to gather at the University of Western Australia in Perth to consider the effects of unification on the (re)writing of German history. Perth's geographical location, it was hoped, would provide some distance—and not only in the literal sense—from the emotional and disputatious climate that prevailed in the new Germany.

That conference, held in September 1993, was generously supported by the Deutsche Forschungsgemeinschaft, the International Office of the University of Western Australia, and the Office of the Vice-Chancellor, Professor Fay Gale. In the wake of the conference, the editors, endeavoring to reinforce the interdisciplinary scope of the project, invited a number of scholars from the United States and from western and eastern Germany to contribute essays on aspects of the unification process. With the exception of the chapters by Lutz Niethammer and Hermann Kurthen, all the contributions were written for this volume. Lutz Niethammer's essay is an abridged version of his contribution (in German) to Antonia Grunenberg's collection *Welche Geschichte wählen wir?* (1992), and Hermann Kurthen's "Defining the Fatherland" is a revised and extended version of his article "Germany at the Crossroads: National Identity and the Challenge of Immigration," which appeared in the *International Migration Review*, vol. 29 (1995).

The editors are grateful to the contributors and to all those who helped make the Perth conference a success.

Introduction

PETER MONTEATH and REINHARD ALTER

1.

The revolutions in the German Democratic Republic (GDR) and other parts of eastern Europe were a bewildering experience for many historians. In 1989 of all years, in the midst of the bicentennial commemoration of the French Revolution, they might have been alert to the possibility of revolution in Europe. At this time more than any other, one might have expected a heightened awareness of the capacity of popularly held resentments and hopes to bring about sudden and radical changes. However, the extraordinary revolutionary potential in eastern and central Europe in the late 1980s—above all, the widespread expressions of popular discontent in the form of mass gatherings and protests, the large-scale exodus from the GDR to the West, and Gorbachev's obvious disinclination to interfere—went unrecognized by almost everyone, including many of the participants themselves.

More disconcerting than historians' failure to predict the sudden demise of the Soviet Empire and the collapse of the communist regimes of eastern Europe was the fact that they had not even allowed for the possibility that such changes might occur in the foreseeable, let alone the immediate, future. In this respect they were not much different from most people, among whom only a very small number could credibly claim foreknowledge of these revolutionary events.

Suggestions that historians were rendered speechless by their failure to predict the events of 1989 are exaggerated, however.[1] Having digested the initial shock and come to terms with their failure as forecasters (which, after all, is not their role), historians soon got on with the task of explaining the past and illuminating its links with the present. Failure to prognosticate by no means implied an unwillingness to analyze. One obvious approach was to see the events of

1

1989–90 in Germany in the light of comparable events in German and European history; the establishment of points of similarity and of difference is, after all, a commonly used strategy for achieving historical understanding.

As chance would have it, the central and symbolically the most loaded event of 1989–90, the fall of the Berlin Wall, occurred on probably the most notorious date in modern German history. Presumably, the revolutionary events of 1918, the attempted putsch of 1923, and Crystal Night in 1938 were not at the forefront of Socialist Unity Party secretary Günter Schabowski's mind when he announced the lifting of travel restrictions for GDR citizens on 9 November 1989. Although the symbolic importance of 9 November could not slip by historians unnoticed, other kinds of comparisons promised to be more fruitful and instructive. Above all, historians were eager to position the events of 1989–90 in Germany in two broader contexts. In the first place, the revolutionary changes in the GDR demanded to be seen in the context of the eastern European revolutions of that year. Second, the unexpected sequel to the revolution—namely, the unification of Germany on 3 October 1990—could be comprehended in the context of earlier attempts at German unification.

In terms of revolutionary history, the most obvious point of comparison was with the French Revolution, not only because of the fortuitous timing but also because of the nature and the perceived historical magnitude of the events in question. Adopting this comparative perspective allowed a number of striking points of similarity to be observed. In France in 1789, as in eastern Europe in 1989, the revolutionary movements were genuinely popular movements, unthinkable without the enthusiastic participation of broad sections of the populations concerned. In both cases, large numbers were mobilized in protest against regimes that were widely perceived to have forfeited all claim to legitimacy. In the outrage against existing conditions, even some of the minor details are uncannily similar—the occupation of the *Stasi* headquarters in Berlin in January 1990, for example, has been seen as the modern equivalent of the storming of the Bastille.[2] Moreover, the ideological principles that converted basic resentment into support for the creation of a new order in France in 1789 and eastern Europe in 1989 were remarkably similar. The classical liberal plea for the trinity of "liberty, equality, fraternity" was just as relevant and as problematic in 1989 as it had been two centuries earlier.

In 1989 as in 1789, the revolutionary movements acquired a national impetus. Historical orthodoxy views the French Revolution as the seminal event in the development of European nationalism, as claims for popular rule led inevitably to demands to define the populace and as the surviving anciens régimes of continental Europe waged war against revolutionary France. Two hundred years later, revolutionary movements throughout eastern Europe were almost synonymous with national attempts at liberation from the oppressive but by now decaying Soviet Empire. The case of the GDR was unique, simply because of the existence of another German state outside the Soviet sphere of influence. For this reason, the national dimension of the revolution was at first retarded, but from an initial position of only marginal significance, it was to become the dominant feature as the course of the revolution changed.

In other respects, the revolutions of 1989 were notably different from the French and other European revolutions. With the exception of Romania, they were largely bloodless. Gorbachev's candid proclamation of the retreat of Soviet interests from their eastern European sphere of influence, together with the rapid evaporation of political will among the governments concerned, meant that no "Chinese solution" was applied. The relative peacefulness of the revolutions has indeed led some to question whether the term "revolution" is appropriate at all. Germans often prefer the much less emotive term *Wende* (turn) to describe events. Timothy Garton Ash has proposed the neologism "refolution" to indicate the combination of revolutionary and reformist elements at work, especially in Hungary and Poland.[3] The relatively nonviolent quality of the revolution, however, should not minimize the profundity of the changes it heralded in Germany and elsewhere. In all cases, the events of 1989 led to changes not just of governments but of entire political systems and to the substitution of free markets for planned economies, not to mention the profound social, cultural, and psychological changes that inevitably followed. Nevertheless, the fact that such far-reaching changes could be introduced without bloodshed allows room for some faith in human progress and the hope that history does not merely repeat itself.

In their international dimensions as well, the revolutions of 1989 were vastly different from previous European revolutions. The crucial role of the Soviet withdrawal from its eastern European sphere of influence has already been alluded to. This Soviet tolerance and goodwill toward eastern Europe, and more especially toward Germany, were not unique. The revolutionary movements were almost universally welcomed and encouraged. Moreover, there was widespread optimism concerning the sort of international environment that could result from such political changes. Instead of a continent divided in two through Germany, the eastern European revolutions, together with the unification of Germany, offered the opportunity for the creation of a united Europe that was committed to the upholding of liberal democratic principles. This was in stark contrast to the international context of the French Revolution, which incurred the wrath of much of Europe and led to its deep and lasting division. The same could be said of the 1917 Russian Revolution. But the 1989 revolutions presented the possibility of a radically different, unifying outcome. Instead of causing the division of Europe, they held the promise of uniting the continent. As Jürgen Kocka pointed out, "as a consequence of the revolutions of 1989, in terms of conceptions of economic order, constitutional principles and official political philosophy, Europe is less fragmented than at any other point in the last 200 years."[4]

There are certainly strong ideological similarities between 1989 events and earlier European revolutions; the key difference, however, is that by 1989, the ideals that inspired the overthrow of governments could hardly be described as radical or new. On the contrary, the ideological content of the revolutions was old hat. Liberal as well as national ideals had inspired earlier revolutions on German soil, most notably in 1848–49. They had played an important role in the revolutionary aftermath of the First World War, culminating in the creation of a German Republic based on liberal democratic principles. But in Germany, with its propensity for turning points that fail to turn (to borrow A. J. P. Taylor's dictum about the 1848 revolution),[5] and indeed throughout eastern Europe, liberal ideals had proved less than durable. Apart from passionately held notions of a "third way" between liberalism and communism and hope for the realization of a "Swedish model," the revolutions of 1989 were marked by a commitment to the revolutionary principles of an earlier era. These were "catch-up revolutions," as eastern Europeans struggled finally to achieve the advantages, both materially and in terms of a democratic political culture, of which their histories had deprived them.[6] As Timothy Garton Ash noted wistfully: "The ideas whose time has come are old, familiar, well-tested ones. (It is the new ideas whose time has passed.)"[7] Conservatives predictably rejoiced in the failure of these new ideas and in the repositioning of 1917 and its Bolshevik Revolution, which Marxist orthodoxy viewed as signaling the end of the era of bourgeois preeminence and the first step in the creation of a communist utopia, as a mere precursor to the events of 1989. For some, this signaled the final discrediting of all systems of utopian thought; for others, the apparent triumph of liberal capitalism implied the very end of history.[8]

Although German historians were sensitive to the international dimensions of the revolutionary events in the East, they were especially eager to place them in a national historical context. Germany, after all, was a special case. Here it was not just a matter of the achievement of a liberal democratic revolution in a former eastern bloc country. The German revolution led unexpectedly to unification, achieved within eleven months of the fall of the Berlin Wall. As with the revolutionary events within the GDR that preceded it, the course of events took place with breathtaking and bewildering rapidity. Historians and others again looked to historical parallels to make sense of the unexpected. Indeed, the public debate about unification, both within Germany and beyond its borders, was frequently couched in historical terms. As Konrad Jarausch noted: "Unification offered a return to and an escape from history. The debate about the legitimacy and form of unity was saturated with references to the past."[9] For the opponents of unification, references to similarities with previous unifications (1871 was the obvious point of comparison, but allusions to the 1938 *Anschluß* could be used to add some heat to the debate) helped justify their fear of repeating past mistakes. Supporters of unification dwelt on those things that distinguished the situation in 1989–90 from less felicitous attempts at nationhood in the past.

The similarities between 1871 and 1990 are manifold. Though the degrees of sophistication vary enormously, both the Second Reich created in 1871 and the unified Germany of 1990 are constitutional states constructed according to federal principles and with some commitment (in the case of the Second Reich in only a rudimentary form) to social welfare. These elements had also been present in Weimar Germany but did not manage to survive the "national revolution" of 1933. Furthermore, in 1871 as in 1990, they were established within the political framework of the so-called *Kleindeutschland* (Small Germany) solution to "the German problem," that is, without the incorporation of Austrian territory into a Greater Germany.

Comparisons of the ideologies that motivated and framed the unifications of 1871 and 1990 are difficult but instructive. Since the 1850s, a pragmatic *Realpolitik* had been able to justify itself as the only effective antidote to a weak-willed and vacillating liberalism that had been ingloriously defeated in 1848–49 and remained very much on the defensive throughout the Second Reich. But although the ideological cornerstone that was laid at the founding of a unified, modern German nation on 3 October 1990 was the liberal one that had been conspicuously absent at the unification of 1871, the political culture of the united Germany in the early 1990s manifested considerable confusion and discord. Fault lines appeared not only between East and West but also within the western part of Germany. The antiutopian campaigns of publicists and historians such as Joachim Fest, Wolf Jobst Siedler, or Arnulf Baring[10] heralded administrative and technical efficiency as the cardinal virtue needed to rescue the moribund economy and purge the corrupted political culture of the GDR. The belief in a more or less automatic correlation between economic success and political democracy—which had, to some extent, been shaken by the oil crises of 1973 and 1979—regained much of its currency. The propensity to regard the free market "as the cure for all ills, social and political as well as economic"[11] was clearly demonstrated by the overwhelming support in the eastern part of Germany for the Christian Democrats at the decisive elections of 18 March 1990. The election result (192 seats for the Christian Democratic Union [CDU] and 88 seats for the Social Democrats) reflected the eagerness of many East Germans at this early stage of the unification process to trust in the capacity of the market to repair the East German economy without major social costs.

In some important respects, the absorption of the GDR into the Federal Republic continued the Prussian tradition of an administratively steered "revolution from above," and, like previous German attempts at revolution, the events of 1989–90 "strangely combined revolutionary and national with restorative elements."[12] But whereas the efforts of liberals in the German Empire, especially since the 1890s, to adapt to a rapidly advancing capitalist industrial modernity were hampered by the legacy of German liberalism's genesis as a preindustrial movement,[13] the problem in 1989–90 was not so much a lack of self-confidence but rather an overweening belief in the capacity of the functional elites to synchronize an "antiquated" GDR with the modern, liberal democracy that had been consummated in the Federal Republic. No doubt the polemical tone that could be heard in the assertion of the superiority of the West over the failed socialist experiment in the GDR was partially motivated by growing anxiety about the effects of the unification process on the already precarious balance between the "social" and the "market" elements of the social market economy, which many West Germans saw, and continue to see, as the key to the economic and political success of the Federal Republic.

The geopolitical differences between 1871 and 1990 outweigh the similarities. Most obviously, key institutions such as the army and the civil service had not been subject to parliamentary control in Bismarck's Empire. Moreover, the unification of 1990 took place with the consent and even goodwill of Germany's European neighbors, near and distant. Indeed, without such consent, in particular from the Soviet Union, the unification of 1990 is totally inconceivable. It also helps explain the relatively peaceful course of unification in 1990, which was in stark contrast to the series of wars that Bismarck had so craftily precipitated to achieve unification in 1870–71. The nation he created was much larger than present-day Germany and the population within its borders more heterogeneous than today. Then, there were significant minorities of Poles, Danes, Alsatians, and Lorrainians. German borders were disputed and openly contested at various points between 1871 and 1945. With the exception of the Kohl government's prevarication in 1990 on the issue of the border with Poland, the borders of contemporary Germany appear stable and incontestable; its minorities are a result of migration, and they are therefore uninterested in questions of territorial revision. The united Germany of 1990, as Heinrich August Winkler pointed out days before unification, sees itself as complete and, with the exception of a number of officials in some of the organizations representing ethnic Germans driven from their homelands in eastern Europe, has no unsolved nationality problems.[14]

The territorial differences between Germany in 1871 and Germany in 1990 raise a minor question of terminology. Historians often speak of the "reunification" of Germany, since a unitary German nation-state had already been in existence from 1871 to 1945, albeit one whose borders changed a number of times. At the same time, there is a good argument for the use of the term "unification" in reference to 1990, since it brought together two states that had never previously been connected and whose combined territory did not correspond to any previous geopolitical configuration. Both terms are acceptable and in this volume are used interchangeably; nevertheless, the fact that the choice of terminology is an issue at all is a gauge of how intensely historical the unification debate has become.

To what extent the society contained within the borders of Germany after 3 October 1990 differs from that of Bismarck's Germany is a much more sensitive issue. The superficial differences are marked. The dominant conservative elites of the Second Reich who doggedly blocked all attempts at any far-reaching democratization and who diverted attention from internal tension through reckless foreign policy ventures have long since disappeared. German society is overtly much more democratic; its commitment to upholding Western liberal values domestically, and peace and stability internationally, is scarcely questioned. Nevertheless, the temptation remains to identify elements of continuity and consistency in German history. In particular, some critical observers of the unification process have raised fears about a certain consistency of German character that appears to survive any apparent political turning points. This was evident in the year of unification. In July 1990, British Prime Minister Margaret Thatcher invited a group of prominent experts on Germany (Timothy Garton Ash, Gordon Craig, Hugh Trevor-Roper, Fritz Stern, Norman Stone, and George Urban) to discuss the implications of a united Germany. This was a private meeting, but a memorandum prepared by Thatcher's private secretary, Charles Powell, was leaked to *The Independent on Sunday* and to *Der Spiegel*. Not all those present were convinced that the memorandum was an accurate reflection of the proceedings; apparently, Powell's Tory views played more than just a mediating role. Interesting nonetheless was the memorandum's recording of typically German attributes from the past that, it was thought, could be expected to manifest themselves in the future: "their insensitivity to the feelings of others (most noticeable in their behaviour over the Polish border), their obsession with themselves, a strong inclination to self-pity, and a longing to be liked. Some even less flattering attributes were also mentioned as an abiding part of the German character: in alphabetical order, *angst*, aggressiveness, assertiveness, bullying, egotism, inferiority complex, sentimentality. Two further aspects of the German character were cited as reasons for concern about the future. First, a capacity for excess, to overdo things, to kick over the traces. Second, a tendency to over-estimate their own strength and capabilities."[15] The conclusions reached, at least as Powell recorded them, were that "we should be nice to the Germans. But even the optimists had some unease, not for the present and the immediate future, but for what might lie further down the road than we can yet see."[16] What lies further down the road is not necessarily indicated by the more conspicuous manifestations of right-wing radicalism in the shape of violent skinheads, but by the less palpable and more complex attitudes of the majority and by the social and cultural factors shaping them. Historiography, as Jürgen Kocka has suggested, needs to concern itself less with the dramatic turning points in history and historical experience, which the events of 1989 and 1990 initially seemed to call for, and more with history as structural continuity.[17]

2.

This volume examines the implications of the dramatic political events of 1989–90 for the writing of German history. From a variety of perspectives, the contributions assess the impact of unification on historiography. In doing so, they raise a broad range of questions:

the consequences of an altered perspective, the role of historical writing in the formation of (a new?) national identity, the ways in which the GDR is being consigned to the past, the institutional ramifications of practicing history in the unified Germany. The contributors represent a variety of ideological standpoints and cultural backgrounds. Nonetheless they share the belief that historical writing will do far more than merely reflect the changed historical circumstances: it will play an important role in deciding the kind of Germany that establishes itself in the heart of Europe.

Konrad Jarausch's contribution introduces many of the issues and options confronting historians since the fall of the Berlin Wall. A central issue that he identifies is that of the nation-state and its place in German history. This question is, of course, not peculiar to postunification historical debate. As Jarausch indicates, the role of the German nation-state was debated extensively by historians in both the Federal Republic and the GDR before 1989. From the viewpoint of a divided Germany, it seemed logical to condemn the German nation-state as a catastrophic political arrangement that had plunged Europe into two world wars and an unparalleled act of genocide. Though the approaches differed markedly, historians in both the Federal Republic of Germany (FRG) and the GDR highlighted the failings of the unified Germany as it had existed from 1871 to 1945 and moved to revise the analytical category of the nation-state in their work. The theoretical justification for this was obvious enough in the GDR, with its wholesale and exclusive adoption of Marxist theory, but in the Federal Republic as well, partly under the influence of Fritz Fischer's groundbreaking work in the early 1960s, it expressed itself in a focus on social history and a devotion to *Alltagsgeschichte* (the history of everyday life) in the 1970s and 1980s. According to conservative critics of this dominant tendency in German historiography, it blunted any alertness to the possibility of radical political changes at a national or international level. Had there not been such an abandonment of *histoire événementielle* and the analytical category of the nation, they argued, the events of 1989–90 might have been predicted by historians rather than greeted with stunned silence.

Several years before unification, the *Historikerstreit* (historians' dispute), triggered in the middle of 1986, signaled a tendency toward the renationalization of German historiography. Although Ernst Nolte and his supporters in the *Historikerstreit* appeared to have been defeated intellectually, history in a sense supported their cause. Jarausch detects the postunification rehabilitation of the nation-state as an analytical category, a tendency that is likely to lead away from social

history and back to a more traditional form of political and diplomatic history. It might also engender a more positive reevaluation of
the history of the unified Germany that existed from 1871 to 1945.
From this perspective, a united Germany looks more "normal" than
it did from the pre-1990 viewpoint of a divided Germany. Such a
trend is resisted by adherents of the political Left, who, as during the
Historikerstreit, warn of the dangers of a revived nationalism and insist on the continuing relevance of critical historical approaches to
the Second and Third Reichs.

Jarausch points to the implications of these developments for the
question of national identity, which is taken up in greater detail in
the contributions by Hans-Georg Betz and Hermann Kurthen. In Germany as much as in any other country, historians have been accorded
the role of defining and promoting a sense of national identity. It is
in what Eric Hobsbawm and Terence Ranger have labeled "the invention of tradition" that the origins of the modern historical profession
in Germany are to be found.[18] This certainly applies to nineteenth-
century Germany and remains relevant through the Weimar and Nazi
periods. Although the postwar German states made earnest attempts
to establish their identities by appealing to ideals that were distinctly
internationalist, the temptation to claim the status of heir to an indis-
putably German past was never fully overcome. This temptation became especially evident in the final decade of the GDR, when historians
of a so-called socialist German nation went to considerable lengths to
project their state as the legitimate heir to all progressive tendencies
in the German past. Similarly, in the Federal Republic in the 1980s,
proponents of the creation of a positive national identity asserted that
turning to history could offer some refuge in the face of increasing
uncertainties.

The closeness of the link between history and identity in Gemany
is itself historically explicable. Germany was, in Helmut Plessner's
words, "the belated nation," not achieving political unity until relatively late in the nineteenth century. And even then, the German nation was unable to enjoy long periods of stability. Lacking institutional
and territorial stability over a prolonged period, Germany's need to
locate a shared identity in a common past was particularly acute.
Whether German attempts to establish national identity by locating a
common history have been successful is a contentious issue. Certainly
from the perspective of 1945, these attempts could only be seen as
disastrous. Under Hitler, German "identity" was developed to the point
of a murderous national chauvinism that was ultimately self-destruc-
tive, to say nothing of its horrendous impact on the rest of the globe.

It was little wonder, then, that at an official level the two postwar German states undertook the construction of "postnational" identities. As a socialist state, the GDR understood itself as a broader system of states that was unwaveringly internationalist in outlook. Through the Council for Mutual Economic Assistance (COMECON) and the Warsaw Pact, it tied itself institutionally as well as ideologically to an international socialist order. As for the Federal Republic, the move to a postnational order involved looking to the West and adopting Western values and institutions. The nature of Germany's postnational identity, which Hans-Georg Betz examines in some detail, was expressed most succinctly in the term *Verfassungspatriotismus* (constitutional patriotism), coined by the political scientist Dolf Sternberger and popularized above all by Jürgen Habermas. On an ideological level, it entailed a commitment to the principles of liberal democracy and the free market economy, principles that were enshrined in the Basic Law. Institutionally, it manifested itself most obviously in the creation of a federal parliamentary system of government and a central role in the North Atlantic Treaty Organization (NATO) and what is now the European Union. The Federal Republic thus became what Betz labels a "civilian power" rather than a military power, its identity stemming from a legitimate pride in its political system and a powerful economy whose benefits were shared widely through the agency of the welfare state.

In these postnational approaches to the problem of identity, history had only a limited role to play. Both postwar German states were eager to distance themselves from the history of a unified German nation-state, especially the Third Reich, though each predictably identified dangerous elements of continuity from the pre-1945 era in the other. In this scheme of things, historical references, when used at all, played an overwhelmingly negative role in the construction of identity. For example, by taking Auschwitz as the central symbol of the history of unified Germany, the notion of an identity tied to a unitary German nation-state was totally discredited.

Unification raised new questions and created new problems of German identity. Because each of the postwar states had partially defined itself *against* the other, the sudden disappearance of one of those states was potentially troublesome. Above all, unification raised the possibility of again employing history to establish an identity for the new, united Germany. From the perspective of October 1990 and beyond, the history of a unified Germany no longer looks quite so abnormal; indeed, it appears to have been restored to a "natural" state of affairs. Given also the above-mentioned tendency in both German states in the 1980s to appropriate history for the creation of identity, the maintenance of a postnational identity appears to be seriously threatened. This was most clearly illustrated by the decision to install Berlin as the capital of the unified Germany. Close though the Bundestag vote was, the abandonment of Bonn for the old imperial capital was dense with historical symbolism.[19] Bonn had stood for cosmopolitanism, for the cultivation of ties with the West, and for a certain modesty of presence in international affairs. Historically, Berlin has connoted German nationalism and imperialism, the rejection of the West, and a weighty presence in central and eastern Europe. The power of symbolism is easily overestimated, yet the choice of Berlin as the capital gave enormous impetus to a new, historically reconstructed German identity.

A certain "renationalization" of German identity is perhaps inevitable; at the very least, it is apparent that the advocates of a postnational identity have been driven to take the defensive. There appears to be one area, however, in which there is a strong argument for a firmer commitment to Western values rather than an abandonment of them, and that is in the area of citizenship, a subject discussed in some detail by Hans-Georg Betz and Hermann Kurthen. The Federal Republic's restrictive citizenship law is archaic. It grants citizenship to those who are citizens of Germany as it existed in 1937 or are descendants of such citizens. In effect, it defines citizenship in terms of "race" rather than residence on German territory. In this way, citizenship is denied to the many who have migrated to postwar Germany for whatever reason but cannot claim membership of the *Volk*. Such exclusiveness has its historical basis—if borders and institutions were merely transient, then at least the *Volk* could provide a certain sense of permanence. In the context of the early history of the Federal Republic, the law even had a distinctly inclusive dimension, since it left open the possibility of accepting all those Germans who found themselves outside the country's radically redrawn borders. But today the law may well be a contributing factor in the intolerance toward foreigners that seemed to increase markedly after unification. Resistance to change nonetheless remains strong, and Chancellor Kohl himself has affirmed that "Germany is not a country of immigration."[20]

Those who support the construction of a new identity for the united Germany usually proceed from the assumption that Germany has become a "normal" nation. The political organization of Europe into unitary nation-states is taken to be a "natural" state of affairs (although nation-states and nationalism are inventions of the last two centuries). Division into two states is viewed as an abnormal state of affairs, a punishment for previous sins that could not legitimately be regarded as a permanent arrangement. That period of punishment having been consigned to the past, Germany was entitled to assume its position as a normal European nation-state boasting institutions and values comparable to those of other nation-states such as Britain or France.

This claim to normalcy has been widely and hotly contested. For historians, it has proved particularly problematical, because it runs counter to a widely held notion in modern German historiography— namely, the idea of a *Sonderweg*, a peculiarly "German" path of economic and political modernization: Germany had modernized in such a way as to diverge from what was regarded as the standard Western model of development. Whereas in nations such as Britain, France, and the United States economic modernization in the nineteenth and early twentieth centuries was accompanied by progress in the social and political realms, in Germany there was resistance to change in these areas. The dominant social group remained the Prussian landed aristocracy, which successfully blocked any attempts at a fundamental democratization of the political system but at the same time allowed and even promoted economic growth. Despite its astounding economic performance, Germany thus remained socially and politically different from the other modernizing powers. There was an apparent disjunction, a unique combination of modern and feudal elements that distinguished Germany from the "normality" of the West.

Before 1945, this apparent divergence from the West was not necessarily seen in negative terms. In fact, there was a pre-1945 positive version of the *Sonderweg* thesis that claimed to identify much that was praiseworthy in Germany's path of development in the late nineteenth century, when the united Germany recorded unparalleled economic growth and established itself as the most dynamic force on the continent. Moreover, this development appeared to take place within a stable political framework, characterized by widespread consensus, and without jettisoning earnestly held national cultural values. Economic progress did not appear to be inhibited by continued affirmation of traditional, apolitical cultural values of German *Innerlichkeit* (inwardness). Not only did these values fail to inhibit cultural chauvinism; they also helped to sustain nationalism, imperialism, and militarism, as Thomas Mann's *Betrachtungen eines Unpolitischen* (Reflections of a Nonpolitical Man) eloquently testified toward the end of the First World War.

But from a post-1945 perspective of German history, it was impossible not to attribute more sinister qualities to this special path of development. Germany had become aggressive and chauvinistic, twice within thirty years precipitating wars of imperialist expansion. The focus was placed more sharply on the undemocratic nature of German society, a society that had never experienced the liberating effects of a bourgeois revolution such as those that had transformed and above all democratized Britain and France. Instead, the old elites had clung doggedly to their enormous political privileges, successfully resisting pressure from below for democratic reform. Germany was in a kind of time warp—an extremely modern and dynamic economy was developing within an increasingly archaic political and social framework. This lack of synchronization engendered deep tensions. Instead of leading to revolution or even reform, however, these tensions were successfully manipulated by the ruling elites to their own advantage, inciting popular hypernationalism and xenophobia and ultimately leading Germany into war as a solution to what was essentially a domestic crisis.

Although a damning indictment of modern Germany, for contemporary Germans, the *Sonderweg* thesis at least had the redeeming feature of identifying 1945 as the end point of the *Sonderweg*. Military catastrophe and total collapse, according to this view, destroyed the old Germany and with it the conditions underpinning the *Sonderweg*. The destruction of the *Junker* caste through the loss or redistribution of their lands had weakened the social foundations of conservative versions of a *Sonderweg*. Moreover, the division of what remained of Germany into two separate states, both with radically different political orders from the one that preceded them, ensured that 1945 was a genuine caesura. The Federal Republic, at least, was free to take its place alongside "normal" Western states. Although not a nation-state, it nevertheless succeeded in combining Western liberal democratic values with a capitalist free-market economy.

Although of seminal importance in the historiography of modern Germany, the critical version of the *Sonderweg* thesis has always had its detractors. It disconcerted conservative historians because it emphasized that Hitler was no mere "accident in the works" but the culmination of a lengthy process dating back to 1871 or even earlier and strongly involving the economic, social, and political elites. If Germany was "peculiar" in any way, the detractors argued, it was a geographical peculiarity stemming from its position in the center of Europe. Lacking natural boundaries and saddled with a multiplicity of neighbors, it displayed an understandable propensity to go to war over territorial claims.

More recently, the "critical" version of a German *Sonderweg* has come under attack from the British Marxist historians Geoffrey Eley and David Blackbourn, who were troubled by the ready identification of the now defunct feudal elites as the source of Germany's straying from the "normal" path of development.[21] Germany might not have had the overt bourgeois revolution that the Western tradition considered obligatory, and it might not have been a paragon of democratic virtue, but it does not follow that there was no influential bourgeoisie. On the contrary, there was a significant bourgeois class, but one that had acquiesced in an authoritarian political framework because it provided this class with the conditions in which it could do business. The other troubling thing about the *Sonderweg* thesis from the viewpoint of Blackbourn and Eley is that it posits a "normal" Western path of modernization based primarily on the experience of Britain, France, and the United States. From the late twentieth century, it is easier to see just how varied the paths to modernization have been around the globe. Asia in particular delivers numerous examples of rapid economic development taking place within authoritarian political frameworks and apparently feudal social structures. If anything, the paths of modernization followed there are closer to the German model, rendering British, French, and U.S. models exceptional. In any case, the notion that there was a single, normal path of development needed to be abandoned, and if there was no normality, there could be no "peculiarities" either.

German unification threatens to discredit the *Sonderweg* thesis further; at the very least, it will provide a test of its elasticity. From the perspective of 1990 and beyond, Germany appears to be a normal European nation-state. Whether appearances are deceptive is the question explored in the contributions by Lutz Niethammer, Reinhard Kühnl, and Reinhard Alter. All three resist the "normalization" of German history; countering the temptation to interpret 1945 as a turning point whose achievements are confirmed and extended by the events of 1989–90, they seek structural continuities that run through those crucial dates and implicitly warn of the possibility of the reemergence of dangerous elements from a "special" past.

Unification, as Niethammer points out in his contribution, brought with it a new set of contradictions and paradoxes, largely bearing on the complicated interrelationship between foreign and domestic policy as a consequence of Germany's return to a central location in Europe. The fact that the unification of Germany has been taking place within the framework of European integration, Niethammer suggests, speaks against the continuance of a *Sonderweg*. Nevertheless, Germany's central position in Europe may indicate the return of some elements of the *Sonderweg*—even if they are no longer being pursued consciously—in terms of both mentalities and the interventionist tendencies of the state in relation to society and the economy. Kühnl points to the lack of resolute action against right-wing extremism in the unified Germany and warns of structural conditions that have favored extreme right-wing ideologies, both in the socioeconomic elites and among the mass of the population—above all, the middle classes. Alter discusses the defensive and ideologically integrative role envisaged for Germany's literary culture by influential critics and publicists since the fall of the wall, and he examines this role in the light of previous attempts—above all, in the *Historikerstreit* of 1986–87—to rewrite history with a view to constructing a homogeneous national identity that reconciles economic dynamism with political stability.

Claus Leggewie contributes a sociological perspective to the problem of historical continuities and breaks. He reflects on the likelihood of a new political generation formed by the fall of the wall and the unification process and sees the concept of "generations" as an important criterion of historical periodization. Leggewie anticipates that the new generation in whose lives the events of 1989 played a formative part will articulate itself primarily in the arena of popular culture: subscribing neither to pragmatic party politics nor to alternative ideologies and movements, the new, largely de-ideologized culture represented by "generation X" will leaven the political culture, and as a consequence, less formal modes of social organization will affect the language of mainstream political movements.

3.

The writing of GDR history was practiced by eastern and western bloc historians for decades. Their work, by and large, was profoundly influenced by the Cold War climate in which it was written. The Marxist historians in the GDR saw their state as the culmination of all progressive elements in German history and its officially decreed antifascism as a counter to the persistence of fascist tendencies in the other German state. In the West, GDR history was often written in concurrence with the totalitarianism theory, which was especially popular at the height of the Cold War in the 1950s and again in the Reagan-Thatcher decade of the 1980s. By identifying a series of common features, this theory conflated National Socialism and Soviet communism, viewing them as equally repulsive versions of totalitarian rule. At the same time, eastern bloc states such as the GDR were interpreted as extensions of Stalinist modes of rule, in principle, therefore, comparable with Nazi Germany. The diametrically opposed fascism and totalitarianism theses did little to establish an adequately nuanced reading of the GDR past.

The events of 1989–90 demand a rewriting of the history of all the countries of the eastern bloc. Those historians and publicists who adhere to the totalitarianism thesis (and thus interpret the GDR as a kind of extension of the Nazi past) will not seize the opportunity to cast aside the rigid ideological framework of the Cold War and to write histories that will achieve a fresh awareness of previously unrecognized complexities.

Some early indications suggest the predominance of the totalitarian thesis. At a popular level in particular, there is an obsession with the GDR regime's machinery of coercion and surveillance, usually in the form of an almost ghoulish fascination with the state security police, the *Stasi*. This fascination excelled itself in 1990 with the heated debate over what to do with the 180 kilometers of files on some six million citizens that the *Stasi* had managed to put together in the course of its wretched existence. The dispute became "a symbolic struggle over control of the GDR's past."[22] A comparable preoccupation with the trappings of power at the cost of analyzing the modus operandi of the political system as a whole was evident in the interest attracted by attempts to bring the leading figures of the regime to justice.

In her contribution to this book, Mary Fulbrook criticizes the perpetuation of the black and white imagery of the Cold War era in historical writing on the GDR since the fall of the wall and resists the temptation to demonize the "villains" and to salute the "heroes" of GDR history. She calls for a social history that allows for a clearer view of the interplay between state and society at various stages in the history of the GDR. Like a number of other contributors to the volume, Fulbrook is skeptical about the role of history in the construction of a national "identity" and asks that future reevaluations of German history raise an awareness of the ambiguities and dilemmas inherent in all forms of social organization, be they capitalist or communist.

As Hermann Weber warns in his essay, the media's sensationalist treatment of the *Stasi* has threatened to inhibit a more successful coming to terms with the East German past. Indeed, there are worrying parallels between this focus on the *Stasi* and other "totalitarian" aspects of the GDR and the postwar confrontation with the Nazi past. Above all, there is a similar tendency to locate the blame for the existence of a repressive state apparatus in the contribution of a relatively small group of individuals ruling ruthlessly from on high and applying various strategies of terror to bludgeon an innocent population into submission. In short, there has been a kind of witch-hunt, a search for convenient scapegoats to exculpate the bulk of the population, to ease consciences and consign the experiences of the mass of the people in eastern Germany to an unreachable past. This tendency is especially clear in the treatment of those prominent individuals accused of having cooperated with the *Stasi*. The outstanding example is Manfred Stolpe, a former church leader who was elected state governor of Brandenburg, only to be subjected to censure when the Gauck authority revealed that he had informed on the Protestant church. Stolpe possessed the perspicacity to note that the *Stasi* debate demonstrated "in how short a time it was forgotten what the conditions of a dictatorship were." In a statement that is of importance not just for historians, he went on to recommend: "One must distinguish between the criticism of the system and the criticism of the biography of the people. The danger which I see at present is that coming to terms with the past can be appropriated for political ends or even commercialized in the form of sensationalist news."[23] To identify the GDR past with just a few of its leading representatives, as Hermann Weber warns, runs the risk of repressing the past. It cannot lead to the necessary process of self-analysis; on the contrary, it can result in "a kind of cheap revision of history."[24]

How long it will take to work beyond a continuation of a distinctly Manichaean Cold War perspective remains to be seen. The broad range of research possibilities awaiting historians who adopt new perspectives is evident in the essay by John Moses and Gregory Munro. They offer a rewriting of GDR history that employs an analytical category hitherto largely neglected in this area—namely, the church. Its importance in GDR history became apparent relatively late, when it was the key gathering point for opposition elements and, ultimately, a crucial instrument for overthrowing the regime. The perception of the role of the church is likely to remain a subject of some controversy. On the one hand, it was an effective and articulate source of opposition to Socialist Unity Party (SED) rule. On the other hand, by providing a common roof for diverse oppositional elements, it might have facilitated the state's control over its enemies. In any case, a closer examination of its role in the GDR and its overthrow is a necessary step in rewriting GDR history, a step that was inconceivable given the circumscriptions of the official GDR brand of Marxist historiography.

The rewriting of the GDR past can also extend to a reexamination of GDR historiography, which, like the state with which it enjoyed a symbiotic relationship, has come to a sudden end. This task is undertaken here by Wolfgang Ruge in the form of a critical (and self-critical) reappraisal of East German research on Nazi Germany, a topic now consigned, as Saul Friedlander puts it, "to a twice-distant past, that is, to 'mere history.'"[25] It was the immediacy of that Nazi past that determined the character of its historiography in the GDR and accounted for its strengths and weaknesses. East German historians were committed to ensuring that the evils of fascism would never be repeated; their work, they believed, could and should be devoted to this goal. In making this commitment, they bound their profession too closely to the injunctions of a regime that professed similarly admirable antifascist sentiments. Genuine though those initial sentiments no doubt were, in their later form of a state-sponsored and state-imposed "antifascism," they became self-serving and unconvincing. For the historians, however, the commitment to the ideology could not be separated from an obligation to the state; their work became one-sided, narrow, and, at worst, blatantly propagandistic.

Having largely served the interests of a regime that is now defunct, East German historiography faces an uncertain fate. Its theoretical underpinnings have been severely shaken by the collapse of communism—1989, after all, was not supposed to *follow* 1917. The question of whether Marxist historiography has a future at all, not just in the former GDR but everywhere else as well, can be raised.[26] But it is in the former GDR specifically that the crisis has been most acute. The many weaknesses of the practice of history in the GDR have been exposed to the point of ridicule; its strengths are in danger of falling victim to the selective amnesia that has accompanied the triumph of the West.

At one level, the fate of East German history and historiography will be decided in the institutions, that is, in the universities and research institutes. Developments there will largely determine whether an East German intellectual identity generally and East German history specifically will survive in the new Germany.

A leading German representative of the so-called '68 generation, Rudi Dutschke, envisaged a "long march through the institutions" in order to fulfill his generation's reform program. If the events of 1989–90 signal a change of generation, as has been suggested, then the new generation is confronted with a similar task. The experience of the institutions of the former GDR indicates that the march ahead will be a much shorter one; it will be more akin to a romp. Among the first victims of the changes at the institutional level were the historians, who, along with many of their colleagues in the universities and academies of the former GDR, found themselves cut off from any form of institutional base, having been judged unfit to practice their profession.

The fate of the universities is considered here from two perspectives, one an East German (Siegfried Hoyer), the other a non-German (Peter Monteath), one a participant, the other an observer. Both accounts are institute specific, one dealing with the University of Leipzig, the other with Jena, site of Napoleon's military triumph in 1806 and of the alleged end of history. In both cases, the procedures implemented were harsh and painful for many, a clear reminder that unification was carried out very much on the West's terms. The willingness with which some Westerners sought opportunities offered by this period of radical change, and the eagerness with which some Easterners have welcomed and facilitated the arrival of the new order, help explain the extent of the West's victory in the institutions and beyond. In terms not only of the institutional but also of the intellectual remaking of Germany, the fate of the universities can be seen as a kind of microcosm of the unification process.

None of the historians represented in this volume has enjoyed the advantage of great distance from the events described, at least not in a temporal sense. This collection, which was not finalized until after the October 1994 federal elections, is the product of a period of great flux and uncertainty. Even several years after revolution and unification, the possibilities for the future remain open. At one end of the spectrum, the opportunity presents itself to overcome the old East–West division through the creation of a unified Europe, in which Germany is allocated the crucial role of bridging East and West to promote a breadth and depth of political and economic security as never before experienced in Europe. At the other end lies the possibility that revived German nationalism could assume a chauvinist character, triggering nationalist and regionalist revivals across Europe and casting it back into a period of political instability and economic misery. The contributions collected here go some way toward identifying the course charted thus far by the unified Germany in its search for a new identity and a new place in Europe, but uncertainties abound.

NOTES

Reinhard Alter died in 1996, soon after the completion of this collection.

1. See especially Harold James, *Vom Historikerstreit zum Historikerschweigen: Die Wiedergeburt des Nationalstaates*, Berlin, 1993.

2. For example, Konrad Jarausch, *The Rush to German Unity*, New York and Oxford, 1994, 96.
3. Timothy Garton Ash, *In Europe's Name: Germany and the Divided Continent*, New York, 1993, 344.
4. Jürgen Kocka, "Revolution und Nation 1989. Zur historischen Einordnung der gegenwärtigen Ereignisse," in Rainer Eckert, Wolfgang Küttler, and Gustav Seeber (eds.), *Krise-Umbruch-Neubeginn. Eine kritische und selbstkritische Dokumentation der DDR-Geschichtswissenschaft 1989/90*, Stuttgart, 1993, 86–7.
5. "German history reached its turning-point and failed to turn. This was the fateful essence of 1848." A. J. P. Taylor, *The Course of German History: A Survey of the Development of Germany Since 1918*, London, 1945, 68.
6. The term "catch-up revolutions" is used by Jürgen Kocka in "Umbrüche-aber ohne neue utopische Ideen. Die Sogkraft des Nationalen und der Beitrag der Bundesrepublik zur Revolution in der DDR," in Udo Wengst (ed.), *Historiker betrachten Deutschland. Beiträge zum Vereinigungsprozeß und zur Haupstadtdiskussion (Februar 1990–Juni 1991)*, Bonn and Berlin, 1992, 99. Originally in *Frankfurter Rundschau*, 11 July 1990.
7. Timothy Garton Ash, *The Magic Lantern*, New York, 1990, 154.
8. Joachim Fest, *Der zerstörte Traum. Das Ende des utopischen Zeitalters*, Berlin, 1991; Francis Fukuyama, *The End of History and the Last Man*, London, 1992.
9. Jarausch, *The Rush to German Unity*, 182.
10. Fest, *Der zerstörte Traum*; Arnulf Baring, *Deutschland, was nun? Ein Gespräch mit Dirk Rumberg und Wolf Jobst Siedler*, Berlin, 1991.
11. Tomothy Garton Ash: *We the People. The Revolution of '89 Witnessed in Warsaw, Budapest, Berlin & Prague*, London, 1990, 152.
12. Jarausch, *The Rush to German Unity*, 202. See also Charles S. Maier, "The DDR Upheaval of November 1989 and the Issue of German Revolution," in Konrad H. Jarausch and Matthias Middell (eds.), *Nach dem Erdbeben: (Re-)konstruktionen ostdeutscher Geschichte und Geschichtswissenschaft*, Leipzig, 1993.
13. Dieter Langewiesche, *Liberalismus in Deutschland*, Frankfurt, 1988, 216.
14. Heinrich August Winkler, "Der unverhoffte Nationalstaat. Deutsche Einheit: Die Vorzeichen sind günstiger als 1871," in Wengst (ed.), *Historiker betrachten Deutschland*, 169 (originally in *Die Zeit*, 28 September 1990).
15. Charles Powell, "What the PM Learnt About the Germans," in Harold James and Marla Stone (eds.), *When the Wall Came Down: Reactions to German Unification*, New York and London, 1992, 234.
16. Powell, "What the PM Learnt About the Germans," 239.
17. Jürgen Kocka, "Sozialgeschichte der neunziger Jahre," in *Die neue Gesellschaft/Frankfurter Hefte* 40 (1993): 1127.
18. Eric Hobsbawm and Terence Ranger, *The Invention of Tradition*, Cambridge and New York, 1983.
19. For the reactions of historians to this debate, see especially the seven contributions by historians in Wengst, *Historiker betrachten Deutschland*, 213–64.
20. Quoted in *Der Spiegel*, 15 March 1993, 53.
21. David Blackbourn and Geoffrey Eley, *The Peculiarities of German History: Bourgeois Society and Politics in Nineteenth-Century Germany*, Oxford, 1984.

22. Jarausch, *The Rush to German Unity*, 173.
23. Manfred Stolpe, "Keine Bürger zweiter Klasse," in J. Kogel, W. Schütte, and H. Zimmermann (eds.), *Neues Deutschland. Innenansichten einer wiedervereinigten Nation*, Frankfurt, 1993.
24. Anne-Marie Le Gloannec, "On German Identity," *Daedalus* 123, no. 1 (Winter 1994): 140.
25. Saul Friedlander, *Memory, History, and the Extermination of the Jews of Europe*, Bloomington, 1993, 90.
26. As it is, for example, by Wolfgang Küttler in his chapter "Hat 'marxistische' Geschichtsschreibung noch eine Zukunft?" in Konrad Jarausch (ed.), *Zwischen Parteilichkeit und Professionalität. Bilanz der Geschichtswissenschaft der DDR*, Berlin, 1991, 165–84.

1

Normalization or Renationalization? On Reinterpreting the German Past

KONRAD JARAUSCH

The implications of the caesura of 1989–90 for German history are still largely unclear. Unification may assume its place in the series of radical changes in 1918, 1933, and 1945, but its uneven consequences, which affect the East far more than the West, complicate any attempt to come to terms with it intellectually. Initial judgments correctly stressed that the collapse of post-Stalinism ended the Cold War, and the re-creation of a reduced but united Germany completed the postwar era.[1] It remains to be seen, however, what effects the unexpected return of the nation-state will have on the basic structure of the national master narrative. Instead of ending in division indicating German blame, unification has provided a new point of departure suggestive of a drama of guilt, atonement, and redemption.

On the opinion pages and in talk shows, the radical change has led to a curious confusion of ideological fronts. Adherents of the Right and the Left had defined themselves through a particular understanding of the German catastrophes of the twentieth century. Whereas the Right, despite declarations of loyalty to Europe, regretted the demise of the nation-state, the Left interpreted division as a just punishment and a precondition for peace between East and West. As the historical foundations of the respective political camps have now become redundant, the diagnoses of the present and hopes for the future that are to be constructed upon these foundations have also disappeared. It is no wonder that intellectuals are now discussing the fortuitously ambiguous questions "What's Left?" and "What's Right?"[2]

A central element in this debate is the legitimacy of the nation-state. This is no coincidence, because the construction of a common history played a key role in the constitution of a national identity in the nineteenth century. At that time, historians became involved in the dispute over the alternatives of a "Greater Germany" or a "Small Germany" in the creation of a German state. And members of the Prussian School, such as Heinrich von Treitschke, made a considerable contribution to Bismarck's founding of the Reich. In the postwar era, the discrediting of national traditions as a result of National Socialism turned the tables, with the result that critical intellectuals began to search for other, regional or international, orientations. Progressive circles, in particular, effectively tabooed the term "nation" as the root of all evil.[3] Therefore the unexpected return of the nation-state was bound to raise this question anew.

In this debate, conservative circles propagate a restoration of the concept of nation with the argument of "normalization." In an essay that attracted widespread attention, Bonn political scientist Hans-Peter Schwarz asserts that unification offered Germany a chance to overcome its identity neurosis and to become a normal nation-state in Europe. "After wandering astray for a long time, the country has finally returned to itself." Left-wing critics have responded that a renationalization would promote hostility to foreigners and would legitimate dangerous right-wing trends. In his controversial reply, Frankfurt social philosopher Jürgen Habermas labeled the attempt at normalization "the second great lie of the Federal Republic."[4] This battle for the authority to interpret the past, which also informed the debate about the resistance, raises the central question: in which direction is German historical self-understanding developing since the unexpected unification?

Although this is a matter concerning the past, professional historians thus far have hardly intervened in the discussion. Following its own logic, normal research continues without worrying about such issues. Other controversies such as poststructuralist approaches in cultural history or coping with a double totalitarian past arouse emotions much more. But precisely because the eastern European embracing of nationalism and western Europe's relapse into it appear to be so unnecessary, Eric Hobsbawm's warning has to be taken seriously: "For historians it is extraordinarily important to be conscious of their responsibility, which rests above all in not allowing themselves to be influenced by the passions of the politics of identity—even if they experience them themselves."[5] The following observations are an attempt to discuss critically some aspects of the debate on the nation in German historical consciousness.

1.

After the Second World War, the hypertrophy of nationalism caused by National Socialism led to a distancing from the nation. Part of the international criticism of German history, which drew a direct line from Luther via Frederick the Great and Bismarck to Hitler, was so vehement and superficial as to be viewed more correctly as war propaganda. But even serious academic studies by democratically inclined emigrants such as Hans Rothfels, Hans Rosenberg, and Hajo Holborn attacked the national historical tradition. In the same way, Anglo-American authors such as Gordon Craig, Fritz Stern, and George Mosse laid the blame for the catastrophes of the twentieth century on the excesses of German nationalism.[6] Although the historical profession in the main was dismissive of external criticism, international scholars were able to exert influence in the German-speaking world through translations and visits that promoted a change in historical thinking.

At the same time, Marxist authors in East Germany pronounced their judgment of the national conservative past in the harshest terms. It is true that the SED leadership initially supported the goal of a united, socialist Germany, but the "antifascist-democratic revolution" also followed the Soviet model and propagated proletarian internationalism. Although most historians continued to assume that in the future a socialist-led unification would take place, they denounced nationalism as an ideological construct of the ruling classes. After the Berlin Wall was built, the existence of two different states forced a rethinking that attempted to legitimate the coexistence of different systems. Despite doubts of a substantive nature, many historians in the 1970s went one step further and supported the formulation of the party thesis of a separate "socialist nation."[7]

In the early stages of the Federal Republic, leading historians therefore had to "contend with a flood of accusations against German history and German polity." Thus the conservative Gerhard Ritter contemplated "the German problem" in order to examine whether these attacks were justified and whether they would necessarily "give us cause to reconceptualize German history." Because of their responsibility for the world wars, Ritter explicitly distanced himself from the exaggerated nationalism of the Pan-Germans and labeled National Socialism "a kind of romantic convulsion." But "as a German who loves his fatherland," he did not want to abandon entirely the collective

craving for admiration; rather, he sought a form of nationalism puri-
fied of excesses.[8] Although Catholic or liberal researchers confronted
the tradition more critically, to a large extent, a sense of national responsibility was representative of the first generation of postwar West
German historians.

Not until the Fischer controversy of the 1960s was the close nexus
between history and nationalism broken in the Federal Republic. It is
sometimes overlooked that Hamburg professor Fritz Fischer, in his
studies of the First World War, also piled up terrifying evidence of
the fateful role of nationalism as an ideology that justified inner repression and external expansion. The history profession reacted so
sharply to the accusation of war guilt in 1914 because it feared that a
German admission of responsibility would place in question "the continuity of the nation-state tradition" as such. Driven forward by the
student revolts at the end of the 1960s, Fischer's criticism of Germany
led to a clear dissociation, especially among his own students, from
the fundamental patriotic consensus among historians. This discussion delegitimized the realization of national aspirations as the goal
of German history and declared it a problem instead.[9]

The social history of the 1970s fueled this denationalization
substantively, methodologically, and ideologically. The Bielefeld School's
rejection of the primacy of foreign policy fundamentally shifted research interests toward an examination of the social determinants of
historical development. The critique of historicist hermeneutics and
the turn to theory-driven analysis rendered the fixation with a national master narrative obsolete. Systematic comparison with other
societies produced the provocative thesis of a German special path of
development, or *Sonderweg*. This path was not compared positively
with democratic norms, as Thomas Mann had done in the First World
War, but negatively, with reference to inner repression and outward
aggression.[10] The consequence of such a perspective was a critical
attitude toward the past that demanded a rigorous commitment to a
Western system of values.

At the beginning of the 1980s, the academic view of German history therefore appeared to be largely denationalized. In the Anglo-
Saxon realm, the German national state was sometimes considered as
a seventy-five-year-long episode, and many scholars concentrated on
conflicts between regions, classes, and minorities instead.[11] Occupied
with the historical legitimation of the status of the GDR as a separate
state, East German researchers also polemicized against the alleged
national tendencies in bourgeois historiography.[12] In the Federal Republic, the history of everyday life (*Alltagsgeschichte*) steered atten-

tion to the life experiences of the common people and local spaces, far removed from national pathos. The awareness of the danger of too close a link between nationalism and historiography, gained over decades of self-criticism, seemed to have discredited this attitude forever. As representatives of a "postnational democracy," many German historians had now become less nationalistic than their foreign colleagues.[13]

This consistent denationalization finally produced reactions on a variety of fronts. In comparison with earlier excitement, the international discussion became noticeably calmer. American political scientist David Calleo, for example, argued for greater understanding of the legitimate aims of a national German policy. Even the Marxist criticism of the *Sonderweg* thesis offered by Geoff Eley and David Blackbourn led to a denial of the exceptional character of German development and a relativization of the English norm as a point of comparison. At the same time, other researchers began to judge the scientific and local political achievements of the Kaiser's Germany more positively.[14] Although among the Anglo-American public the Holocaust trauma continued to dominate, a more differentiated view of the German question established itself among specialist historians.

In the GDR, dealings with the past were eased as a result of the "Legacy and Tradition" (*Erbe und Tradition*) campaign. In the early 1980s, the SED leadership attempted to increase the acceptance of the regime by a broadened understanding of German history. Although it continued to base its own state on the revolutionary legacy of the workers' movement, the party now appealed to the general traditions of the Prussian past. An astounded public registered the change in direction through the return of the statue of Frederick the Great on horseback to its position on Unter den Linden. In the impressive biography of Bismarck by Engelberg, unmistakeably national tones were evident to which even a Western public could relate. This turn from legacy to tradition may not have been intended to bring about reunification—rather, it was meant to strengthen East German independence—but the broadening of historical consciousness signaled a more relaxed East German relationship to the nation.[15]

In the Federal Republic, the historians' dispute (*Historikerstreit*) of the mid-1980s was similarly aimed toward the attempted "normalization" of the German past. Although terms of the controversy were often unintelligible to outsiders, the debate essentially revolved around the place of the Third Reich in the course of German history. Without doubt, Ernst Nolte's initial provocative claim—namely, that Nazi atrocities were justified as a reaction to previously committed Bolshevik atrocities—implied a relativization of Nazi crimes. Even Andreas Hillgruber's greater sympathy for the Wehrmacht's defensive battle against the Red Army in 1945 than for the victims of the Judeocide tended toward a cleansing of the German past.[16] The outrage of progressive historians and publicists led by Habermas may have succeeded in once again refuting these attempts to play down the Nazi past, but increasingly critical positions were forced onto the defensive.

Among the broader public, the defeated arguments did find some acceptance. Although the critics largely dominated the media and the schools, at a popular level an unexpectedly strong nationalistic current continued to grow in strength; it was beyond the reach of academic influence, because it was based on positive memories of the Third Reich. In particular in East Germany, detached from the West, national characteristics remained strong for economic and political reasons. In West Germany, surveys indicated rather a negative view of nationalism, which was compensated by pride in growing affluence.[17] In both German states there developed a complicated identity debate that showed that, despite alternatives, the question of a national self-understanding remained unresolved.[18]

2.

Unification has noticeably strengthened diverse tendencies toward a renationalization of German self-understanding. Although it is still too early to reach a final judgment, there are some indications of a "new German audacity in dealing with the past." A never-ending series of xenophobic riots, desecrations of Jewish cemeteries, and political indiscretions (such as Bitburg) has awakened in the non-German West fears of a "Fourth Reich." The asylum crisis and the ensuing citizenship debate also gave cause for concern, because they promoted ethnic xenophobia.[19] The attacks may finally have evoked an impressive counterreaction from citizens and politicians, but the xenophobic tendencies have pointed to the potency of a nationalism long thought overcome.[20]

The real danger lies in the legitimation of populist relapses through corrections to official history. Although academic production proceeds slowly, there are increasing indications of a return to nationalism among professional historians. Because unity weakens the responsibility of the first nation-state for the catastrophes of the world wars by recalling a peaceful normality, "the re-evaluation of the Bismarck Reich [has] already begun." Instead of continuing to function as a structural precursor of the Third Reich in the sense of Fischer or Wehler, the German Empire of 1871–1918 is restored as a norm of German nation-statehood.[21] Such critical minds as Wolfgang J. Mommsen have barely perceptibly begun to use national vocabulary without the qualifiers considered standard until recently. The rethinking is so irresistible because it is presented as a necessary correction to previous overcompensations.[22]

At first, unification provided impetus for intensified research on national themes. The nation-state perspective, which for decades had been overshadowed by local case studies or international comparisons, has been revived and thrust into the center of historical interest. Now the nation is experiencing an unexpected boom in the feature pages, on talk shows, in journals, and at conferences. Even if it is inspired by fashion, this return to the nation offers an opportunity for Germans to become acquainted with progress in international research on nationalism. Instead of proceeding from political nation building, historians of other countries have begun to examine the invention of nations in the cultural processes of the construction of identity. As this promises to shed new light on old questions, the application of such approaches to German developments can only be welcomed.[23] The debates about modernization crises or political religion at the last German historical congress in Leipzig took some first steps in this direction.

A further consequence of the renewed interest is the de-tabooing of the nation as an analytical category. The unexpected continuation of the nation-state supports a previously contested form of viewing the past, according to which the states created in the aftermath of the Second World War were considered to have shared, interconnected histories.[24] In a provocative essay, U.S.-based English historian Harold James draws a logical consequence from the shock of 1989: "The nation reappears as the main player on the historical stage." Targeting the postnational moralizing of the structural historians, he denounces "the myths of critical history" and calls the nation-state a fixed point in the "raging stream of instabilities." Although the rehabilitation of the nation as a central category is overdue, this plea overlooks the analytical mark, because it attributes to the nation-state not just factual but also normative power.[25]

The return of a unified national history also reinvigorates traditional methodologies. In the West German methodology debate of the 1970s, nationally thinking hermeneuticists locked horns with historical social scientists working comparatively. As a result of unification, Erlangen historian Gregor Schöllgen pleads for the rehabilitation of the previously unfashionable diplomatic history and holds social history responsible for the widespread disinterest among the educated in foreign policy issues. In a bitter attack on the intellectual disengagement from issues of power, he demands a "strengthened concentration on the urgent, central questions of today . . . concerning the role of Germany in Europe and the world." Schöllgen's polemic in favor of responsible power politics illustrates the nexus between methodological rethinking and the reemergence of conservative tendencies in politics.[26]

At the same time, old geopolitical interpretations of Germany as the "land of the middle" in Europe are the focus of renewed attention.[27] In this way, the westward orientation of the old Federal Republic, one of the fundamental changes in political culture after the Second World War, received fresh scrutiny. One widely discussed collection, edited by historian and publicist Rainer Zitelmann, emphasizes that it "will become increasingly clear in the coming years" that the westward orientation "by no means remains adequate and by itself is no longer capable of offering a reliable orientation." For the editor, it is a matter of "soberly discussing the opportunities and risks of being bound to the West," of doing away with the "almost mystical transfiguration of 'the West,'" and of rehabilitating the proponents of neutrality as the true champions of national unity. In another essay, Zitelmann welcomes unification as an opportunity to break the intellectual reflex, stemming from the Left, of German self-hatred.[28]

The national and power political approach also renders fashionable a more affirmative attitude toward the past. In contrast to the criticism of unification evident among many intellectuals, Göttingen academic Karlheinz Weissmann presents a positive justification for German unity that goes beyond the official government line. His treatise argues explicitly in favor of re-establishing links with German traditions as the basis for a stronger role in Europe. As the representative of a generation untroubled by the past, distancing itself from the left-wing generation of '68, Weissmann justifies the turn to the Right historically: "The strongest argument for the nation-state is that there is neither a practical nor a theoretical alternative." Like other neoconservative spirits, this young historian promotes not so much a turning back to history per se as a reorientation toward a particular kind of German nation-state tradition.[29]

Finally unity offers an opportunity to question the intellectual hegemony of the national skeptics. The unexpected course of history suggests a criticism of the political myopia of those historians who supported cooperation with the GDR in order to preserve peace. In a merciless attack on such "German errors," Regensburg jurist Jens Hacker points to the reservations of the social historians concerning German unity in order to denounce them as "apologists and accomplices of the SED-regime in the West." With great relish he displays a voluminous file of quotations from German historians, attacks advocates of the two-state theory such as Hans Mommsen, and praises only proponents of reunification such as Andreas Hillgruber. "It is important to note the extent to which German historians considered the unnatural division of Germany good, necessary and preferably permanent."[30]

The result of these tendencies is a partly subtle, partly blatant renationalization of German national consciousness. The desire for a historical "feeling of togetherness," evident already in the foundation of the *Haus der Geschichte* in Bonn and the German Historical Museum in Berlin, is understandable in the context of an extended Federal Republic.[31] But the proponents of a reorientation toward the nation go further and aim for nothing less than a basic change in German historical consciousness. Intellectuals such as Botho Strauss are restoring respectability to national positions, while critical voices such as Klaus Hartung argue that "the nation does not belong to the Right" in order to provoke the Left "to use the opportunity to play a role in determining German identity."[32] These individual statements may not appear particularly noteworthy, but considered together, the neonational advances are part of a broader rethinking that would like to brighten the dark image of the German past in order to strengthen self-confidence and change the face of politics.

It is possible to speculate on a number of reasons for the revitalized public interest in the nation. The return of the nation-state would inevitably reactivate older, previously suppressed modes of thought. Also, a level of weariness with alternatives such as European union or proletarian internationalism, brought about by the bureaucratization of Brussels or the collapse of "real socialism," made room for other kinds of identity. At the same time, the rhetoric of nation offers politicians a proven means of justifying the costs of unity and playing down the economic and psychological difficulties of growing together. Just as the unification crisis indicates that a German nation does not already exist as a quasi-natural entity, national appeals are an attempt paradoxically to reconstitute the nation in the collective consciousness after 1990.[33]

3.

How should critical historians react to this change of climate? One widespread response is simply to ignore "the new national thinking" in order to limit the effect of its arguments through systematic nonrecognition. Another approach is to attempt to solve the problem by academicizing it, that is, by making the revival of nationalism itself an object of research. But in the long term, neither understandable silence nor necessary analysis can come to terms with the new right-wing tendencies, because they underestimate the political dynamism of the national appeals. Not only right-wing extremism but also the respectable middle seeks in national solidarity an emotional cement for the attainment of inner unity. This is the argument put forward by CDU party whip Wolfgang Schäuble: "The bond which holds such a community together and gives it identity is the nation."[34]

Alarmed by such views, pugnacious supporters of the Left warn of the new "German dangers." Out of fear of the return of the past, they conclude: "The nationalization of Germany, as it occurred between 1890 and 1914, has to be averted this time." With a hint of hysteria, liberal newspapers crusade against the new nationalism, as if one could prevent its revival with ingenious polemics. Similarly, the doyen of the Bielefeld School, Hans-Ulrich Wehler, warns of the "new dreams of the intellectuals," of a "mystified nationalism." Even Jürgen Habermas dismisses the new revisionism as the "third rehashing of ideas by a young conservative group" and suggests that instead of supporting "the dubious future of the nation-state" it would be better to work toward the formation of transnational entities. Thus many critics are maintaining their antinationalism all the more resolutely.[35]

In contrast, intellectuals of the New Right are propagating a committed continuation of the change. The controversial Brigitte Seebacher-Brandt rails "against intellectual conformism," and others condemn the progressive consensus as an informal but all the more effective force for "political correctness," a sort of left-wing philistinism. In the battle for intellectual hegemony, Weissmann labels the neoconservatives the first opinion camp in the united country and boldly demands: "Think the nation." Although more flexible in his views, writer Peter Schneider interprets "the growing brutalization of the political debate" as a left-wing overreaction to the breaches of taboo by apostate former allies. Even one of the editors of the *Frankfurter Allgemeine Zeitung*, Joachim Fest, promotes as a cure for the alleged decay of values the formation of a new German national consciousness. It is no accident that a new conservative manifesto draws on the controversial pronouncements of writer Botho Strauss in order to demand a return to "normality, that is a self-confident nationhood."[36]

Between these fronts, some historians are attempting to develop a democratic patriotism. In eloquent essays, classical scholar and historian Christian Meier presents a program that urges Germans to create a new, westward-oriented nation. Contemporary historian Heinrich August Winkler also argues for a "new formation of the German nation" with a firm European orientation and Western values.[37] Instead of persisting with the negation of the need for national cohesion, these moderate intellectuals react to unification by interpreting the return of the nation as a challenge to shape the new Germany democratically. Without denying the guilt of the past, as a kind of inoculation they endeavor to create an identity that aims to prevent a relapse into extreme nationalism by producing a tolerant and nonetheless genuine patriotism.

To gain influence on the political center, some neoconservatives now proclaim a revolt of the rightist sons against their left-wing fathers, the erstwhile rebels of 1968. Literary critic Ulrich Greiner thus interprets the ideological debate as a battle of the generations, a "conflict between the '68ers and a new generation of authors and critics, eager to climb onto the podium, who are at the age now of the '68ers then."[38] The danger does not lie with the established intellectuals but with the possibility that the thirty-year-olds, influenced by unification, might identify with national issues and implement a change of historical paradigms: "It could become the great intellectual achievement of the 'post-1989 generation' if it takes up the challenge of restoring to Germany its conception of itself as the land of the middle."[39]

Which of these tendencies will ultimately prevail? At the moment, the critics still seem to hold the better cards, because leftist intellectuals have considerable influence on the media and on academe. At the same time, the great majority of the population appears to show little interest in national slogans. According to surveys, the number of committed nationalists among the adult population is under 10 percent, and it is somewhat larger only among adolescents, depending on the phrasing of the question. West Germans in particular remain relatively lacking in pride in their country, and the new citizens of the Federal Republic are more inclined once again to identify themselves as East Germans.[40] Even if an openly distorted image of the Third Reich is limited to less than one-seventh of the population, there exists a broader reservoir of citizens who repress the past (almost one-quarter) or excuse it (one-fifth). It is precisely these unstable groups that are susceptible to the nationalist message.[41]

Finally, this historical-political debate raises the question of what kind of nation the Germans want to be. When they articulate it at all, neoconservative ideologues normally proceed from a closed concept of the German nation, one based on ethnic origins, a common language and culture, and a centralist-authoritarian state. More liberal thinkers prefer an open, Western concept of nation that is based on citizenship, tolerates cultural and regional differences, and guarantees the human rights of its members. Although the current debate often conflates nationalist rhetoric with national thinking, both not only are developmentally related but also have fundamentally different effects. In contrast to liberal patriotism, Hagen Schulze warns against the destructive effects of the principle of ethnocracy: "Not the idea of the nation has to be overcome in Europe, but the fiction of a fateful, objective and inescapable unity of people, nation, history, language and state."[42]

Both positions contain certain dangers. As the abuse of ethnic nationalism by the Nazis indicates, the attempt to re-create an unbroken national consciousness involves the risk of straying into racism, xenophobia, imperialism, and repression. It is hoped that the structural sources of the old nationalism have largely dried up with the disappearance of the traditional elites, but the power of the media and the spread of right-wing violence suggest that new forms of chauvinism might quickly arise. In this situation, the experience of the Weimar Republic indicates that constitutional or economic patriotism alone cannot offer a stable basis for democracy in the long term. If one looks to other Western democracies, one certainly finds popular pride in the state without it being accompanied by arrogance. The bitterness of the German debate on general principles is in itself a sign of a deep-seated tension that is preventing a calm approach to the past and the future.[43]

Perhaps historians can help overcome this polarization by contributing to the development of a democratic self-consciousness. As an institutionalized conscience, they must repeatedly draw attention to the catastrophes of German history caused by the excesses of nationalism. Should they not invoke a minority tradition that, in Herder's cosmopolitan sense, was thoroughly patriotic and democratically oriented and that inspired the Revolution of 1848, social democracy, and the Weimar Republic? In contrast to the forced homogenization of ethnic nationalism, a democratic patriotism demands the recognition of breaks and alternatives that again and again have been suppressed by the prevailing chauvinism. Only the critical recovery of the histories of different and conflicting identities can make the formation of a sense of community possible—a community that not only tolerates but celebrates these contradictions.[44]

How one answers the question of normalization depends largely on how one defines "normalcy." Since the dark shadows of the German past cannot be erased, the neoconservative attempt at an aggressive renationalization must arouse vehement contradiction. But after the return of the national state, the attitude of postnationalism also seems insufficient, because a permanent sense of insecurity among the Germans helps neither European integration nor international cooperation. A way out of this dilemma could be a partial normalization that attempts to democratize the guilt-laden category of the nation. As custodians of collective memory, German historians in East and West, in Germany and outside it, have a particular responsibility to resist all nationalist tendencies from the start. But at the same time, they confront the challenge of developing democratic perspectives for dealing with a restored national state in a unifying Europe.[45]

NOTES ·

This chapter was translated by Peter Monteath.

1. Karl Dietrich Bracher, "Zeitgeschichtliche Anmerkungen zum 'Zeitenbruch' von 1989/90," *Neue Züricher Zeitung*, 20 January 1991; Klaus Tenfelde, "1914 bis 1990—Einheit der Epoche," *Aus Politik und Zeitgeschichte* 40 (1992): 3 ff.; and Jürgen Kocka (ed.), *Historische DDR-Forschung. Aufsätze und Studien*, Berlin, 1993, 9 ff.

2. Compare the series in *Die Zeit* on "What's Left" in 1992 with the series of articles in the *Frankfurter Allgemeine Zeitung* on "What's Right" in April 1994.

3. George Iggers, *Deutsche Geschichtswissenschaft. Eine Kritik der traditionellen Geschichtsauffassung von Herder bis zur Gegenwart*, Munich, 1971; George Iggers (ed.), *The Social History of Politics: Critical Perspectives in West German Historical Writing Since 1945*, Leamington Spa, 1985.

4. Hans-Peter Schwarz, "Das Ende der Identitätsneurose," *Rheinische Merkur*, 7 September 1990; Jürgen Habermas, "Wir sind wieder 'normal' geworden," *Die Zeit*, 18 December 1992.

5. Michael Geyer and Konrad Jarausch, "Great Men and Postmodern Ruptures. Overcoming the 'Belatedness' in German Historiography," *German Studies Review* 28, no. 2 (May 1995); Konrad Jarausch and Matthias Middell (eds.), *Nach dem Erdbeben. (Re-)Konstruktionen ostdeutscher Geschichte und Geschichtswissenschaft*, Leipzig, 1994; and Eric Hobsbawm, "Die Erfindung der Vergangenheit," *Die Zeit*, 9 September 1994.

6. Fritz Stern, "German History in America, 1884–1984," *Central European History* 19 (1986): 131 ff.; Konrad Jarausch, "German Social History American Style," *Journal of Social History* 19 (1985): 349 ff.

7. Hermann Axen, *Zur Entwicklung der sozialistischen Nation der DDR*, Berlin, 1973; Jürgen Hofmann, *Ein neues Deutschland soll es sein. Zur Frage*

der Nation in der Geschichte der DDR und der Politik der SED, Berlin, 1989; and Alexander Fischer and Günter Heydemann (eds.), *Geschichtswissenschaft in der DDR*, 2 vols., Berlin, 1988.

8. Gerhard Ritter, *Das deutsche Problem. Grundfragen deutschen Staatslebens gestern und heute*, Munich, 1962, 7 ff., 196 ff. See also Klaus Schwabe and Rolf Reichardt, *Gerhard Ritter. Ein politischer Historiker in seinen Briefen*, Boppard, 1988.

9. Fritz Fischer, *Bündnis der Eliten. Zur Kontinuität der Machtstrukturen in Deutschland 1871–1945*, Düsseldorf, 1979, 93 ff.; see also John A. Moses, *The Politics of Illusion: The Fischer Controversy in German Historiography*, London, 1975.

10. Hans-Ulrich Wehler, *Das deutsche Kaiserreich 1871–1918*, 4th ed., Göttingen, 1980; and Jürgen Kocka, "Deutsche Geschichte vor Hitler. Zur Diskussion über den 'deutschen Sonderweg,'" in Kocka, *Geschichte als Aufklärung*, Göttingen, 1989, 101 ff.

11. James J. Sheehan, "What Is German History? Reflections on the Role of the Nation in German History and Historiography," *Journal of Modern History* 53 (1991): 1 ff.; and Michael Geyer and Konrad Jarausch, "The Future of the German Past: Transatlantic Reflections for the 1990s," *Central European History* 22 (1989): 227 ff.

12. Gerhard Lozek et al. (eds.), *Unbewältigte Vergangenheit. Handbuch zur Auseinandersetzung mit der westdeutschen bürgerlichen Geschichtsschreibung*, 2d ed., Berlin, 1971.

13. Winfried Schulze, *Deutsche Geschichtswissenschaft nach 1945*, Munich, 1989; Hans-Ulrich Wehler, "Historiography in Germany Today," in Jürgen Habermas (ed.), *Observations on the "Spiritual Situation of the Age,"* Cambridge, 1987, 221 ff.

14. David Calleo, *The German Problem Reconsidered: Germany and the World Order, 1870 to the Present*, Cambridge, 1978; David Blackbourn and Geoff Eley, *Mythen deutscher Geschichtsschreibung. Die gescheiterte bürgerliche Revolution von 1848*, Frankfurt, 1980; Jack Dukes and Joachim Remak (eds.), *Wilhelmian Germany: The Other Side*, Boulder, CO, 1988.

15. Helmut Meier and Walter Schmidt (eds.), *Erbe und Tradition in der DDR. Die Diskussion der Historiker*, Berlin, 1988; Georg Iggers, "Die Geschichtswissenschaft in der ehemaligen DDR aus Sicht der USA," in Konrad Jarausch (ed.), *Zwischen Parteilichkeit und Professionalität. Bilanz der Geschichtswissenschaft der DDR*, Berlin, 1991, 57 ff.; and Jan H. Brinks, *Die DDR-Geschichtswissenschaft auf dem Weg zur deutschen Einheit*, Frankfurt, 1992.

16. Charles S. Maier, *The Unmasterable Past*, Cambridge, MA, 1988; Konrad H. Jarausch, "Removing the Nazi Stain? The Quarrel of the German Historians," *German Studies Review* 11 (1988): 285 f.

17. Gebhard Schweigler, *Nationalbewußtsein in der BRD und der DDR*, Düsseldorf, 1973; Werner Weidenfeld (ed.), *Politische Kultur und deutsche Frage. Materialen zum Staats- und Nationalbewußtsein in der Bundesrepublik Deutschland*, Cologne 1987; Heinz Niemann, *Meinungsforschung in der DDR. Die geheimen Berichte des Instituts für Meinungsforschung an das Politbüro der SED*, Cologne, 1993.

18. Thomas M. Gauly, *Die Last der Geschichte. Kontroversen zur deutschen Identität*, Cologne, 1988; Studienzentrum Weikersheim (ed.), *Deutsche Identität heute*, Stuttgart, 1983.

19. Volker Ulrich, "Die neue Dreistigkeit," *Die Zeit*, 6 November 1992; Reinhard Kühnl, *Gefahr von rechts? Vergangenheit und Gegenwart der extremen Rechten*, Heilbronn, 1990.

20. Klaus Hartung, "Wider den linken Alarmismus," *Die Zeit*, 27 November 1992; "Nach Mölln ein Volk im Schock," *Spiegel*, 7 December 1992; Richard von Weizsäcker, "The Dignity of Man Is Inviolable," *Statements and Speeches* 15 (1992), no. 17; Helmut Kohl, "Erklärung," ibid., no. 18.

21. Jürgen Kocka, "Die deutsche Einheit und die Sozialwissenschaften," *Tagesspiegel*, 16 September 1992; Kocka, "Zwischen Sonderweg und Bürgergesellschaft," ibid., 17 September 1992.

22. Keynote address by Wolfgang J. Mommsen, "Der Ort der DDR in der deutschen Geschichte," Potsdam Conference of the Forschungsschwerpunkt Zeithistorische Studien, 6 June 1993. See also his essay "Die Geschichtswissenschaft nach der 'demokratischen Revolution' in Ostmitteleuropa," *Neue Rundschau* 105 (1994): 75 ff.

23. Peter Alter, *Nationalismus*, Frankfurt, 1985; Benedict Anderson, *Imagined Communities: Reflections on the Origins and Spread of Nationalism*, London, 1983; Otto Dann, *Nation und Nationalismus in Deutschland 1770–1990*, 2d ed., Munich, 1994.

24. For example, Christoph Klessmann, *Die doppelte Staatsgründung. Deutsche Geschichte, 1945–1955*, Göttingen, 1982, and Michael Lemke, "'Doppelte Alleinvertretung.' Die nationalen Vereinigungskonzepte der beiden deutschen Regierungen und die Grundzüge ihrer politischen Realisierung in der DDR," *Zeitschrift für Geschichtswissenschaft* 40 (1992): 531 ff.

25. Harold James, *Vom Historikerstreit zum Historikerschweigen*, Berlin, 1993, and *A German Identity*, London, 1989.

26. Gregor Schöllgen, *Angst vor der Macht. Die Deutschen und ihre Außenpolitik*, Frankfurt, 1993. See also Michael Stürmer, *Die Grenzen der Macht. Begegnungen der Deutschen mit der Geschichte*, Berlin, 1990, 178 ff.

27. Hagen Schulze, *Gibt es überhaupt eine deutsche Geschichte?* Berlin, 1989; Gregor Schöllgen, *Das Land der Mitte Europas. Stadien deutscher Außenpolitik von Friedrich dem Großen bis zur Gegenwart*, Munich, 1992.

28. Rainer Zitelmann, Karlheinz Weissmann, and Michael Grossheim (eds.), *Westbindung. Chancen und Risiken für Deutschland*, Frankfurt, 1993, 9 ff.; Zitelmann, "Wiedervereinigung und deutscher Selbsthaß: Probleme mit dem eigenen Volk," in Werner Weidenfeld (ed.), *Deutschland. Eine Nation—doppelte Geschichte*, Cologne, 1993, 235 ff.

29. Karlheinz Weissmann, *Rückruf in die Geschichte. Die deutsche Herausforderung*, Frankfurt, 1992, and "Wiederkehr eines Totgesagten: Der Nationalstaat am Ende des 20. Jahrhunderts," *Aus Politik und Zeitgeschichte* 43 (Summer 1993): 3ff.

30. Jens Hacker, *Deutsche Irrtümer. Schönfärber und Helfershelfer der SED-Diktatur im Westen*, Berlin, 1992, 352 ff.

31. Haus der Geschichte der Bundesrepublik Deutschland, *Zeiträume. Konzept, Architektur, Ausstellungen*, Berlin, 1994; Deutsches Historisches Museum, *Prospekt*, Berlin, 1994.

32. Botho Strauss, "Anschwellender Bockgesang," *Spiegel*, 8 February 1993, and "Der eigentliche Skandal," *Spiegel*, 18 April 1994; Klaus Hartung, "Die Nation gehört nicht der Rechten," *Die Zeit*, 29 October 1993; Ulrich Greiner, "Der Seher auf dem Markt," *Die Zeit*, 29 April 1994.

33. Karl-Rudolf Korte, *Nation und Nationalstaat. Bausteine einer europäischen Identität*, Melle, 1993; Axel Knoblich, Antonio Peter, and Erik Natter (eds.), *Auf dem Weg zu einer gesamtdeutschen Identität*, Cologne, 1993; Dietrich Mühlberg, "Die DDR als Gegenstand kulturhistorischer Forschung," *Mitteilungen aus der kulturwissenschaftlichen Forschung* 33 (1993): 7–85.
34. Ulrich Wyrwa, "Nationen in Europa. Von den Rändern und der Mitte her," *Werkstatt Geschichte* 3 (1994): 3–13; Wolfgang Schäuble, "Der Platz in der Mitte," *Frankfurter Allgemeine Zeitung*, 6 July 1994; interview, *Spiegel* 38 (1994); Wolfgang Schäuble, *Und der Zukunft zugewandt*, Berlin, 1994.
35. Peter Glotz, "Deutsche Gefahren," *Spiegel* 17 (1994); Rudolf Walther, "Was ist 'nationale Identität'?" *Die Zeit*, 19 August 1994; Hans-Ulrich Wehler, "Gurus und Irrlichter. Die neuen Träume der Intellektuellen," *Frankfurter Allgemeine Zeitung*, 6 May 1994; Jürgen Habermas, "Gelähmte Politik," *Spiegel* 28 (1993).
36. Brigitte Seebacher-Brandt, "Strudel im Meinungsstrom. Gegen geistigen Konformismus," *Frankfurter Allgemeine Zeitung*, 18 April 1994; Karlheinz Weissmann, "Die Nation denken. Wir sind keine Verschwörer," ibid., 22 April 1994; Jan Ross, "Schwellendes Philistertum," ibid., 9 May 1994; Heimo Schwilk and Ulrich Schacht (eds.), *Die selbstbewußte Nation. "Anschwellender Bockgesang" und weitere Beiträge zu einer deutschen Debatte*, Frankfurt, 1994.
37. Christian Meier, "Die Republik denken," *Frankfurter Allgemeine Zeitung*, 29 April 1994, and *Die Nation die keine sein will*, Munich, 1991; Heinrich August Winkler, "Für den Westen—ohne Vorbehalt," *Die Zeit*, 26 November 1993; Winkler, "Nationalismus, Nationalstaat und nationale Frage in Deutschland seit 1945," *Aus Politik und Zeitgeschichte*, 40 (1991): 12 ff.
38. Ulrich Greiner, "Die Neunundachtziger," *Die Zeit*, 16 September 1994. Rainer Zitelmann, "Position und Begriff. Über eine neue demokratische Rechte," *Die selbstbewußte Nation*, 163 ff.
39. Karlheinz Weissmann, "Der 'Westen' in der deutschen Historiographie nach 1945," and Ansgar Graz, "(Historiker-) Streit unter Adenauers Enkeln," in Zitelmann et al. (eds.), *Westbindung*, 343 ff., 365 ff.
40. Erik Natter, "Wie sehen sich die Deutschen selbst? Empirisches Material aus West- und Ostdeutschland," in *Auf dem Weg zu einer gesamtdeutschen Identität*, 19 ff.; and youth survey in *Spiegel* 38 (1994).
41. Felix Phillip Lutz, "Verantwortungsbewußtsein und Wohlstandschauvinismus. Die Bedeutung historisch-politischer Einstellungen der Deutschen nach der Einheit," in Weidenfeld (ed.), *Deutschland. Eine Nation—doppelte Geschichte*, 157 ff.
42. Rogers Brubaker, *Citizenship and Nationhood in France and Germany*, Cambridge, 1992; Daniel Cohn-Bendit and Thomas Schnaid, *Heimat Babylon. Das Wagnis der multikulturellen Demokratie*, Hamburg, 1992; Hagen Schulze, *Staat und Nation in der europäischen Geschichte*, Munich, 1994, 377 ff.
43. Werner Weidenfeld, "Deutschland nach der Vereinigung. Vom Modernisierungsschock zur inneren Einheit," in Weidenfeld (ed.), *Deutschland. Eine Nation—doppelte Geschichte*, 13 ff.; Antonia Grunenberg (ed.), *Welche Geschichte wählen wir?* Hamburg, 1992.
44. Bernd Faulenbach, "'Nation' und 'Modernisierung' in der deutschen Geschichte," in Zitelmann et al. (eds.), *Westbindung*, 103 ff.; Faulenbach, "Probleme des Umgangs mit der Vergangenheit im vereinigten Deutschland. Zur Gegenwartsbedeutung der jüngsten deutschen Geschichte," in

Weidenfeld (ed.), *Deutschland. Eine Nation—doppelte Geschichte*, 175 ff.

45. Martin Walser, "Über freie und unfreie Rede," *Der Spiegel*, 7 November 1994, versus Glotz, *Normalisierung*, 11 ff.; Jürgen Gebhardt, "Verfassungspatriotismus als Identitätskonzept der Nation," *Aus Politik und Zeitgeschichte* 43 (1993): 29 ff.; Jürgen Kocka, "Das Problem der Nation in der deutschen Geschichte 1870–1945," in Kocka, *Geschichte als Aufklärung*, 82 ff.

2

Perplexed Normalcy: German Identity After Unification

HANS-GEORG BETZ

For the past 150 years, the German problem has dominated European history. Too strong to be thoroughly integrated into the confines of Europe, but not strong enough to escape Europe and become a world power, Germany persistently remained a focal point of unrest. The national catastrophe of 1945 (unconditional surrender and occupation) and ensuing division finally appeared to have solved the German problem. However, the dramatic events of 1989 that led to unification showed that this was only temporary.

The following discussion deals with a question that is intricately connected to the German problem, namely, the question of national identity. It is based on the premise that after unification the question of German national identity has once again become problematic. For a number of reasons, unified Germany has been unable to adopt the former Federal Republic's identity. At the same time, the transformation of the international environment is increasingly forcing the Germans to come to terms with their new strategic position. The result has been a new German problem.

DEVELOPMENT OF A WEST GERMAN IDENTITY

Throughout much of modern history, Germans have spent a great deal of time and effort in search of their identity. As Friedrich Nietzsche put it in one of his less flattering observations on the German soul, if there is one enduring trait that characterizes the Germans, it is "that the question 'what is German' never dies out among them."[1] More

40

than any other nation in Europe, Germany has suffered from bouts of anxiety regarding its national identity that regularly culminated in identity crises.

A number of reasons have been advanced to explain why, despite great efforts, Germans have failed to develop a stable and secure national identity. In his influential book on the Germans, cultural anthropologist Norbert Elias goes so far as to trace the German identity problem back to the catastrophe of the Thirty Years War, which impoverished, weakened, and divided the German lands at a time when the other great European powers achieved territorial and political consolidation. In Elias's view, the psychological result of this experience of collective weakness was a sense of humiliation and insecurity, which led to the notion that, as a "latecomer," Germany was in a perpetual race to catch up with the rest of the world.[2]

For others, the German inability to construct a durable sense of identity results primarily from the absence of successful and enduring democratic traditions in German history. Thus political scientist Wolfgang Rudzio recently bemoaned the fact that compared with other Western democracies such as France or the United States, German democracy generally lacks "a historical myth." The history of democracy in Germany was too much "a history of defeats" for it to serve as a point of orientation.[3]

Undoubtedly the most significant reason for the recurring crises of national identity that occasionally shook the preunification Federal Republic was the catastrophe of 1945. In the face of total defeat, occupation, and finally a divided country, and confronted with the horrors of Nazi mass murder committed in the name of the German people, the Germans chose in large part to avoid dealing with the problems of their national traditions and identity. In the wake of Auschwitz and Berlin, it appeared that German identity could be defined only negatively. Germany once again was soulless, or, as sociologist and liberal political theorist Ralf Dahrendorf characterized the former Federal Republic in the second half of the 1980s, "not a nation, not a culture, hardly a society but an entity, a country which has been successful economically and one in which economic success has been closely linked to the success of political institutions."[4]

Empirical studies largely supported the contention that Germany was far from a "normal" nation. Cross-national surveys on national pride regularly found the Germans on the low end of the list. In 1970, for example, in a survey among nationals from six European Community (EC) member states, 70 percent of the Belgian, 65 percent of the French, 62 percent of the Italian, 54 percent of the Dutch, but only 37 percent of the German respondents said that they were absolutely proud of their nationality. In the late 1980s, only 21 percent of German respondents said that they were very proud of their nationality, compared with 87 percent of American, 58 percent of British, and 53 percent of Austrian respondents. Only Japanese respondents showed a similarly low level of national pride as the Germans. Similar results were found regarding willingness to defend one's country. Whereas 71 percent of American and 62 percent of British respondents declared that in case of war they would be prepared to defend their country, the corresponding number among German respondents amounted to little more than a third.[5] These findings seemed to suggest that postwar German identity (at least in the former Federal Republic) was of a profoundly pathological nature. Germans constituted an "injured nation" suffering from permanent damages they had largely inflicted upon themselves.[6]

However, what this diagnosis tended to ignore was the fact that in modern advanced industrial and postindustrial societies, the level of national pride might not necessarily be the only, or even best, evidence of national self-consciousness. In fact, a sizable amount of evidence suggests that by the 1980s, the former Federal Republic had developed a particular Federal Republican identity and self-consciousness, which derived their legitimation from nontraditional sources. Surveys revealed striking shifts over time with regard to what West Germans considered the most important sources of national pride (in answer to the question: "what are you most proud of regarding our country?"). In 1959, traditions and customs topped the list (36 percent), followed by the economy (33 percent) and countryside and nature (17 percent), with the political system ranking relatively low on the scale (6 percent). Twenty years later, the picture had radically changed. In 1978, the political system already ranked second (31 percent) behind the economy (40 percent) but ahead of traditions and customs (25 percent) and far ahead of countryside and nature (14 percent). Finally, in 1988, more than half the population said that they were proud of the Basic Law, closely followed by the economy and the welfare state (39 percent).[7]

Even if the latter results are not completely comparable with earlier ones, they confirm the general trend. They show that by the late 1980s, the citizens of the Federal Republic had attained what one might characterize as a postnational, postconventional, even postmodern identity.[8] Its emergence coincided with broader trends of sociocultural liberalization, social fragmentation, and individualization; the formation of "taste cultures" and new postconventional milieus; and the emergence of new political forces such as new social movements and the Greens, which generally were seen as the most visible symptoms of the "Americanization" of West German society.[9] In response, many observers, particularly left-leaning West Germans, concluded that the acceptance of a political order constituted by rights of self-determination and political participation indicated that "the idea that political order is bound to the collective values of a nation separated from other nations as a 'community of fate' via ethnic, historic, and cultural categories," which in the past had defined German identity, had finally been overcome.[10]

Two additional features completed West Germany's postnational identity. One was the particular enthusiasm with which the West Germans pursued the idea of a united Europe. No other member of the EC showed greater support for common European goals than West Germany. Thus, throughout the 1970s, roughly 70 percent of the West German population said that they were in favor of the EC developing into a united Europe. At the same time, between 60 and 65 percent said that they would regret it if the EC were to be dissolved.[11] These survey results, together with other evidence, suggest that a considerable majority of the West German population shared the view that "because the Federal Republic was not a nation-state she seemed particularly suited to promoting the supranational integration of western Europe."[12]

The other important feature of West Germany's postnational identity has been characterized by political scientist Hanns W. Maull as "civilian power." On this view, what differentiated the Federal Republic (and Japan) from traditional powers such as the United States, France, or Great Britain was the fact that the latter still relied to a significant extent on military power, whereas the former had turned into primarily trading states. West Germany's relations toward the outside world were essentially determined by three distinct features: first, West Germany had accepted the necessity of cooperating with others in the pursuit of its national objectives; second, it concentrated primarily on economic and diplomatic means to secure its national goals; and third, it increasingly pushed for the development of supranational structures to confront and solve critical issues of international management.

In the process, the Federal Republic developed not only both constitutional and political mechanisms safeguarding against any unilateral use of military force but also a strong aversion to the use of military force in general. This led West German elites, as well as the general public, to underestimate the continued relevance of military

force in international relations; it fostered "a certain lack of awareness and understanding of the importance of Germany's attitudes and
policies in the overall context of international relations"; and it led to
a tendency "to assume the 'moral high ground' vis-à-vis those who
are more willing to contemplate and implement the use of force."[13]
These tendencies might help explain why occasional outbursts of anti-
Americanism in the Federal Republic (for example, during the controversy over the stationing of new American intermediate nuclear
weapons on West German soil in the early 1980s) took on a particularly emotionally charged character.[14]

The evidence provided so far suggests that over a period of several
decades, the Federal Republic succeeded in developing a distinct identity. This identity was grounded in a growing acceptance of, and even
something like pride in, the constitutional and political system, even
if, as Ralf Dahrendorf and others repeatedly noted, the acceptance of
the political system was closely linked at first to the success of the
economy and later increasingly to the welfare state. This, however,
was hardly cause for alarm. To a certain degree, it might even be
considered proof of normalization and convergence with other Western democracies whose publics were hardly less output-oriented than
the West Germans.

West Germany's transformation into a civilian power was not without
its critics, who charged that Germans had gone from being *machtbesessen*
(obsessed with power) in the past to being *machtvergessen* (oblivious
to power) in the present.[15] Again, however, one could suggest that
this was nothing but the logical consequence of the catastrophe of
1945. Rather than supporting the notion that Germany was an "injured nation," the fact that the West Germans were particularly reluctant to defend their own country was perhaps the most telling evidence
that the majority of the population had internalized the lessons of
their past.

CONFRONTING THE PAST

If West Germany succeeded in constructing a new postconventional
identity, its basis was the notion that 1945 marked both a clear break
with the German past and a new beginning (the myth of the *Stunde
null*, the zero hour). West Germany's identity was not only *machtvergessen*, but also to a large extent *geschichtslos* (devoid of history). In
the face of Auschwitz, the majority of West Germans chose largely to
avoid a confrontation with the past.[16] In the immediate postwar years,
the occupying powers forced the Germans to confront the reality of

the Nazi crimes. However, with the founding of the Federal Republic, there emerged a widely shared political and societal consensus to put the Nazi crimes to rest. This consensus was only on rare occasions disturbed. With time, a growing number of West Germans agreed with the statement that there should not be so much talk about the Holocaust, that one should rather draw a line under the past (in the late 1980s, two-thirds of the West German population agreed with that statement).[17] At the same time, sentiments were growing stronger that after forty years West Germany had earned the right no longer to be reminded of its past. As Bavaria's former minister-president Franz Josef Strauss put it, "a people that has created such an economic miracle has a right not to be constantly reminded of Auschwitz."[18]

The result, however, was less than convincing. More often than not, it ended in public embarrassment and public-relations disasters, including Bitburg (1985), the *Historikerstreit* (1986–88), the resignation of Philipp Jenninger, president of the Bundestag (1988), the resignation of CDU presidential candidate Steffen Heitmann (1993), and the scandal surrounding the sentence of the Mannheim state court in the case against the chairman of the right-wing extremist National Democratic Party (NPD), Günter Deckert (1994).[19] The last case in particular is paradigmatic.

Accused of having publicly agreed with the views of Fred Leuchter, an American expert in gas chamber construction who repeatedly stated that the gas chambers in Auschwitz could not have been used for mass gassings, Deckert was sentenced to one year in prison with probation. After Deckert appealed to the Federal Court of Justice, the latter referred the case to the state court in Mannheim. Although the Mannheim court would not go so far as to repeal the earlier sentence, the judges showed a surprising amount of understanding for the accused. Among other things, the court attested to the fact that he was "strong of character," a "responsible personality with clear principle." Furthermore, the court noted that the accused was not an anti-Semite in the sense of the Nazi ideology, but that he took "bitter offense that the Jews continued to insist on the Holocaust and that almost fifty years after the end of the war they still made financial, political, and moral demands on Germany . . . while the mass crimes committed by other peoples remained unpunished."[20]

The ensuing uproar in the German media should not obscure the fact that the judges' opinion only reflected sentiments and resentments that have been widespread among the West German public.[21] The court decision marked only the most recent instance in a series of scarcely hidden attempts to promote understanding for both the (German) perpetrators of past crimes (e.g., in Bitburg) and the large number of Germans who tacitly supported the Nazis' attitudes—if not their actions—toward Jews and other minorities (e.g., Philipp Jenninger's speech), to create empathy for their motives and their particular situation (e.g., some aspects of the *Historikerstreit*), and to exculpate them of any guilt. This could only reaffirm the impression that the Germans were considerably more sympathetic toward the perpetrators than their victims.[22]

The Germans' continued difficulties in coming to terms with their past is perhaps the most significant evidence that despite considerable progress elsewhere, the Federal Republic is still far from being a "normal" nation. This became clear once again in the late 1980s with the sudden rise of the radical right-wing populist Republikaner. Among other things, Schönhuber's party demanded the "decriminalization of German history" and an "objective interpretation" that no longer reduced all of German history to Auschwitz, and it called for Germany's acceptance as a normal nation.[23]

The sudden success of the Republikaner reflected yet another aspect of the Germans' problems with their identity—namely, how to confront the growing influx of immigrants and refugees and the new reality that the Federal Republic was rapidly turning into a multicultural society. Some West German intellectuals have argued that multiculturalism implies above all that minorities have the opportunity to preserve and develop their culture and identity and that the majority makes an effort to understand and tolerate alien cultures and, if necessary, contributes (above all, financially) to their preservation.[24] For this, West Germans were largely unprepared. To be sure, surveys found that in the 1980s, West German attitudes toward foreign immigrants and "guest workers" were changing to a considerable extent. Between 1980 and 1990, the number of West Germans who thought that immigrant workers should adapt their lifestyles to that of the Germans fell from 45 to 34 percent; the proportion of those who said that foreign workers should choose their spouses from among themselves declined from 33 to 18 percent; and the number of those who thought that foreign workers should be sent home when jobs get scarce dropped from 38 to 20 percent.[25]

However, the dramatic increase in the number of immigrants and refugees in the late 1980s led to an equally dramatic rise in xenophobia and racism in the Federal Republic. Not only did a growing number of West Germans think that the number of foreign immigrants in the Federal Republic was too high, they also thought that the number of all immigrants and refugees (even German resettlers from the east) should be drastically reduced to prevent an "invasion of the poor" from "flooding" the country.[26] At the same time, Germans grew increasingly willing to support even the most extremist positions. In early 1989, for example, 24 percent of the population agreed with the statement that the Germans should take care to keep Germanness (*das Deutsche*) pure and prevent the mixing of peoples (*Völkervermischung*).[27] Even if only a minority of Germans were prepared to express their fears and anxieties about a threatened foreignization (*Überfremdung*) in such drastic terms, the increasingly hysterical overtones of the public debate clearly showed that Germans were far from willing to accept the new realities. In fact, when the Allensbach Institute asked in January 1992 to what degree Germans supported a multicultural society, only 48 percent of the population of the former Federal Republic knew what multiculturalism meant, and only half of those who knew what it meant supported it.[28]

The discussion so far suggests that by the late 1980s the Federal Republic had developed its own distinct identity. This identity was not without ambiguities. On the one hand, the West Germans had largely embraced Western-style democratic values. What appeared problematic was the fact that this loyalty to the political system was largely dependent on the success of the economic system. On the other hand, the Federal Republic faced continued problems with its historical legacy, which ensured that West German society remained in a state of limbo while at the same time engendering growing feelings of resentment. The refugee and immigrant crisis of the late 1980s only exacerbated these tensions. The debate about multiculturalism and its consequences for German society showed above all else that its postnational identity had its limits.

THE NATIONAL QUESTION

Any account of the evolution and transformation of Germany's postwar identity would be incomplete without a discussion of the central issue: the attitudes toward division and unification. Here we find evidence of a growing divergence between pretension and reality that supports the main contention of the first part of our argument. Looking back at the evolution of public views on unification in the former Federal Republic, one finds at least three developments.[29] First, as regards the overall support for unification, one finds throughout the postwar period that a large majority of West Germans came out in favor of unification. Although there was a decline from the early 90 percent support in the 1960s, by the 1980s, about 80 percent of the

West German public still favored unification, with only a marginal 3 to 5 percent objecting to it and the rest largely showing indifference.

At the same time, the number of those believing that unification could still be achieved dropped precipitously. Until the mid-1960s, a small majority of West Germans thought that unification was a real possibility. However, with the advent of Ostpolitik in the late 1960s, the number of those expecting unification dropped to around 10 percent in the early 1970s; after a brief increase in the early and mid-1980s, it fell to a mere 3 percent in 1987. At the same time, fewer and fewer West Germans considered unification an important issue on the political agenda. In 1955, a third of the West German population considered reunification the most important question for the Federal Republic, but by the early 1980s, unification had virtually disappeared as an important societal and political issue (less than 0.5 percent in 1983).[30] The longer the division of Germany lasted, the more realistic the West German public grew about the prospects of eventual unification. A similar development appears to have occurred in the GDR.[31] Manfred Kuechler was probably right when he observed that with growing separation in both Germanies, "the public had accepted the existence of two German states as a fact. The very idea of unification continued to be appealing, though on a more pragmatic level some degree of liberalization in the East . . . seemed to satisfy the vast majority of all Germans."[32] In fact, in a survey conducted in March 1989— a mere nine months before the opening of the wall—by the Emnid Institute for *Der Spiegel*, 44 percent of the West German population agreed with the statement that the German question was no longer open, that one had to understand that reunification was no longer an option.[33]

Similar changes occurred with regard to West German attitudes toward the GDR. It is important to understand that the Federal Republic derived both its self-understanding and its legitimation to a considerable extent from a strict demarcation from the GDR. Or, as French political scientist Anne-Marie Le Gloannec put it, "its ideological foundations—from 1949 to 1990—were necessarily premised on the existence of a second German state."[34] This could not help but shape West Germans' attitudes toward the "other Germany" and might explain why these attitudes were so ambiguous. Generally it can be said that West Germans were quite sympathetic to the East Germans as a people and quite hostile to East Germany as a state. In 1984, for example, 83 percent of West German respondents recognized the existence of two German *states*; at the same time, 73 percent said that they considered the Germans in east and west as *one people*. This might also explain why only a small minority of West Germans (24 percent), when asked what Germans could be proud of, mentioned the achievements of East German athletes (compared with 54 percent who said that they were proud of the achievements of West German athletes).[35]

At the same time, a growing number of West Germans appear to have abandoned the notion of one nation in favor of considering East and West Germany not only as two German states but as two German nations. Thus, between 1974 and 1984, the proportion of West Germans who said that the Federal Republic of Germany (FRG) and the GDR represented one nation decreased from 70 to 42 percent, whereas the number of those who said that the two states did not constitute a nation increased from 29 to 53 percent.[36] The pattern was similar with regard to questions about what constitutes "Germany." Ever since the question was raised for the first time in the late 1970s, more than half the West German respondents associated "Germany" with the Federal Republic; only between 25 and 30 percent associated it with both the Federal Republic and the GDR (1989 results: FRG only, 54 percent; FRG and GDR, 29 percent; Germany within the borders of 1937, 16 percent).[37] Only a minority of West Germans, however, went so far as to consider the GDR a completely foreign country. Between 1973 and 1987, the number of those who did so increased from 22 to 32 percent. The overwhelming majority, however, although "differentiating between two German states of one German people," was unwilling to give up the common historical roots."[38]

There were, however, clearly distinguishable groups that were quite willing to do just that. Polls showed that national sentiments were least developed among young West Germans and among followers of the West German Greens. In 1987, for example, only 65 percent of those aged fourteen to twenty-nine (compared with 78 percent of the whole population) considered themselves members of one German people; 51 percent of the West Germans of that age group (compared with 32 percent of the whole population) considered the GDR a foreign country. The results were even more dramatic for the West German Greens. In 1989, for example, 65 percent of Green supporters thought that the German question was no longer open, compared with 52 percent of West Germans aged eighteen to twenty-nine and 44 percent of the whole population.[39]

The evidence provided in this section suggests that as West German society gradually adopted its own distinct postconventional identity, it gradually drifted away from the notion of the common nation. As West Germany acquired its own identity, West Germans grew increasingly indifferent to their brothers and sisters on the other side of the border. This was particularly true for younger and better educated citizens of the Federal Republic. "West Germans, living in an open and mobile society, part and parcel of the western world, subject to democratic influences and global trends, looked upon the GDR as another world, closed and stale, with which they had few affinities, if any."[40] For a growing number of citizens of the former Federal Republic, Paris, Milan, Palma de Mallorca, and even New York were infinitely closer than Dresden, Leipzig, or Rostock. From this, one might even conclude that the Federal Republic owed the fact that a distinct West German identity could emerge and take shape in the late 1970s to the continued division of the German nation.

CRISIS OF POSTCONVENTIONAL IDENTITY

Just when there were some strong indications that, at least as far as the former Federal Republic was concerned, the question of German identity had finally been resolved, the end of the Cold War appeared to reopen the German problem anew. For many foreign as well as German observers, German unification once again forced the Germans to reassess their collective identity.[41] As historian Heinrich August Winkler put it, the Federal Republican self-understanding of a "post-national democracy among nation-states does not apply to unified Germany. The New Federal Republic *is* a nation-state—though clearly of a more postclassical than classical nature."[42]

However, the argument that the search for German identity in the early 1990s was primarily due to unification conveniently overlooks the fact that in the late 1980s, West Germany's postnational identity was already suffering from serious strains. In the past, West Germany's identity was largely tied to economic performance, which, in turn, contributed to growing pride in the country's constitutional and political system. In the late 1980s, however, there were a number of signs indicating that both the economy and the political system were confronting a major structural crisis. At the same time, Germans harbored growing doubts about the future of European integration. What remained largely intact was support for Germany's position as a civilian power.

Given the Federal Republic's strong position in the international economy throughout the 1980s, Germans were largely unprepared for the structural crisis that affected their country in the early 1990s. In the early 1980s, German per capita growth was still among the highest in the world. Germany was still the number-two exporter, only marginally behind the United States and comfortably ahead of Japan. What this image obscured, however, was the fact that the country was facing deep structural problems that it largely failed to resolve. In the mid-1980s, the Federal Republic was already experiencing rapidly growing mass unemployment, a growing number of long-term unemployed, and the emergence of a new type of poverty that contributed to the growing gap between the average citizen and an increasing number of marginalized groups, putting a strain on the social system.[43] Yet what was perhaps most alarming was the fact that because of a rigid, immobile, and inflexible socioeconomic system, the Federal Republic appeared to be less and less capable of competing in a rapidly changing global economy. Weighed down by the combined burden of high taxes, overregulation, high labor and social costs, and a rigid labor market, in the late 1980s, the *Standort Deutschland* was on the verge of losing much of its previous attractiveness. Although the "pervasiveness of wealth and affluence helped to distract from structural problems," the Federal Republic was not only at risk of losing "its hard-won rank in world-wide competition" but also at risk of losing out "in those areas where she was recently preeminent."[44] Unification only compounded the country's economic and financial problems, while acting as a lens magnifying Germany's weaknesses with regard to its global competitiveness.[45] Surveys from the late 1980s support the contention that already before unification, a sizable proportion of the West German public had become skeptical about West Germany's economic future. When asked in early 1989 what kind of life their children would have in the future, almost twice as many West Germans thought that it would be worse (39 percent) as thought that it would be better than their own (20 percent). Pessimism increased after unification. Between early 1990 and late 1993, the number of former West Germans who said that they faced the future with some anxiety increased from 26 to 54 percent.[46]

The late 1980s also saw a dramatic rise in popular disaffection with political parties, the political class, and politics in general.[47] The main symptoms were rapidly declining confidence in the average citizen's ability to influence major political decisions, growing voter abstention in state and federal elections, and the rise of radical right-wing populist parties and regional protest parties. Between 1980 and 1989 alone, the number of West Germans who thought that they had no influence on politics increased from 48 to 63 percent, and those who thought that the political parties were interested only in votes and not in what the people thought rose from 63 to 75 percent. The growing loss of confidence in the political system was also reflected in increasing rates of abstention. In the 1980 federal election, turnout was 88.6 percent of the vote, but in the first all-German election of 1990, turnout dropped to 78.6 percent of eligible voters (in the former Federal Republic; in the former GDR it was even lower). This was the lowest turnout since 1949, when it had been 78.5 percent.[48]

A growing number of West Germans were prepared to vote for new, nontraditional parties. Thus the spectacular gains of the radical right-wing Republikaner in the European elections of 1989 can largely be attributed to massive voter protest against the established parties.[49] Although unification reversed these trends, the reversal proved only temporary. In the early 1990s, annual surveys conducted for the Interior Ministry showed once again an alarming decline in public satisfaction with democracy and the political system. Whereas in the 1980s the proportion of the population that was satisfied with democracy had never dropped below 70 percent, by 1993, that number had fallen to 54 percent in the west; in the east it amounted to little more than 40 percent. What was more, compared with 1989, there was a marked increase in dissatisfaction with the political system among the supporters of all major parties, including supporters of the center-right coalition.[50]

The deterioration of the Federal Republic's position in the emerging global economy and the growing perception that the political class was largely unprepared to confront the challenges facing the new Germany appear to have considerably shaken public confidence. Perhaps Germany's most widely read newsweekly, *Der Spiegel*, expressed the sense of anxiety best when it warned that Germany threatened to become a "second league player."[51] However, despite the most serious economic crisis since the foundation of the republic, and despite what represented probably the most profound erosion of popular confidence in the democratic system, Germany remained relatively stable, although a wave of xenophobic attacks on foreign residents, the growth of skinhead and neo-Nazi groups, and occasional electoral successes of radical right-wing parties in the early 1990s were reason for concern. In this sense, at least, Germany had become a "normal" nation, neither better nor worse than its neighbors. However, the new reality of mass unemployment, growing pockets of poverty, and widespread fears of individual socioeconomic decline and marginalization inevitably undermined Germany's postnational identity, which to a great extent had been founded on pride in economic achievement, material prosperity, and social welfare.

The situation was similar with respect to German attitudes toward European integration. Whereas in the early decades of the Federal

Republic a majority of West German citizens was overly enthusiastic about the idea of a united Europe, in the late 1980s they grew increasingly skeptical about its prospects and pragmatic about Germany's membership in the European Union (EU). In 1976, almost half of the West German population felt strongly attracted to the notion of being a European, but by 1989, that number had declined to 38 percent.[52] One of the most important reasons behind these new sentiments was the question of the currency union, that is, the replacement of the symbol of German economic success, the D-Mark, by a rather sterile bureaucratic invention, the European Currency Union (ECU). As recently as 1970, 52 percent of the West German population supported the idea of abolishing the D-Mark in favor of a uniform European currency. Twelve years later, a mere third of the population still supported it; 45 percent were against it. In the early 1990s, opposition grew even more: in 1994, 70 percent said that they were against replacing the D-Mark with a European currency.[53] At the same time, polls found a growing number of Germans who saw a threat to German culture in the process of European integration. Between 1991 and 1993, the number of those who agreed grew from 15 to 23 percent, and the number of those who disagreed strongly decreased from 42 to 26 percent. It appears that the two developments were linked: for a significant proportion of the German population, the abolition of the D-Mark in favor of a common European currency represented a direct attack on their identity.[54]

The 1980s also witnessed growing German realism regarding the costs and benefits of European union. In the 1980s, polls revealed a considerable drop in the number of those who considered German membership in the European Union "a good thing": from 61 percent in 1979 to 53 percent in 1989. By 1994, the number had declined to 41 percent. Polls also found that a growing number of Germans believed that the process of European integration should be slowed rather than accelerated. In 1988, 14 percent thought that it should be slowed, and 33 percent opted for acceleration. By 1993, 35 percent thought that integration should be slowed, with 19 percent in favor of acceleration.[55]

The decrease in German enthusiasm for European union in the 1980s and 1990s is not difficult to explain. The image of Brussels as a distant, anonymous bureaucratic machine over which the average citizen has no control, and frustration over a European Parliament that has no real power, "subdue on all sides enthusiasm for Europe—not least of all for the West Germans, for whom 'Europe' substituted for national identity."[56] But this negative image of European union also marked the emergence of a new realism on the part of the Germans.

European identity was a viable option only as long as there was some assurance that the other western Europeans shared a commitment to the gradual dissolution of their nation-states in a united Europe. As western Europeans have grown more skeptical about the project of a united Europe, it is not surprising that Germans too have had to re-think their position. One could hardly expect the Germans to be the only ones to hold on to a dream that the rest of western Europe had long since abandoned.[57] The shift from Euro-enthusiasm to more prag-matic cost-benefit calculations was thus another indication that Ger-many was on its way to becoming a normal western European nation.

THE WALL IN THE HEAD

It is possible to interpret the transformation of German attitudes to-ward European integration as part of a more comprehensive and sin-ister development. From this perspective, the former Federal Republic had given up some of its sovereignty to supranational organizations in order to attain sovereignty, including the possibility of reunification. Once Germany had attained its goal, the country was free to liberate itself from the ties that had helped "tame" the Germans in the past. According to a 1994 survey, more than half the German population refused to give up national independence in favor of a unified European state, which could be read as a further symptom of the "renationali-zation" of the German question.[58]

A number of arguments contradict this view. First, unification did not lead to greater national pride. In 1990, 70 percent of West Ger-mans said that they were proud to be Germans; in late 1992, 69 per-cent.[59] Second, although in the early 1990s it became increasingly clear that a growing number of Germans regarded the prospects of a Euro-pean union with a mixture of apathy and skepticism, the political class continued to push for integration. As Hans-Peter Schwarz pointed out, at the "very moment that Germany was regaining the status of a united nation and major European Power, it decided to limit its own autonomy and to function as a unit of the EU." In what British histo-rian Timothy Garton Ash called "a symbolic act of profound signifi-cance," in December 1992 the unified German state amended the famous article 23 of the Basic Law on which German unification had been based to commit Germany to "the realization of a united Europe" through the European Union as envisaged by the Maastricht Treaty.[60]

Finally, there has been the fallout from unification itself. As has become painfully obvious, unification has turned out quite differently from what many observers expected in 1990. As many polls show, the West German public was hardly prepared for a quick unification of the two German states. Once unification appeared inevitable, a majority of the West German public supported it, however reluctantly. In December 1989, for example, when asked whether Germany should be united or remain as two independent countries, 41 percent opted for the second solution. In the spring of 1990, only 19 percent said that they were "very pleased" about unification (as compared with 41 percent in the east); 26 percent were either not pleased or indifferent (as compared with only 9 percent in the east).[61]

After unification, West German disenchantment with unification continued to grow, and with it, resentment toward their new fellow citizens (*Mitbürger*). Between early 1991 and late 1992, polls noted that the earlier joy over unification was gradually giving way to growing worries about the problems associated with it. In May 1993, the renowned Allensbach Institute warned that the Germans were "feeling less and less like a united people." Other German observers warned of a growing "wall in our heads."[62]

In 1990, West German responses to the idea of unification were already quite different from those in the eastern part of the country. For West Germans, unification meant above all economic problems. In view of the mounting financial problems created by unification, West Germans expected that Germany would be preoccupied with its own problems for years to come. Rising financial demands from the east appeared to confirm these expectations, challenging the West German public's willingness to sacrifice a part of its affluence for the East Germans—a willingness that was soon exhausted. In 1993, more than two-thirds opposed greater financial aid to the east.[63] Initial joy soon gave way first to skepticism and then to growing resentment.

In no other group were skepticism and resentment as pronounced as among the intellectual and political Left. For the Left, reunification meant a return to a nationalist past that the Federal Republic appeared to have overcome, a return to the crass materialism that had characterized West German society in the 1950s and 1960s, and a return to the authoritarianism of the Adenauer period. According to this view, the vast majority of the population in the former GDR had developed what sociologist Martin Greiffenhagen called a "lower-class authoritarianism," characterized by obedience to hierarchy, apathy, and a lack of trust—characteristics that were bound to affect the political culture of postunification Germany. In the words of political scientist Michael Minkenberg, unified Germany "inherited from the GDR a modified subject culture which was derived from the authoritarian traditions of the *Obrigkeitsstaat*." As a result, East Germans could be expected to adopt behavioral patterns reminiscent of those of West Germans in the 1950s: "ritualistic conformity with authorities, retreatism, and rebellion." Greiffenhagen's fears went in a similar direction. For him, the way unification had been achieved—largely from above—threatened to reawaken traditional aspects of West German political culture. Once again, economic efficiency threatened to become the sole criterion "for the value or non-value (*Wert oder Unwert*) of a political regime."[64]

It is hardly surprising that those groups that had fought hardest against nationalist and authoritarian tendencies in the Federal Republic were least enthusiastic about unification. Particularly among the post-'68 Left, many considered the division of Germany to be just punishment for the atrocities committed by Germans in the past. If nothing else, unification for them meant that Germany had escaped the shadows of Auschwitz. In the past, division had served as a constant reminder of the crimes committed in the German name, and unification threatened to absolve the Germans from historical responsibility.[65] In response, the great majority of the New Left and their supporters rejected unification. Thus in 1990, almost half of Green supporters said that they were not pleased with or were indifferent toward German unification.[66]

Studies carried out at the time of unification showed that East Germans generally tended to be more materialistic and, to a limited degree, more authoritarian than their West German counterparts. At the same time, however, easterners were considerably more socially oriented than their western cousins. Although younger East Germans appeared to be particularly susceptible to adopting radical right-wing attitudes, East Germans as a whole were, if anything, more immune to right-wing thinking than were West Germans.[67] Thus in 1994, only 4 percent of respondents in the east "strongly" agreed with the statement that Jews are exploiting the Holocaust for their own purposes. In the west, 18 percent agreed strongly. Similarly, 56 percent of West Germans, but ony 36 percent of East Germans, said that they wanted to draw a line under the past. Polls on the question of refugees revealed similar tendencies. In 1993, 31 percent in the east, but only 19 percent in the west, said that Germany should accept without restrictions people who fled human rights violations in their countries.[68] These results contradict the notion that East Germans are particularly authoritarian. On the contrary, as Russell Dalton recently argued, East German attitudes toward democracy have rivaled, if not excelled, the expression of democratic norms in the west.[69]

PERPLEXED NORMALCY

The evidence accumulated during the past few years suggests that unification has not led to the rise of a new nationalism in Germany. If anything, unified Germany seems to be as much an artificial entity as was the former Federal Republic or the GDR. In fact, evidence suggests that since unification, the two parts of Germany have grown further apart. In 1990, the majority of East Germans said that they considered themselves above all to be Germans, but two years later, a majority said that they considered themselves East Germans. By 1993, East Germans were rediscovering "their" GDR. The result was a diffuse GDR nostalgia, which found expression both in the increased demand for East German products and in the renaissance of a number of GDR ideological positions. Thus in 1993, 56 percent of the East German population said that they believed that in a hundred years people would say that socialism had had its good sides (16 percent in the west); 29 percent believed that only through socialism could human beings attain true equality (11 percent in the west); and 14 percent believed that a reformed socialism would be better for the future of Germany than the established market-oriented system of the Federal Republic. Given the revival of GDR consciousness, it was hardly surprising that the Party of Democratic Socialism (PDS)—SED successor organization and representive par excellence of GDR nostalgia—reemerged as a serious political force in the early 1990s.[70]

Unification, rather than settling the question of German identity once and for all, has raised it anew. Could there be a German identity if the main foundations of the Federal Republic's postconventional identity had not been eroded and a new, national identity was not in the making? And what about Germany's past? As historian Christian Meier put it, either the Germans are a nation and thus have to carry historical responsibility, or they are just a bunch of people who happened to grow up between Rhine and Oder (or migrated there) and thus can hardly be held responsible for the crimes committed half a century ago.[71]

I suggest that there is a solution. Yet ironically, this solution already seems to have become the major source of a new German problem. If there is anything left of the former Federal Republic's postconventional identity, it is the sense that Germany has been and still is a civilian power. Since the notion of civilian power is, among others, also an expression of the lessons learned from the past, it should satisfy those who see it as their foremost task to keep memory alive. At the same time, it goes well with the broader sociocultural changes that occurred in the former Federal Republic during the 1980s. Nothing could better confirm this than a poll conducted at the time of unification that asked West Germans how they envisioned Germany by the year 2000. Forty percent of the respondents answered "like Switzerland," and another 29 percent answered "like Sweden," two "small neutral but wealthy countries, geographically tucked away from the brunt of world conflicts."[72]

Nothing in the evolution of the political climate in Germany since unification suggests that these sentiments have abated. Only a few critics of the current political climate have dared to ask the hard questions: "Is this really the lesson to be learned from Nazi fascism, that since we are responsible for the worst war crimes in history, we have the moral duty (and privilege) to restrict ourselves for all eternity to taking care of business, leaving other people to offer their lives for human rights?"[73] For the majority, the transformation of the international environment after the end of the Cold War only reinforced the prevailing mood. As a recent white paper on the security of the Federal Republic put it: "Germany has gained most from the revolutionary political changes in Europe. It has achieved its unity with approval of all its neighbors, and the world powers, and now has full sovereignty." The united Germany "is surrounded solely by democratic states, friends and partners."[74] Under these circumstances, it is hardly surprising that the newly unified Germans are particularly reluctant to behave like a traditional European power.

Young Germans in particular appear to take the civilian nature of German power as a given. A survey of German youth for the weekly *Der Spiegel* found that although the vast majority of German youth considered the established German sociopolitical system worthy of being defended (80 percent yes, 19 percent no), only 19 percent said that they would take part in *Bundeswehr* missions to defend Germany. As many as 53 percent said that they would not take part in any *Bundeswehr* missions.[75] Given these sentiments, it is hardly surprising that after unification the number of conscientious objectors to mandatory military service dramatically increased.

Ironically, in the early 1990s, unified Germany appears to have come rather close to what others always wanted Germany to be: a peaceful, satiated nation without hegemonic pretensions that no longer threatens its neighbors. However, just when the ideal was about to turn into reality, both the German political establishment and the public at large, which had taken great pride in Germany's postconventional identity, are "coming to the painful realization that both at home and abroad such attitudes no longer work." In the 1980s, right-wing politicians, academics, and intellectuals called on the Germans to become a "normal nation" again. Now that Germany has finally become normal again (at least in terms of its territorial unity and national sovereignty), Germans appear perplexed as to what to do with their normalcy. As a result, the world once again is faced with a German problem.

As U.S. security analyst Ronald Asmus put it, if the "old German Question centered on the issue of German unity, then the new German Question focuses on what geopolitical role a reunited Germany will now assume in Europe and beyond."[76] In order to come to terms with this question, German society will first have to come to the realization that the "holiday from world politics" (Christian Meier) that the Germans have been taking for the past forty-five years is just about over. Given the extent to which Germany identifies itself as a civilian power, its task will be anything but easy.

NOTES

1. Friedrich Nietzsche, *Beyond Good and Evil*, §244.
2. Norbert Elias, *Studien über die Deutschen: Machtkämpfe und Habitusentwicklung im 19. und 20. Jahrhundert*, Frankfurt, 1992, 12–4.
3. Wolfgang Rudzio, *Das politische System der Bundesrepublik Deutschland*, 3d ed., Opladen, 1991, 480; see also Martin Greiffenhagen and Sylvia Greiffenhagen, *Ein schwieriges Vaterland: Zur politischen Kultur im vereinigten Deutschland*, Munich and Leipzig, 1993, 34–7.
4. Ralf Dahrendorf, "The Search for German Identity: An Illusory Endeavor?" in Wolfgang Pollak and Derek Rutter (eds. and trans.), *German Identity—Forty Years After Zero*, 3d ed., Sankt Augustin, 1987, 141; see also Elisabeth Noelle-Neumann and Renate Köcher, *Die verletzte Nation: Über den Versuch der Deutschen, ihren Charakter zu ändern*, Stuttgart, 1987.
5. Elisabeth Noelle-Neumann, *Eine demoskopische Deutschstunde*, Zurich, 1983, 96–8; Fritz Plasser and Peter A. Ulram, "Politischer Kulturvergleich: Deutschland, Österreich und die Schweiz," in Fritz Plasser and Peter A. Ulram (eds.), *Staatsbürger oder Untertanen?* Frankfurt, Berne, New York, and Paris, 1991, 40.
6. Noelle-Neumann and Köcher, *Die verletzte Nation*; see also Werner Weidenfeld, *Ratlose Normalität: Die Deutschen auf der Suche nach sich selbst*, Zurich, 1984.
7. Hans-Joachim Veen, "National Identity and Political Priorities in Eastern and Western Germany," paper presented at the annual meeting of the American Political Science Association, Washington, DC, 1993, 12; ALLBUS 1988, cited in Greiffenhagen and Greiffenhagen, *Ein schwieriges Vaterland*, 400.

8. See Werner Weidenfeld and Karl-Rudolf Korte, *Die Deutschen: Profil einer Nation*, Stuttgart, 1991, 149.

9. See, among others, Joachim Raschke, "Politik und Wertwandel in den westlichen Demokratien," *Aus Politik und Zeitgeschichte* B36/80 (September 1980): 23–45; Siegfried Schumann, "Wahlverhalten," *Politische Studien* 321 (January/February 1992): 67–95; Gerhard Schulze, *Die Erlebnisgesellschaft*, Frankfurt and New York, 1993; Michael Vester, Peter von Oertzen, Heiko Geiling, Thomas Hermann, and Dagmar Müller, *Soziale Milieus im gesell–schaftlichen Strukturwandel*, Cologne, 1993.

10. M. Rainer Lepsius, cited in Jürgen Habermas, "Yet Again: German Identity—A Unified Nation of Angry DM-Burghers?" *New German Critique* 52 (Winter 1991): 89.

11. Elisabeth Noelle-Neumann and Edgar Piel, *Allensbacher Jahrbuch der Demoskopie 1978–1983*, Munich, New York, London, and Paris, 1983, 598, 605.

12. Heinrich August Winkler, "Rebuilding of a Nation: The Germans Before and After Unification," *Daedalus* 123 (Winter 1994): 107; see also Hans-Peter Schwarz, "Germany's National and European Interests," *Daedalus* 123 (Spring 1994): 82–3.

13. Hanns W. Maull, "Germany and Japan: The New Civilian Powers," *Foreign Affairs* 69 (Winter 1990–91): 92–3; "Germany's New Foreign Policy," *AICGS Seminar Papers*, no. 5, American Institute for Contemporary German Studies, Washington, DC, January 1993, 5–6.

14. See Harald Mueller and Thomas Risse-Kappen, "Origins of Estrangement: The Peace Movement and the Changed Image of America in West Germany," *International Security* 12 (Summer 1987): 52–88.

15. Hans-Peter Schwarz, *Die gezähmten Deutschen: Von der Machtbesessenheit zur Machtvergessenheit*, Stuttgart, 1985; "Die Unlust an der Nation," *Rheinischer Merkur* 9 (September 1994): 4.

16. See Felix Ph. Lutz, "Empirisches Datenmaterial zum historisch-politischen Bewußtsein," in *Bundesrepublik Deutschland: Geschichte—Bewußtsein*, Bonn, 1989, 154–8

17. See Werner Bergmann and Rainer Erb, *Antisemitismus in der Bundesrepublik Deutschland*, Opladen, 1991, 236–9.

18. Cited in Martin Greiffenhagen, "Die Bundesrepublik Deutschland 1945–1990," *Aus Politik und Zeitgeschichte* B1-2/91 (January 1991): 16.

19. For a discussion of some of these events and their significance, see, among others, Richard J. Evans, *In Hitler's Shadow: West German Historians and the Attempt to Escape from the Nazi Past*, New York, 1989; Wolfgang Gessenharter, *Kippt die Republik? Die Neue Rechte und ihre Unterstützung durch Politik und Medien*, Munich, 1994.

20. *Frankfurter Allgemeine Zeitung*, 10 August 1994, 3; see also Patrick Behners, "Objektive Selbstzerstörung," *Frankfurter Allgemeine Zeitung*, 15 August 1994, 21.

21. In March 1989, 46 percent of the West German public thought that the amount of reparations West Germany paid to Jews living in the Federal Republic was too high, 47 percent thought that it was appropriate, and 5 percent thought that it was too low. At the same time, 39 percent agreed that the reason foreigners continued to bring up German guilt was that they were envious of the industrious nature and prosperity of the Ger-

mans (Emnid survey, "Zeitgeschichte," March 1989). In late 1991, 18 percent of the West German public agreed with the statement that "many Jews try to gain an advantage from the past of the Third Reich and to let the Germans pay for it." Thirty-nine percent thought that there was some truth to that statement, 23 percent said that it was not true, 17 percent said that it was impossible to say, and 3 percent refused to respond (Emnid survey on anti-Semitism, November–December 1991). In January 1994, 18 percent of West Germans strongly agreed and 26 percent somewhat agreed with the statement that "Jews are exploiting the National Socialist Holocaust for their own purposes." Eighteen percent did not know or refused to answer. Only 13 percent strongly disagreed with the statement, and 25 percent somewhat disagreed. See "Current German Attitudes Toward Jews and Other Minorities: A Survey of Public Opinion," American Jewish Committee, Washington, DC, 1994.

22. One need only think of how the Federal Republic has treated officials involved with the Nazis and some of the victims of the Nazi regime. The former receive generous pensions, and more often than not, the latter have had to endure humiliating treatment by West German bureaucracy to receive reparation. Some groups, such as Sinti and Roma or slave laborers, are still waiting to see their claims recognized by German authorities and industry.

23. See Hans-Georg Betz, *Postmodern Politics in Germany*, New York, 1991, 119–21.

24. Axel Schulte, "Multikulturelle Gesellschaft: Chance, Ideologie oder Bedrohung," *Aus Politik und Zeitgeschichte*, B23–24 (June 1990): 3–15; on the debate on multiculturalism, see also Daniel Cohn-Bendit and Thomas Schmid, *Heimat Babylon: Das Wagnis der multikulturellen Demokratie*, Hamburg, 1992, and Ute Knight and Wolfgang Kowalsky, *Deutschland nur den Deutschen?* Erlangen, Bonn, and Vienna, 1991.

25. Statistisches Bundesamt (ed.), *Datenreport 1992*, Bonn, 1992, 615–7.

26. In the fall of 1991, for instance, only 13 percent of West Germans thought that Germany should take in all ethnic German resettlers from the former Soviet Union and Poland. Forty-three percent wanted to see their number reduced to a certain extent, and 44 percent supported a strong reduction (Emnid poll, August, September 1992). See also Manfred Richter, *Sturm auf Europa*, Munich, 1990, and Jan Werner, *Die Invasion der Armen*, Munich, 1992.

27. Emnid survey, "Zeitgeschichte," March 1989; when Emnid asked the question again in 1991, the results were almost identical.

28. "Allensbacher Berichte," no. 9, 1992.

29. For a comprehensive discussion of these trends, see Gerhard Herdegen, "Perspektiven und Begrenzungen," *Deutschland Archiv* 20, no. 12 (1987): 1259–73; Silke Jansen, "Zwei deutsche Staaten—zwei deutsche Nationen?" *Deutschland Archiv* 22, no. 10 (1989): 1132–43; Manfred Kuechler, "Framing Unification: Issue Salience and Mass Sentiment 1989–1991," in Russell J. Dalton (ed.), *The New Germany Votes*, Providence and Oxford, 1993.

30. See Noelle-Neumann and Piel, *Allensbacher Jahrbuch der Demoskopie 1978–1983*, 334.

31. See Weidenfeld and Korte, *Die Deutschen*, 137–8.

32. Kuechler, "Framing Unification," 31.

33. Emnid survey, "Zeitgeschichte," March 1989.
34. Anne-Marie Le Gloannec, "On German Identity," *Daedalus* 123 (Winter 1994): 133; see also her account in *La Nation orpheline*, Paris, 1989.
35. See Gerhard Herdegen, "Einstellungen der Deutschen (West) zur nationalen Identität," in Dirk Berg-Schlosser and Jakob Schissler (eds.), *Politische Kultur in Deutschland*, PVS-Sonderheft, no. 18, Opladen, 1987, 214.
36. See Lutz, "Empirisches Datenmaterial," 164; see also Jansen, "Zwei deutsche Staaten," 1136–7.
37. Emnid survey, "Zeitgeschichte," March 1989; see also Jansen, "Zwei deutsche Staaten," 1138–9.
38. Jansen, "Zwei deutsche Staaten," 1139; see also Herdegen, "Perspektiven und Begrenzungen," 1260–2.
39. Jansen, "Zwei deutsche Staaten," 1142; Emnid survey, "Zeitgeschichte," March 1989.
40. Le Gloannec, "On German Identity"; see also Helga Welsh, "The Divided Past and the Difficulties of German Unification," *German Politics & Society* 30 (Fall 1993): 77.
41. See, among others, Jacques Le Rider, "Un an après l'unification: retour à la normalité de la nation allemande?" *Politique étrangère* 56, no. 4 (1991): 913–27; Le Gloannec, "On German Identity": Peter H. Merkl, "A New German Identity," in Gordon Smith, William E. Paterson, Peter H. Merkl, and Stephen Padgett (eds.), *Developments in German Politics*, Durham, 1992; Weidenfeld and Korte, *Die Deutschen*, 146–52; Greiffenhagen and Greiffenhagen, *Ein schwieriges Vaterland*, 40–48; and especially Lothar Probst, "Krise der Demokratie und Suche nach nationaler Identität," *Die neue Gesellschaft/Frankfurter Hefte* 41 (March 1994): 233–7.
42. Winkler, "Rebuilding of a Nation," 108.
43. See Peter Rosenberg, *Das soziale Netz vor der Zerreißprobe?* Frankfurt, 1990; Peter Krause, "Einkommensarmut in der Bundesrepublik Deutschland," *Aus Politik und Zeitgeschichte* B49/92 (November 1992): 3–17; Jürgen Jäger, "Arbeitslosigkeit in der vereinigten Bundesrepublik Deutschland," *Aus Politik und Zeitgeschichte* B35/93 (August 1993): 3–15; Walter Hanesch et al., *Armut in Deutschland*, Reinbek, 1994.
44. Kenneth Dyson, "Economic Policy," in Gordon Smith, William E. Paterson, and Peter Merkl (eds.), *Developments in German Politics*, Durham, 1989, 153; Kurt J. Lauk, "Germany at the Crossroads: On the Efficiency of the German Economy," *Daedalus* 123 (Winter 1994): 62–3.
45. For an official comprehensive diagnosis of Germany's economic problems and solutions, see Bundesministerium für Wirtschaft, *Zukunftssicherung des Standorts Deutschland*, Bonn, 1993.
46. Emnid survey, "Zeitgeschichte," March 1989; Peter Gluchowski and Carsten Zelle, "Vom Optimismus zum Realismus: Ostdeutschland auf dem Weg in das bundesrepublikanische politische System," in Fritz Plasser and Peter A. Ulram (eds.), *Transformation oder Stagnation*, Schriftenreihe des Zentrums für angewandte Politikforschung, no. 2, Vienna, 1993, 134.
47. Among the vast literature on *Parteien-* and *Politikverdrossenheit*, see particularly Erwin K. Scheuch and Ute Scheuch, *Cliquen, Klüngel und Karrieren*, Reinbek, 1992; Karl Starzacher, Konrad Schacht, Bernd Friedrich, and Thomas Leif (eds.), *Protestwähler und Wahlverweigerer: Krise der Demokratie?* Cologne, 1992; Hans Rattinger, "Abkehr von den Parteien? Dimensionen

der Politikverdrossenheit," *Aus Politik und Zeitgeschichte* B11/93 (March 1993): 24–35; Thomas Darnstädt and Gerhard Spörl, "Streunende Hunde im Staat," *Der Spiegel* 13 (1993): 142–59.

48. See Rudzio, *Das politische System der Bundesrepublik Deutschland*, 122–3; Forschungsgruppe Wahlen, *Bundestagswahl 1990*, Berichte der Forschungsgruppe Wahlen e.V., no. 61, Mannheim, 1990, 8.

49. See Dieter Roth, "Sind die Republikaner die fünfte Partei?" *Aus Politik und Zeitgeschichte* B41-42 (October 1989): 10–20.

50. See Institut für praxisorientierte Sozialforschung, *Einstellungen zu aktuellen Fragen der Innenpolitik 1993*, Mannheim, 1993, 28.

51. "Abstieg in die zweite Liga," *Der Spiegel* 19 (1993): 138–47.

52. Hans-Joachim Veen et al., *Trends in der öffentlichen Meinung im Vorfeld der Europawahl 1989*, St. Augustin, 1989, 7.

53. See Noelle-Neumann and Piel, *Allensbacher Jahrbuch der Demoskopie 1978–1983*, 603; Ulrich von Wilamowitz-Moellendorf, *Meinungstrends im Vorfeld der Europawahl*, St. Augustin, 1993, 7–9; Peter R. Weilemann et al., *Die Europawahl in der Bundesrepublik Deutschland vom 12. Juni 1994*, St. Augustin, 1994, B3.

54. See United States Information Agency (USIA), "European Integration: The German Perspective," Office of Research, USIA, Washington, DC, 1993. A youth survey conducted in 1994 for *Der Spiegel* gives an indication to what degree even young Germans aged fourteen to twenty-nine identify Germany with the D-Mark. When asked what they thought of when they heard the word "Germany," 79 percent of the respondents said "D-Mark." "Mercedes-Benz" came in a distant second with 54 percent. *Der Spiegel* 38 (1994): 81.

55. See von Wilamowitz-Moellendorff, *Meinungstrends*, 1–4; Ronald D. Asmus, *German Strategy and Opinion After the Wall 1990–1993*, Santa Monica, 1994, 47.

56. Winkler, "Rebuilding of a Nation," 120.

57. See Christian Meier, "Am Ende der alten Bundesrepublik," *Merkur* 544 (July 1994): 368; Schwarz, "Germany's National and European Interests," 87.

58. Weilemann et al., *Die Europawahl*, B3; on Germany's renationalization, see especially Jürgen Habermas, "The Second Life Fiction of the Federal Republic: We Have Become 'Normal' Again," *New Left Review* 197 (January/February 1993): 58–66.

59. Weidenfeld and Korte, *Die Deutschen*, 131; Institut für praxisorientierte Sozialforschung, *Zur Lage der Jugend in Ost-und Westdeutschland*, Mannheim, 1993, 70.

60. Schwarz, "Germany's National and European Interests," 84; Timothy Garton Ash, *In Europe's Name*, New York, 1993, 385.

61. Forschungsgruppe Wahlen, ZDF Politbarometer, December 1989; Kuechler, "Framing Unification," 37.

62. "Erst vereint, nun entzweit," *Der Spiegel* 3 (1993): 52; Elisabeth Noelle-Neumann, "Wird sich jetzt fremd, was zusammengehört?" *Frankfurter Allgemeine Zeitung*, 19 May 1993, 5.

63. Hans-Dieter Klingemann and Richard Hofferbert, "Germany: A New 'Wall in the Mind'?" *Journal of Democracy* 5 (January 1994): 39.

64. Greiffenhagen, "Die Bundesrepublik Deutschland 1945–1990," 25; Michael

Minkenberg, "The Wall After the Wall," *Comparative Politics* 26 (October 1993): 60–1; Greiffenhagen and Greiffenhagen, *Ein schwieriges Vaterland*, 374–5.

65. See Rainer Zitelmann, "Wiedervereinigung und deutscher Selbsthass," *Deutschlandarchiv* 24 (August 1992): 812–4.

66. Kuechler, "Framing Unification," 37.

67. See Harry Müller and Wilfried Schubarth, "Rechtsextremismus und aktuelle Befindlichkeiten von Jugendlichen in den neuen Bundesländern," *Aus Politik und Zeitgeschichte* B38/92 (September 1992): 16–28, which documents significant levels of right-wing extremist attitudes among East German youth.

68. See Peter Gluchowski and Carsten Zelle, "Demokratisierung in Ostdeutschland," in Peter Gerlich, Fritz Plasser, and Peter A. Ulram (eds.), *Regimewechsel: Demokratisierung und politische Kultur in Ost-Mitteleuropa*, Vienna, Cologne, and Graz, 1992, 240–5; American Jewish Committee, "Current German Attitudes," table 19; USIA, "European Integration," 26.

69. Russell J. Dalton, "Communists and Democrats: Democratic Attitudes in the Two Germanies," *British Journal of Political Science*, forthcoming.

70. Patrick Moreau and Viola Neu, *Die PDS zwischen Linksextremismus und Linkspopulismus*, Interne Studie N. 76/1994, St. Augustin, 1994, 80.

71. Meier, "Am Ende der alten Bundesrepublik," 569.

72. Merkl, "A New German Identity," 329.

73. Peter Schneider, "Standing Aside in Self-Deluding Virtue," *International Herald Tribune*, 1 June 1993.

74. Federal Ministry of Defense, *White Paper 1994*, Bonn, 1994, 24.

75. See "Wann möchten Sie sterben?" *Der Spiegel* 38 (1994): 70, 84.

76. Schwarz, "Germany's National and European Interests," 92; Asmus, *German Strategy and Opinion After the Wall*, 5.

3

Defining the Fatherland: Immigration and Nationhood in Pre- and Postunification Germany

HERMANN KURTHEN

THE QUEST FOR NATIONAL IDENTITY

German unification in 1989–90, triggered by mass emigration from the east and later highlighted by violent incidents against asylum seekers, exacerbated long-standing contradictions and tensions regarding the postwar realities of immigration and ethnocultural diversity. The unexpected and for some time uncontrolled immigration during and after unification under unfavorable economic, political, and social conditions exposed resentments that predate the collapse of the Cold War order and German unification. But skinhead street violence and the crude display of Nazi symbols by right-wing extremists, as well as populist xenophobic slogans of the right-wing Republican party, which attracted so much domestic and foreign attention in 1991–92, are not a simple repetition of ills that led to the collapse of the Weimar Republic in 1933. They indicate fears, insecurity, and a polarization of the German population about the ongoing ethnic and cultural diffusion as a result of postwar and postunification immigration and its consequences for the cultural, social, and political fabric of the country. In other words, the issue of immigration has become a battlefield on which different concepts of the future of the nation-state and of cultural and national identity are being fought out. In Germany, the discussion is taking place between two extreme positions, one that denies that Germany is de facto an immigration country,[1] and one that compares Germany with traditional immigration societies such as the United States, Canada, and Australia.

Is immigration a recent phenomenon in Germany? The answer is a clear no. Yet it cannot be ignored that Germany's migration history is different from that of other nations with regard to processes of nation building, patterns of territorial expansion, the scale of settlement, and national identity formation. To understand the ambiguities of the Federal Republic's attempts to cope with the consequences of large-scale immigration and to accept its role as an immigration country, it is useful to look at the historical context, in particular the difficulties of German nation building and Germany's search for a national identity in the past and present.

First, the geographical position in the heart of Europe and the lack of natural boundaries that would separate or protect people and cultures from uncontrolled migration have made this densely populated region not only a crossroads and a marketplace for goods, capital, and services but also a target of migration, of wars, and of cultural exchange for centuries. Invaders, refugees, migrants, and traders have contributed to the emergence of a unique economic, social, political, and cultural ensemble. In the age of nationalism, the emerging nation-states began to control political and ethnic borders and restrict migration movements more effectively. Drawing boundaries and using their inclusive and exclusive capacities, states constituted principles of citizenship and molded scattered tribal and cultural identities into homogenized ethnocultural units, which, in the case of Germany, have been defined incompletely and in simplified terms as the *German nation*.

Second, nation building, or mobilization of the idea of nationalism for political purposes, occurred in Germany under different and more complicated circumstances than in neighboring countries. The unique structure of the Holy Roman Empire as a vessel for a multitude of diverse and often opposing political, religious, cultural, and ethnic conditions contributed to the flourishing of diversity, exchange, hostile as well as peaceful encounters, and tolerance. Only after Prussia put an end to Hapsburg claims to be the legitimate successors of the remnants of the Holy Roman Empire in central Europe in 1866, and only after Prussian victory against France in 1870–71, was the political unification of Germany accomplished. In quick succession, Germany experienced a constitutional monarchy, three revolutions, two dictatorships (one fascist, one communist), and two democratic republics. It suffered from two devastating defeats in world wars, followed by dismemberment, expulsions, and massive refugee movements, all of which undoubtedly had an impact on Germany's definition of nationhood, its national identity, its symbols, and its institutions. It was not until 1990 that Germany's political borders, particularly in the east, were once and for all clearly defined and accepted inside and outside of Germany. Still, the issue of nationhood, the question of what constitutes *Germanness*, has not yet been resolved, as will be demonstrated.

In the German case, the ideology of *völkisch* ethnic nationalism has complicated the belated process of nation building and blurred the perception of past and present ethnic diversity, including a sober appreciation of the benefits of immigration. Upholding the notion of ethnocultural homogeneity also impeded the embracing of universalistic constitutional and liberal democratic political principles. *Völkisch* nationalism, or, in academic terms, "state-centered political rights on the basis of nationhood,"[2] not only suppressed institutions and memories of more than a thousand years of ethnocultural and tribal diversity based on large and continuous in- and out-migrations in central Europe, it also promoted in the twentieth century a drift to fascism, racism, and anti-Semitism. But *völkisch* nationalism did not end with the defeat of Nazi Germany and the establishment of a democratic republic in the western part of the country in 1948–49. Unification, and the rise of xenophobia and ethnocentrist sentiments in its aftermath, revealed unresolved contradictions between the exclusive idea of the nation-state and the inclusive ideas of republican and universal principles of human and civil rights, between rigid citizenship regulations and a liberal asylum law, between the notion of the ethnocultural homogeneity of the nation-state and the increasing diversity created by immigration and refugee movements.

Having pointed out the importance of migration movements and the defining principles of nationhood for Germany's national fabric in the past, present, and the future, I first sketch the pre- and postwar history of migration on the territories that became the German nation-state in the late nineteenth century. My intention is to illustrate that immigration waves and the formation of ethnocultural entities cannot be ignored as central constituents of peoples that were later defined as "imagined" national communities.[3] I then explain why this history was deliberately forgotten during Germany's nation building for the higher good of *völkisch* nationalism. Then, after a brief overview of the effects of the main postwar immigration and refugee waves on the domestic situation in the Federal Republic, I describe the origins of the contradictory nature of the current citizenship and naturalization regulations and the need to redefine Germany's legal framework, immigration policy, and national identity after unification.

A NATION OF MIGRANTS: A HISTORICAL OVERVIEW

The first migration movement sufficiently documented and laid down in popular narratives, myths, and tales since Germanic tribes settled 3,000 or 4,000 years ago in northern and central European areas occurred during the great migration of peoples in A.D. 400, when dozens of tribes crossed central Europe on their way from the north and east to the south and west. In the following centuries, the Huns and Goths attempted to overrun what the Romans had conquered, populated, and "civilized" since Caesar's acquisitions in the south and the west of central Europe. In the second part of the first millennium, the Vikings settled on the coast of the North Sea and the Baltic. Slavic tribes crossed the Elbe River before they mixed with German colonizers, who, since the thirteenth century, had settled in the east along the Neisse and Vistula Rivers and further on along the Baltic coast, which later came under Swedish domination and influence for centuries.

Massive intra- and extramigrations happened, particularly in the early Middle Ages and during the Germanic colonization of the east by the Hanse Union and Teutonic knights. More followed during and after the Lutheran Reformation period with its endless religious wars, when mercenaries from all over Europe crisscrossed German territories, not only devastating the country and murdering its populations but also staying or leaving illegitimate offspring behind. Later, in the seventeenth and eighteenth centuries, an almost endless stream of religious émigrés settled in various parts of central Europe. Prussia, for example, attracted Lutherans in the seventeenth century from Salzburg-Austria, Huguenots from France (Edict of Potsdam 1685), and Jews from eastern Europe and Russia. The expansion of the Prussian Empire and its incorporation of parts of Poland also led to an increase of settlement activities supported by the government to *Germanize* the new Slavic conquest.[4]

During the period of overseas colonization after the discovery of the New World, German-speaking emigrants settled in British, French, Spanish, and Portuguese colonies, particularly in North America and Latin America. German mercenaries fought in America for the British as well as for American independence. When the hostilities ended, many stayed in North America; others returned. At the end of the nineteenth century, with rapid domestic industrialization, Germany became a passageway as well as a source and a destination of emigration and immigration. Soon the outflow of German emigrants was outweighed by the influx of labor migrants. Germany became an immigration rather than an emigration country. But these changes were also the result of political unification under Prussian hegemony in the late nineteenth century.

The economic growth of the German Empire attracted hundreds of thousands of labor migrants and seasonal workers from Italy, Russia, Poland, and the eastern parts of Prussia to build industries on the Rhine, in Silesia, and around Berlin or to support the agrarian demand for cheap manual labor. After the establishment of a German empire, colonists, administrators, and soldiers were sent out to settle in newly acquired African and Asian territories. But German colonies, annexed by the victorious allies after World War I, were too short-lived to create strong political and cultural links with peoples in Africa and Asia. In contrast to traditional outward-colonizing countries such as France and Britain, or inward-colonizing countries such as the United States and Canada, Germany did not gain experience with absorbing non-European people, cultures, languages, and religions. Further, the notion of national homogeneity was not challenged in Germany by massive postcolonial remigration movements of white and non-white persons from former overseas colonies, in particular after World War II, as was the case in the United Kingdom, France, the Netherlands, and Belgium.

In the twentieth century, new categories of migration evolved. The mass mobilization of manpower during World War I and the redrawing of boundaries after the war led to the first forced migrations and refugee movements in this century.[5] Following the Paris Treaties in 1919, the victors carved out of the collapsed German, Austro-Hungarian, and Russian Empires new, ethnically mixed nation-states in central and eastern Europe. The cession of parts of the former German Empire to its neighbors led to the expulsion or remigration of a significant number of ethnic Germans to Weimar Germany. Additionally, the restless and impoverished postwar years fueled emigration to countries overseas.[6] After the demise of the short-lived Weimar Republic, another huge politically induced migration movement followed. In this case, émigrés were forced to leave Nazi Germany for political, religious, ethnic, and "racial" reasons. However, at the same time, the armament industry in Germany was attracting laborers, particularly from Mussolini's Italy and other neighboring countries such as Austria, Poland, and Czechoslovakia. After the beginning of World War II, the Nazis themselves, despite their racist ideology and policies, contributed to a further wave of migration. Altogether, about eight million laborers, including two million prisoners and concentration camp inmates, from all over Europe had to work for the Nazi war effort in the Reich. The war and the division of Europe after

1945 left millions of displaced persons from former Nazi prisons and camps (among them 200,000 Jews) without a homeland. These included members of eastern European military units fighting with the German army and eastern European refugees fleeing communist oppression. After a waiting period, most left the occupied western German zones for other overseas destinations. Only a fraction of those stayed in Germany itself.

In other words, Germany was for centuries a land that experienced vast in- and out-migrations, contributing to religious, ethnic, and cultural diversity on its territory. How could these facts be forgotten or ignored in the age of nationalism? Why did *völkisch* elements of nationhood become so important and remain part of Germany's national identity until today? The peculiarities of Germany's nation building since the late nineteenth century may provide an answer to these questions.

Originally attracting the hopes and fantasies of German literati and the rising bourgeoisie, the French Revolution in 1789, with its republican ideas of enlightenment and human and civil rights, lost its attractiveness and its legitimacy because of the atrocities of the revolution and the succeeding Napoleonic imperialist policy of conquest and oppression. The humiliating defeat, occupation, territorial and organizational dismemberment, and reorganization of the German states, coupled with other factors, gave rise to a popular nationalist and anti-French German freedom movement in the early nineteenth century.[7] Neither the multitude of smaller principalities, nor the larger multiethnic and culturally diverse entities of Prussia and Austria, nor even commonly shared political principles provided a realistic focus of national identification that went beyond a pride in Germanic ethnocultural achievements and national self-determination against alien influence and foreign domination. For this reason, ethnic nationalism became the rallying point of a nation that had yet to be founded politically and territorially. *Völkisch* nationalism "was not only seen as an ideology supporting German interests, but as a doctrine of universal validity equal with demotic nationalism."[8] Since civil and human rights were not an inherent part of ethnic nationalism, democracy was never perceived as absolutely necessary for the advancement of ethnic nationalism. In fact, democratic and national movements became separated.[9] In contrast to inclusive republican ideals, ethnic nationalism invited exclusionary politics to preserve unity against external threats and internal centripetal regional, religious, and social forces. One consequence was the suppression of such diversity for the higher good of ethnocultural homogenization and national advancement. Ascriptive and particularistic definitions were used to construct a homogeneous national identity.[10] In other words, the ethnic nation-state created and enforced its own ideology, instruments, and symbols of "belongingness."

In the German (as in the Italian) case, belated political unification after the Franco-Prussian War in 1870–71 contributed to the development of nationalistic fervor as a compensation for their neighbors' imperialist striving for a place in the sun and led to the suppression of elements of past and present diversity. Perverted nationalism also provided fertile ground and a rationalization for xenophobia, nativism, and anti-Semitism, "much older and more universal tendencies than nationalism . . . against alien elements in their own midst."[11] Bismarck's domestic struggles to Germanize the Slavic minority in Prussia and to subdue cultural, political, and religious resistance by the Catholic Church, the socialists, and minorities in Alsace-Lorraine and elsewhere duplicated the pressures of homogenization that had already been successfully implemented in France and England during their much earlier attempts at nation building in the seventeenth and eighteenth centuries.[12] However, the Wilhelmine Empire was belated insofar as these policies in the late nineteenth and early twentieth centuries had lost much of the legitimacy of their predecessors. Instead, *völkische Sammlung* (Pan-Germanism), which opposed *Gesellschaft* with *Gemeinschaft*, Western *Zivilisation* with *Kultur*, liberal democracy with authoritarian law and order (*Obrigkeitsstaat*), became a trademark of illiberalism, chauvinism, and racism that left tracks in German political culture that were later followed by National Socialism.

Considering centuries-old German regionalism and tribalism and the lingering class conflicts in the Second Reich, the molding of Germany into a national homogeneous unit might not have succeeded as quickly or as completely had World War I not given it new and potent nourishment. The bloody war, Germany's struggle to escape the perceived encirclement by hostile powers that were supposedly out to destroy the country's status as a *Kulturnation* and a great power, and finally Germany's humiliating defeat combined with international isolation and ostracism to nurture feelings of national kinship and a common fate that blurred ethnic, cultural, and class differences.[13] The racist policies of the Nazis built on the fertile ground of the political and economic instabilities of the Weimar Republic, of nationalistic humiliation and corresponding ethnocentric and racist hubris, further erasing a sober appreciation of diversity and pluralism. Certainly World War II as well as World War I left scars in postwar Germany's self-understanding as a fictitious homogeneous entity or *Volks- und Schicksalsgemeinschaft*, that is, a national community with a shared destiny in good and bad times and collective feelings of anger, guilt, and shame.

Ironically, after unconditional surrender, the expulsion of millions of ethnic Germans from their eastern homelands, and years of occupation, a partitioned country evolved under the supervision of the victorious allies that represented a nation "ethnoculturally homogeneous" to an extent that even the Nazis had not dreamed about, though considerably reduced in population, size, and power status. The rebuilding of the divided country from the rubble helped rebuild national pride, solidarity, and identity, this time bolstered by confidence in superior economic, monetary, and technological abilities that would peacefully conquer markets and win the confidence of consumers around the world. The West Germans thus established in a very short time a stable political culture on the liberal foundations of their postwar constitution.

But the ghosts of the past were not banished. The economic miracle (*Wirtschaftswunder*), emerging constitutional patriotism,[14] and the new cosmopolitan outlook of Germany were hiding the continuing existence of *völkisch* definitions of nationhood embodied by restrictive citizenship and naturalization regulations alongside liberal republican and universalistic principles, represented most notably by the postwar constitution and its stipulation of an individual right of asylum. The unresolved contradictions of inclusive republican principles and exclusive *völkisch* principles and the notion of ethnocultural homogeneity were exacerbated by postwar economic and political developments and, in particular, by migration movements. *Modell Deutschland* (a term invented by former chancellor Helmut Schmidt in his late-1970 election campaign to create identification and gloss over domestic antagonisms) lost its assumed glitter under the strains of postunification recession and unprecedented migrations, a growth of xenophobic and ethnocentric resentment, and a wave of right-wing violence.

It is estimated that about 16.6 million people, or 25 percent of the 64 million persons living within the territory of West Germany in 1990, migrated into West Germany between 1950 and 1994. These figures include 7 million foreign residents, 4.64 million East German émigrés, 3.3 million ethnic German resettlers, and about 1.67 million non-Germans (1.45 million naturalized persons and 211,000 asylum seekers). The presence of millions of migrant laborers, resettlers, asylum seekers, and other types of migrants or residents[15] contradicts the assertion that Germany is not an immigration society, and it challenges the traditional definition of *Germanness* and the notion of ethnic and cultural homogeneity. In the following sections, I briefly describe the four major postwar migrations that helped make the Bonn Republic, against its will, a "culturally and ethnically pluralistic country of immigration"[16] and triggered the current identity crisis in Germany.

VICTIMS OF WAR AND EXPULSION

World War II caused the largest refugee and migration drama the world has ever seen. Naturally, Germans were strongly affected by these events. First, Hitler arranged with Mussolini and Stalin for the expatriation of ethnic Germans from South Tyrol and the Baltic. Then, after the Nazi attack on the Soviet Union in 1941, Stalin ordered the deportation of approximately 1.5 million ethnic Germans from their centuries-old autonomous settlements in the Volga region into Gulag camps, scattered areas in Siberia, and other places east of the Ural Mountains as a collective reprisal for alleged collaboration. One out of three of these ethnic Germans did not survive this expulsion.

In central Europe and Germany itself, millions of German civilians became victims of revenge, expulsion, and foreign occupation in the last months of the war and during the postwar years until 1950. Following the Yalta and Potsdam agreements, German-speaking residents were forcibly expelled from the Sudetenland in Czechoslovakia and from German provinces east of the Oder and Neisse Rivers occupied by Poland and the Soviet Union, areas that they had settled centuries ago. The first German postwar census in 1946 found that 9.7 million residents had been moved out of these disputed territories. Between 1946 and 1950, 12 million *Vertriebene* (expellees) from eastern German provinces and eastern European settlements suffered from violent expulsion and ethnic cleansing. About 1.6 to 2 million starved, were killed, or perished during their exodus.[17]

When West Germans were allowed to travel abroad again, they left in search of better lives in North and South America, South Africa, and Australia. Over two million exhausted German emigrants fled war-devastated Germany between 1950 and 1960; two and a half million emigrated between 1960 and 1990.

EAST–WEST REFUGEES

During the occupation of Germany by the four victorious allies, 1.3 million people moved from the Soviet zone of occupation into the three western zones and the western parts of Berlin. From the 1950s, a total of about 3.8 million East Germans fled across the "green border" from communist expropriation and oppression, and 500,000 pro-communists moved into East Germany. Significant losses of population through migration to the west served to destabilize the East German system. Between 1950 and 1961, some 2.6 million people migrated from east to west—a considerable number, considering the total East German population of 17 million.[18] The number of east–west migrants dropped to a trickle after the Iron Curtain was sealed with a concrete wall, barbed wire, and minefields in August 1961. At the same time, however, moving across the border for "family reunification" became legal, providing a limited number of East Germans with the opportunity to transfer legally (*Übersiedler*). Between 1962 and 1988, 560,000 people left—68 percent with official papers, and 32 percent as "illegal" refugees. These numbers increased rapidly before and after the opening of the Berlin Wall in 1989 and dropped slowly after unification. The most spectacular migration peak occurred in 1989, when 344,000 people—2 percent of the East German population, and 3 percent of the labor force—left for West Germany. This was a major factor in the dissolution of the communist regime in the east. It is estimated that in the aftermath of unification between 1990 and 1993, about 1.4 million East Germans and East Berliners settled in the west. With the economic upswing in the east after 1993–94, a reverse internal migration took place. The Federal Statistical Office estimated the number of west–east migrants between 1989 and 1993 at more than 350,000 persons, among them many East Germans who had left earlier.

Ethnic Germans Return to the Fatherland

Another unresolved legacy of World War II and its aftermath are so-called ethnic German resettlers (*Aussiedler*). As relations between the Federal Republic, eastern Europe, and the Soviet Union improved through the West German *Ostpolitik* in the 1970s, ethnic Germans increasingly were allowed to leave homelands that had been seized by Poland, Russia, and the former Czechoslovakia after the Yalta and Potsdam agreements in 1945. The largest group arrived from various Russian and Asian provinces of the former Soviet Union, representing survivors of the two to three million ethnic Germans who had been deported by Stalin. This resettlement program was Europe's biggest mass migration since the late 1940s. It resembled the return of émigrés and resettlers from ethnic enclaves in Russia to Finland, Greece, and Israel and the remigration of colonial subjects to the United Kingdom, France, the Netherlands, Belgium, Portugal, Italy, and Spain. Besides an estimated 3 to 3.5 million Germans, about 1.5 million persons with legal entitlements are currently waiting for remigration into Western countries.[19]

Ironically, the conservative-liberal Kohl government, which opposes defining Germany as an immigration country, has strongly supported the resettlement of ethnic Germans since the 1980s. Their admission was declared an act of patriotism and an alternative to non-German immigrants who were ethnoculturally more distant and less willing to integrate but who were needed to compensate for low German birthrates and labor market shortages. A number of reasons were put forward for the adoption of this resettlement policy. First, in the immediate postwar decade, repatriation was seen as a humanitarian gesture toward collectively persecuted German citizens and ethnics who happened to live in former eastern German lands or in the eastern European diaspora. In fact, many resettlers decided to leave their former homelands because of subtle or open ethnic discrimination and oppression. Second, it was an anticommunist instrument to support those who wanted to leave the Soviet Union for political, economic, and family reunification reasons. In fact, it was applied only to eastern European Germans and could not be claimed by ethnic Germans who lived in the Western Hemisphere or under similar undemocratic regimes as in the east.[20] Third, according to international law, the Federal Republic was seen as the successor state of the Third Reich and, among others, was held responsible for those who suffered from persecution and deportation as a result of the war. Therefore, the West German postwar constitution (paragraph 116 of the Basic Law) and the war-related Compensation Act stipulated that persons with proof that they, their parents, or their grandparents were citizens of the German Reich within the German borders of 1937, or refugees and resettlers from the communist eastern parts of Europe and Russia with reliable evidence of ethnic German background (*Volkszugehörigkeit*), could not be refused application for naturalization.[21]

After the demise of the Soviet Union and the ensuing turmoil in the East, the number of resettlers willing to migrate increased dramatically. The number of those prepared to give up their possessions and social ties would have been smaller had West Germany's economic wealth, social security, and democratic accomplishments not been additional attractions. But like the earlier migrations described, the integration of resettlers into West German society has not been without friction. Many immigrants had been isolated in peasant enclaves in eastern Europe and behind the Ural Mountains for decades and have memories dating back to prewar Germany. Many do not even speak German, or they speak an odd kind of archaic German dialect. Although they tend to stick together in clans and families, they are willing to assimilate to their new *Heimat* after they have overcome the first culture shocks. Initially, they are put in special reception camps, informed about their new rights, and, after a screening process, given German documents. Then, following a quota system, they are distributed among the federal German states and munici-palities. Resettlers are fairly well housed and are given full unemployment benefits, German language courses, and job retraining if needed. They are also aided in finding jobs, which is often not easy.

Rising numbers of arrivals and the costs of the mass influx (esti-mated to be at least US$6 billion a year) have created resentment among some Germans, who fear for their own jobs, housing prospects, or cultural alienation. In 1989, 58 percent of respondents to an Allensbach survey thought that "too much" was being done officially for resettlers. In contrast, only 6 percent thought that "too little" was being done.[22] The German government now wants to persuade would-be resettlers to stay in their respective countries. Several measures have been im-plemented to make life more attractive for ethnic Germans abroad. In 1990, the Polish government agreed, for example, to grant Germans living in Poland minority rights, including the use of their own hith-erto outlawed language. In 1992, Germany gave about US$100 mil-lion to the governments of Romania, Russia, Kazakhstan, the Ukraine, and other former Soviet republics to help them resettle ethnic Ger-mans in their former communities or to improve their lots where they currently live. Another US$70 million was given to support the small private businesses of potential resettlers and to aid them with cloth-ing, food, and medicine. German-language teachers and schoolbooks were sent to these areas, and cultural centers and TV satellite receivers were built in an effort to induce potential migrants to remain.

Since July 1990, Germany has started to control the potential immi-gration of millions by passing the *Aussiedler-Aufnahmegesetz*, which requires applications for an *Aufnahmebescheid* (reception permit) at German consulates or embassies in the country of origin.[23] Now it can take months or even years after application and a thorough ex-amination of claims before ethnic German immigrants receive entry visas to Germany. Moreover, since 1992, an annual cap of about 250,000 resettlers limits their immigration.

Critics within and outside Germany have proposed an end to the continuation of special preferences and privileges to ethnic German minorities from the east because—so the argument goes—after unifi-cation and the liberalization in the former Soviet Union and eastern Europe, the motives that legitimated the resettler program after World War II, that is, the threat of expulsion or oppression, have disappeared.[24] Yet, in the course of a search for national roots and cultural identity, particularly in eastern Europe, the imagined or real ethnocultural bonds have not ceased to exist in the minds of the resettlers themselves and in the politics of the conservative Kohl government. The proponents of continued resettlement argue that Germany needs immigrants willing to assimilate to compensate for Germany's low birthrate. Moreover, it is argued, Germany cannot continue to accept historical and moral responsibilities for victims of Nazi aggression and at the same time ignore the plight of those Germans who were punished as war aliens in enemy territory or suffered as tokens of revenge against Nazi aggression. To deny ethnic Germans immigration into a land that they perceive as the place to pursue their happiness would be unjustified, because they should have the same right of return as other diaspora groups in Russia, such as Jews, Greeks, Spaniards, or Hungarians.

The constitutional rights of resettlement have not been challenged yet, and public opinion in Germany is still inclined to accept the immigration of people with a real or an assumed affiliation with German culture, history, language, ancestry, and traditions. Had the resettlers become assimilated into their former homelands in eastern Europe and the Soviet Union instead of being collectively discriminated and labeled as separate "ethnics," their wish to immigrate might be weaker and the task of removing their immigration privileges would be easier. Even if these moral and ethnic responsibilities are contested or become more questionable, the fact that Germany needs immigrants for demographic and economic reasons suggests a continuous preference for resettlers from the East. The preference for immigrants with ethnocultural affinities or historical ties to the host country will continue as long as the definition of national belonging is based on real or imagined ascriptive criteria rather than on individual inclination and confession.

GUEST-WORKER IMMIGRATION

A fourth group of migrants resulted from the economic recovery of western Europe after World War II. From the mid-1950s, West German industry developed a strong demand for manual labor that could not be supplied sufficiently by the domestic labor force, especially after the erection of the Berlin Wall brought the constant flow of migrants from East Germany to the Federal Republic to a complete stop. The so-called *Gastarbeiter* rotation system was established, whereby foreign workers from mostly Mediterranean countries were supposed to stay for one to three years and then return to their home countries. This system did not work because it was against the long-term interests of both the workers and their employers.

Ever since the first signs of world recession at the end of 1973, the German and other European governments imposed a virtual ban on new recruitment from outside the European Community. But this *Anwerbestop* (recruitment stop) had a paradoxical effect. Knowing that they might lose their work permits if they left Germany for more than three months, many migrants decided to stay. Immigration based on family reunion, protected by the Basic Law and the European Convention of Human Rights, became the largest immigration category, representing about 50,000 to 100,000 persons annually, or 90 percent of all immigrants after 1974. Additionally, births of foreigners' offspring continued to rise. In 1992, the annual foreigner birthrate reached 100,000 (Turks 45,000). Consequently, despite the recruitment ban and an incentive scheme for voluntary departure in 1983–84, the overall foreign population continued to rise after 1973, whereas the working population became stagnant. At the end of 1993, 27 percent of the 6.88 million foreigners and 34 percent of the 4.42 million former *Gastarbeiter* labor migrants had resided in Germany for more than twenty years, having arrived in the Federal Republic before the recruitment stop in 1973.[25] Having lived more than five years in Germany, currently about 85 percent of all *Ausländer* (foreigners) have permanent work and indefinite residence permits, regardless of their employment status. Turkish migrants and their offspring now represent the largest immigrant group in Germany, with roughly 2 million (1994). The next most numerous groups are ex-Yugoslavs (1.3 million), followed by Italians (563,000), Greeks (352,000), Spaniards, and Portuguese. These original "guest workers" total about 4.5 million persons. An additional 2.5 million are from other European, American, Asian, and African countries, among them 260,000 Poles, the largest group of non-typical migrants. Altogether, about 7 million *Ausländer*, or about 10 percent of the population of West Germany and 2 percent of East Germany's population, live and work in the united Germany.[26]

THE ALIEN LAW: A SUBSTITUTE FOR IMMIGRATION LEGISLATION

The *Ausländerrecht* (Alien Law),[27] enacted early in the guest-worker rotation scheme in April 1965, became a substitute for the nonexistent immigration law. It reflects the doctrine that Germany is not an immigration country and the expectation of temporary residential status for labor migrants.[28] It regulates the legal status of foreigners and their family members, and it grants formal legal equality in matters of civil and criminal law, as well as material access to the system of social security (welfare, health, unemployment, retirement), with the exception of full political and voting rights, military service, and civil service employment.[29] The Alien Law also establishes the conditions under which family reunion or deportation can occur. Extraditions are possible, for example, on grounds of anticonstitutional activities, a criminal record, or "failure to earn a living." The administration can also reject an application for a permit if the "interests of the Federal Republic might be endangered." However, a reform of the law in 1990–91 limited the discretion of the administration in interpreting these provisions. Administrative and civil courts play an important role in providing legal aid and in protecting and expanding the status and rights of foreigners. For example, court orders can be suspended until an appeal to a higher court has been heard, and persons with low income are entitled to free counsel to sue the administration if they cannot pay the court expenses and legal fees.

The stated goal of the Alien Law is the integration and equal treatment of foreigners in society, in education, and at the workplace, without questioning their right of cultural or religious autonomy. It is not intended to assimilate or Germanize non-Germans, but it is expected that they will accept the constitutional laws and the existing social order in Germany.[30] In its interpretation of the Alien Law, Germany is bound to civil liberties and human rights such as free movement, free speech, and protection against discrimination regulated by the Basic Law (constitution), as well as to various international and supranational conventions such as the International Labor Organization (ILO) Charter for Migrants, the European Convention on Human Rights, the European Social Charter, European Union law, and bilateral treaties.[31] EU regulations in particular override many national regulations, including the right to vote in local and regional elections since 1995. EU members also need neither work permits nor residence permits. Additional regulations exist for citizens of states associated with the EU, such as Turkey. Members of these nations receive a limited work permit after four years of residence, whereas other applicants may have to wait eight years. Unlimited residence permits are granted to non-EU citizens after five years on the condition that they have housing and are able to understand and speak German. Only children under age sixteen do not need residence permits. Resident aliens married to German spouses must wait only five years for naturalization, or three years when family members come from countries or areas where the German language is spoken, such as Romania, Italy, Switzerland, Austria, Belgium, or Denmark. Children not born in Germany but adopted by parents with German citizenship are immediately naturalized.

The participation of foreigners in public affairs passed through several phases. Before the debate about voting rights gained momentum, foreigners were represented by elected or appointed foreigners' councils (in big cities), city councils, social affairs departments, and *Ausländerbeauftragte* (representatives of foreigners similar to ombudsmen in the Swedish model) on national, state, and federal levels. At the local level especially, this system was successful in many municipalities (for example, in Berlin and Frankfurt) in promoting and integrating the demands and concerns of resident aliens. Innumerable activities and aid programs in support of the needs of immigrants and asylum seekers have also been initiated by the Protestant and Catholic Churches, unions, public and private agencies, and a great number of private and voluntary grassroots and neighborhood organizations, some of which are subsidized by federal and state funds. Foreigners have increasingly organized themselves in hundreds of self-help groups, associations, and semipolitical organizations, creating an elite of ethnic entrepreneurs. In addition, democratic political parties have opened their ranks for membership. For example, in 1994, the Green Party had a naturalized twenty-eight-year-old Turk elected as party deputy in the *Bundestag* (national parliament). The state of Saarland decided in the summer of 1995 to allow all foreign residents the right to vote. Three of the most populous states—Berlin, Baden-Württemberg, and North-Rhine Westphalia—have announced plans to follow this example, and it seems only a matter of time before this issue is resolved nationally.

THE CRISIS OF GERMAN IMMIGRATION POLICY

The original concept of a rotating guest-worker system did not take into account that "humans came when labor migrants were requested." Neither the receiving German society nor the migrants were prepared for the accompanying human problems of immigration or the sociocultural implications of ethnic and cultural diversity.[32] As Lewis Edinger pointed out, "too many migrants came from too many countries in too short a time to be easily integrated into a state that lacked a distinct national identity of its own."[33] First, the domestic infrastructure was not sufficiently prepared to absorb millions of migrants and their families; then their cultural integration and public acceptance came onto the agenda. As in the first postwar economic crisis in 1966–67, and later in the 1970s and 1980s, when Germany's economy was suffering from rising unemployment and tax and price increases, immigrant minorities became an easy target for resentment and frustration among certain segments of the population. Hidden or suppressed ethnic and cultural conflicts, economic fears, and xenophobic hostility surfaced. But it was not until 1989–90 that huge, unexpected migrations of an unprecedented scale occurred. Germany began receiving as many legal immigrants, including East German refugees, resettlers, and asylum seekers, as the traditional immigration countries of Australia, Canada, and the United States combined, on a territory sixteen times more densely populated and fifty-four times smaller than the North American continent. Sixty to 70 percent of all asylum seekers entering the EU applied, and hundreds of thousands of civil war refugees from the former Yugoslavia flocked to Germany.

However, it was not just competition for jobs and housing or economic frustration that fueled the utilitarian perception of labor migrants as temporary guest-workers who could be sent home when jobs became scarce in Germany or, worse still, boosted xenophobic and ethnocentric resentment.[34] Postwar migrations and German unification exacerbated unresolved contradictions between national identity and reality, that is, between the official ideology of not being an immigration country and the reality of increasing cultural pluralism and ethnic diversity. The established political and economic elite in particular had failed to initiate a public debate and to prepare the German population for the consequences of de facto immigration, that is, the need to accept the integration of resident aliens and to relish emerging multiculturalism. Instead, short-term solutions were applied, and many Germans and politicians held on to the self-deceptive notion that Germany is not and will not be an immigration country for non-Germans.

THE CHALLENGES OF ASYLUM

As soon as the universalistic and humanitarian entitlements of the asylum provisions were put into practice, allowing hundreds of thousands of asylum seekers to enter Germany, the unresolved conflict between the exclusive ethnic definition of nationhood embodied in citizenship laws or ethnic naturalization regulations (paragraph 116 of the Basic Law) and the liberal human rights principles of the constitution represented by the asylum law (paragraph 16 of the Basic Law) became visible.

The asylum provisions, which have been called the most generous in the Western world, were a reaction to an excessively rigid interpretation and practice of principles of nationhood that led to the expatriation of hundreds of thousands of citizens under National Socialist rule after 1933. However, the practicability of the asylum law, enacted in war-devastated Germany in 1949 primarily as a moral gesture to victims of Nazism (many of whom were involved in framing the law), was largely untested until the late 1970s and early 1980s. Therefore, the potentially disruptive nature of Germany's asylum provisions in the context of its rigid immigration policies went unrecognized for a long period.

The authors of the asylum law assumed that only asylum seekers from political, religious, and other forms of oppression would apply and that political and economic refugees could be easily distinguished or deterred from applying. Applicants using fraudulent means—for example, deliberately destroying their documents before entry to delay the process of extradition—were neither known nor anticipated at the time the law was framed. In fact, the law wanted to protect those without documents, because under Nazi rule, Germany's neighbors often sent refugees without papers back to Germany, where they were perceived as illegal immigrants or vagrants and sent to prisons and labor camps. The law of 1949 deliberately went beyond the international norms of its time in establishing a new and universalistic standard. The Federal Republic felt a unique moral obligation toward all political refugees of the world. By opening its doors, it would expiate its guilt for the violent extradition of hundreds of thousands because of their race, ethnic origin, or political or religious beliefs. Finally, it was assumed that Germany and the German people would be able and willing at any time in the future to fulfill and heed the moral obligations and intentions of the asylum provisions.

In other words, the asylum law rested on highly idealistic assumptions, thus inviting abuse and failure. It was also assumed that the number of applicants would remain small and therefore administrable, and that extradition would be enforced, thereby avoiding the creation of a large number of de facto refugee immigrants. But the long and thorough legal process required for considering asylum requests and legal objections for individual cases (asylum quotas and other collective screening policies were not allowed) did not correspond to the postwar realities of worldwide refugee movements and the sudden applications by hundreds of thousands. It was not foreseen that the asylum law would become a substitute for immigration, the only way for non-EU foreigners to enter West Germany legally without a visa. Over the years, as the approval ratio dropped significantly from 57 percent in 1973 to 5 percent after 1990, it became more and more evident that most applicants were de facto immigrants or temporary sojourners seeking employment. Finally, the costs of taking refugees were not anticipated. For example, in 1992–93 the estimated total annual costs for administration, health care, court trials, translation, and extradition by air or land amounted to about US$22 billion.[35]

A number of factors contributed to an increase in undocumented immigration and a rise in the number of asylum seekers, particularly from poor countries in Africa and Asia since the late 1970s and, more recently, from eastern Europe and the Balkans. On the one hand, acknowledged push factors such as political oppression, civil unrest and war, environmental pollution, high unemployment, and economic depravation increased the potential number of applicants. On the other hand, tales about the economic paradise in West Germany (induced, in some cases, by commercial traffickers) and the desire to find an escape route into prosperity and security added momentum. Third, the easing of emigration restrictions in eastern Europe after the collapse of the Iron Curtain between East and West removed the sheltering of the Federal Republic from large East–West migrations. Finally, because the asylum article in the 1949 constitution declared that no one arriving on German soil and claiming asylum could be turned away without a fair individual investigation, Germany permitted these applicants to stay. Continued generous handling of rejected asylum seekers, that is, the nonenforcement of most extraditions, fueled rising applications. In addition, rejected applicants could delay their extradition for two, three, or more years by legal appeals.

The conservative-liberal Kohl government initially tried to restrain administratively the growing number of applicants and avoid a public debate about Germany's immigration and asylum policies. To reduce the waiting period and address other shortcomings, the asylum law was revised several times: from 1982, it regulated the applicants' benefits (mostly food stamps instead of cash); from 1991, it allowed gainful employment under certain conditions, it set conditions for freedom of movement, and collective housing in local communities was reorganized. But these administrative amendments had no significant effect on waiting periods and the continuing influx, particularly because the courts and the judiciary did not comply with the policy measures and because extradition of rejected asylum applicants was not enforced.[36] Sixty to 70 percent of those rejected as de jure refugees were allowed to stay and work indefinitely as de facto asylum seekers; others decided to stay as undocumented illegals. For example, only 3,060 of 115,000 rejected asylum seekers were extradited in 1990. In the same year, some 500,000 asylum seekers were thought to be in the de facto category; another 580,000 cases were bona fide asylum seekers pending or awaiting an appeal; about 40,000 were quota refugees (*Kontingenzflüchtlinge*), that is, mostly "boat people" from Indochina or fugitives from military and right-wing regimes such as Chile, Iran, and Turkey; 110,000 belonged to the category of accepted asylum seekers (*Asylbewerber*); and 30,000 were categorized as stateless persons. Altogether, about 1.26 million asylum seekers lived in Germany at that time, constituting 1.6 percent of Germany's population. In other words, the country hosted as many asylum seekers after unification as it had accepted applications between 1950 and 1990.[37] In addition, more than 300,000 civil war refugees from the former Yugoslavia were accepted in the early 1990s. Serbs, Croats, Bosnians, and others who waived their rights to asylum were given temporary residence, work permits, and welfare support.[38]

Before violent clashes and anti-asylum-seeker riots made worldwide headlines in 1991–92, refugees were already perceived by the public as abusing the asylum law. Although the integration of smaller, more educated, and culturally closer groups of asylum seekers—for example, Russian Jews—was not a reason for public concern, hatred and prejudice were directed against the more publicly visible and ethnoculturally different people from Africa, Asia, and eastern Europe, such as Vietnamese and Romanian Gypsies (Sinti and Roma), some of them begging and panhandling at street corners and train stations. Insensitive remarks by politicians using growing ethnic tensions for shortsighted political gain,[39] public rumors, and exaggerated media reports about street crime, prostitution, drug dealing, illegal employment, welfare fraud, faked marriages, and so forth made refugees easy scapegoats in a climate of postunification depression, particularly in the unemployment-stricken east. Moreover, the policy of redistributing refugees was poorly implemented. In some rural municipalities, 40 percent of all welfare recipients were asylum seekers, giving the native population the impression that refugees were taking over their community life and taking advantage of generous welfare provisions financed by the working taxpayers.[40] Finally, administrative mistakes, incompetence, and the ill will of law-enforcement agencies aggravated or even triggered incidents. For example, the housing of asylum seekers in East German residential areas with high conflict potential and insufficient protection, as in the case of Rostock and Hoyerswerda, gave rise to frequent violent attacks by right-wing fringe groups, skinheads, soccer hooligans, youth gangs, drunks, and other individuals.[41]

Even though Chancellor Kohl had officially stated in August 1986 that Germany must prevent any abuse of the law, promising measures to better enforce it without violating its liberal and humanitarian spirit, the seemingly uncontrolled influx of asylum seekers (438,000 in 1992, compared with 57,000 in 1987), the supposedly lax handling of asylum administration and deportation, and the postunification economic and social strains exacerbated suppressed feelings of xenophobia and racism that had already aided the rise of the far-right Republican party in the 1980s.[42] The public got the impression that there was a lack of leadership, since the government was unable to live up to its promises and enact efficient measures to prevent Germany from becoming an immigration country against its will.[43]

Such an atmosphere played into the hands of right-wing extremists and the Republican party more successfully than in previous years. Under the new climate of national reanimation and redistribution of resources, they demanded as a solution a drastic reduction of asylum seekers, foreigners, and ethnic German resettlers, implying that they were defending economic interests, cultural rights, national sovereignty, and self-determination of the native population. Their strategy was to exploit the fears of social disruption, economic hardship, discontent, declining wealth, job competition, social stagnation, loss of traditional values, and cultural alienation.[44] *Heimatverlust* (loss of home), Balkanization or *Überfremdung* (foreignization), and *Überflutung* (swamping) became popular slogans in the west and in the east in the aftermath of unification.[45] Although the use of Nazi symbolism by the skinhead youth movement evoked ghostly remembrances of the Nazi past, it was not this provocative breaking of taboos by an isolated and politically unattractive and impotent fringe but the subtle or open ethnocentrism and xenophobic resentment of a significant minority of the population that posed a threat to political culture and the public climate. There was an expectation that labor migrants would fully assimilate and then return home whenever it was economically convenient. Resentment was based on a tendency to evaluate and rank people according to their physiognomy and national and cultural background (what has been called cultural "Western racism")[46] rather than on ultranationalist hubris and biological racism. Another characteristic of the public mood was a new kind of "affluence nationalism" and "welfare chauvinism," that is, fear of losing control over the preservation of economic wealth, political stability, and social security, the trademarks of postwar prosperity and progress. In fact, polls indicated that there were widespread fears about the strong D-Mark being devalued, alleged exploitation of the generous social security and welfare system, and a Balkanization of society and culture through immigration and the importation of exotic feuds, fundamentalist religions, and strange mores that would undermine order, consensus, and ethnocultural homogeneity. Although in some segments of the population antiforeigner and antirefugee resentment could be explained by competition for jobs, housing, education, apprenticeships, and so forth, attitudes were often not grounded in personal experience or spatial proximity but in *perceived* competition and *projected* threats allegedly posed by asylum seekers and foreigners to society and to personal well-being. Such perceptions were often fostered by sensationalist media reports and influenced by the atmosphere in which issues were discussed in public and among *Stammtisch* (pub culture) peer groups.[47]

This combination of alienation, depravation, and resentment led to violent acts and the development of a new far-right subculture, particularly in smaller communities among status-insecure young males with low income, low education, traditional materialist value orientations, and authoritarian personality traits.[48] It is also no coincidence that the first widely reported hostile incidents happened in the east, which was struggling to overcome the economic legacy of forty years of socialism coupled with a lack of exposure to liberal democratic traditions and ethnocultural diversity.

After the issue was aired publicly by right-wing extremists, and after vile assaults became a daily event, democratic parties, politicians, intellectuals, and the public started to react, and a fierce political debate about the pros and cons of Germany's asylum law, immigration and citizenship policies, and right-wing radicalism began. This debate revealed a deep split and polarization of the electorate and the parliamentary parties, centering on the questions of how to cope with the sudden outburst of hatred and violence and how to restore a stable political culture and control the damage to Germany's image abroad.

The first political signals given to the public by the governing conservative-liberal coalition, however, were weak and ambiguous. Instead of creating awareness about the issues at hand, the government focused incessantly on the abuse of the law and concentrated on technical solutions and promises. By talking about an "asylum crisis" and pointing to the lengthy and costly judicial appeal process through civil courts, as well as the costs of administration and accommodation, the coalition was unable to curb public resentment and frustration. Over the course of months, the Christian Democrats, Liberals, and Social Democrats became entangled in a legalistic political battle about changes to the relevant section of the constitution. In an attempt to ease the rising public resentment and anger, during the summer of 1992, all parties agreed to a reduction in the processing time for asylum applicants to six weeks and a prompt expulsion of those rejected. But this and other purely administrative measures proved impracticable or insufficient. Finally, all three major parties found a compromise in the winter of 1992 and the spring of 1993, keeping the individual right of asylum and defining refugees on the basis of the Geneva Refugee Convention.[49] An addendum to the asylum article in the Basic Law confirmed the continued guarantee of protection against political oppression but stipulated that applicants from non-oppressive (particularly neighboring) so-called safe countries could be turned back at the border unless they presented clear evidence of political, racial, or religious persecution.

Now, in accordance with Germany's EU partners and the Schengen Treaty of 1995, asylum applicants turned back from EU countries cannot apply a second time and will be returned to the country of first entry (*Drittstaaten-Regelung*).[50] In other words, applicants to EU and neighboring countries can no longer seek "the safest haven" according to their personal preferences.[51] But tensions dissipated only when tighter asylum regulations and enforced border controls were followed by massive public demonstrations and a bold government crackdown on right-wing activities. The number of violent incidents involving right-wing opponents of foreigners and asylum seekers dropped from 2,223 in 1992 to 860 registered violent acts in 1994. Over the same period, the total number of asylum seekers fell from 438,000 to about 127,000, and then dropped to 58,700 during the first six months of 1995.

The public debate and political actions of 1992–93 marked a turning point and indicated a clear distancing of the overwhelming majority of Germans from xenophobia, ethnocentrism, and racial prejudice, as demonstrated by poll results, surveys, and the devastating election results for the organized political right fringe.[52] Nonetheless, the central question of what constitutes national identity has not been sufficiently answered. The contradiction contained in a *völkisch* definition of the nation versus liberal elements in the constitution and laws, and the fiction that Germany can maintain, in spite of immigration, its "homogeneous" fabric, is not yet resolved and is certain to resurface. Postunification developments demonstrate that a policy of procrastination has a polarizing effect on German political culture and may deepen a schism in the traditional party system along an axis of new and old politics.[53]

From the perspective of "traditional" immigration countries, it may be difficult to understand why—after the lesson of the asylum conflict—immigration is still an emotionally charged issue. To find an answer, one has to take a further look at German citizenship and naturalization regulations. It is true that the significance of ethnocultural homogeneity for national identity and the higher good of one's nation is not specifically German and can also be found in other nations in public statements by politicians, in the philosophical underpinnings of laws dealing with immigration and citizenship, and in the motives that fuel xenophobia, ethnocentrism, racism, and nationalism.[54] What makes Germany different from the discourse in neighboring European or Western countries are its specific cultural traditions, its historical experience with and awareness of immigration, and its *völkisch* implications. The reform of the asylum law adapted the German regulations to the less liberal law of its neighbors, but it did not resolve the problem of nationhood. The persisting question of Germany's national identity is particularly reflected in Germany's citizenship law and naturalization procedures.

WHO IS A GERMAN? INTRICACIES OF CITIZENSHIP AND NATURALIZATION

The main contents of the present version of the German citizenship law can be traced back to the nineteenth-century notion of an identity of "nation" (*ethnos*, *Volk*) and "state" (*demos*), where a state is typically defined as ethnoculturally homogeneous based on a common language, history, ancestry, moral principles, social values, and other commonalities. Citizenship in this context reflects three dimensions: ethnic membership, state membership, and political citizen rights. In the German case, the ethnic or *völkisch* dimension obtained a special weight and independence that overshadowed the two others.[55] This can be explained by Germany's belated struggle for national self-determination and its search for a distinct national identity, as discussed earlier.

The concept of the ethnic nation-state goes back to the philosophical origins of German idealism and romanticism, for example, in Herder's idea that each nation has a distinctive identity based on a common language, history, ancestry, and culture and that its citizens therefore have natural rights to political self-determination and protection by the state. In other words, in contrast with the French and U.S. concepts of nation building, in which states are born out of a political revolution or founded on immigration, the cultural nation-building concept assumes that primarily ethnocultural and ancestral ties should constitute the basis of a political *civitas*.[56] Consequently, the granting of citizenship was related to the parental, ancestral principle (*ius sanguinis*), in contrast to granting citizenship on territorial and political principles (*ius solis*). However, these concepts never existed in a pure form in reality. A third principle, *ius domicilii*, that is, naturalization under certain conditions after a period of residence, has been established in modern states.

It was not until 1842, in the aftermath of the national awakening that had occurred in German territories in the wake of the Napoleonic Wars, that Prussia switched (for bureaucratic rather than nationalist reasons) from the feudal and much older principle of place of birth and residence to the ancestral principle. After German unification under Prussian hegemony, and against the particularist resistance of the federal member states, the German Empire upheld the priority of the ancestral principle for nationalist reasons of identification and integration and refined it in the citizenship law (*Reichs- und Staatsangehörigkeitsgesetz*) of 1913, which is still valid today with some modifications.[57]

A literal translation of the Latin *ius sanguinis* has misled some observers into identifying it with the perverted, racialized, pseudobiological Nuremberg Laws of 1935.[58] However, the present German citizenship law, which is similar to that of other European, particularly Scandinavian, states, is guided not by crude biology but by the following considerations and political circumstances that influenced the liberal founders of the German postwar constitution in their decision not to abandon elements of *ius sanguinis* in 1948–49.[59]

First, the postwar policy of the allied victors themselves stipulated a collective and ethnic definition of *Germanness*. Germans were to be isolated and contained in the four occupation zones until 1949 and collectively punished or reeducated. At the time, German lawmakers believed that the referral to common ethnocultural bonds would guarantee national stability, identity, and continuity while Germany was still recovering from the devastating effects of World War II and emerging Cold War division. The West German government tried to avoid at all costs an official recognition of the involuntary division of Germany. Therefore, claims of a separate East German citizenship were resisted in the west, and East Germans were automatically granted German citizenship. Moreover, West Germany wanted to be a safe haven for Germans suffering either from violent expulsion and ethnic cleansing after 1945 or from communist oppression. Finally, and in contrast to policies pursued under Bismarck and Hitler, the Federal Republic had no intention of Germanizing as many non-Germans as possible via immigration or the *ius soli*. For example, the automatic naturalization of persons born on German territory, such as the off-spring of displaced persons waiting desperately to leave Germany once and for all, was voided.

Accordingly, foreigners living in Germany were considered subjects of another *demos*. Only if they had proved their willingness to assimi-late to the life, language, and culture of the German *demos* could they apply for naturalization. In other words, the Federal Republic based its citizenship regulations on two principles: *ius sanguinis* and *ius domicilii*. Children with at least one parent holding German citizen-ship, regardless of race, ethnicity, gender, and other ascriptive crite-ria, were defined as Germans, that is, they had a right to the same citizenship as their parents. Families from pre–World War II eastern German provinces, or persons considered ethnic Germans in their eastern European homelands, were granted German citizenship upon application, based on the war-related Compensation Act and para-graph 116 of the Basic Law (see above). Citizenship could also be acquired through adoption of a child by parents with German citi-zenship or through naturalization, that is, according to *ius domicilii*.[60] Subsequently, rights of temporary residents and labor migrants (eu-phemistically called guest-workers) were regulated by the Alien Law, which offered integration without naturalization (see above). Because, by definition, foreigners were seen as transient, their naturalization was considered an exception until the reform of 1990, though natu-ralization was neither impossible nor unusual.[61] But as a consequence of the doctrine of not being an immigration country, Germany has had a comparatively low level of naturalization. The German law dis-tinguishes between *Anspruchseinbürgerungen* (entitled naturalizations), mostly used for spouses of German citizens, adoptions, and the like, and *Ermessenseinbürgerungen* (discretionary naturalizations), which apply to the regular naturalization of foreigners. In the latter case, the natu-ralization administration has greater latitude to reject applicants. The annual naturalization rate of immigrants (ethnic Germans as well as non-Germans) was, until the closing of the Iron Curtain, about 0.5 percent of the total population. The percentage has increased con-stantly since 1975 and quadrupled since unification. Between 1973 and 1993, 30 percent of a total 1.21 million naturalizations were discre-tionary and 67 percent were entitled. According to Eurostats, between 1990 and 1993, Germany issued a total of 129,000 passports based on discretionary naturalizations. However, if the entitled naturalizations of resettlers are included, the total annual naturalization rate is cur-rently about 200,000. This compares with between 55,000 and 60,000 naturalizations annually in the United Kingdom and France.

In the past, German officials defended their restrictive policy with the argument that naturalizations should occur at the end of a "successful integration" process. Germany, it was argued, was not encouraging citizenship or assuming that the majority of foreigners and their offspring would seek it. However, this is disputed by critics, since the resettlement program of ethnic eastern European Germans reflects a de facto attempt to re-Germanize ethnic Germans who, in many cases, preserved only remote linguistic bonds with Germany. Finally, as the argument of government officials goes,[62] any measure to encourage naturalization would be unpopular with Germans and with the migrants themselves. This view refers to polls indicating that fewer than 10 percent of all foreigners are interested in applying for German citizenship.[63]

It is true that not everybody living and working in Germany has a desire to become a German citizen. In fact, many older migrants seem to be reluctant to apply for German citizenship because of their continuing identification with their homelands, cultures, languages, and religions. The preservation or development of a sense of national pride and the practical bonds and pressures from sending countries also play a role.[64] But the disinterest of many residents (especially Turks) in assimilation and naturalization is not only a result of self-chosen segregation in ethnic colonies but also an outcome of experienced rejection by Germans.[65] There is little of the U.S.-style "melting pot" or even "salad bowl" atmosphere in Germany yet.

However, segregation is a different story for the so-called second and third generations, the offspring of the migrants born or educated in Germany. The majority are leaning toward assimilation into German society. Therefore, naturalization regulations were eased through a reform of the Alien Law that was passed on 7 July 1990 and became valid on 1 January 1991. The *Gesetz über die Einreise und den Aufenthalt von Ausländern im Bundesgebiet* (law relating to the entry and residency of foreigners on the territory of the Federal Republic) provided that the offspring of labor migrants in Germany could become naturalized if they were between the ages of sixteen and twenty-three, had resided in Germany for at least eight years, had been educated in Germany for six years, and were willing to give up their former citizenship. The naturalization fee was US$60 (formerly about US$3,000). Ethnic assimilation, proof of German language proficiency, and identification with German culture were no longer necessary prerequisites for naturalization. Additional requirements existed for foreigners over the age of twenty-three, namely, fifteen years residence and proof of guaranteed subsistence in Germany. Applications had to be made before the end of 1995; otherwise, the regular naturalization conditions apply.[66]

The 1990 regulations are a sign that the German government is trying to close the gap between de facto immigration and the restrictive definition of naturalization for *Ausländer*. The new measures indicate a liberalization toward the principle of *ius domicilii* and also incorporate elements of *ius soli*, giving those born on Germany territory a privileged access to citizenship. Even conservatives, who until recently blocked sweeping reforms, are now advocating the general naturalization of all newborn children of foreigners in Germany and supporting a further reduction of discretionary powers of the naturalization administration.[67] Moreover, the increasing number of persons with dual or multiple citizenships (granted mostly to ethnic Germans in Poland and immigrants from Turkey and the former Yugoslavia) indicates a willingness to give up the state monopoly on the definition of citizenship and to share national sovereignty rights.[68] Other proposals include an extension of *ius soli* rights and the granting of foreigners with a certain time of residence the option to choose between an "active" and a "resting" citizenship.[69]

Although the new measures are a step in the right direction, the continuing coexistence of inclusive and exclusive definitions of nationhood in law, rhetoric, and political practice still nurtures public confusion and political polarization around the issues of citizenship, immigration, and asylum in the aftermath of unification. Resettlers are counted not as immigrants but as nationals returning to their *ethnos*, whereas labor migrants and asylum seekers, among them large numbers of de facto immigrants, are still perceived de jure as temporary aliens. The only officially acknowledged non-German immigrants in this scheme are second- and third-generation descendants of labor migrants, resident aliens applying for naturalization, and recognized refugees and naturalized persons. Furthermore, the *völkisch* notion of *ius sanguinis* and of a homogeneous *Volk* based on the identity of *demos* and *ethnos*, and the fiction that Germany is not an immigration country, remain official dogma, albeit weakened in its material effects.

It is this insufficient recognition of large and ethnoculturally diverse groups of people who wish to immigrate that nurtures xenophobia and cultural racism. It is not primarily an inability or an unwillingness to feed and house immigrants that has led to the tensions that predate unification and the polarization after unification, but rather the unpreparedness of the public and the politicians to face the reality of immigration. The resulting ambiguity is further exacerbated by the coexistence of inclusive republican, civil, and universal human rights principles with exclusive elements in the definition of nationhood and in political rhetoric. The abstract idea of national homogeneity and the fear that immigration poses a threat are at the heart of the problem. They prevent the development of a discourse that is able to appreciate and seriously assess the benefits of immigration, that is, its short- and long-term economic, cultural, and demographic advantages. Only recently—with the support of a growing percentage of citizens born and educated after the war—have the established parties and the legal system introduced reforms that reflect current realities more pragmatically. But a new assessment of immigration and of national identity that values increasing ethnic diversity and cultural pluralism will not be easily accomplished, because the current ambiguities have origins reaching back to the very foundations of the nation-state and of modern German history, and to the roots of collective memory.

CONCLUSION: THE FUTURE OF THE FATHERLAND

Using the example of the German definition of nationhood, this essay has elaborated on how migrations and the social construction of identities interact. In the age of nationalism, Germany underwent extreme phases in defining nationhood, which led to the suppression of its history of extensive in- and out-migration and of cultural and ethnic diversity. Germany's belated nation building supported the development of nationalist fervor, which was further promoted by antiliberal and authoritarian traditions, the lack of the colonial experience of absorbing non-European people, the paranoia of encirclement by hostile powers, the collective humiliations after both world wars that shook and almost destroyed the country, the racist discourse of the Nazi era and the following depression and collective humiliation, ethnic cleansing during and after World War II that fell back on the Germans, the artificial Cold War division, and deep collective anger, guilt, and shame. All these circumstances upheld a notion of a national identity that overemphasized ethnocultural homogeneity and an inward-looking, self-centered collective identity. Germans, despite their impressive cultural achievements, were by geographical location and tradition "inlanders" rather than cosmopolitan, with the exception, perhaps, of those in the northern seafaring cities.

Their experience with nation-state building led the Germans to believe that it is necessary to draw exclusive boundaries to preserve unity against external threats and internal centripetal regional, religious, social, and cultural forces. The nation-state created and enforced its own ideology. Exclusive and inclusive citizenship and naturalization regulations were used to mold a collective and overarching sense of national "belongingness." The century-old history of migration in central Europe and the experiences with cultural, ethnic, and religious diversity were forgotten or ignored for the higher good of homogenization for the purpose of national advancement. *Völkisch* nationalism, a reaction to oppression and foreign domination, served to create identity, cohesion, and solidarity, but it later became a vehicle of oppression itself and—in its extreme manifestations—an instrument of violent inclusion and exclusion.[70] But we have seen that recent migrations in the wake of economic, political, and cultural globalization create conditions under which the narrow concept of *völkisch* nationalism becomes an obstacle. Thus, the global exchange of goods, capital, services, and labor has a civilizing function and creates conditions that may give way to more universal and multicultural concepts of belongingness.

There is little doubt that the immigration waves after World War II made Germany an immigration country against its will. The massive influx of refugees from East Germany, resettlers, and asylum seekers after German unification in 1990 has exacerbated the underlying tensions of universal versus *völkisch* and national principles in German law, culture, and society. It is estimated that—excluding immediate postwar population shifts—between 1950 and 1994, almost 16 million people, or a quarter of the population currently living in West Germany, took up residence in that territory. Germany was politically, legally, culturally, and ideologically unprepared to deal with the realities of immigration and their consequences: ethnic diversity and cultural pluralism. But the fact of immigration and its consequences cannot be reversed without cutting links to the world and Germany's European neighbors. Even opponents of continuous immigration recognize that foreigners and their consumption, trade links, investments, savings, pensions, and taxes are essential for Germany's wealth and well-being, and that foreigners contribute their fair share to secure and maintain economic prosperity, social welfare, and political stability. With their labor, they perform essential jobs that Germans do not want. They are engaged in trades and niches that enrich the economy and society. A mass exodus would have harmful consequences for the Germans themselves and for their neighbors.[71]

Under the given conditions of a still ambiguous and unreceptive environment, relatively few immigrants have felt encouraged to become integrated into German society. Economically, the mass of labor migrants was confined to an ethnic substrata, employed mostly in industries and occupations that were no longer attractive to German labor.[72] Only recently has an expanding stratum of ethnic entrepreneurs begun to develop, and social differentiation within ethnic groups is taking place. Some groups are more easily integrated into the societal fabric than others. Many Turks, for example, tend to live segregated in ethnic enclaves, particularly in larger cities and urban agglomerations.

It was not until the mid-1980s, with a new generation slowly taking over positions of power and intellectual discourse, that the political agenda changed in favor of a more realistic policy on foreigners. A reform of the Alien Law was set in motion on the national level, and recently the citizenship regulations and the asylum law have been overhauled. Along with other unforeseen consequences of unification, European integration, and international responsibilities, postunification Germany is facing a series of changes greater than the sum of all changes that took place in the preceding decades. German democracy and political culture are undergoing a difficult process of readjusting and redefining national interests and identity in the 1990s, taking into account domestic interests, integration capacities, and humanitarian concerns.[73] In this process, Germany has to come to grips with its status as an immigration society and the unavoidable consequences of increasing ethnic and cultural diversity. It has to finally shed the relics of *völkisch* or ethnic nationalism and, by doing so, may become a model of a postnational nation that transfers part of its national sovereignty, institutions, national symbols, and identities to supranational entities, such as the EU or the United Nations.

The German government and public have to reform and modernize themselves to regain a new stability and postnational identity that mirror the realities of transnational migration and refugee flows, European and global integration, the development of new denizen rights, and supranational memberships[74] and the adherence to the republican, civil, and universalist principles of Germany's postwar constitution, democratic institutions, and political culture. Acceptance of the new diversity and pluralism makes it more likely that domestic and neighborly peace and the postwar democratic traditions and liberal outlook of united Germany will be preserved. The emotionally charged issue of immigration and diversity may well constitute one of the most difficult tasks that united Germany will face for some time to come.[75]

NOTES

The author is grateful for helpful comments by Kay Losey, Bev Wiggins, and Konrad Jarausch. Parts of this chapter are based on an earlier abridged article, "Germany at the Crossroads: National Identity and the Challenges of Immigration," published in *International Migration Review* 29, no. 4 (1995): 914–38.

1. Peter J. Katzenstein, *Policy and Politics in West Germany*, Philadelphia, 1987, 218–39.
2. Craig Calhoun, "Nationalism and Ethnicity," *Annual Review of Sociology* 19 (1993): 216.
3. Benedict Anderson, *Imagined Communities: Reflections on the Origin and Spread of Nationalism*, London, 1991.
4. See Klaus Bade (ed.), *Neue Heimat im Westen. Vertriebene, Flüchtlinge, Aussiedler*, Münster, 1990.
5. See Ulrich Herbert, *Geschichte der Ausländerbeschäftigung in Deutschland 1880 bis 1980*, Berlin, 1986.
6. See Hans-Ulrich Wehler, *The German Empire 1871–1918*, Providence, RI, 1985.
7. See Elie Kedourie, *Nationalism*, Cambridge, MA, 1993, and John Breuilly, *Nationalism and the State*, Manchester, 1982.
8. E. K. Francis, *Interethnic Relations: An Essay in Sociology and Theory*, New York, 1976, 78.
9. Calhoun points out that nations in the everyday meaning are treated metaphorically as individuals rather than as webs of social relationships. Such a personification of nations places an emphasis on sameness, which often makes nationalism an enemy of pluralism, democracy, and (transnational) equality. Moreover, it suggests that national identities should take precedence over other competing identities. Calhoun, "Nationalism and Ethnicity," 211–39. For a similar assessment, see Robert Miles and Nora Räthzel, "Migration and the Homogeneity of the Nation State," in Hedwig Rudolph and Mirjana Morokvasic (eds.), *Bridging States and Markets: International Migration in the Early 1990s*, Berlin, 1993, 67.
10. Mathias Bös, "Ethnisierung des Rechts? Staatsbürgerschaft in Deutschland, Frankreich, Großbritannien und den U.S.A.," *KZfSS* 45, no. 4 (1993): 639.
11. Francis, *Interethnic Relations*, 83.
12. Peter O'Brien, "German-Polish Migration: The Elusive Search for a German Nation-State," *International Migration Review* 26, no. 2 (1992): 373–87.
13. The "nationalization" of politics had its breakthrough with the proclamation of national self-determination as a state-building principle at the end of World War I, when feudal concepts of supranational dynasties or princely states no longer seemed a viable means of state organization. Even the Soviets, who deliberately tried to overcome the bourgeois concept of nationalism, were not able to suppress the concept and therefore included it as a cornerstone in their governmental framework.
14. Jürgen Habermas (ed.), *Stichworte zur "Geistigen Situation der Zeit,"* Frankfurt, 1979, 7–35.

15. Besides the types of immigrants described in the text, six categories of temporary residents can be distinguished: invisibles (businesspeople, technicians, managers, professionals, academics); gap-fillers (seasonal, temporary, or project-tied immigrant workers, particularly in service sectors—estimated at 500,000 persons); undocumented illegal workers and tourists with expired visas (an estimated 650,000 persons in 1990); members of NATO and their families or, until 1994, Russian occupying military forces; about 100,000 transborder commuters; and citizens of EU member-states (more than half a million persons). See W. R. Boehning, "Integration and Immigration Pressures in Western Europe," *International Labour Review* 130, no. 4 (1991): 445–8.
16. Katzenstein, *Policy and Politics in West Germany*, 225.
17. Alfred M. de Zayas, *The German Expellees. Victims in War and Peace*, New York, 1993.
18. Gerhard Heilig, Thomas Büttner, and Wolfgang Lutz, "Germany's Population: Turbulent Past, Uncertain Future," *Population Bulletin* 45, no. 4 (1990): 24 f.
19. Boehning, "Integration and Immigration Pressures in Western Europe," 448.
20. Inge Weber-Newerth, "Ethnic Germans Come 'Home to the Fatherland,'" *Debatte. Review of Contemporary German Affairs* 3, no. 1 (1995): 134 f.
21. The *Bundesvertriebenengesetz* (expellee law) of 1956 defines in article 6 a member of the German people (*Volkszugehöriger*) as a person who professed in his or her former homeland to belong to the German people (*Volkstum*). This claim has to be certified by certain characteristics, for example, ancestry, language, education, cultural practice. Included are persons who became German citizens through collective naturalization proceedings (*Sammeleinbürgerungen*) between 1938 and 1945 and did not subsequently relinquish German citizenship. Proof of descent is most frequently applied, because other characteristics were often suppressed by postwar communist regimes. The application of these criteria is highly controversial, particularly as they concern applicants from *Volkslisten*, who were often selected by Nazis only because they were deemed suitable for Germanization.
22. Ardagh, *Germany and the Germans: After Unification*, London and New York, 1994, 294.
23. See also Jost Halfmann, "Immigration and the Changing Concept of Citizenship in Germany," unpublished paper, GSA Conference, Washington, DC, October 1993, 17.
24. Halfmann, "Immigration and the Changing Concept of Citizenship in Germany"; Christiane Lemke, "Crossing Borders and Building Barriers. Citizenship and the Process of European Integration," paper prepared for the German Studies Association Conference, Washington, DC, 5–10 October 1993; Daniel Kanstroom, "Wer sind wir wieder? Laws of Asylum, Immigration and Citizenship in the Struggle for the Soul of the New Germany," *Yale Journal of International Law* 18 (1993): 155–211.
25. The number of foreigners from befriended socialist and Third World countries (Vietnam, Mozambique, Cuba, and Poland) living in the former East Germany to compensate for demographic deficits and labor shortages remained comparatively small and insignificant (150,000–200,000 persons).

In contrast to West Germany, no efforts were made to integrate these laborers. They were strictly isolated from the population (as were the half million Red Army soldiers and their families). They were not allowed to stay and settle down with their families and had to return after a certain period of time. The collapse of East German industry after unification led to a premature end of most labor contracts. The majority of "socialist" guest-workers were encouraged to leave the country with a return fee of several thousand U.S. dollars. See Bundeszentrale für politische Bildung (ed.), *Ausländer*, Bonn, 1993, 6 f.

26. Data from Statistisches Bundesamt, 31 December 1993; cf. *Deutschland Nachrichten* 8 (April 1994): 1.

27. For an overview, see Winfried Kissrow, *Ausländerrecht einschließlich Asylrecht*, 11th ed., Cologne, 1992.

28. Depending on length of residence, citizenship, family, and occupational status, different work and residence regulations exist. Four types of residence status have been established: *Aufenthaltserlaubnis* (residence permit), *Aufenthaltsberechtigung* (extended residence permit similar to the U.S. resident alien status), *Aufenthaltsbewilligung* (short-term residence permit), and *Aufenthaltsbefugnis* (permit granted because of humanitarian or political considerations). See Kissrow, *Ausländerrecht*, 6 ff.

29. In the field of education and training, special basic language and vocational training programs for foreigners have been established. Because educational efforts in the Federal Republic are controlled by the federal states, educational programs vary tremendously in the degree to which they address the special linguistic, religious, and cultural needs of foreign children. In Berlin alone, 320 Turkish teachers are on the government payroll.

30. Besides the official policy of integration of long-term residents and their families, two other policy measures declared by the Kohl government in 1983 are still valid today: the limitation on a further influx of (labor) immigrants, and the encouragement of those willing to return to their former homelands. A financially aided return program initiated in 1983–84 was not as successful as expected—only about 250,000 people left.

31. Roger Blanpain, "Equality and Prohibition of Discrimination in Employment," in Blanpain (ed.), *Comparative Labour Law and Industrial Relations*. 2d rev. ed., Deventer and Boston, 1985, 457 ff.

32. See Jürgen Fijalkowski, "Gastarbeiter als industrielle Reservearmee," *Archiv für Sozialgeschichte* 24 (1984): 399–456, and "Die Bundesrepublik und das Migrationsproblem: historische Erfahrungen und aktuelle Herausforderungen," in Manfred Knapp (ed.), *Migration im neuen Europa*, Stuttgart, 1994, 113–28.

33. Edinger (1986), 54, cited in Marilyn Hoskin, *New Immigrants and Democratic Society: Minority Integration in Western Democracies*, New York, 1991, 14.

34. Klaus F. Geiger, "Einstellungen zur multikulturellen Gesellschaft. Ergebnisse von Repräsentativbefragungen in der Bundesrepublik," *Migration* 9 (1991): 11–48, and *Spiegel Spezial* "Das Profil der Deutschen" (January 1991).

35. Applicant families receive a monthly benefit of between US$250 to $340. Most of it consists of food instead of cash, and it comes in addition to free housing, schooling, and health benefits. The annual costs were esti-

mated to be about US$10 billion in 1993 and US$8 billion in 1994. See *Migration News* 2, no. 12 (1995).

36. The poor enforcement was caused by a liberal interpretation of the Geneva Convention's definition of de facto asylum seekers and by non-extradition of families and individuals who were undergoing medical treatment or of applicants who married German citizens. Most asylum seekers from "third" countries with long, pending cases also were spared from deportation. Moreover, court decisions were often prolonged due to the lack of cooperation of the country of origin, nonexisting documents, and backlogs of court cases because of a shortage of qualified administrative personnel and translators.

37. About 211,000, or 9.4 percent, of 2.258 million asylum seekers between 1950 and 1994 were given official political refugee status. However, these numbers are not absolutely accurate, because first and second applications were in some cases included. See Dietrich Thränhardt, "Die Ursprünge von Rassismus und Fremdenfeindlichkeit in der Konkurrenzdemokratie," *Leviathan* 21, no. 3 (1993): n. 50.

38. Josef Bielmeier and Gottfried Stein, *Stichwort: Neues Asylrecht in Deutschland und Europa*, Munich, 1994.

39. Some observers speculated that the scapegoating of foreigners had the "indispensable function of holding together a precariously united people profoundly divided into Ossies (East Germans) and Wessies (West Germans)." See O'Brien, "German-Polish Migration," 384.

40. Opinion polls indicated that three-quarters of the population thought that the authorities were "too generous" toward asylum seekers, and only 4 percent found them "too mean" (Ardagh, *Germany and the Germans*, 291). A majority in Germany supported refugee quotas and the extradition of economic refugees abusing the law. More than one-third supported a reduction of the numbers of those who applied for asylum.

41. Thränhardt, "Die Ursprünge von Rassismus," 352, n. 54 f.

42. Manfred Kuechler, "Germans and 'Others': Racism, Xenophobia, or 'Legitimate Conservatism'?" *German Politics* 3, no. 1 (1994): 47–74.

43. Hoskin, *New Immigrants and Democratic Society*, 7.

44. Ardagh, *Germany and the Germans*, 289.

45. In contradiction to the xenophobic notion that Germany was "swamped" by persons from distant and non-European cultures, statistics indicate that the number of asylum seekers from Turkey, Asia, and Africa decreased from 33 to 15 percent of all applicants between 1986 and 1993, in comparison with asylum seekers from eastern Europe and Russia. It was not so much the absolute number of Third World applicants as their visibility that made them targets of prejudice and fear.

46. Dieter Fuchs, Jürgen Gerhards, and Edeltraud Roller, "'Wir und die anderen.' Ethnozentrismus in den 12 Ländern der EG," *Kölner Zeitschrift für Soziologie und Sozialpsychologie* 45, no. 2 (1993).

47. See Geiger, "Einstellungen zur multikulturellen Gesellschaft," 28.

48. A growing body of research has investigated the origins of youth street violence, particularly in the east. The following factors were said to have triggered the development of a deviant subculture after unification: high unemployment, weak family and religious bonds, lack of youth infrastructure, an ideological vacuum, and an identity crisis. See Klaus Farin

and Eberhard Seidel-Pielen, *Rechtsruck. Rassismus im neuen Deutschland*, Berlin, 1992, 67–75; Armin Pfahl-Traughber, *Rechtsextremismus. Eine kritische Bestandsaufnahme nach der Wiedervereinigung*, Bonn, 1993, 195–201; Thränhardt, "Die Ursprünge von Rassismus," 353.

49. The Geneva Convention gives asylum seekers no automatic right of entrance and a legally recoverable individual right of refugee status, as in the German asylum law. The convention rules only on the legal status of those accepted as asylum seekers and their right not to be expelled to a country that would threaten their lives or freedoms. The Convention is the norm of the less liberal regulations of Germany's European neighbors, the United States, and other Western immigration countries.

50. On 24 September 1992, Germany and Romania signed an agreement to deport about 60,000 Gypsies and 40,000 other Romanians. Under the accord, Romania will take back all its citizens who live illegally in Germany. Germany offered US$20 million to pay for their deportation and job training programs in their homelands. *Migration World*, 20, no. 5 (1992): 3.

51. The reform of the Asylum Law was followed by bilateral agreements of return between Germany and Austria, Poland, Romania (September 1992), Bulgaria (September 1994), and the Czech Republic (October 1994), in exchange for financial and economic assistance, support for EU and NATO application, a liberalization of the bilateral border regime, and easier labor market access. See Hedwig Rudolph, "Dynamics of Immigration in a Nonimmigrant Country: Germany," in Heinz Fassmann and Rainer Münz (eds.), *European Migration in the Late Twentieth Century. Historical Patterns, Actual Trends, and Social Implications*, Aldershot, 1994, 113–26.

52. The public's association of right-wing parties, such as the Republikaner party, with xenophobic violence led to their delegitimization, particularly after the shocking arson attacks in Mölln, which significantly increased public awareness and solidarity with the victims. See Kuechler, "Germans and 'Others'"; Thränhardt, "Die Ursprünge von Rassismus," 352.

53. See Hermann Kurthen and Michael Minkenberg, "Germany in Transition: Immigration, Racism and the Extreme Right," *Nations and Nationalism* 1, no. 2 (1995): 175–96.

54. Recent political and legal changes in the United Kingdom, France, Sweden, and the United States indicate a trend to handle immigration, citizenship, naturalization, and asylum more restrictively, thus leading to a renationalization and "racialization" of immigration policies instead of a liberalization, as had been hoped by liberals and supporters of a global trend toward more universalism. See Frank Bovenkerk, Robert Miles, and Gilles Verbunt, "Racism, Migration and the State in Western Europe: A Case for Comparative Analysis," *International Sociology* 5, no. 4 (1990); Robert Miles and Nora Räthzel, "Migration and the Homogeneity of the Nation State," in Hedwig Rudolph and Mirjana Morokvasic (eds.), *Bridging States and Markets: International Migration in the Early 1990s*, Berlin, 1993, 65–92; Mathias Bös, "Ethnisierung des Rechts? Staatsbürgerschaft in Deutschland, Frankreich, Großbritannien und den USA," *Kölner Zeitschrift für Soziologie und Sozialpsychologie* 45, no. 4 (1993): 619–43; Thränhardt, "Die Ursprünge von Rassismus," 1993.

55. Albrecht Funk, "Wer ist Deutscher, wer ist Deutsche?" forthcoming in *Leviathan*.

56. Kymlicka has correctly pointed out that the founding fathers of U.S. civic nationalism had to emphasize political principles because they shared the same ethnic characteristics (language, religion, and literature) with the English. But the focus on universalist political principles (applicable at that time to white males only) did not replace the cultural component of U.S. national identity. In fact, a noncultural definition of civic nationalism is hard to comprehend. The current "culture wars" in U.S. society about multiculturalism and the canon reflect an ethnocultural struggle about U.S. nationhood, as does, for example, the heated debate in France about Muslim immigrant women wearing the *tschador* (head scarf) in public. Will Kymlicka, *Multicultural Citizenship. A Liberal Theory of Minority Rights*, Oxford, 1995, 200, n. 15.

57. Albrecht Funk, "Inclusion and Exclusion in the Legal Construction of Citizenship in Nineteenth Century Germany," unpublished paper prepared for the German Studies Conference, Chicago, September 1995.

58. See Kanstroom, "'Wer sind wir wieder?'" 192 f.

59. Bös, "Ethnisierung des Rechts?" 626, 638.

60. Naturalization requires a voluntary and permanent desire to remain in Germany, basic knowledge of the polity, and a pledge to the democratic foundations of the Federal Republic. This also implies active command of the German language, eight years residency in Germany, a secure job, legal competence, and no criminal record (regulations from 17 December 1977).

61. The often repeated allegation, even in serious academic works, that labor migrants (in particular Turks) who were allegedly "completely assimilated" and "living their whole lives" in Germany were "not allowed to gain citizenship" runs counter to the facts (see, for example, Kymlicka, *Multicultural Citizenship*, 23).

62. Kanstroom, "'Wer sind wir wieder?'" 13.

63. Hoskin, *New Immigrants and Democratic Society*, 37.

64. Turkey, for example, does not allow expatriates to inherit or own real estate in Turkey.

65. According to the Federal Statistical Office, in 1991, 10 percent of all marriages were between Germans and foreigners (a total of 455,000), but only 1 percent were between Germans and (mostly Muslim) Turks.

66. *Deutsches Ausländerrecht*, Munich, 1991, 10 f.

67. See *Migration News* 2, no. 2 (1995).

68. In 1991, over 6,000 applicants in 27,295 discretionary naturalization cases were granted dual or multiple citizenship. About 60 percent of those applicants had Turkish citizenship; 20 percent were from Poland and the former Yugoslavia. Of those persons granted single citizenship, 40 percent were from the former Yugoslavia and Poland, and about 20 percent were from the former Czechoslovakia and Turkey. See also *Der Spiegel* 24 (1993): 26 f.; and *Migration News* 2, no. 2 (1995).

69. Herta Däubler-Gmelin, "Von der Ausländer- zur Einwanderungspolitik: Brauchen wir eine neue Einwanderungspolitik?" in Friedrich-Ebert-Stiftung (ed.), *Von der Ausländer- zur Einwanderungspolitik*, no. 32, Bonn, 1994, 7–24. Halfmann, "Immigration and the Changing Concept," 18.

70. Bös, "Ethnisierung des Rechts?" 639.

71. Hans Dietrich von Loeffelholz, "Zuwanderung: Erfahrungen und

Perspektiven der Zuwanderung in die Bundesrepublik aus ökonomischer Sicht," in Friedrich-Ebert-Stiftung (ed.), *Von der Ausländer- zur Einwanderungspolitik*, 41–60.

72. Hermann Kurthen, Helmut Gillmeister, and Jürgen Fijalkowski, *Ausländerbeschäftigung in der Krise?* Berlin, 1989.

73. Ursula Mehrländer and Günther Schultze, "Einwanderungskonzepte für die Bundesrepublik Deutschland," in Friedrich-Ebert-Stiftung (ed.), *Von der Ausländer- zur Einwanderungspolitik*, no. 32, Bonn, 1994, 25–40.

74. Yasemin Soysal, *Limits of Citizenship: Migrants and Postnational Membership in Europe*, Chicago, 1994.

75. Hoskin, *New Immigrants and Democratic Society*, 146 f.

4

The "Generation of 1989": A New Political Generation?

CLAUS LEGGEWIE

The year 1989 represents a deep caesura not only for European history but also for societies throughout the world. "Nothing can remain as it was," Willy Brandt remarked when the Berlin Wall fell, and in this he was of one mind with many of his contemporaries. That most improbable and momentous of events, the opening of the Iron Curtain, which had been thought by the whole of humanity to be unassailable for all eternity, invites us to mark the end of the century with 1989— a short century, which had not really started until August 1914.

How should we characterize the train of events that began in 1989? Participants and observers alike use the neutral term *Wende* (turn) when they refer to the events of 1989. This word is also a navigational term suggesting a turn of 180 degrees, that is, a complete change of course. We are probably justified in ascribing a revolutionary quality to the events of 1988–90—revolutionary in the original sense of the word, denoting a return to the good old order of things and connoting social and political restoration. The "revolution" of 1989 was actually less remarkable for creating new realities than for restoring old ones—from the conditions of private ownership and the capitalist market economy to the traditional political parties and systems. Generally, the protagonists of 1989 no longer identified themselves with a strong belief in history or progress. They contented themselves with toppling a decaying, partially totalitarian, and increasingly intolerable ancien régime to make way for a system modeled on the Western democracies and market economies.

The participants in the events of 1989 came from the ranks of social movements, from civil rights organizations such as Solidarity in Poland and Charta 77, and from among the governing classes, church groups, and artistic and intellectual circles. As a rule, they were middle-aged, and insofar as they were not subject to political persecution and social marginalization, they were well established professionally and socially. It is clear now, half a decade after the *Wende*, that they are not spearheading the transformation to a postsocialist regime. On the contrary, they once again find themselves in opposition, or else they have taken a "private," more or less apolitical stance. These "eighty-niners," whose biographical similarities and differences have yet to be analyzed, have most definitely not formed a "political generation."

Leaving aside individual circumstances and the structural factors that are inherent in the process of transformation in eastern and central Europe, this might have something to do with the fact that the eighty-niners were no longer young when they were confronted with the opening of the Iron Curtain. But generations are usually formed when their members are young—in late adolescence or early adulthood, when external events still have a strong and even decisive formative influence. Potential eighty-niners, then, would have been those between sixteen and twenty-five years old in the annus mirabilis of 1989 and thus especially receptive to a political dynamism that they had not triggered themselves. It is true that in eastern and central Europe, members of this age group—school and university students, members of youth movements, and adherents of various subcultures—actively participated in the new turn of events; that is, they could be mobilized for street protests and for reform initiatives. The overwhelming majority of youth in the Europe of 1989, however, experienced the events of that year as a community of TV consumers. Young people's connections with 1989 are indirect and secondary, even if the often vividly recalled events are described in terms of a fundamental and decisive caesura. In any case, events such as the disaster at the Chernobyl nuclear reactor (1986) or the Gulf War (1990–91) were more profoundly shocking, and more far-reaching in the reactions they evinced, than the fall of the wall, which has taken on a somewhat episodic, abstract character. In both East and West, there is a general sense that events since 1989 have been passively endured rather than consciously shaped.

The "objective" circumstances, then, were more conducive to the formation of a new (political) generation after 1989 than were the subjective experiences of young people. Could there be a generation of eighty-niners nevertheless? This is the subject of the unavoidably speculative reflections that follow. It is first necessary to elucidate a concept of generations that seeks to explain how those of a similar age can also come to be of a like mind. The second step will be to combine the concept of generations with the insights of sociological research into the specific characteristics of contemporary youth. Finally, we can try to assess the likelihood of a new political generation.

HOW THOSE OF A SIMILAR AGE COME TO BE OF A LIKE MIND: THE CONCEPT OF GENERATIONS

To be born in the same or almost the same year is a biographical accident and sociologically insignificant. It is true that in everyday life one often observes that people of about the same age seek out one another's company and can communicate with and understand one another spontaneously, or at least they can readily discuss specific topics. For young people in particular, the peer group represents an extremely strong formative community of action and interaction. Thus the mere accident of belonging to the same vintage and stepping into the world together does indeed establish a collective consciousness that is effective in both microsocial and macrosocial contexts and can go beyond merely sporadic communication and superficial friendliness.

But not all age cohorts make up a generational identity. This evidently requires special circumstances. The preeminent sociologist in this area, Karl Mannheim, defined three elements that are necessary for an "objective" generational "location" (*Lagerung*) to develop into a subjectively experienced, stable "generation unit."[1] A marked, biographically formative central historical event must have been experienced with a considerable degree of intensity by young people in a group context as well as in relevant social institutions. For this to occur, certain social preconditions must be met. Above all, it is necessary that the youthful years be clearly distinguished from other phases of life (childhood, adulthood), which has occurred on a mass scale only since the end of the nineteenth century. And there must be social meeting places where young people can articulate plans for their future lives and where historically and politically significant turning points are registered (e.g., in youth groups, universities). I return to this issue shortly, with reference to generationally significant features that have been particularly effective in twentieth-century German history.

A "generation" can first of all be characterized as a specific mode of collective consciousness, as a variant of the genus of "we-feelings." It can be an effective bonding agent—not unlike other collective identities such as ethnic origin and affiliation, sense of national community, patriotism or nationalism, class consciousness, and communities based on worldview or religion. Compared with collective identities such as these, a generation seems to involve a relatively loose bonding among its individual members. The concept of generations, of course, presupposes neither a stable sense of place nor a common lot that is any more enduring than the vagaries of historical circumstance, such as *ethnos* and nation. The notion of generations presupposes that social structures are viewed (and very strictly so) in their temporality; that is, *specific* historical events intervene in the drawn-out process of social transformation and crystallize in *particular* age groups.

The concept of generations is therefore one of the most important criteria of historical periodization, even if it is only an optional criterion, and under favorable circumstances, it can become significant in the accustomed everyday world. Furthermore, generational location is distinct from class location: an age cohort, which by definition transcends classes and social strata, does not come about as the result of common interests; the latter are rather the consequence of some momentary interaction, the result of a subjective feeling of participating in a shared experience. Nor is this feeling based on a set of beliefs or a rational program that can be easily or clearly articulated, but on a more general and a more heterogeneous sense of shared values. In this way—as temporary collectives—generations adopt manifold aspects of the social structure and, in turn, they contribute to it a particular stamp, or style, arising from similarities in age and consciousness of the times.

Generations thus come about through the effects of a significant and memorable historical occurrence (and hence a feeling of belongingness) upon adolescents and young adults in the context of social milieus and institutions that radiate into the rest of society. This can be illustrated by the example of the generational movement (not typical only of Germany) called the *Wandervögel*, which took shape around 1900 as an age cohort bound together by shared experience and by a common front against the "old world" (i.e., the world of the older generation) and which carried over into later stages of personal development the peculiar sense of self that had been formed in their earlier association and cooperation. The peer group was determined to make its presence felt in the various clubs and associations and in other forums of the *Wandervögel*, thus reinforcing age-specific perceptions of the present and blueprints for the future. In this way, a new cultural exemplar or model could unfold and then extend far beyond the limited (in this case, even marginal) milieu that produced it. And it was able to outlast the specific circumstances that prevailed in the late nineteenth century.

It was according to this model—and from these historical origins—

that the politicized youth movements of the interwar years (which at this stage had already taken on an international quality) developed, including the totalitarian Hitler Youth movement. In Germany, an autonomous generational variant was the so-called *Flakhelfer* (paramilitary antiaircraft gunners at the end of the war), which also existed in a modified form among the western European allies. We can call them the "forty-fivers": young adults whose paramilitary experience helped them recognize the profound caesura (and the historical opportunity) represented by the end of the war, who grasped the initiative and who still constitute the majority of the political and economic elites in the Federal Republic and in other societies. It is no exaggeration or psychological projection to ascribe to this generation of *Flakhelfer* common forms of consciousness and patterns of behavior with long-term effects. No matter how much those born around 1928 might be segmented according to their origins in a variety of social structures, their age has produced a powerful social affinity. In the form of a generational bond lasting several decades, it has grown stronger.

With the "sixty-eighters," a generation once again emerged, and on a global scale. They are the latest obvious example of a durable generational identity. They have (quite rightly) had a "cultural revolutionary" identity attributed to them. This goes far beyond the small core of activists in the student movement, and it is not restricted to the localities where they staged their spectacular protests. Despite their initially eccentric identity as a small radical minority, the sixty-eighters were both the symbol of and the driving force behind the transformation of values in the affluent democratic industrial societies (with offshoots in some of the countries of "real existing socialism" and in some Third World countries). At the same time, the sixty-eighters put generational conflict back onto the agenda and confirmed a well-established truth of functional sociology: that in highly developed modern industrial societies, accelerated social change presupposes a transfer of know-how within generational collectives—a dense network that communicates sociocultural and technical innovations within stable and independent youthful peer groups and is capable of adopting and developing innovations that occur in rapid succession.

THE YOUTH OF TODAY:
GENERATION X—RAREFIED OR UNIVERSAL?

Studies of generations often exhaust themselves in the superficial examination of trends or in ephemeral portraits of the current subcultures. These may contain some of the elements that make up a generation, but generations arise only over long periods of time and independently of what is likely to be fashionable at a given time. It is possible, however, to draw conclusions about the potential character of a generation from the peculiarities of youthful subgroups. The youth of today, those between sixteen and twenty-five years old (others stretch the definition of "youth" to include those from thirteen to thirty, to accommodate earlier maturity and an extended postadolescence), are fundamentally different from previous age cohorts in a number of respects. Most noteworthy is the dramatic overturning of the age pyramid in the affluent industrial societies, which has led to the rarefaction of the sixteen- to twenty-five-year-olds when compared with older cohorts. In contrast with the situation until the middle of the twentieth century in the Northern Hemisphere (and in a spectacular manner in those regions of the Southern Hemisphere with high birthrates), young people in all societies are numerically marginalized.

At the same time, the cultural quality we call youthfulness is detaching itself from its biological moorings and functioning as a kind of cultural code that is "in the air" and thus freely available to all, regardless of age. The dictum "forever young" is leading to an intermingling of the lifestyles of the various age groups, and in the process, the sense of a shared generational experience is becoming more plausible: attributes of biological age are relative and highly inclusive; it is the generational attributes that are effectively exclusive— that is, they bring about restrictive social attitudes and behavior. To this extent, we may assume a degree of conflict between those who are over thirty and those who are under thirty—a conflict that no longer takes the form of classical political differences between the generations but rather manifests itself as cultural *distance*. In the 1980s, a new cultural model arose that had to do with the end of the classical industrial society based on labor and with the functional transformation of the service industries. In the meantime, the application and mastery of digital technologies have become routine, although clearly the young enjoy the advantage of greater competence in this area. In popular culture, new directions in style are on the move (rap, rave, techno). With the recognizable but nonetheless indistinct label "Generation X," these styles are making their way into film, literature, and music, and they are claiming an increasing amount of space in advertising and in the world of political symbolism. In this area, a large amount of cultural capital is accumulating. Consequently, the political upheaval of 1989 (a topic I take up again presently) expresses itself culturally rather than in the narrower arena of politics. This being the case, the focus on political youth movements, most recently on the sixty-eighters, seems anachronistic.

Behind this struggle for recognition, which is typical of multicultural societies, there is a latent conflict of interest between young and old. In affluent industrial societies, sociopolitical patterns of regulation are bound by the classical "pact between the generations," which has become obsolete because of the aforementioned demographic change. To affirm this pact and to set it in concrete would amount to an agreement of title favoring the older and the middle generations at the expense of the rising generation. Demographic relativization, the national debt, and the destruction of the environment all conspire to disadvantage the young, given that they will have to pay the price for the ecological, fiscal, and sociopolitical "sins" of their parents and grandparents, or at least they will have to direct much of their huge potential inheritance toward repair work.

Other fault lines run through the potential generation of eighty-niners. The most important of these since the fall of the wall is the mental divide between East and West. This gap is not decreasing as rapidly as was at first expected but is being perpetuated and increased by the consequences of the reunification of Europe. The evaluation of 1989 and its consequences is thus becoming a controversial issue within the age cohorts. But only at first glance does this look like an obstacle to the emergence of a generation. Experience has shown that generations do not come about on the basis of shared convictions but through a common focus on pivotal events (such as the end of the war, the student revolts) that do not require a normative consensus. The decisive question, then, is whether the date 1989 will remain a focal point—directly or indirectly—for communication among the generations.

Gender-specific perceptions and ways of life must also be considered when the issue of generations is discussed. Until now—as illustrated in the examples of the *Flakhelfer* and to a large extent the sixty-eighters—male perceptions and male constructions of meaning have been the focus of debate; in discussions about generational types, girls and young women have long stood in the shadows. Nowadays, an internal battle for recognition runs through age groups, because male perceptions are no longer accepted unquestioningly as the dominant ones; instead, competing interpretations are available. This difference need not prevent or hinder the emergence of generations. A double perspective can even strengthen the unity of an unfolding generation, given the demands within the women's movement for generational succession, and given the concrete moves to change the guard.

A further source of plurality is a kind of *ethnic layering* as a consequence of several decades of immigration. In the youthful age cohort, members of the second or third generation of immigrants play a greater role in terms of numbers than they did in earlier generations. The familiar, everyday, multicultural ambience of circles of friends, and of leisure groups generally, has increased no less than have ethnocentric modes of perception, both in the majority culture (most obviously and aggressively among right-wing skinheads) and among those minorities (e.g., religious and revivalist fundamentalists) that tend to nurture tensions with other minorities (as is the case with young Kurds and Turks). Despite the distance they keep from one another, these ethnic groups demonstrate so many similarities that they can be brought together in broadly overlapping youth cultures, and they can even be mobilized politically—for example, the *generation beur* in France. Evidently, generations can also arise in a heterogeneous cultural environment, and here too, generation almost seems to compensate for the pluralization of lifestyles.

In short, pluralizing processes that mirror variations in lifestyle occurring within society as a whole must not be seen as insuperable obstacles to the formation of generations. One could go so far as to suggest the converse: the more that classes and social strata disintegrate, the more palpable the fragility of nations as "imagined communities"[2] becomes; and the more that biological differences in age can be minimized by cultural options and conscious choice, the more self-evidently the formation of a generation suggests itself as a way of reducing cultural complexity and making cultural conflicts "meaningful."

This is borne out by the astonishing consistency of youthful peer groups that seek to compensate for the breakdown of the traditional nuclear family, the disappearance of old high school class reunions and of social clubs, and the effects of solitary media consumption. Groups whose members are more or less of the same age can still be considered the chief source of communal experience. And so they remain the decisive medium for the reception and interpretation of relevant historical events and turning points—that is, for the formation of a new generation. The ways in which Generation X has portrayed itself in novels, films, and everyday discussions (not only within the culture industry) can serve as a good example of how the question of the generations is posed anew and how it is shaped by novel structural guidelines. This means that even the construction of a generation is subject to generational change.

The "Eighty-niners": A Political Generation?

"Eighty-niner" was the name given in the media debates in the Federal Republic to those who called the cultural hegemony of the sixty-eighters into question. The label was also attached to those on the political Right, including right-wing radicals, who wanted to revise thoroughly the model of the "old" Federal Republic as conceived by both the *Flakhelfer* and the generation of 1968 (including the historical position adopted by the Federal Republic in relation to National Socialism, i.e., as the successor state to the Third Reich). The pretenders who gathered under the banner of "89" to storm the cultural Bastille tended to be in their mid-thirties and were considering a step up the career ladder or a political paradigm shift—and this did not amount to the emergence of a new political generation. The debate between the generations was thoroughly conventional, and it proceeded on the terms of the standard and familiar culture; or it set out to discredit antipathetic leaders of public opinion who had by now lost faith in their own opinions.

There is a broad acceptance of the overgeneralization that sixteen- to twenty-five-year-olds are "unpolitical." It is true that people of this age group seem to be less interested (certainly less so than people of the same age group in the 1960s and 1970s) in participating in conventional politics (parties, elections) or in unconventional politics (social movements, demonstrations). But it would be wrong to conclude that this is an unpolitical generation of apathetic couch potatoes. The reluctance of this age group to throw itself into party politics, as the *Flakhelfer* generation had done, or to embrace the political culture of the alternative social movements of the 1970s is in fact quite consciously motivated. It is not worthwhile for the members of this age group to involve themselves in conventional politics: they are not numerically strong enough. And the days have passed when it was still possible for youthful avant-garde movements to be taken seriously. The system of historical coordinates has shifted considerably in the years since 1989. Together with the old world order, as everyone knows, the grand narratives of modernity have also had their day: a movement that fancied itself to be at one with historical progress would very smartly be ridiculed for its pathos. Neither does the clearcut Left-Right classification of the nineteenth century look convincing. And youth cultures no longer display their innovative potential in the sense of "creative shocks" but rather as anonymous samplers and collage makers. The nature of creativeness and innovation—which are the hallmarks of any claim to form a generation—has itself undergone a transformation.

It seems plausible, therefore, that any claims made by the new generation will first be articulated in the cultural realm, and from here they may be carried over into the political dimensions of culture. In popular culture, which once played a decisive role in disseminating the ideas of 1968, new trends, new methods of production, and new codes are emerging. They no longer break radically with the past, but they recycle and resample an almost unimaginable range of fragments from earlier movements and trends. This is evident—artistically as well as technically—in the contemporary music scene, which is dominated by rap and techno, and it is combining in interesting ways with developments on the labor market and in career structures: newcomers to the labor market immediately find themselves under great pressure to be flexible, and they try to avoid leading the insecure life of an employee by pursuing novel and precarious modes of economic independence. A third labor market has existed for some time now—a market that produces totally different attitudes on the part of the "employed" than in any previous growth phase in the postwar economies.

If taken in combination, these trends (political de-ideologization, the new vernaculars of popular culture, far-reaching changes in technology and the labor market) can produce a new cultural model. This model would be radically different from that of its precursors in Europe—from both the generation of postwar reconstruction and the generation that embodied the transformation of values. The retrospective expectation that a new "skeptical generation" may be on the horizon is just as misleading as the fixation on the prototypical political generation of 1968. The activities of the generation of 1989 can be described as "subpolitical" in the sense that its members acquiesce neither in the pragmatic and competitive spirit of party politics nor in the subjective, ideological aspects of the alternative movements, but they campaign as directly as possible for political objectives pertaining to concrete changes in their professional and working lives, or they seek to create the symbols of political solidarity in all ideological shadings.

Impulses like these are just as difficult for traditional large organizations such as parties, associations, and unions to articulate as they are for traditional mass movements. At the end of the twentieth century, it seems that we may well have to learn to think in paradoxes: informal organizations and individualized movements will most likely take shape. Examples of this can be found in the leisure and sporting activities of young people. Phenomena such as the worldwide Nintendo club or far-flung streetball tournaments do not fit into the orthodox framework of research into social organization and social movements. This is especially so in the case of rave and love parades, which galvanize hundreds of thousands of people and cannot be understood through the traditional methods of research into youth culture.

Furthermore, these processes of social mobilization have discounted the nation-state, which until recently was the main framework for the formation of generations. The generation of 1968 propagated an abstract and traditional internationalism; its subtext was always inextricable from the national political culture. Today, the younger age groups are driven by a dialectic of tribalization and globalization that is undermining and sometimes invalidating the reference systems of national cultures. Campaigners and activists that enjoy a high degree of popularity and respect among the young, such as Greenpeace or Benetton, have long been operating transnationally. Their logos are understood irrespective of national boundaries, and it is evident by now that they are indebted to the new cultural patterns. The language of political communication has no choice but to adjust to this situation. It is a language that in recent years has become imbued more and more with questions concerning the future—as the established political system's answer to the rhetoric of political transformation and the postulate of generational change.

Finally, three hypothetical conclusions can be drawn:

1. Age is becoming an increasingly important criterion for social stratification and a more significant political attribute. In voting behavior as well as in other areas of political participation, age differences have become more relevant than the more accustomed sociodemographic characteristics. This is to some degree part of a biopolitical turn coming in the wake of other indicators such as gender, place of origin, and race that have entered into the (in these respects, value-free) liberal-universalist discourse. It is possible, however, that this tendency is also indicative of the increasingly brittle foundations of what has been understood as virtually a "contractual" arrangement between the generations upon which all sociopolitical calculations are based. If this contract is no longer adhered to, age differences will become increasingly fraught with conflict, and the political systems of Western democracies have not provided for the formal resolution of conflicts such as this. The Western democracies are being perceived more and more as illegitimate gerontocracies that are no longer up to the task of confronting the problems of the future and seem incapable of solving them. A coalition of the middle and older generations to safeguard their assets would have the effect of marginalizing the younger generation, and the latter's abandonment of the customary political procedures means that, to a certain degree, it also tends to marginalize itself. It is remarkable that under entirely different circumstances—an explosive increase in the younger age cohorts—the same consequences are becoming evident in the underdeveloped South: there too, the under-

thirties are being excluded from labor markets, from social security systems, and from political leadership functions. In some instances, this has already manifested itself in conflicts such as the Algerian "bread rebellion" of 1988 and the subsequent Islamic offensive.

2. In liberal democracies, where the need for self-legitimation is high, generational change is considered to be indispensable for the regeneration of the political system. In this context, 1989 merely supplied the objective occasion for a fresh change of generations. In the East, the protagonists of a peaceful revolution were thrust aside; in the West, the overwhelming majority of the old elites remained where they were. In the process of the founding of the European confederation, this could have problematic consequences. On the political level, the failure to effect a change of generations could occur indirectly and surreptitiously—"through the back door"—as a consequence of significant changes in technological and cultural dynamics necessitating a caesura in the political system.

3. Leaving aside its increasingly shallow representation by the media, Generation X is a fascinating object of study. Until now, it has cleverly avoided any quick and easy identification by deliberately presenting itself as an unknown quantity (X), and it thus appears to be the no-name generation. This combination of superior self-representation and delayed coming-out is an ingenious mode of self-generation that can embrace, repudiate, or accommodate itself to each of the numerous offerings of external agencies such as advertising and the fashion industry. At the same time, the cultural gulf vis-à-vis the older generation grows wider in the course of these communicative strategies and altercations, for let us not forget the real purpose of the formation of generations: to demonstrate that we are not like you, and that you will not keep up with the changes we are making.

NOTES

This chapter was translated by Reinhard Alter.
1. Karl Mannheim, "The Problem of Generations," in Mannheim, *Essays on the Sociology of Knowledge*, 5th ed., London, 1972, 276–320.
2. The term is derived from Benedict Anderson's book *Imagined Communities: Reflections on the Origins and Spread of Nationalism*, London, 1983.

5

The German Sonderweg Reconsidered: Continuities and Discontinuities in Modern German History

REINHARD KÜHNL

1.

There are good reasons to speak of a German *Sonderweg*, that is, a uniquely German road to modernity.[1] First, both world wars essentially were unleashed by Germany. Although the entire epoch was characterized by imperialism, it must be accepted that German imperialism was particularly aggressive. Second, in no other country was fascism able to achieve such a degree of terror and destructive power and at the same time such a level of mass acclamation and fanaticism.

The conditions that made this possible grew out of a lengthy historical process. That is not to say that these conditions would unavoidably have determined the course of history beyond 1918. Such determinism does not exist in history. Every historical situation is open to alternative lines of development. But it does mean that these historical preconditions provided a certain set of underlying circumstances upon which the political forces of 1918 and thereafter had to act. At the same time, these underlying circumstances favored the development of certain political forces and militated against the effectiveness of others.

These circumstances were related to social hierarchies and political structures, as well as to intellectual traditions. At first they shaped Germany's path toward a bourgeois society, but then they shaped the particular character of bourgeois society itself. They can be summarized briefly as follows.

First of all, Germany did not succeed in staging a bourgeois revolution, neither in the wake of the French Revolution nor in 1848–49. In 1871, the political unity of Germany was indeed achieved, not in the form of a bourgeois-parliamentary national state but in the form of the Prussian-German monarchy, brought about by Prussian bayonets and supported by them. In this authoritarian state, which existed into the twentieth century, the ruling elites considered their position of power a natural state of affairs, whether in the context of the state, the barracks, or the factory. In their eyes, the November Revolution and the establishment of a democratic republic were unnatural and could at best be viewed as temporary aberrations. Despite their positive experiences under the democratic republic during the period of stability of 1924–28, they enthusiastically grasped the opportunity after 1929 to restore the "natural order" and to show who was master in the German house.

Second, since Germany's rise to the status of a major industrial power at the end of the nineteenth century, these elites were simultaneously filled with the conviction that, on an international level, a hegemonic position—a claim to the status of world power—was their birthright, and to this end, the necessary military and ideological instruments of power should be acquired. The defeat of 1918 did not shake this view. On the contrary, they concluded that the next war would have to be better prepared, that if need be, they would have to maneuver carefully for a time. (This was labeled a "policy of peace.")

The defense offered by the ruling elites against all bourgeois-revolutionary, liberal, and democratic endeavors led to the formation of a special German mentality that declared democracy and parliamentarianism un-German. The "German essence," increasingly shaped by *völkisch* nationalism, was combined after 1871 with the moral codex of the Prussian military caste. Now for the middle classes as well, the virtues of discipline, obedience, and authority assumed the highest priority, and the military was regarded as the highest form of human existence. This worldview of the middle classes survived the revolution of 1918. Weimar democracy was viewed as the weapon of the victors, forced upon the German people in order to destroy the German soul and break the will to resist. This inherited worldview combined after 1918 with the stab-in-the-back legend[2] and led to a broad acceptance of all political attempts to restore an authoritarian state and rebuild Germany as a military power.

Finally, from this constellation came a situation in which all right-wing forces, even those that resorted to terrorism, could count on sympathy among broad sections of bourgeois society. In particular, they could expect sympathy from army officers, judges and public prosecutors, church leaders, and university professors.

A central feature of the German path toward bourgeois society was that all steps necessary for modernization were taken "from above" by the state, and that all attempts to influence the process "from below"—all attempts by the people themselves to play an active role in politics—were rigorously suppressed. In the longer term, this had grave consequences not only for the political consciousness of the elites but also for that of the masses ("glorification of the state" and "spirit of subservience"). In this way, the German Reich was able to achieve the highest levels of modernity and effectiveness in its economy and military, yet maintain strongly reactionary elements in the political and intellectual arenas. It is this specific combination, this reactionary modernity, that characterizes the German Reich.

2.

For some years after 1923, it seemed that Germany had become a "normal" parliamentary democracy. However, the German peculiarities again assumed enormous significance when the Great Depression began in 1929. On 2 December 1929, the Reich Association of German Industry (*Reichsverband der Deutschen Industrie,* or RDI) published a memorandum titled "Rise or Fall?"[3] in which a decisive change in the entire economic, financial, and social policy in favor of capital formation was demanded. What was specific to the "German path," however, was not this expression of capitalist interests, which occurred in other countries also. In Germany, an immediate consequence of this expression of interests was the demand that democracy, incapable of achieving the required ends, be abolished and replaced by a national dictatorship. As early as in the discussion of that RDI conference, the president of the Association of Saxon Industrialists drew the conclusion that the realization of these goals "requires a firm and durable government which is earnestly committed to radical change," which could hardly be achieved with the existing parliamentary democracy (the "chaos of the party system").

The interest in strengthening the state executive apparatus and forcing back democratic forms of control and influence was the main content of capital's political efforts in the following years. "The changing or bending of the constitution," as Chancellor Brüning put it retrospectively in his memoirs,[4] was the means with which to achieve not just the dismantling of social services but also the creation of another state, a dictatorship.[5]

In the area of foreign policy, this was accompanied by the readoption of expansionary goals that had failed in 1918. In the economic sphere, a unified European economic area was proposed that would, of course, be under German leadership: "A closed economic bloc from Bordeaux to Odessa will give Europe the backbone it needs to assert its global importance," proclaimed Carl Duisberg, president of the RDI in March 1931.[6] This bloc was also to represent a counterweight to the global power of the United States. "Farsighted elements within German industry" tackled in particular the economic penetration of the "countries of the south-east."[7] In October 1932, the Central European Economic Assembly (*Mitteleuropäischer Wirtschaftstag*), in which not only heavy industry but also the new industries (in particular, IG Farben) were represented, worked out a plan in cooperation with the army and the Foreign Ministry for the division of eastern Europe and presented it to the fascist government of Italy.[8] The plan envisaged consigning Serbia, Old Romania, Bulgaria, and Albania to the Italian sphere of interest; in return, a customs union of Germany and Austria would be set up, and Czechoslovakia and Poland would fall into the German sphere of influence. Furthermore a Danube Federation consisting of Croatia, Slovenia, Hungary, and parts of Romania would be formed as a common area of interest.

The task of the German Reich's political and military leadership was to pursue these interests and goals in such a way as to make them attainable first of all domestically, against the opposition of the German population, and secondly externally, against any opposition from neighboring countries, some of which were still distrustful of Germany. In the domestic sphere, it was a matter of keeping under control and diverting the social discontent that would inevitably arise. In other words, the courses of action open to oppositional elements had to be limited and an atmosphere created in which a strong state and a new power strategy within Europe would be possible and perhaps even demanded. An important element in this would be the existence of "a broad consensus on armament" (with the inclusion of the Social Democratic Party [SPD]) and the avoidance in public of "a discussion on strategy and armament and the role of the Army."[9] Generally speaking, this was achieved.

In external relations, it was crucial to achieve freedom of action, especially freedom to rearm, and to remove the remaining limitations on German sovereignty. For this task, General von Schleicher, who at the time was minister for the army and became chancellor in December 1932, coined the slogan that one must always demand equal rights and the disarmament of others so that "we," in case these demands are rejected, will have world opinion for "us."[10] To be flexible in method but firm in commitment—that was the bottom line, because "if one wants to fight for world dominance one has to prepare well in advance and with unwavering single-mindedness," as Minister for the Army Groener noted as early as 1929.[11]

To promote such goals, in the realm of both domestic and foreign policy, required politically effective forces. The ruling elites in the economy, the military, and the upper echelons of the bureaucracy were by no means committed to the forces of the extreme Right. In general, they were not committed to any particular form of political rule or even to any particular party coalition. For them, these were questions not of principle but of pragmatism that had to be dealt with according to concrete circumstances. In this there were also differing opinions and interests.

In principle, all existing political forces had to be taken into strategic consideration, including the forces of the extreme Right. The army viewed the organizations of the extreme Right as valuable in a national sense, simply because they cultivated a martial spirit and, with the support of the army, carried out military training and possessed a clear image of the enemy: the Left. The intentions and goals of Hitler were perfectly in order, claimed Minister of the Army Groener, during a conversation with the Führer in January 1932, but he was "a dreamer and a zealot" (*Schwarmgeist*).[12] Thus arose the concept of "taming." The bourgeois parties and governments noted with satisfaction that the extreme Right branded the Jews, the Left, and the Versailles Treaty as being responsible for Germany's social plight—an ideological position that, from the capitalist viewpoint, was not exactly one of compromise.

Such an ideological position became more urgently necessary as social misery, discontent, and fear grew among the masses, especially as voters·deserted the bourgeois parties in large numbers. Not much more could be gained from financing the traditional parties, which, in the eyes of the masses, had failed, or from employing a policy of "money against mass," as it was put by Brauweiler, managing director of the Organization of German Employer Associations (*Vereinigung Deutscher Arbeitgeberverbände*). Only a new, unused force could be of assistance. The longer the crisis continued, the more urgent it became "to mobilize the masses for their own interests against the interests of industrial workers. This is precisely what Hitler offered."[13] This is how Fritz Fischer summarized the basic situation.

In any case, the result of these efforts was that after all other plans to establish a dictatorship had proved themselves inadequate (presidential dictatorship) or unachievable (military dictatorship), the alliance with the leadership of the Nazi Party was cemented, and Hitler's government formed in January 1933.

3.

"Bonn is not Weimar." This comforting formula of Establishment politics often finds its counter in the no less sweeping fear that "things haven't changed at all." But in fact, history is always a contradictory unity of continuities and discontinuities, and even the discontinuities are causally connected to the past; they contain elements of the past. Thus it is appropriate to look for both the continuities and the discontinuities in a comparison between Weimar and Bonn.

The reason for the possibility of continuities lies first of all in the fact that fundamental interests have been maintained that are, in turn, based on capitalist property relations. Capitalist pressure to reduce the costs of labor and social services as a response to economic crisis and global competition leads to demands that are certainly comparable with those of 1929. This, however, is not peculiar to Germany. The question to be examined here is whether elements of the German "special path" continue to exist or whether this came to a definitive end in 1945. Let us consider briefly the special German conditions outlined earlier.

First, the ruling elites, after the defeat suffered in 1945 and almost fifty years of experience with a parliamentary system and compromises with unions, have without doubt undergone a change of mentality. They too now take the parliamentary system, the existence of unions, and political parties for granted. They have had to adjust to them in the pursuit of their own interests and goals, especially as similar institutions and structures exist in all other countries within the European Community and NATO.

This does not mean that they eschew efforts to increase the power of the executive within this institutional framework or to limit the development of democratic, left-wing forces. The history of constitutional and legal changes—the military laws of 1955, the emergency laws of 1968, the recent discussions about arming the police, fatal shootings, and bugging operations—is a clear indication of a desire to contain left-wing opposition. And even today, the option of resorting to openly authoritarian forms of rule cannot be ruled out entirely. But in contrast to the Weimar Republic, parliamentary democracy today is not constantly being called into question, and the "master of one's own house" mentality of the employers does not exist in the same uninhibited form that it once did.

Second, the defeat of 1945 made a much greater impression than that of 1918 on the consciousness of the masses and also on that of the elites, simply because of the total occupation of Germany. New stab-in-the-back legends, even though the Right did propagate them, could not have a widespread impact under these circumstances. Also, the commitment of the Federal Republic to international treaties and organizations occurred in a much more intensive manner than was the case in the Weimar Republic.

At that time too, the Western powers had undertaken to tie Germany to a series of international obligations. This was attempted through the Versailles Treaty; through military and economic control agencies; through the Locarno Pact (1925), under which Germany recognized its western (but not its eastern) borders; through entry into the League of Nations (1926), which committed Germany to the peaceful resolution of international conflicts; and through the Kellogg Pact (1928), which proscribed war as an instrument of politics (although without introducing binding measures to achieve this). Within a few years (1932–35), this apparently firm web of obligations was torn. The circumstances that allowed the German Reich to achieve this need to be analyzed closely,[14] but it is sufficient here to draw attention to two factors: the army was a national army that was not integrated into an international alliance system, and the power elites in the Western democracies regarded the communist threat as being so grave that they did not recognize the fascist project, that is, the terrorizing destruction of the Left at home and rearmament for the purpose of destroying the Soviet Union abroad. Instead, they treated fascism with obvious goodwill.

The integration of the Federal Republic, however, involved the military from the beginning, and the Western powers maintained their military presence in Germany. As far as the process of integration into western Europe is concerned, both economically and politically, it achieved a quality far superior to all the tentative efforts in Weimar times. It may be that it could reach a point of stagnation for a lengthy period, but it could not be reversed.

Economic competition between the nation-states has not been eliminated as a result of this development, but it has been limited (whereby the fundamentally incompatible economic systems have played a role). And indeed, since the 1970s, the Federal Republic has again emerged as the strongest industrial power in Europe (like the German Reich from the end of the nineteenth century and then again from the end of the 1920s), and more ambitious claims for great power status can again be heard.

Ideologically, such endeavors were articulated from the mid-1980s in particular: first in the campaign for the stengthening of national feeling, for national identity,[15] and then in the historians' dispute (*Historikerstreit*). The key argument in the position of the Right in the historians' dispute was that the crimes of German fascism had to be "normalized" and "historicized," that they could no longer act as constraints on the development of a new German power politics.[16]

Since the absorption of the former GDR into the Federal Republic, the claims to great power status have again become apparent among the ruling elites. To a growing extent, national interests and national sovereignty are again being emphasized, along with the possession of military instruments of power and the ability to deploy them world-wide.[17] In my opinion, however, it is clear that the limitations on such national ambitions are more effective than they once were.

Third, the ideology of the "German essence," which was allegedly incompatible with democracy, has largely lost its potency since 1945. Despite all the attempts of the Right to denounce the opening of the Federal Republic to the West and to depict its bourgeois-democratic values as a "reeducation" that was destroying the German soul, these efforts have had little impact even in bourgeois circles. It is true, how-ever, that since the absorption of the GDR, there has been a renewed growth of activity by right-wing forces in the press and academe, despite their less than convincing contribution to the historians' dis-pute. Now they have staged a direct attack against the Westerniza-tion of Germany, which was (again) presented as a threat to German identity.[18] It is evident that central motifs of the Right from the Weimar period, particularly from the "conservative revolution," are being adopted here.

Without doubt, such arguments, often formulated in connection with the work of Ernst Nolte, are on the point of achieving certain effects. The intellectuals of the New Right work together with the right wing of the conservative parties on journals and in publishing houses, acad-emies, and symposia. The bourgeois newspapers, even those that re-gard themselves as liberal, such as the *Frankfurter Allgemeine Zeitung*, give them free rein, and leading politicians (such as Wolfgang Schäuble) are again propagating the nation as a community of values and of fate. Thus for some years now, authors of the German Right (such as Nietzsche, Spengler, Moeller, and van den Bruck), as well as central concepts of this tradition (*Volk*, nation, national consciousness, na-tional identity—all these in a *völkisch* sense), have indeed been expe-riencing a remarkable renaissance.

At the same time, similar efforts to resuscitate militaristic values have had little noticeable effect. The time of the glorification of the military as an exemplary way of life has definitively passed. Particularly crucial in this respect were the experiences of the fascist war and defeat, not to mention the student movement of 1968 and the peace movement at the beginning of the 1980s, both of which strengthened antimilitarism.

4.

All this has worsened the structural conditions from which extreme right-wing ideologies and parties might have benefited. This is true, first of all, for the attitude of the elites in the media, in the churches, in schools and academe, and in part also in the legal system and the civil service. The changes in the churches and in academe have been particularly striking. They both offered massive support in the battle against democracy and in Germany's shift to the Right at the time of the Weimar Republic. In both areas, however, a strong critical potential of considerable proportions has formed since the 1960s, and it is now offering solid resistance to the extreme Right. Moreover, the universities have gained enormously in significance in the broader political arena, as the proportion of the population receiving a university education has increased from about 3 percent in the 1920s to almost 35 percent today. And it is of some importance that the membership of student societies has fallen from over 50 percent in the Weimar Republic and 30 percent in the 1950s to 3 percent after 1968. Even since the election of the CDU in 1982 and the "national success" of 1989–90, it has not grown appreciably, despite massive support from the highest quarters.[19] The worsening structural conditions for the success of right-wing ideologies and parties have affected not merely sections of the elites but also the great majority of the population, whose basic political beliefs, especially as far as the middle classes are concerned, have undergone fundamental changes since the Weimar Republic and now approximate the norm of the western European democracies.

It must be borne in mind, however, that the ability of the committed antifascist forces to organize themselves effectively is much less developed than it was in the Weimar Republic and has even deteriorated since the 1980s. The candlelight parades after the murders in Mölln[20] clearly demonstrate to what extent an antifascist potential exists on the level of beliefs. But at the same time, they show that the capacity to act is largely confined to occasional expressions of opinion. Unions and churches offer a certain organizational basis, but the mainstream political parties, in stark contrast to the Weimar Republic, hardly represent a support base.

Naturally, the power elites today take all relevant political forces into consideration—including the extreme Right. In France, for example, the Front National, with its antiforeigner invective, has prepared the way for the ruling conservative government to introduce tightened laws concerning foreigners and receive broad support from the population in the process. Did not the events of Rostock demonstrate the interconnectedness of extreme right-wing activities and the plans of the ruling conservatives? Did the extreme Right not create the preconditions under which changes to the asylum law could be pushed through? Were these not the preconditions under which the SPD could be brought to a policy position that, until four years ago, was represented only by the right-wing Republicans—the preconditions, that is, that led the general population to call for radical measures against the "flood of foreigners"? And was this interconnectedness between the extreme Right and the ruling conservatives merely a matter of practical convenience, or were there indications of some form of collusion? Beyond this, an even more fundamental question is why the extreme Right has for decades been given a free hand in the propagation of even the wildest forms of nationalism and racism, even though it is known from experience the murderous consequences that can result. Why are terrorist attacks invariably identified by the relevant authorities as being without political motive, even before any detailed information is available? And if it really is no longer possible to disguise the fact that the extreme Right is responsible for an attack, why is it that the police and legal system respond with such leniency?

All this seems to indicate a continuation of the *Sonderweg*—a peculiarly German path. These elements are especially evident in the understanding of people and nation not as a community of all those who inhabit a particular territory but as a particular ethnic group, that is, not *demos* but *ethnos*. This concept derives from nineteenth-century *völkisch* nationalism, combining romantic and social Darwinist beliefs. It cannot conceal distinctively racist elements (whereby the ethnic community is defined in racial terms); it is deeply rooted in the mass consciousness of the Germans, and it determines the thinking of large sections of the elites. It penetrates as far as the Basic Law, the Nationality Law, and laws relating to foreigners.

In this instance, the *völkisch* nationalism and racism of the extreme Right are carried by a broad body of convictions that in Germany have been regarded as natural for over a hundred years: that a deep and lasting difference exists between "us Germans" and "the others," who consequently are labeled "foreigners" rather than "migrants," as in other Western countries. Just where this position stems from politically becomes clear when one notices that the Right in France and other European countries regards Germany as a model to be imitated.

In the area of foreign policy as well, this *völkisch* nationalism contains dangerous elements that are strongly reminiscent of the revisionist policy of the Weimar Right concerning the eastern borders. They manifest themselves in the federal government's claim to have a say in matters concerning the "Germans" in Poland, the Czech Republic, Russia, and other countries, including territorial claims. For decades, the Federal Republic claimed territorial legal rights from its eastern neighbors, and not until 1990 was it forced by international pressure to recognize its eastern borders. As late as the winter of 1989–90, Chancellor Kohl, conscious of newly achieved national strength, declared in Moscow and Warsaw that the recognition of the eastern borders was not an issue for the Federal Republic. In June 1993, leading Christian Social Union (CSU) politicians demanded the right of domicile for Sudeten Germans, not for the area where they had been living for fifty years, but where they had lived in 1945–46. In this case too, when the extreme Right demands the annexation of all "German" areas from Silesia to Alsace and from South Tirol to "North Schleswig," it bases itself on *völkisch*-German ideas, the same base on which official policy rests.

The consequences that can arise when an ethnic definition of nationality provides the basis for the formation of states are now evident in the conflicts of eastern Europe and in the new Estonian constitution, which excludes more than a third of the population from all political rights—to a certain extent, following the German model. The consequences are particularly drastic in what was once Yugoslavia. Against the wishes of most of its European Community and NATO partners, the Federal Republic advocated this ethnic definition with the utmost energy, pushing through the recognition of Slovenia and Croatia as independent states and, in the process, adding fuel to the fire. Applied across the board, this definition would set all of eastern Europe on fire and could also have considerable explosive consequences in France, Great Britain, and Spain.

5.

On balance, it can be said that in Germany's social conditions and ideological traditions, there are now, as there were earlier, conditions

that bring forth and favor extremist right-wing tendencies. Their prospects improve during economic and political crises, when fears grow
among broad cross sections of the population.

These extreme right-wing ideologies and organizations can gain
influence on the formation of political opinion when they tackle real
problems of concern to the population and when they offer simple
solutions to those seeking ready answers. In doing so, they massively
exploit existing fears, prejudices, and stereotypes. Whether it stems
from latent sympathy for the fundamentals of right-wing politics, or
whether it comes from the fear of losing contact with the mood of
the masses, this pressure from the extreme Right is exerted on the
mainstream parties, which gradually give in to it. In individual cases,
we need to examine whether extreme right-wing activities are not
granted some freedom of maneuver in order to produce effects that
might appear useful for one's own cause. And generally, of course, it
has to be asked in regard to the ideologies of the extreme Right whose
interests they serve. If Jews and foreigners are portrayed as being the
prime sources of social and cultural threats, then that is a convenient
solution for government as well as for business.

These considerations should indicate that the extreme Right is a
politically potent force even before it becomes a mass party or plays
a role in government. It can influence politics even when it is not
well represented in governments or in parliaments. This danger is
especially great in the Federal Republic (but of course not just there),
because one cannot exclude the possibility that mass support could
still grow considerably, and then the right wing of the CDU would
be more voluble in asking whether these parties might not be considered possible coalition partners, naturally only "to avoid the worst."
There is already a range of examples of this tendency, and not just
from the 1960s after the rise of the NPD.

The extreme Right even today has its roots in mainstream German
society, not somewhere in the margins. This is often understood in
such a way as to locate the causes of insecurity and xenophobia in
developments that affect society generally. No doubt that is so, but it
should be added that those who promote extreme right-wing developments, as well as those who profit from them, also have their place
in the mainstream. This danger of the indirect impact of extreme right-
wing activities can therefore be clearly recognized.

In contrast, the danger that the extreme Right will participate directly in government at the state or federal level appears to be slight.
Or perhaps I should say that, until recently, it seemed limited. For
the first time in a European democracy since 1945—namely, in Italy—

a party of the extreme Right was able to participate in government. This could break the taboos that until now have existed in other countries too. It is obvious that such desires to participate in government are felt in the right wing of the moderate Right in the Federal Republic. Militating against this is the fact that Germany continues to be viewed critically by its allies. This exercises a controlling influence that is strengthened by the need for political and economic elites to take other countries into consideration for the sake of the export economy.

The dangers that stem from the continuities of the "special German development" are certainly not to be regarded as dramatic, but they remain great enough to encourage an intensive search for counterstrategies.

NOTES

This chapter was translated by Peter Monteath.

1. On the German *Sonderweg*, see especially G. Lukács, *Die Zerstörung der Vernunft*, Neuwied, 1962; and H. Grebing (ed.), *Der "Deutsche Sonderweg" in Europa 1806–1945. Eine Kritik*, Stuttgart, 1986. For intellectual history, that is, work on the "special mentality of the Germans," see K. D. Bracher, *The German Dictatorship*, Cologne, 1969, chap. 1. As it is not possible in the available space to present in full the evidence and the grounds for the following theses, I refer to those of my works that deal with them in detail: *Die Weimarer Republik. Errichtung, Machtstruktur und Zerstörung einer Demokratie. Ein Lehrstück*, 3d. ed., Heilbronn, 1993; *Faschismustheorien. Ein Leitfaden*, 4th ed., Heilbronn, 1990; *Der Faschismus. Ursachen, Herrschaftsstruktur, Aktualität. Eine Einführung*, 2d ed., Heilbronn, 1988; *Der deutsche Faschismus in Quellen und Dokumenten*, 6th ed., Cologne, 1987; *Formen bürgerlicher Herrschaft. Liberalismus-Faschismus*, 12th ed., Reinbek b. Hamburg, 1986; *Gefahr von rechts? Vergangenheit und Gegenwart der extremen Rechten*, 3d ed., Heilbronn, 1993; *Streit ums Geschichtsbild. Die "Historiker-Debatte." Dokumentation, Darstellung und Kritik*, Cologne, 1987.
2. According to the stab-in-the-back legend, the German army was stabbed in the back by the civilian government, which sued for peace in November 1918, thus depriving German forces of the opportunity to achieve victory on the battlefield. Moreover, Germany then had to suffer the allegedly avoidable ignomiy of the Versailles Treaty, which was imposed by the victors.
3. Extracts in my volume *Der deutsche Faschismus in Quellen und Dokumenten*, 70 ff.
4. Heinrich Brüning, *Memoiren 1918–1934*, Stuttgart 1970, 146.

5. How the path to fascism via the presidential governments of the years before 1933 was completed is presented and analyzed in detail in the two Marburg dissertations: Axel Schildt, *Militärdiktatur mit Massenbasis?* Frankfurt and New York, 1981; and Ulrike Hörster-Philipps, *Konservative Politik in der Endphase der Weimarer Republik*, Cologne, 1982.
6. Extracts in R. Opitz (ed.), *Europastrategien des deutschen Kapitals 1900–1945*, Cologne, 1977, 581 f.
7. Company report by Tilo von Wilmowsky, president of the Central European Economic Assembly, on 22 November 1938, concerning German industry's plans in the years 1929–31 for southeast Europe, published in my volume *Der deutsche Faschismus in Quellen und Dokumenten*, 72 ff.
8. Schildt, *Militärdiktatur mit Massenbasis?* 63.
9. Michael Geyer, *Deutsche Rüstungspolitik 1860–1980*, Frankfurt, 1984, 127.
10. Cited in T. Vogelsang, "Neue Dokumente zur Geschichte der Reichswehr, 1930–1933," *Vierteljahrshefte für Zeitgeschichte* 4 (1954): 397 ff.
11. Cited in Schildt, *Militärdiktatur mit Massenbasis?* 66.
12. Extracts in Kühnl, *Der deutsche Faschismus*, 148 f.
13. F. Fischer, *Bündnis der Eliten*, Düsseldorf, 1979, 71.
14. See W. Deist et al., *Ursachen und Voraussetzungen des Zweiten Weltkrieges*, Frankfurt, 1989; D. Eichholtz and K. Pätzold (eds.), *Der Weg in den Krieg*, Cologne, 1989, in particular the contributions by Eichholz and Hass.
15. See R. Kühnl, *Nation, Nationalismus, Nationale Frage*, Cologne, 1986, chap. 1, "Der neue Nationalismus in der Bundesrepublik"; A. Klönne, *Zurück zur Nation? Kontroversen zur deutschen Frage*, Cologne, 1984.
16. I have discussed this in greater detail in my examination of the *Historikerstreit*, "Streit ums Geschichtsbild"; see also *"Historikerstreit,"* Munich and Zurich, 1987; H.-U. Wehler, *Entsorgung der deutschen Vergangenheit? Ein polemischer Essay zum "Historikerstreit,"* Munich, 1988.
17. Compare, for example, the "guidelines" of the Federal Defence Ministry from November 1992, in which the deployment of the armed forces is to be considered if, among other possibilities, national interests (for example, access to raw materials) are threatened. See also E. Spoo (ed.), *Kohl-Zeit. Ein Kanzler und sein Deutschland*, Cologne, 1991.
18. For example, an entire range of publications and publishers has been influenced by the relevant writings of the group surrounding Berlin historian R. Zitelmann. On the New Right generally, see M. Venner, *Nationale Identität. Die Neue Rechte und die Grauzone zwischen Konservatismus und Rechtsextremismus*, Cologne, 1994. See also M. Feit, *Die "Neue Rechte" in der Bundesrepublik*, Frankfurt and New York, 1987.
19. See L. Elm, D. Heither and D. Schäfer (eds.), *Füxe, Burschen, Alte Herren. Studentische Korporationen vom Wartburgfest bis heute*, Cologne, 1992. The statistics normally refer to the proportion of male students.
20. On 22 November 1992, neo-Nazis firebombed an apartment house in Mölln, near Hamburg, injuring eight Turkish residents and killing one Turkish grandmother and two girls.

The German Sonderweg
After Unification

LUTZ NIETHAMMER

1.

The debate about the German *Sonderweg* is almost as old as German historiography and certainly as old as the creation of a belated (and failed) German nation-state in the center of Europe in 1871. Underlying this debate was the endeavor to define the peculiarity of the German path to modernity in relation to Western traditions—an ideal type of national development ascribed variously to France, England, and above all the United States. The doctrine that prevailed among German historians in the Second and Third Reichs saw the "peculiarity" of the German path positively, whereas the liberal and some of the left-wing émigrés from the Third Reich saw it as the beginning of the Germans' aberrant path into barbarism. This latter view is shared by the most influential members of the generation of West German historians that established itself in the academic world during the period of modernization in the Federal Republic since the 1960s. For these historians, the self-destruction of the German *Sonderweg* as a consequence of the Third Reich was completed when the Federal Republic was integrated into the West. A bipolar world has not only made it possible for the West Germans to turn their gaze from the trail of blood that stains German history; it has virtually guaranteed that they do so.

West Germany is no longer a state, but it does dominate the new German nation-state. Although the nation is now unified as one state, there are two societies, two communities of experience, deeply riven in many directions. This has occurred in a phase during which the nations of western Europe are planning to relinquish essential elements of their nationhood to a regional polity, a network of federated but heterogeneous supranational agencies. Furthermore, the participating nations (including the German nation) all have new problems relating to nationalities, not unlike those in the United States. This is true insofar as the ethnic pedestal upon which a sense of nationhood was built among the majority of the populace has been challenged since the 1960s and increasingly since the 1980s in western European nations as well as in the United States. The source of the challenge is found in transnational migration movements from the poorer regions of Europe and from other parts of the world, and also in a multicultural diffusion of the established national culture. Hatred of foreigners is a politically more hazardous force in Europe than in the United States, because the foreigners here are in the minority.

In more traditional terms, too, the situation of the new Germany has changed completely when seen in relation to the unequal parts into which it was previously divided. Germany has returned to the center of Europe, and there is even the general conviction that it is unchallenged as the strongest economic power on the continent. This perception is widespread, despite the fact that one-quarter of Germany's potential has been devastated by the shock of the free market and must be helped back onto its feet through state aid. In the global arena, Germany finds itself exposed to unaccustomed difficulties, because it is now expected to exercise the sovereignty of a middle power, which in reality it possesses only partially and is unaccustomed to exercising. At the same time, Germany is admonished about its hubris during the Third Reich. In the east, it faces a volatile region that had hitherto been stabilized by Soviet rule but is now being rendered unpredictable by a plethora of simultaneously igniting flash points. Large-scale movements of population are to be expected, and in this process it will not help Europe's new middle to insist on the universal recognition of all borders, even though it has only recently recognized them itself, often at the cost of ongoing pain for some. The new neighbors in the east are torn between their memories of German rule by violence in the Second World War and their hopes for a changed Germany as a guarantor of welfare and order.

The main difference between the new situation and the old, divided Germany is that traditional elements of German history from before the Third Reich or even from before the First World War are becoming evident in these new circumstances, and not only as perceived by the Germans. Perhaps, therefore, the German *Sonderweg* did not come to an end with the fall of the Third Reich after all. Was the dual path taken by Germany in the postwar decades merely a (widely unrecognized) variant of historically determined German peculiarities, and is the *Sonderweg* therefore continuing?

The question is not rhetorical, because it can be answered neither with a clear yes nor with a simple no—irrespective of whether one would prefer a positive or a negative response. It may well be that many West Germans would like to think that only minor adjustments have been required of them since 1989. Some West Germans, however, feel passively normalized, so to speak, as they construct bridges that span the undulating intellectual landscape of the twentieth century, starting again with the Second Reich and talking of regained global power in tones reminiscent of an officers' mess. Both responses are merely extreme variations of the prolonged process of learning to come to terms with a world without superpowers and perceiving it—and thereby oneself—in a differentiated manner. The question of whether the German *Sonderweg* will continue therefore needs to be considered.

2.

The origins of a consciousness of the German *Sonderweg* are found in the rejection of the French Revolution in nineteenth-century Germany. The critical turning point came with the desire to become like the United States.

During the period when it acquired a positive meaning, the German *Sonderweg* was essentially characterized by four elements: the notion of the German mind (*Geist*) as the supreme achievement of the educated middle class, the geopolitics of Germany's central position in Europe, a mixed constitution, and a state-sponsored cooperative economy. The German *Geist* distinguished itself from Western rationalism through its depth and inwardness (the legacy of the Reformation), through its elevation and objectivity (a legacy of German idealism), and through its undogmatic realism (a legacy of German historicism). In contrast to France, Germany's location in the middle of Europe had thwarted the democratic-revolutionary potential of absolutism operating within an existing nation-state. It also prevented a maritime-based global expansion such as England had achieved, releasing Germany from the concert of rival European great powers. Germany's central location, which was also held responsible for the sense of insecurity caused by the pincer movement of aggressive neighbors (the nightmare of coalitions between Western and Eastern powers), dictated the primacy of foreign policy. This, in turn, produced a state intent on guaranteeing external security while suppressing attempts at internal reform. Finally, Germany's central location in the age of imperialist expansion—in contrast to successful rivals from earlier times, who had divided other continents up among themselves—led it to countenance the possibility of establishing hegemony within Europe. In this respect, the colonization of the underdeveloped areas in eastern Europe appeared to be a natural starting point.

The model of the German *Sonderweg* contained a set of arguments that ran counter to the systemic union of rationalism, individualism, and the free market, which was the basis of the Western model. It also prevented the synchronization of the free market with its economic infrastructure. However, the German model held a special appeal when seen from the viewpoint of latecomers to the process of modernization who sought to harness the state's resources and to adopt a realistic perspective on their development that was appropriate for prevailing conditions. Indeed, in the twentieth century, these arguments had a more significant influence on development models adopted in the Second and Third Worlds than did the classic model of Western modernization.

The basic disadvantage of these arguments for a German *Sonderweg* was a tendency toward the formation of authoritarian societies. The German model had at least three problems: insofar as society had entrusted itself to the state, it became dependent on the state's ability to assert itself externally and was affected internally by the state's legitimation crises; in its traditional role, the state tied society firmly to power relationships that were more typical of premodern societies; and in this combination of authoritarian inwardness, objectification of authority, and relativist pragmatism, the German model rendered society helpless against any kind of hegemonic tendencies in a state that had dispensed with all organized political opposition.

3.

The post-1945 critiques of the German *Sonderweg*, made with the Third Reich in mind, were now formulated more concisely, in a sociologically more specific context, and, in view of West Germany's place within the Western world, in a more focused manner. Essentially, the debate concerned the role of segments of society in the modernization process and the attempt to synchronize those elements that were out of step with one another by accelarating progress or abandoning the social structures and conditions that retarded modernization. All in all, these critiques concluded that (objectively) the German *Sonderweg* had brought about its own demise and (subjectively) that it remained the permanent task of the Germans to overcome it.

There was an alternative line of tradition to that of the German *Geist*. Its origins were in the Enlightenment, and it continued in modern times in the work of Karl Marx and Sigmund Freud and then, to an even greater extent, in the early reception of Max Weber. This, at least, was the case until the ambivalence of modernity and its uncertain future became more and more evident. Germany's central location had come to an end with the Second World War, which had resulted in West Germany's integration with the West and had disburdened society of the *Junker* class (a bulwark of archaic statehood, a seedbed for an autonomous military, and a pressure group that advocated state intervention in the interests of the armaments industry and the wealthy landowners).

At the same time, the primacy of foreign policy could also be consigned to the past. It had been superseded by the division of Germany into two states and by the predictable and reliable orientation of the Federal Republic toward the West. It is true that the primacy of foreign policy was retained as a basic point of orientation in the conflict between the superpowers. But insofar as foreign policy had become rigid in both German states and pointed in opposite directions, neither of which offered an alternative to the other, it relieved the respective societies of the need to search openly for international orientation. Moreover, it enabled them to concentrate on adapting to the roles and requirements of the camp in which each of them was located. Integration into western and eastern blocs, and the resulting diminution of political sovereignty, removed the military potential of the two powers from their national framework, although this potential remained significant.

More problematical has been the diagnosis of an inadequately developed bourgeoisie in a society in which the influence of the bourgeoisie has traditionally been disproportionate to its state of maturity. One could divide the German bourgeoisie into the educated but poor on the one hand, and the uneducated but wealthy on the other. This would have the advantage of explaining the political-cultural hegemony of the residual late feudal aristocracy. But how does this help distinguish Germany from England? One could also envisage the bourgeoisie as a power caught in the vise between between late feudalism and the revolutionary workers' movement; the involuntary cooperation between these two could then be branded as "social imperialism." But who could fail to recognize the pivotal role of the bourgeoisie in the founding of the Weimar Republic through its participation in the Corporatist Union of Capital and Labor (*Zentralarbeitsgemeinschaft*) or in the demise of the Republic in 1933? And who would have believed that the possessors of new and old wealth in the postfascist Adenauer era would be seen as the epitome of liberalism? The suggestion of a bourgeois society devoid of a bourgeoisie sounded so much like the old complaint that Weimar was a "republic without republicans" that it became difficult to distinguish clearly the boundaries between subjective attitudes and objective fate.

It was here that the most sensitive criticism entered the debate—sensitive not least because it originated outside of Germany, namely, in one of the "model" countries: Great Britain. This gave the debate a subjective turn: the German Reich had not suffered so much from the lack of a bourgeoisie but rather from a bourgeoisie that was not favorably enough disposed toward democracy. This may have inspired extensive empirical research on the German bourgeoisie in the nineteenth century, but the only result was the idea that in this form the German bourgeoisie did not allow its natural affinity with the liberal norm to develop. Other critics stepped into the breach and broadened the scope of their attack. The development of England was deprived of its normative character and was declared a special case in its own right. The corporative interplay of capital and labor was interpreted as a sign not of the weakness but rather of the strength of the property-owning bourgeoisie, and a closer analysis of the extent of the collusion (including Auschwitz) of the bourgeoisie with the functional elites in the Third Reich reduced the prospect of establishing a bourgeois society that did indeed consist of bourgeois democrats.

In the critical versions of the German *Sonderweg*, its integrative center, the German *Geist*, gave way to a structural and comparative approach that focused on the anonymous process of modernization. In this way, the German *Geist* could be interpreted as an ideological impediment to the optimization of growth—growth that was both sensible and necessary. Ecological, philosophical, and historical arguments that were hostile to growth burgeoned since the 1970s. Socioeconomic growth was viewed as catastrophic when its global environmental and social costs were taken into account. At the same time, key phrases such as "growth limits" and "sustainability" were adopted in arguments for a reduction of economic activity to levels consistent with the supply of renewable resources. Philosophers have criticized in their entirety the grand schemes of human development, from which modernization theory was derived, because these schemes were at odds with actual human experience. They seemed to originate partially in myth, and their narratives appeared as abstract constructions. Moreover, history had shown that the questions overlooked by the project of modernity were questions of central importance, such as nature, gender, and the exclusion of the other. So it became clear that modernity was itself historically specific and not necessarily a universal category.

The longer the Federal Republic lasted and the more clearly it transformed itself, beginning in the 1960s, from a society in a phase of
reconstruction to one in a phase of modernization, the more irrefuta-
ble was the view that the critique of the German *Sonderweg* had transformed itself from a political critique into a historical affirmation of
existing conditions. For liberal minorities in prewar German society,
and for the German émigré community, the comparison with the West
had been fundamental to their criticisms of German society and to
their own conception of a utopia. However, if the diagnosis made by
Ralf Dahrendorf at the end of the Adenauer era is correct, the critique of the *Sonderweg* failed to live up to its high expectations in the
wake of the Third Reich. Dahrendorf argued that the destructive dynamism of National Socialism had also brought about the destruction
of the peculiarities of German society through the agency of the war
and the Allied invasion. This alone would have been enough to di-
minish the relevance of a *Sonderweg* after 1945 and to turn it into an
antiquated critique of the historical epochs that preceded postwar
Germany.

4.

With the collapse of the communist regimes in eastern and central
Europe and with the absorption of the GDR into the Federal Republic, the postwar era in Germany came to an end. Unification in the
center of Europe immediately creates a new perspective on the histories of the two Germanies and the ways in which they constructed
their identities. Naturally, one should not attempt to gloss over the
differences between a pluralistic debate about society and an authoritarian imposition of a social order. The latter produces a quick but
merely provisional result, incapable of confronting new challenges,
whereas the former requires a long period before a prevailing model
establishes itself, which then develops qualities of durability and integration. Nevertheless, one can hardly overlook the fact that already
by the end of the 1940s in the east and at least since the 1970s in the
west, the prevailing expressions of identity linked a fractured national
continuity with a sense of societal purpose appropriate to the ideological camp in which each part of Germany found itself. Thus the
two German societies became dependent on the capacity of the superpowers to provide them with models for development.

In searching for the functional equivalents of national traditions in
postwar Germany, one should look beyond these models. With their
derivative character and their cognitive and material orientation, they

ultimately lack a sense of shared values, because they have no basis in the emotionally self-evident sense of an identity that is acquired through experience. For those born after the Third Reich in particular, the attempt to fill this vacuum made for a confrontation with the Nazi past that became more and more intensive as the decades of division progressed. In the process, the post-1945 generation specifically negated the link with the nation, as well as constructions of national identity. In the final years of division, this ever-increasing negative interrogation of the past became a central element of the search for a new political identity. But before this occurred, even at the beginning of the 1960s, it had become apparent that there was a preparedness to assume actively the responsibility for Germany's Nazi past in the manner of the so-called expression of atonement initiative (*Aktion Sühnezeichen*). This was the case, for example, in certain circles of young academics, who for the most part regarded themselves as being emphatically postnational. Their stance was interpreted as nationalism in a negative and morally loaded form. In the east, where the failure to achieve material gains became increasingly obvious, far greater damage was done to society's perception of itself. Negative nationalism, in the form of the officially sanctioned doctrine of antifascism, had already been imposed on the generation that had grown up in the Third Reich. In its manipulative distortion of history, and in its role as a "converted" generation's substitute for meaning, morality, and identity, the capacity of this antifascism to negate the German national past was noticeably reduced in following generations. For them, the nation, in the shape of an idealized vision of life in the west (made even more enticing by a fascination with the forbidden), had assumed positive power and practical significance.

5.

The end of Germany's political and ideological division can be understood in a variety of ways. This is true, at least, in a period of transition, when it is not yet clear which forces will prevail in the new constellation. Currently, the dominant interpretation is that of annexation. According to this interpretation, the eastern model has rendered itself redundant, and what was once the driving force of the east has been replaced by a vacuum or a chaos in the process of imploding. The constructive forces in the east were merely making up ground on the west, removing the distinction between the two. The world now has a single pole, and history is—as some would have it—at an end, given the absence of viable political alternatives. Others believe that to apply this conclusion concerning modern industrial societies to the world in general would be to misjudge the actual state of power relations around the globe, as well as the nature of the relationship between social order and state power. Far from predicting an end of history, they expect that when history is relieved of the strictures of universal ideological blocs, certain variants of traditional history might be revitalized. This could be in the form of conflicts stemming from a neo-Malthusian paradigm of overpopulation and migration, or the return of the tradition of power politics, in which state-based forces engage one another. Alternatively, these two forms could be combined in a manner that can no longer be fully understood. It will be some time before an analytical approach can establish which prediction is correct. It is hardly likely that the bipolar world order will be replaced by a pax americana, as even the first test of the new world order, the Gulf War, demonstrated. The limitations of the vastly superior firepower of the U.S. forces were revealed when they were matched against a minor power. For Germany, this means that the future of the unified nation cannot simply be extrapolated spatially and numerically from the history of West Germany. In this regard, one has to take seriously the fact that postwar Germany danced to two different tunes and that each of the separate states possessed more power and influence than its size alone would have indicated. One cannot discount the possibility that in the multipolar international context that has now replaced the stabilizing competition of the bipolar world, unified Germany's central location may cause some of the elements of the German *Sonderweg* to reappear.

It is immediately clear what speaks against this. German unification has taken place within the framework of and in conjunction with European unification. For this reason, a *Sonderweg* in a society creating its own separate order is as unlikely as the revival of international power politics. These things are imaginable at best in some dissipated form, because the German economy is even more interested in the continental market than are its other partners. Moreover, sovereignty in the areas of military and foreign policy was reduced from the beginning—and this was demonstratively reaffirmed during the unification process—through a federal power structure and through overarching systems of alliances.

The second factor speaking against the *Sonderweg* is the German *Geist*. In its old form, with its claim to world-historical greatness based on the outstanding creativity of German classicism, romanticism, and historicism, the German *Geist* has ceased to exist. It endures only as a particular mentality, one that revolves around an uncertainty about

Germany's own history and identity. It is a provincial variation on the theme of overlapping cultural currents within the club of the wealthiest industrial and postindustrial societies. If one confines one's attention to this question of mentalities, the "peculiarities" of Germany's position cannot be overlooked. The (West) Germans are the only ones among the former European colonial powers who have engaged with their own imperialist past in a discourse that increasingly has concerned their entire culture. Having met with total defeat, Germany is one of the few nations for which the experience of the greatest and most devastating war in history possesses largely negative connotations. Since then, any attempt to justify war as an instrument of politics has completely lacked any basis of support in German society. Even the deployment of military forces for the purpose of regaining national unity and sovereignty was, in the final analysis, politically inconceivable in both postwar German societies. It is also indicative of the German mentality that only in Germany has the ecological crisis led to a widespread crisis of political orientation, even if there was not a corresponding change in actual behavior or in the structures that gave rise to the problem in the first place. In this respect, the sudden appearance of ecology on the list of priorities of all the parties appears to be a direct response to the rapid and vigorous modernization and economic transformation of both German postwar societies and to the limited capacity of traditional environments and political structures to cope with change. Our politicians never grow tired of preaching to us about the dialectical unity of economic and ecological concerns; they are less inclined, however, to point out that the dynamics of this dialectic have to do with the particular qualities of Germany's delayed and failed imperialism. There is no longer a particular quality of the German *Geist* that one is aware of in the way that one was so strongly aware of it in the nineteenth and early twentieth centuries, but there do seem to be unconscious peculiarities of the German mentality.

6.

To follow the course of the new situation into the future and judge it historically according to the standards of the German *Sonderweg* can be no more than speculation. But the memory of the old blood trail of the *Sonderweg* leading into the Third Reich at least provides a scent.

Let us begin with the lack of a bourgeoisie, at least of a bourgeoisie capable of providing a modern understanding of the project of bourgeois society. The old diagnosis was that the bourgeoisie in Germany was unsuited for this purpose because it was, in the ideal-typical sense, incompatible with itself. The greater part of it had come into existence prematurely in the free cities of the Holy Roman Empire, where it assumed typically bourgeois features. From early on, the bourgeois upbringing was officially chained to the political order. And even among the haute bourgeoisie, the entrepreneurial spirit was not accepted as a natural component of their self-understanding but rather was spread among the nouveaux riches at the margins of aristocratic decadence. It was, however, also characteristic of the political discontinuities in twentieth-century Germany that politics was the classic playground of the upwardly mobile. Under all regimes, one could expect from this segment of society that it would clamber from the bottom to the very top within a single generation. Even in the Federal Republic, the political tip of the bourgeois iceberg remained precarious, culturally insecure, socially corruptible, and lacking in political independence. This was the case despite the fact that immigration patterns of the 1940s and 1950s meant that there was an unprecedented preponderance of the upper classes, stemming from the influx of eastern and central German aristocrats as well as the politically compromised and socially more active section of the bourgeoisie there.

To that we must now add what is left of the bourgeoisie of the GDR, whose members had to reconcile themselves to their fate of possessing only residual historical importance. The leading elements here were the so-called *Blockflöten*,[1] those who played the tunes required of them and who were well skilled in the art of maximizing personal gain through collaboration. The other functional elites in the east consisted essentially of social climbers who were often incompetent in their new roles. And those who survived the changeover period in positions of responsibility had generally already cut themselves loose from any political or moral ties. A significant continuity factor in the GDR's bourgeoisie was a core group comprising socialist intellectuals and cultural functionaries—often from Jewish backgrounds and progressively inclined—who had returned from emigration to take part in the project of a new Germany. They committed themselves to this project and then suffered in the process of putting it into effect. As a result of unification, the driving forces of a bourgeois society in Germany have become not stronger but weaker, because of the lower than average number of middle-class people in the population of the five new states, and also because of a further fragmentation of life experience.

One could say that since bourgeois society was translated back into "civil society" to achieve a postsocialist future for eastern Europe, the idea of the bourgeoisie as the necessary core of a bourgeois society had become outmoded. Moreover, in West Germany, that bourgeois society had long since been supplanted by functional elites and foci for political responsibility drawn from all classes, but predominantly from the middle classes. Even in such a social-liberal reformulation of the project of civil society, the possible population growth from eastern Europe would in fact work against this project, because the limited scope and the fragmented backgrounds of populations such as these are more reminiscent of the weak points in the bourgeoisie in Wilhelmine Germany than of the recent bourgeois forces in Poland or Hungary, for instance, where they are small and highly fragmented.

Finally, there is an alternative, left-wing formulation of the project of civil society located between the state and private enterprise, which takes the form of a long-term program pursued by a minority in east and west. Politically, however, this minority formulated its program in the context of two German states, and in the first years after the fall of the wall, these alternatives proved to be incompatible with unification. In both societies, in view of the prevailing tendency to reduce unification to an economic problem, alternative scenarios became less and less influential. This applies to the opposition groups close to the church and to civil movements in the east more than it does to the Greens in the west, not only because most of them could not meet the sudden challenge of pragmatic politics but also because the *Stasi* issue, to which these sensitive groups in particular had been exposed, led them down a path of self-destruction stemming from their preoccupation with the past. In reality, the *Stasi* was an overbureaucratized, marginal component in the GDR's system of political and social control oriented toward the dissenting margins of society, and the subsequent fixation on it has prevented a public discussion of the central sociopolitical problems of GDR society.

Whichever formulation one chooses for the development of an open and politically responsible society, one has to assume that the relative weight of the forces supporting it in the spheres of economics, politics, culture, and society in the old Federal Republic will, at least initially, be reduced as a consequence of unification. And in this most general formulation, a central element of the *Sonderweg* tradition resurfaces.

7.

Attempts by the state to compensate for social weaknesses were once celebrated as "Prussian socialism." Because of the high level of state intervention and corporative involvement, it was viewed from a Western perspective as one of the most important German characteristics. A second proclivity toward tradition thus becomes unmistakable. Both on the western and on the eastern side, the myth of the market may have played a decisive role at the beginning of the unification process, and it may have set the pace. Each society was entirely ignorant of the everyday realities and modalities of the other, and of all industrial societies, the GDR was certainly the one that was the least informed about itself. Trust in the market was, however, lost as a result of the unification process, so within a year, the liberation of GDR society from state patronage led to the largest push toward state intervention in German history since nationalization in the GDR. The government is still able to disguise the extent of this debacle by claiming that unification has been good for West German industry and trade and that state intervention in the east has taken the form of privatization. Moreover, all taxpayers were promised that they would be required to meet the costs of adjustment for a brief period of equalizing living conditions, which should be completed in three to five years and therefore could be financed to a large extent from credit. But even the debates about the so-called tax lie trivialized the failure of the government to draw attention to the onset of state intervention. This failure was reduced to a merely moralistic reproach for dishonesty during the 1990 electoral campaign, and it has demonstrated a very old pattern in the management of national crises in Germany.

Universal suffrage for men in the Wilhelmine Empire—at that time, almost unique in Europe—was introduced as an antidemocratic measure and was motivated by immediate political concerns. It was designed to provide popular support at a time of vulnerability for the newly formed Reich. It was applied inconsistently because of the special powers accorded to the allied principalities, but overall, the dominance of Prussia meant that its effect was blunted. The epoch-making initiation into a peculiarly German social policy did not stem from Bismarck's concern for the needs of working-class families in times of sickness, old age, or death but rather from the desire to gain workers' support for the state and to play them off against the bourgeoisie. This led to the corporative self-administration of the first general insurance scheme in Europe—not to a nation of state-supported pensioners. The fact that this was foreseen by no one was the result of a pragmatic compromise between the authoritarian state and the bourgeoisie. The Corporatist Union of Capital and Labor (*Zentralgemeinschaft*), which in 1916 first acknowledged the trade unions as fundamental pillars of society (with the assistance, incidentally, of the women's movement), had been negotiated by the *Junker* class within the Prussian military. The latter was interested neither in the owners of enterprises nor in workers, and certainly not in the women's movement. The military was concerned, at a precarious stage of the war, about raising productivity levels on the home front. Similarly, the breakthrough to a system of social housing in the Weimar Republic was not a child of the Republic or of the workers' movement, which was then able to expand the system under the conditions of the Republic; rather, it had been ordered in the final months of the war by the army high command, which was drawn from the social elites who for half a century had prevented the intervention of the state in the urban catastrophe brought on by industrialization. They feared an uprising from the soldiers returning to a housing shortage, and for this reason, they resorted pragmatically to models adopted by their earlier opponents from social-liberal reform alliances.

The individual steps that made up the German *Sonderweg* in constitutional and social policy can be seen throughout the twentieth century, including Adenauer's epoch-making scheme to expand pensions according to growth, which gained him the first absolute majority for a conservative party in German history and secured his policy of Western integration against the policy of reunification preferred by the Social Democrats and the Liberals. The moves toward state intervention and progressive social policies in Germany were never achieved through the united strength of the economically disadvantaged. On the contrary, breakthroughs stemmed from preventive strategies by which conservatives in power used their domestic policy in an attempt to shore up the primacy of foreign policy. In doing so, they displayed a remarkable pragmatism in negotiating social compromises and in cementing their position within the state. For the most part, this pragmatism totally ignored expressions of bourgeois interests, and in a short-term perspective, it did so successfully. It also ran counter to liberal principles and postponed indefinitely the fulfillment of state obligations. In this respect, the political economy of reunification stands more in the tradition of occasional massive intervention by the state (whereby the primacy of foreign policy finds support by populist means) than in the tradition of the state-assisted market economy that had established itself in West Germany during the currency reform and the Grand Coalition.

It is not a matter here of positive or negative evaluations but rather of influential societal models and national lines of tradition. The Western model of the primacy of society and of choice in the free market and in the established political institutions was triumphant in the twentieth century. The neoclassical attempt, in the shape of Reaganomics and Thatcherism, to recover the ground that the free capitalist society had lost to the social state—an attempt toward which even the *Wende* in the old Federal Republic had been oriented, albeit with moderate success—failed as a consequence of stagnating economies, excessive state debts, and systemic unemployment. In this sense, the future of the models remains open, even if they are not considered according to the current criterion of economic and social sustainability on a global scale, whereby the future of uncontrolled markets would appear as brief as their past. The political economy of reunification does not point toward these new horizons but toward an older model in central Europe that was thought to have been superseded.

The speed with which reunification was implemented produced the push toward state intervention, with its far-reaching effects. But this haste was not economically motivated, and it is a fairy tale to suggest that its origins were to be found in the aggressiveness of West German capital. Not only the most powerful representatives of West German business but also the best-informed experts in the analysis of the East German and eastern European society issued early warnings about this rapid tempo in the spring of 1990. They could see that the sudden and unabated storm of the global market was about to pass like a hurricane across the hitherto placid territory of the former COMECON countries, where it would leave a trail of destruction through its depleted capital stocks and its already vulnerable social assets. They were right, but it was typical that they were not heeded and that it was possible *not* to heed them. The primacy of politics was established, and this too was correct: if the annexation of the GDR to the Federal Republic was to come about—and for forty years, this had been one of the highest proclaimed goals of the state—then it would happen only if Moscow were prepared to accept the right of self-determination for its western vassals in exchange for the cash necessary for the rebuilding of Soviet society. And it would come about only as long as the population of the GDR saw annexation to the Federal Republic as the fulfillment of their highest goal of self-determination and did not, as in the fall of 1989, fragment into a collection of individuals seeking to exercise their self-determination by moving to the west or by trying to construct a society that was poor but at least had an alternative cultural identity.

The critical period in which both these conditions existed was extremely short. In retrospect, it is apparent that with the double collapse in 1991 of the Soviet Union and of GDR industry, this period was confined to 1990. By seizing this opportunity, irrespective of well-founded economic and political doubts expressed by his opponents and in the face of the hesitancy displayed by business, Helmut Kohl placed himself firmly in the Bismarckian tradition of mediating between the primacy of a national foreign policy on one hand and domestic support for that policy, secured by state guarantees of satisfying populist expectations, on the other. These guarantees manifest themselves in the currency union and the conversion of GDR industry into a state enterprise, albeit with the intention of privatizing it. But as this is possible only in part—at least if employment levels are used as an indicator—the state will have to accept a long-term role in the administration of unprofitable enterprises and in social assistance to a large section of the East German population, at a time when the aftereffects of East German disillusionment have been shaping political culture generally. The differing capacity for accelerated reform in the two German societies has become evident in the open and often challenging (not to say mutually offensive) way in which both sides have conducted themselves. The contrasts, the dashing of expectations, the rejection of old practices, and the loss of values have been abrupt, and they have created an undercurrent of explosive tension.

Bismarck has been accused of exaggerating for tactical reasons the problems created by the social system in the economic and political spheres. This, it was argued, meant the absence of a "domestic foundation for the Reich" (*innere Reichsgründung*), out of which developed over the long term the problem of a "restless Germany" as an excessively dynamic international troublemaker. Certainly one can argue that the comparable constellation of reunification and its long-term effects cannot have such a great impact on the international order as long as European integration proceeds and Germany continues to play a central role in it. This proviso will probably be satisfied, but it is not guaranteed, and it could be subjected to the creeping erosion of its inner cohesiveness as a result of a wider participation in the integration process after the collapse of the Soviet Empire. Such uncertainty could grow—at which point, the circle would be complete—if the expectation proves illusory that Germany will be the motor not only of the unification process but also of the rebuilding of eastern Europe.

8.

This leads us to our final point: the return of Germany to its central location, or *Mittellage*. Certainly in the context of the globalization of the economy and of politics, the significance of the political geography of European nation-states has diminished relative to the late nine-teenth or early twentieth century. At least two dimensions of this central position appear to have a continuing impact, however: the middle in relation to the unstable situation in the east, and, more particularly, the traditional role of the middle as the first point of call for eastern European migrants.

Despite its closer connection with western and southern Europe, German history is linked in a contradictory and highly charged way with eastern and southern Europe—through migration movements, economic and cultural exchange, ethnic mixes, the formation of mul-tinational empires, repressive demographic policies (especially as far as Germany and Russia are concerned), the persecution and extermi-nation of Jews, and huge wars that were catastrophic for both sides. From a West German viewpoint, both the positive and the negative dimensions of this exchange appeared to have come to an end after the Second World War; seen from the perspective of the GDR, the relationship became closer than ever. After the experience of war and mass destruction, Germany as a whole could only appear as funda-mentally threatening to the Slavic nations. Germany thus provided Soviet hegemony with a protective function also. But in the most important central and eastern European nations, the ambivalence of protection and foreign dominance led repeatedly to movements to-ward self-liberation and systemic reform. It was not until there was some willingness on the part of Germany to recognize the borders that had ensued from the Second World War, and thereafter the barely perceptible pressure from Germany to overcome its national division, that the threat felt by eastern European nations receded, thus achiev-ing a fundamental precondition for the disintegration of the eastern bloc. With the collapse of communism, the liberation of eastern Eu-rope from Soviet tutelage, and finally the disintegration of the Soviet Union, both German perspectives are outdated, but so too is the seeming stability of eastern Europe.

In eastern Europe, which even prior to the Third Reich was re-garded as a quasi-colonial target of German expansion and as the locus for the achievement of hegemony in Europe, there are many who, in the face of prevailing material shortages and recrudescent ethnic conflicts, look to Germany as an economic partner and helper and, increasingly, as a guarantor of national independence but can-not entirely abandon their old fear of the Germans. Whether it wants it or not, Germany will be drawn into a hegemonic role in this politi-cally fragmented and economically devastated region. This will amount to a soft, cooperative variation of the old eastward orientation, whose colonialist and fascist aberrations Germans have renounced. But this new orientation has not been prepared conceptually. Consequently, the recent expectations placed upon the Germans find them totally unprepared and lacking a realistic conception of what their new role should be. Their responses to the east fluctuate between heated emotion and fantasy, assuming forms that range from international aid–supply syndrome to the dread of immigration and could even encompass older notions about how Germany might exercise hegemony in the region. This means that, for the present, domestic affairs are difficult to predict for Germany as a partner in an unpredictable region, albeit a partner that is firmly tied to a series of international obligations. If European integration were extended to a large part of this region in the near future, there is no doubt that, as a result of its inner heterogeneity and the strains placed upon its diversity, it would lose some of its integrative power, and the larger nation-states would be able—or even forced—to assume an independent role. At this point at the very latest, one would have to confront the question of which patterns of behavior toward eastern and southern Europe, other than the traditional ones, can be reconciled with a realistic perception of Germany's central position and its power.

9.

It will not be long before the effects of Germany's central location on the migration problem become evident. Throughout its history, Germany has always been a center of transnational migration movements, just as Germany was itself settled primarily by wandering tribes from the east and was influenced by Mediterranean cultures. In the Middle Ages and in the early modern period, there were repeated thrusts of German migration, especially toward the east, then later toward America, and since then primarily from the east toward Germany. Poles and Jews were the most important ethnic groups in this migration, and any consideration of the origins of today's hostility toward foreigners should not overlook that it was the Jews and the Slavs whom the Nazis categorized at the bottom of the racial hierarchy. In this way, they were stigmatized to the point of exclusion, and ultimately they were enslaved and exterminated even outside the territory of the Reich. During the armaments boom in the Second World War, the Third Reich satisfied its need for labor through the mainly enforced acquisition of foreign workers (*Fremdarbeiter*) from all the occupied territories. Among them, the so-called eastern workers (*Ostarbeiter*) from the Soviet Union and Poland were by far the largest group and, after Jews and Gypsies, the group that was treated most harshly and suffered the largest relative casualty rate.

In the postwar period, both German states received long-term benefits from the integration of German expellees from eastern Europe, and the inner-German east–west migration in the 1940s and 1950s greatly boosted West Germany's supply of skilled and committed workers needed for reconstruction. Into the 1960s, both German states thus built a national bridge over Germany's political caesura of 1945, and from the time of its industrialization, Germany repeatedly fetched migrants in large numbers. As was the case then, the Federal Republic continues to open its arms to the remaining German minorities in eastern Europe. Whether the privileging of these refugees from poverty is attributable to a residue of racial ideology or to the belief that they are easily assimilable is a moot point. With a discrepancy between its economic growth and its natural population growth, it is clear that the Federal Republic requires further immigration if it is to preserve for its population the opportunity for upward social mobility and the affordability of relatively high pensions—two of its most important instruments of political migration, as well as stimulants for economic performance.

When the influx of "German" immigrants ceased after the construction of the Berlin Wall in 1961, the Federal Republic satisfied its immigration requirements by recruiting labor from southern and southeastern Europe. However, it refused to admit to itself that this was in fact immigration by employing the term "guest-worker" (*Gastarbeiter*), which had been adopted from the Third Reich. Immigration did not become a pressing political problem until the Federal Republic could no longer maintain this self-deception of using poverty-induced migration to shore up the supply of labor during economic booms. Since then, however, several new factors have exacerbated the immigration problem. The establishment of a post-Maastricht European market, with its goal of freedom of movement across half the continent, promises to increase considerably the level of legal migration to Germany and therefore places growing demands on infrastructure and social policy. At the same time, however, the structural changes in the economy and social policy, increasingly evident since the 1980s, have produced a lasting legacy of structurally conditioned unemployment. Despite this, an increasing number of intercontinental labor and poverty immigrants—alongside a smaller number of political asylum seekers—used legal and illegal means to push for inclusion in the increasingly multicultural society of the wealthy Federal Republic. In addition, the influx of "German" immigrants from eastern Europe increased in the wake of the Conference on Security and Cooperation in Europe (CSCE) agreement and was supplemented by the arrival of East Germans, at first at a moderate rate, but then at a massively increased rate from the fall of 1989. Thereafter, German migration from east to west— which was supposed to be halted by the currency union but in fact was only interrupted temporarily—posed a threat to East Germany's supply of qualified labor as well as to West Germany's infrastructure. As a result of the collapse of East German industry, unemployment, which reached hitherto unheard of proportions in the Federal Republic, became an urgent issue. At the same time, in eastern Europe, the collapse of the Soviet Union and other communist regimes produced a radical increase in situations of economic and ethnic conflict, which normally lead to migration. As the nearest wealthy society, the Federal Republic has assumed a privileged position for those in search of a better or simply a tolerable life. The conflict between East German unemployment and the pressure of east European immigration will become more acute, because both are long-term factors unlikely to dissipate in the foreseeable future.

Just as the social crisis in eastern Europe and especially in the former Soviet Union is coming to a head, West Germany's infrastructure and sociopolitical capacity are overburdened to an extent unknown since the 1950s, when there were considerable integration problems. Already the social and political climate of the country has been contaminated by the accumulated migration problems and the attempts to deal with them. Despite this, there has been no attempt to achieve social consensus on the question of how Germany can remain an open society after having regained its central location in Europe, and how it can control immigration and cope with the consequences of unification. Instead, there is an accumulation of violence and an ideology of rejection among the less privileged members of West and East German society. The political treatment of the issue is confined to questions of procedure relating to the criteria for immigration (asylum law, ethnic identity) and police problems. There appears to be no trend away from the *Heim ins Reich* tradition, but limitations are being applied to the lessons learned from the experience of German émigrés from the Third Reich, namely, that the persecuted should be granted asylum. The failure to perceive problems, and the translation of this failure into a dubious avoidance of problems and a tendency toward historical relapses, is beginning to bring about the kind of breakdown of political culture that has already transformed the problematics of immigration stemming from eastern Europe's ethnic mix into the violent and highly ideologized purity mania of the *völkisch Sonderweg* in central Europe.

10.

As mentioned earlier, the question of whether the German *Sonderweg* will continue is not a rhetorical one. It has to be considered in its various components, of which only a few obvious ones could be discussed here. Other questions, such as those concerning the choice of a capital city or the constitution, also were debated broadly and with reference to their historical dimensions. However, no consensus has been achieved on these questions. The pace of events meant that there were other questions that never caught the attention of the public or, if they did, were immediately dismissed. One example is the missed opportunity to revise the federal structure, which now adds to the disproportions in the size of the states in the west and creates an eastern German patchwork of supposedly historically formed small states with highly variable life expectancies—which is reminiscent of similar missed opportunities in 1871, 1919, and 1932. Another example is the continuing inability, in the face of the largest and most heavily indebted state enterprise a democratic government has ever had to administer, to create economically and socially sustainable forms of decentralized, cooperative enterprises and to rebuild that part of eastern German industry that cannot survive privatization in a manner that does more than adopt merely provisional measures to keep the unemployed in jobs.

Many factors that might suggest a positive response to the question about the *Sonderweg* can still be attributed to the element of suddenness and surprise with which the new situation in Europe confronted the Germans and informed the process of bringing about economic and political unity. Thus, those factors that suggest a continuation of the *Sonderweg* may be temporary ones, and it is possible that they will change with time and further deliberation. At the same time, one cannot overlook the fact that both parts of Germany have stepped away from the protection afforded by the wall, which had set limits on future possibilities and thus might be seen as a symbol of the camouflaged persistence of the *Sonderweg*. Both parts of Germany find themselves in a more complex environment in which there are no longer any simple models to which they can adapt. Not only did the political and functional elites in Germany enter this situation fully unprepared, but in the wake of unification, their understanding of their role and of their ability to perform has changed in relation to the old Federal Republic. The change has not been radical, but it has been relatively unfavorable to the project of an open and functional society and of a credible democracy. The familiar "nonsynchronous" contradictions and tensions between tradition and modernity (*Die Ungleichzeitigkeit des Gleichzeitigen*) have returned to the German consciousness in a regionally concentrated form, and they are more immediately politically relevant than ever before. The avoidance of public debate on the immigration question has continued into the new era. Economically and culturally, it is a highly volatile problem that, as indicated above, is likely to intensify markedly and become a major issue in German domestic and foreign policy. The transformation from a doubly marginal location to resumption of a central location in Europe thus throws up old problems in new forms and so contains the danger of resorting to old models of problem solving.

In a whole range of fundamental questions, this has already occurred during the process of unification, and these mainly involuntary decisions about future directions have already shown some long-term consequences. This is true, above all, in relation to the primacy of foreign policy in the wake of the unification process; as a consequence, Germany has stumbled into a series of not easily solved problems: an illusory trust in the myth of the market, the massive and apparently only short-term state intervention in the economy for the sake of damage control, and the simultaneously depressive and aggressive shock of disappointment after the debacle of broken populist promises that unleashed the hunt for scapegoats. There have been other decisions that demonstrated the same tendency to resort thoughtlessly to past models, but these decisions are at least open to correction at a later point. Examples are the halfhearted decision on the national capital at a time when federalist structures were not functioning effectively, or the creation of a state enterprise that, after only a fraction of eastern German jobs had been secured through privatization, would inevitably fail as the result of regional economic problems, labor market policies, and huge ecological and financial uncertainties.

But clear divergences from the *Sonderweg* tradition are also discernible. The most important of these is that a German *Sonderweg* is no longer consciously pursued. Thus the evidence suggesting that it is continuing is indicative of the power of objective structures and of unconscious modes of perception. A peculiarly German spirit is hardly recognizable anymore when comparisons are made with the cultures of other affluent nations, even if there are distinctive expressions of a German mentality that point to the unconscious continuance of historical experiences, to which one must now add the widespread repression of experiences and problems encountered in the unification process.

It is therefore not unrealistic for leading politicians—and herein may lie the biggest diversion from the *Sonderweg* tradition—to distrust themselves and their people. During and after unification, they did everything to ensure that Germany did not get itself into the position of having to make sovereign decisions, despite the radically changed circumstances and a clear increase in power. Over and above the measures required to clear the way for unification, they have preferred to bind Germany into the federative structures of international relations, which will not allow immediately effective decisions to be made on fundamental military or economic questions. They have attempted, in the face of some distrust, to continue the process of European integration, and they have applied to their eastern neighbors the policy, as practiced in the West, of recognizing borders and promoting reconciliation. The same process that produced the first (in territorial terms) well-satisfied German nation-state also entwined it in postnational and regional structures that will certainly have limits to their development and do not appear capable of any fundamental revision. In this sense, the basic tenets of a German *Sonderweg* have now been diluted, but one can hardly overlook the fact that, after its state of concealment while Germany was divided, it is once again discernible and has not come to rest.

NOTES

This chapter was translated by Peter Monteath and Reinhard Alter.

1. The term *Blockflöten* was applied ironically to the members of the "block" political parties, that is, those parties that were allocated a set number of seats in the parliament of the GDR and whose members in most cases followed the SED's line unquestioningly. The *Blockflöte* is also that most basic of woodwind instruments, the recorder (Eds.).

7

Cultural Modernity and Political Identity: From the Historians' Dispute to the Literature Dispute

REINHARD ALTER

1.

Differences of opinion about the historical and moral singularity or uniqueness of National Socialism have invariably resulted in rival claims as to the "normalcy" of German history before 1933 and after 1945. The Fischer controversy in the 1960s about the origins of the First World War and the interdependence of foreign and domestic policy in the German Empire of 1871–1918 prompted many of the younger generation of historians since the late 1960s to focus their attention more sharply on the social structures of Wilhelmine Germany. The work of "critical" social historians such as Hans-Ulrich Wehler, Jürgen Kocka, Hans-Jürgen Puhle, and others suggested that the roots of National Socialism could no longer be separated cleanly from socio-economic, political, and cultural contradictions and tensions in the course of rapid industrialization since the 1870s. The "deviant" quality of the Nazi period in relation to an essentially "healthy" German path toward a modern industrial democracy had become less feasible, and one of the foundation myths of the Federal Republic was called into question—that the German Empire had been an admittedly paternalist but nonetheless relatively benign society, well on the way to reconciling the demands of modern industrial capitalism and liberal democracy and therefore undeserving of a significant place in the prehistory of National Socialism. In this context, the bitter historians' dispute of 1986–87, in which the location of the National Socialist regime in the continuity of German history was pivotal, can be seen as a "replay of the Fischer Controversy of the 1960s."[1]

Perhaps the most contentious issue to emerge from the ongoing debates in the 1970s and 1980s about the place of the German Empire in the prehistory of National Socialism concerned the respective claims of dynamic socioeconomic modernization and stable political democracy. Did the military defeat of Germany in 1945 mark once and for all the end of the German *Sonderweg*, or authoritarian divergence from a supposedly "normal" progress toward modernization and democratization in western Europe and the United States? Or should we, as Karl Dietrich Bracher has proposed, speak not of a special German path but rather of a special German historical consciousness (*Sonderbewußtsein*) with a marked proclivity to ideologize historical interpretations?[2] And could the *Sonderweg* be understood simply as a retreat to a premodern consciousness, or was it characterized, as the evidence of the "critical" social historians indicates, by "the discrepancy between the somewhat overstrained wish to be modern and the endeavour to preserve older power structures and steering mechanisms"?[3]

Ambiguities such as this have been conspicuous in recent historical constructions of a German national identity—both before and after the collapse of the German Democratic Republic in 1989. The more elusive a German identity was proving, K. D. Bracher observed just as the historians' dispute was coming to the boil in mid-1986, the more agitated the discussions about it were becoming. In Bracher's view, the arguments about a German identity that had been fashionable in the western part of Germany, the Federal Republic, since the late 1970s were inextricably linked with arguments about a German *Sonderweg*; and underlying the dilemma of German identity were the postulates of unification on the one hand and the stabilization of the Federal Republic on the other.[4] It was on the horns of this dilemma that the literary critics of two of Germany's most influential newspapers impaled themselves in 1990 when they attempted to synchronize a historically retarded German Democratic Republic with a robustly modern Federal Republic.

Initially, the literature dispute surrounding East German writer Christa Wolf focused on her alleged opportunism in waiting until June 1990 to publish a modified version of a story, *Was bleibt*, she had written in 1979. According to Wolf's critics, her purpose in delaying publication of the story, which revealed that she had been subjected to surveillance and chicanery by the state security police (the *Stasi*), was to present herself as the victim of repressive cultural politics, whereas in reality, she had lent respectability to the literary culture of the GDR and helped stabilize and legitimate it politically.

It was no coincidence that considerably more critical heat was directed toward Wolf than toward the commissars of official culture in the GDR. The reasons for her ersatz, even scapegoat, function in the cultural divisions that opened up in the process of political unification soon became evident. Like other East German writers such as Stefan Heym and Volker Braun, who were critical of the regime in the GDR but nevertheless remained convinced socialists, Wolf was one of the most prominent advocates of a democratic "third way" between state socialism and a Western market economy. The dispute about Christa Wolf, as Thomas Anz observed, was a dispute about those intellectuals in the GDR who continued to believe in the possibility of realizing a free, democratic socialism in a fundamentally changed GDR—but a GDR that would maintain its independence of the Federal Republic.[5] A common thread running through the attacks in 1990 on the moralism and utopianism of left-liberal intellectuals such as Günter Grass, Jürgen Habermas, and the late Heinrich Böll was that, like the "third way" of their eastern counterparts Wolf, Heym, and Braun, they were impediments to overcoming the sole remaining national "peculiarity" on Germany's road to normalization—the division of the nation into two rival states.

Closer to home, the dispute also involved those West German writers, such as Grass and Walter Jens, who rallied to Christa Wolf's defense in 1990. They, along with Böll, belonged to a generation—with a largely social democratic orientation—that had never forgotten its utopian hopes for a new political and moral beginning after the defeat of the Third Reich and had never stopped pointing to the contradictions between dynamic economic development and the hierarchical and elitist (rather than participatory) model of democracy that prevailed in the Federal Republic in the 1950s and 1960s.[6] Like social philosopher Habermas, writers such as Grass, Böll, and Jens refused to endorse the generally accepted equation of economic prosperity with a democratic political culture. But critics such as Ulrich Greiner of *Die Zeit* and Frank Schirrmacher of the *Frankfurter Allgemeine Zeitung* were not content with declaring the literary canon of the GDR obsolete, nor with bringing into disrepute the utopia (embraced by numerous nonconformist writers in the GDR) of a "third way" between "real existing" socialism and Western capitalism. At issue, as we shall see, was a refurbished literary canon for both parts of Germany, a brand-new period in German literature, and a fresh relationship between societal modernity and cultural modernism. In the interests of the new accord that Greiner and Schirrmacher envisaged between literary and political history, they reorchestrated the arguments of those protagonists in the historians' dispute—for example, Ernst Nolte, Michael Stürmer, Thomas Nipperdey, and Joachim Fest—who had sought to accommodate the respective claims of dynamic economic modernization and stable political democracy in the Federal Republic. The lines of continuity from the historians' dispute of 1986–87 to the literature dispute of 1990 might help us define some of the irksome questions about the relationship between the cultural and the political dimensions of a contemporary German identity.

2.

The interconnections between an integrative political culture in the Federal Republic and the vexed question of historical continuities from 1933–45 until the 1950s were clearly spelled out by Hermann Lübbe in his essay "Der Nationalsozialismus im deutschen Nachkriegsbewußtsein" (National Socialism in the Postwar German Consciousness), published in the *Frankfurter Allgemeine Zeitung* on 24 January 1983. The low key in which the debates about the Nazi past had been held during the formative years of the Federal Republic, Lübbe argued, had been psychologically and politically necessary and desirable so as to make it possible for the postwar population to endorse the new democratic institutions. The large numbers of fellow travelers and active supporters of the Nazi regime could never have been integrated into the new democracy had not a high degree of forbearance been shown toward them.[7] Lübbe went on to cleave the Federal Republic into a stable and secure first period, founded in the consensus of the 1950s, and a discordant and anxious second period beginning in the late 1960s, when allegations by the student protest generation that West Germany's history was one of conservative "restoration" and "lost opportunities" had set in motion a process of political delegitimation of the early history of the Federal Republic and undermined its stable consensus. The ideological polarization in the Federal Republic since the late 1960s, in Lübbe's view, was due entirely to self-righteous "activists of emancipation" and "analysts of denial" (*Verdrängungsanalytiker*) who arrogated to themselves the right "to admit the majority of the populace as patients into their intellectual guardianship."[8]

Lübbe's treatment of continuities and breaks in recent German history begs a question that became one of the sore points of the historians' dispute during 1986–87: to what extent did National Socialism display lines of continuity not only backward to the German Empire of 1871–1918 but also forward to the Federal Republic? The desirability of "historicizing" National Socialism had been raised (partially provoked by Lübbe's essay) by Martin Broszat, director of the Munich Institute for Contemporary History, in 1983 and again, more programmatically, in 1985. The misunderstandings occasioned by Broszat's proposal in the heated debates during 1986–87 about continuities in German history are symptomatic of wider questions about the relationship between politics and culture that manifested themselves in the attempts by a number of literary critics in 1990 to set in motion a kind of cultural reforestation program for a united Germany.

The empirical evidence of a research project led by Broszat from 1975 to 1983 on resistance to National Socialism in Bavaria challenged the prevailing image of the Nazi regime as a monolithic and static system of totalitarian domination under the sway of a charismatic demagogue. The testimony of "normal" people in everyday life during the National Socialist years indicated that the forms of resistance were manifold and often ambiguous. The distinctions between resistance and accommodation to the regime, or even partial affirmation, were by no means as clear-cut as suggested by the standard images of totalitarian manipulation from above. These images served to divert attention from the considerable popular appeal enjoyed by National Socialist propaganda and, consequently, from the economic and social factors, and the longer-term cultural predispositions, that made this possible. Totalitarian models of National Socialism had furnished the heterogeneous political forces in western Germany after 1945 with an ideal common denominator that allowed them to put a safe distance between contemporary society and National Socialism.[9] Broszat's proposal to analyze the socioeconomic, political, and cultural structures of National Socialism in accordance with the same stringent standards of historical research that apply to other, more "normal" periods in German history was also a plea to reintegrate the Nazi period into the continuity of German history before 1933 and after 1945. The "historicization" of National Socialism, in other words, also indicated the need for a critical social and cultural history extending beyond the so-called zero hour of 1945. The "problematical long-term modernizing tendencies and social pathologies which were operative long before 1933 and whose historical after-effects had been declared taboo within the social and legal constitution of the Federal Republic"[10] raised a question about the survival after 1945 of the allegedly "deviant" social character, cultural inclinations, and moral proclivities fostered in the National Socialist years.

The misunderstandings to which Broszat's notion of historicization gave rise did not spring primarily from ambiguities in his argumentation but rather from the paradoxes of economic, social, political, and cultural modernization processes in Germany. It was precisely his endeavor to point to the hazards of modernity without abandoning the entire project that irked the proponents of a "modern" yet "stable" German identity. The main difficulty of an empirically sound and morally sentient historicization of National Socialism, Broszat stressed, was to comprehend—separately *and* jointly—the seemingly conflicting qualities that made up the social, political, and moral character of National Socialism: efficiency (*Erfolgsfähigkeit*) and criminal energy, popular affirmation of the work ethic and destructiveness, complicity and dictatorship.[11]

It is this convergence of bourgeois "normalcy" and moral "deviancy" in National Socialism that most of the historical profession along the whole ideological continuum in the Federal Republic had excluded from its calculations. The "division of labor" between a moral pedagogy entrusted with the National Socialist period and a nostalgic and empathetic historicism reclaiming the supposedly normal and healthy periods in German history demanded, as Broszat had already indicated in an interim research report on the Bavaria Project in 1981, a balance between an ethics based on personal moral conviction (Max Weber's *Gesinnungsethik*) and a critical-historical reworking of the National Socialist past.[12] Weber's categories of "evaluation" and "understanding," which made up the subtitle (The Historian Caught Between Evaluating and Understanding the Hitler Years) of Broszat's initial reference in 1983 to the desirability of historicizing National Socialism, pointed to the intellectual and moral dilemma presented by the apparently conflicting demands of moral pedagogy and disinterested analysis in the historiography of the Federal Republic. As Broszat emphasized on 6 June 1986 in his lecture "Die Ambivalenz der Forderung nach mehr Geschichtsbewußtsein" (The Ambivalence of the Demand for More Historical Consciousness), historicization intended anything but the normalization of historical consciousness or the dulling of moral sensibility.[13]

On the same day, Ernst Nolte ignited the historians' dispute with his essay "Vergangenheit, die nicht vergehen will" (The Past That Will Not Pass). Nolte proposed a version of historical continuity that was the very antithesis of the critical social and political history of the Federal Republic implied in Broszat's understanding of historicization.

3.

Nolte's orchestration of historical continuities circumvents not only material questions such as those Broszat poses about the reasons for the popular appeal of National Socialism but also methodological scruples about the relationship between disinterested historical analysis and moral evaluation. Although Nolte is adamant that National Socialism must be seen in the context of "qualitative ruptures" in European history, beginning with the industrial revolution, these ruptures do not raise questions in his mind about Germany's progress toward modernity. The prehistory of National Socialism, in Nolte's view, is not to be found in the crises of modern industrial capitalism and liberal humanist culture in Germany in the decades before 1914, nor in the precarious relationship between them. National Socialism was Germany's preventive action against the Bolshevist revolution of 1917, and for Nolte, the crisis of modernity manifests itself primarily in the subjection of the "authentic" individual to the tyranny of collectivism in the totalitarian ideologies of fascism and communism. As the replication of the "Asian deed" of the Gulag Archipelago, the Final Solution is largely segregated from the progress of European civilization.

Nolte's version of continuities and breaks in German and European history has unmistakable consequences for the political and cultural history of the Federal Republic. The further the Federal Republic had moved into the vanguard of humanitarian nations, according to Nolte, the more difficult it was to grasp National Socialism's genocide by modern technological means; and the greater the progress toward the "affluent society," the more alien the extremes of Nazi ideology appeared.[14] The "health" of the Federal Republic's body politic is thus defined primarily by a felicitous relationship between capitalism and democracy that had been corrupted by National Socialism. The political and cultural identity of the Federal Republic, then, derives from a dialectic of cultural delegitimation and sociopolitical normalization that runs directly counter to diagnoses such as those by Broszat of the compatibility of bourgeois normalcy with criminality in 1933–45. "The instrumentalization to which the Third Reich owes a good part of its continuing fascination should be prevented," Nolte had declared in 1980. He continued: "Those who criticize the Third Reich in order to strike at the Federal Republic, or even the capitalist system, must be shown to be the fools that they are. Many critical things can be said about the Federal Republic, for example that the artistic and intellectual life of this successful economy consists chiefly of clownishness of an intricate or provocative kind."[15] Nolte's mockery of the alleged vested interests he sees at work in the struggle of a new generation against "the fathers"—he likens these vested interests to the claim by the victims of National Socialism and their descendants to a permanently privileged status—belies the traumas of the student rebellion in the late 1960s and early 1970s, which partially submerged those of 1933[16] and led Nolte and some of his supporters to conflate the critical social history of the 1970s and 1980s with Marxism and revolution. Nolte's "bugaboo" of the National Socialist past, which he sees suspended over the present "like an executioner's sword,"[17] emerges from the "fascism debates" among the New Left in the Federal Republic and, above all, from the neo-Marxist thesis that liberalism lies at the root of fascism.

In his polemical response to Nolte, "A Kind of Settlement of Damages," published in *Die Zeit* on 11 July 1986, Habermas distinguished between "historicization" in Broszat's sense and efforts such as Nolte's to "normalize" German history by shaking off "the mortgages of a past now happily made morally neutral":

> No one desires to oppose seriously meant attempts to strengthen the historical consciousness of the Federal Republic. There are also good reasons for a historicizing portrayal that seeks to gain distance from a past that will not pass. Martin Broszat has written convincingly on this. Those complex connections between the criminality and the dubious normality of everyday life under Nazism, between destruction and vital productivity, between a devastating systematic perspective and an intimate, local perspective, could certainly stand being objectified and brought up to date. Then this pedantic co-option of a short-circuited, moralized past might give way to a more objectified understanding. The careful differentiation between understanding and condemning a shocking past could also help put an end to our hypnotic paralysis. I do not want to impute negative intentions to anyone. There is a simple criterion that distinguishes the people involved in this dispute. The one side assumes that working on a more objectified understanding releases energy for self-reflective remembering and thus expands the space available for autonomously dealing with ambivalent traditions. The other side would like to place revisionist history in the service of a nationalist renovation of conventional identity.[18]

The halfhearted compromise of German neoconservatives with modernity, as Habermas sees it, affirms economic and technological progress while repudiating cultural modernism. Modernity is thus truncated, restricted to instrumental rationality, technical progress, and capitalist growth and development. The process analyzed by Habermas, whereby conservative critics "project the causes, which they do not bring to light, onto the plane of a subversive culture and its advocates,"[19] was operative in the strategy, used since the student revolts of the late 1960s and early 1970s, of calling upon the authority of Max Weber and his category of "value-free" academic inquiry.[20]

The same strategy manifests itself in the inability or unwillingness of Nolte and most of his supporters in the historians' dispute to acknowledge Habermas's central proposition—namely, that National Socialism was "singular" when measured against Idi Amin's Uganda, Pol Pot's Cambodia, or Stalin's Soviet Union, precisely because it was able to take root within a highly modern industrial society and an enlightened humanist culture. This was one of the crucial questions posed by Broszat's notion of historicization. But in a polemical article in support of Nolte printed in *Die Zeit* on 17 October 1986, Thomas Nipperdey—who was noted as the most intrepid opponent of Hans-Ulrich Wehler's insistence that significant elements of National Socialist ideology had originated in the German Empire[21]—explicitly welcomed Broszat's call for the historicization of National Socialism. Nipperdey's quest for congenial pasts, however, tends to promote a restrictive interpretation of liberal democracy in the present, thus standing Broszat's meaning of historicization squarely on its head. The past, Nipperdey complains, "is demasked, politicized, moralized, and even hypermoralized using the omnipotent principle of emancipation. This is the only way the road can be cleared for the monopoly on the future claimed by the utopias."[22] Utopianism and doctrinaire moralism, then, are tacitly equated. No distinctions are made between the utopian "third way" and critics of the *Sonderweg* who are also critics of the modernization process.[23] Consequently, criticism of the German *Sonderweg* turns into a historical affirmation of the prevailing Western economic model and cements the polarity between "normal" and "deviant" politics,[24] which had driven the ideological mills of both Germanies for the duration of the Cold War. In the *Frankfurter Allgemeine Zeitung* of 25 April 1986, Michael Stürmer, at that time Chancellor Kohl's adviser and speechwriter, maintained that the "normalization" of German society rested on the achievements of the 1950s: the political instability in the wake of the oil crises of 1973 and 1979 should have jogged the collective memory in the Federal Republic of Konrad Adenauer's achievement in rectifying Germany's moral and political divergence from the West. The 1950s provided Stürmer with a positive point of reference for the social and political cohesiveness that upheld the economic and political role of the Federal Republic and its central place in the Atlantic Alliance.[25]

The dichotomy between intellectual revolt on the one hand and social stability and homogeneity on the other assumes an irresponsibly utopian Left as the main hindrance to the progress of modernity in Germany—a Left that has subverted the normal and healthy course of German history since 1945. Thomas Nipperdey's essay "Problems of Modernization in Germany" (1979) anticipated the main lines of argument adopted by the neoconservative protagonists in the historians' dispute. In it, Nipperdey concedes that ambivalent responses to modernity in Germany before 1933 facilitated the rise of National Socialism. The decisive caesura, however, came in 1945. The ambiguities of modernity, Nipperdey contends, were promptly resolved in the western part of Germany. The war, total defeat, and reconstruction completed the modernization process. This was "the main tendency and the main outcome of post-war German history—not an alleged restoration. The new capitalism had overcome the modernization crisis of National Socialism and made Germany more homogeneous and more stable than Britain, France or Italy." Discomfiture with modernity, Nipperdey concedes, took on new forms, for example, "intellectual revolt." The critics' alleged undermining of a stable and well-legitimated West German Republic placed them beyond the pale of the culture they were criticizing. Their criticism, in short, had nothing to do with crises *within* modernity; it was merely a revolt *against* modernity.[26] In this neoconservative variant, the new "intimacy between culture and politics," which Habermas diagnosed sarcastically in 1987,[27] maintains that German history has demonstrated a congenial relationship between the bourgeoisie and cultural modernism—or at least with its "moderate" forms, which Nipperdey offered for popular consumption in 1988 with his book *Wie das Bürgertum die Moderne fand* (How the Middle Classes Found Modernity). In its assumption of a relationship of harmony and balance between socioeconomic modernization and cultural modernism, this study could have served as the primer for Ulrich Greiner's and Frank Schirrmacher's attempts in 1990 to restore to literature its autonomy in the face of the "tyranny" of moral engagement.

In this context, Nipperdey's strategy of marginalization is instructive. The purpose of his programmatic, not to say ideological, essay about the development of a middle-class (*bürgerlich*) culture in Germany from the nineteenth to the early twentieth century is to restore to the *bürgerlich* ideal some of the gloss that had become progressively tarnished (and this information he does not share with his readers) since the third decade of the nineteenth century at the latest in the work of writers such as Heinrich Heine and Georg Büchner.[28] In contrast with recent sociohistorical approaches (Wehler, Kocka, and others) that focused on the German middle classes' anxious, sometimes savage, responses to socioeconomic and cultural modernization processes, Nipperdey posits an essentially congenial relationship between *Bürgertum* and cultural modernism. The social and psychological tensions resulting from an increasingly rationalized workaday world are resolved in a "compensatory alternative world" (*kompensatorische Gegenwelt*), where life's restorative cultural "Sundays" permit a therapeutic identification with the rebellious impetus behind much of modern art. They are a time for reflection upon the "real" world, but they remain separate and distinct from it. "Life" and "art," when all is said and done, enjoy a relationship of continuity and balance—a balance to which, in Nipperdey's view, all notions of social and political engagement are anathema. Artistic "autonomy" in this sense puts comfortably to rest just about all modern aesthetic theory in Germany, which—since Benjamin, Marcuse, and Adorno, at least—does anything but resolve tensions between artistic autonomy and social utility. The autonomous impulse behind cultural modernism with which Nipperdey appears to be at cross-purposes is not an integrative but a *self-critical* one: by continually striving to break away from the institutional framework within which it works, modern art ultimately focuses critical attention on this framework and the society it serves.[29] The autonomy of art does not defuse its critical impetus but seeks to rescue it from the integrative and socially stabilizing function that Nipperdey prescribes for it—seemingly unperturbed by the thought that the genesis of the more thorough-going instances of *bürgerlich* self-criticism might have something to do with the intensification of economic and social antagonisms in the nineteenth century. By the late nineteenth century, there was no such thing as an economically, socially, and culturally homogeneous *Bürgertum*. How the German middle classes "found modernity" has a lot to do with the fact that, toward the end of the nineteenth century in particular, they were faced with the dissolution of their traditional social and cultural identity and status.

The essentially moderating function that Nipperdey envisages for art becomes apparent at the point where he writes in praise of the tolerance that the *Bürgertum* has allegedly displayed toward modernist critiques of its culture. In a telling one-word parenthesis, Nipperdey sets definite—although not clearly defined—limits to this tolerance: "what is really conspicuous is the relatively broad approval on the part of the *Bürger* for—moderate—modernity not least in its non-*bürgerlich* form." Nipperdey's penchant for smoothing over critical junctures in German social, political, and cultural history also becomes apparent in his choice of a nineteenth-century literary canon. For him, Theodor Fontane, Wilhelm Raabe, and Theodor Storm represent the right balance of "conciliatoriness, melancholy and criticism" (*Einverständnis, Trauer, Kritik*). But where are the counterexamples? Are Büchner and Heine not "modern"? How "moderate" or "immoderate" is their cultural criticism, or that of Nietzsche, or expressionism? What about Brecht? And was National Socialism's exclusion of "immoderate" modernisms such as expressionism *bürgerlich* or not? How did the Nazis find modernity? Or is the question inadmissible within the framework of Nipperdey's essay because Fritz Fischer was wrong and none of the roots of National Socialist ideology are to be found in the nineteenth century, more specifically in the Wilhelmine Empire?

Nipperdey's selective stocktaking of the nineteenth-century German political and cultural inheritance, then, furnishes one of those "agreeable versions of history" (*zustimmungsfähige Vergangenheiten*) that struck such a false note with Habermas in 1986. Few would agree more than Habermas with Nipperdey's attempt to reevaluate the *bürgerlich* heritage positively. But which heritage? Habermas's essay "Heinrich Heine und die Rolle des Intellektuellen in Deutschland" (1986) holds up Heine as the model for an artistic autonomy that neither polarizes public engagement and artistic integrity nor confuses *influence* within the public sphere with *assimilation* into the political process.[30] *Bürgerlich* culture in Habermas's (positive) sense can be defined in terms of its will and its capacity to measure itself against its own ideals; it tries to close the gulf between politics and morality. In his understandable desire to guard culture against political hegemony, Nipperdey himself succumbs to the temptation of ideology and sets up an unshakable sociology of culture that allows him, willy-nilly, to dispose of an (undefined) "democratic moralism" among (unspecified) artists and intellectuals. The "value-free" historian saddles himself, after all, with a teleology that he would deplore in his allegedly "moralizing" antagonists.

This is precisely the predicament that Martin Broszat had warned against when he pointed out that the tensions between moral engagement (*Gesinnung*) and "value-free" inquiry cannot be resolved unilaterally, in favor of the former. It is no coincidence that in his summary assessment of the historians' dispute on 21 April 1987, Joachim Fest left out the interventions of social historians such as Jürgen Kocka or Hans and Wolfgang Mommsen (and of Broszat himself), who attempted to see the dispute in the historical context of the Federal Republic. Instead, Fest targeted Habermas's polemical response to Ernst Nolte's

"Vergangenheit, die nicht vergehen will" and, in the process, willfully misinterpreted Broszat's proposal that National Socialism be historicized. "Strictly speaking," Fest asserted, "Nolte did nothing but take up the suggestion by Broszat and others that National Socialism be historicized. It was clear to anyone with any sense for the topic . . . that this transition would be beset with difficulties. But that the most incensed objections would come from those who from the beginning were the spokesmen of historicization—this was no less surprising than the recognition that yesterday's enlighteners are today's intolerant mythologues, people who want to prevent questions from being posed." Fest charges that "Habermas and the partisans of hegemonic discourse are not only pleading for a static image of the Nazi regime but are also at loggerheads with the changing times" and that "this makes them the advocates of a hopeless cause."[31]

The endeavor to portray Habermas and, by association, his supporters among the "critical" social historians as protagonists of an obsolete discourse and advocates of a lost cause was also apparent in Fest's long article in defense of Nolte, which appeared in the *Frankfurter Allgemeine Zeitung* on 29 August 1986. In answer to Habermas's crucial question as to the ability of National Socialism to establish itself in a modern, cultured industrial society, Fest evades the issue by accusing his antagonist of a "master race attitude" that assumes "the Nazi distinction according to which there are higher peoples and more primitive peoples who do not even know about the commandment against killing."[32] Fest further distracts attention from the issue through a highly generalized interpretation of Nolte's objections to the causal relationship between the totalitarian movements of communism and National Socialism: communism goes back to "a set of great humanitarian ideas," whereas National Socialism stems from "inferior thoughts of folkish sectarians."[33] The main issue—the place of National Socialism in the continuity of German and European political, social, and cultural history—is thus consigned to oblivion, as is the question about the relationship between the conservative elites and the Nazi Party, the origins of modern racial anti-Semitism, and social Darwinism before 1914, and the vexed question as to whether the radical "antibourgeois" attitudes of the antidemocratic Right in the Weimar Republic might have arisen from the disappointment of specifically middle-class aspirations and values.[34] The final and decisive step in Fest's bid to synchronize intellectual and cultural attitudes in the Federal Republic with a modern economy and society is to mistake the diagnostician for the disease and, accordingly, to consign Habermas to the domain of premodern, indeed "fossilized," categories, "deeply rooted in the intellectual battles of yesterday and yesteryear," when the boundary separating ideological opponents was seen as one "between conservative and progressive, between German-national and liberal historians."[35]

Fest's strong tendency during the 1980s to homogenize "national" and "liberal" traditions in Germany—a tendency that became even stronger after the fall of the Berlin Wall—is conducive to a doubly apologetic critique of the *Sonderweg* of the kind identified by Detlev Peukert in the latter stages of the historians' dispute. If National Socialism was seen as having retarded the modernization process, Peukert wrote, then the Federal Republic had successfully made up the leeway in the 1950s and erased all traces of the *Sonderweg*. If, however, the Third Reich was seen as having accelerated the process of modernization, then it was possible to divide the legacy of National Socialism into the commendable side of modernity, such as the Volkswagen, the autobahns, and mass entertainment, on the one hand and the criminal aspects on the other. In either event, the consequence is a construction of historical continuity that closes to view the ongoing contradictions within societal modernity and is inclined to invoke a facile equation of modernization with progress and democracy[36] and to discount those democratic traditions in Germany, as Hans-Ulrich Wehler wrote on the first anniversary of the fall of the wall, that warn of the broad spectrum of political and moral alibis legitimated by nationalism in the guise of normality.[37] In the process of unification, those versions of normalization that keep awake the memory of the Holocaust appear to be on the defensive against those that seek to bracket it out of the continuity of German history.[38] Exemplary for the period immediately after unification is Fest's book *Die Zerstörung eines Traums. Das Ende des utopischen Zeitalters* (The Destruction of a Dream. On the End of the Utopian Age), published in 1991. There, Fest constructs a simple dichotomy between pragmatic socioeconomic modernity and irresponsible political utopianism, discounts the economic and social conditions that gave rise to utopian ideas in the first place, and jettisons the self-critical impetus inherent in the tradition of the European Enlightenment, thus conflating the totalitarian potential of "system utopias" with the diagnostic potential of utopian guideposts.[39]

The endeavor to assert the primacy of (modern) pragmatic rationality over all variants of (backward-looking) utopian thought was evident in the attempts by Fest and others in 1986–87 to redefine Broszat's "historicization" so as to deemphasize the aftereffects of 1933–45 on the formative years of the Federal Republic rather than stressing, as Broszat did, the "problematical long-term modernizing tendencies and social pathologies" of modernization in Germany before 1933 and after 1945. Early in 1987, the young literary critic Frank Schirrmacher, Fest's protégé at the *Frankfurter Allgemeine Zeitung*, recognized the crucial importance of Broszat's notion of historicization for the historians' dispute. "A fruitful future discussion," Schirrmacher wrote in the *Frankfurter Allgemeine Zeitung* on 11 February 1987, "would need to show where Martin Broszat's much earlier—and barely criticized—proposal to 'historicize' National Socialism diverges from the conservative positions in the current Historians' Dispute.... For we have accustomed ourselves to ... a certain morally unequivocal form of memory, but it is one without practical consequences. From here it is only a small step to the rhetoric of political innocence on days of national mourning." Broszat, too, had been wary of facile and routine moral condemnations of National Socialism,[40] and a similar skepticism informs Ulrich Greiner's criticisms in 1990 of the moralizing tendencies in both East and West German literature.

The problem is that the skepticism of literary critics such as Greiner and Schirrmacher obscures rather than elucidates the historical categories they adduce in support of their criticisms of Christa Wolf. These criticisms, and the discourse that emerged from them about the failure of the intellectuals in Germany, did indeed become "something like a second historians' debate," as Andreas Huyssen suggested.[41] Both debates are inextricably linked with questions of longer-term continuities and breaks in German history: the Weimar Republic had failed to resolve the contradictions of the German Empire of 1871–1918 between cultural modernity and a backward political system,[42] and the Federal Republic prided itself upon having resolved this contradiction. Even "critical" social historians such as Winkler, Wehler, and Kocka do not begrudge Nolte, Stürmer, Fest, or Nipperdey their pride in the achievement of a viable liberal democracy in the Federal Republic. Moreover, they share this pride with their conservative antagonists, and they even agree with them that the authoritarian political system of the GDR was largely attributable to its retarded economic organization. At first glance, a new consensus appeared to have been achieved in 1990 between the "conservative" and the "critical" camps among western German historians: they agreed emphatically about the need for an end to the German *Sonderweg*.

But this consensus did not and does not extend to the belief on the part of the "critical" historians that a democratic political culture emerged more or less automatically from the economic success story of the Federal Republic. Fest's view of the socioeconomic Westerniza-tion or "normalization" of the eastern part of the reunified Germany, for instance, seeks retroactively to invalidate critical perspectives on the modernization process in Germany, such as those advanced by Kocka, Mommsen, Wehler, and, in particular, Habermas in the historians' dispute. In a mirror image of the conservative *Sonderweg* thesis that had been operative since the German Empire of 1871–1918 (as an ideology of integration that served to reconcile the disparities between socioeconomic modernity and neofeudal political structures, undercut the liberal and emancipatory agenda of the bourgeoisie, homogenize disparate social classes, and marginalize all opposition),[43] the enemy now is not modernity but rather the *fear* of modernity, as exemplified by Wolf and other protagonists of a "third way" in the GDR and by a broadly and loosely defined "Left" in the Federal Republic (Grass, Böll, Jens, Habermas). In the lead-up to unification in 1990, the latter-day "normalizers," it seems, had not shaken off the need for "enemy images" that accompanied the constitutive phase of German nationhood after 1871.

4.

In 1990, Christa Wolf's most outspoken critics, Ulrich Greiner and Frank Schirrmacher, both situated her in the anachronistic tradition of the German *Sonderweg*. The aesthetic variant of the *Sonderweg* in contemporary Germany, according to Greiner, is *Gesinnungsästhetik*— the aesthetics of moral engagement, which subjugates works of art to the dictates of history and ideology. But when Greiner and Schirrmacher conflate aesthetic categories with the historical category of the *Sonderweg*, they permit themselves highly elastic definitions of illiberal cultural traditions in Germany. *Gesinnungsästhetik*, Greiner writes, is a variant of the *Sonderweg*, and it is the common denominator of the "fortunately now defunct literature of East and West Germany."[44] Defined as everything that is alien to a vibrant and modern Western democracy, the *Sonderweg* thus offers itself as a handy line of demarcation to separate German literary history into premodern (servile, deviant) and modern (democratic, normal) strands. It cleanly severs sociopolitical instability from democratic "normality," the premodern and totalitarian past of the GDR from the status quo of the Federal Republic, politically ruinous utopianism from a stable political and cultural identity. The *Sonderweg* is extended lengthwise to include historical epochs and ideological positions as different as the German Empire of 1871–1918 and the German Democratic Republic, Thomas Mann's "power-protected inwardness" (in the sense of economic, social, and cultural security under the protective umbrella of the monarchy) and the search for a "third way" by East German writers. And the *Sonderweg* is stretched sideways to encompass West German authors such as Heinrich Böll, Günter Grass, Walter Jens, Siegfried Lenz, and Peter Weiss—authors, not coincidentally, who never tired of criticizing what they saw as the "restoration" of conservative social attitudes and values in the Federal Republic of the 1950s. Like Jürgen Habermas or Ralph Giordano, they believed that the "second guilt" of the Federal Republic had much to do with the fact that its democratic political constitution antedated a thorough and comprehensive correction of its historical consciousness.[45]

Greiner asserted his own standpoint as "liberal." He did so by distancing himself from the doctrinaire moralism of the West German Left. This "League of the Righteous" (*Bündnis der Aufrechten*), according to Greiner, was still intent on maintaining that old polarization of Left and Right that German unification had finally rendered obsolete. But despite later attempts to distance himself from Schirrmacher's (admittedly more radical) position,[46] Greiner in 1990 shared with Schirrmacher a highly elastic definition of the *Sonderweg* that made for a monolithic image of the Left and obliterated the kind of intellectual distinctions that are basic to the liberal position he claimed to uphold—distinctions such as those between critical self-reflection and doctrinaire ideology or between the diagnostic usefulness of utopian guideposts and the totalitarian seductiveness of "system utopias" (J. Strasser). The more broadly conceived the fear of modern industrial capitalism and political pluralism underlying traditional conservative versions of the *Sonderweg*, the more narrowly defined the socioeconomic "modernity" in the western part of Germany, which was to play host to a rejuvenated cultural modernism. On this point, Greiner's argument differed in degree, but not in substance or in method, from that of Schirrmacher of the *Frankfurter Allgemeine Zeitung*.

Schirrmacher, in effect, endeavored to traduce all critical perspectives on western Germany's road to democratic normality since 1945. In the process, utopianism served as a handy sobriquet for a broadly defined intellectual Left in the Federal Republic. Schirrmacher distinguished even more sharply than Greiner between a robust, self-confident western modernity and a timorous eastern servility. Christa Wolf, he wrote in the *Frankfurter Allgemeine Zeitung* on 2 June 1990, could conceive of the society in which she lived "only as a larger-scale variant of the petit bourgeois, authoritarian family structure."[47] The "authoritarian character" thus serves as the lodestone to construct a line of illiberal continuity from the German Empire and the Third Reich through to the GDR—a line that brackets out all questions about continuities from the Third Reich to the Federal Republic. "It is conspicuous," Schirrmacher observed, "that the authoritarian character structure, which was frequently nothing more than opportunism and which has often been attributed to the intellectuals in the German Empire and in the Third Reich, continued to play a role here [in the GDR]—so much so that the forty years of the GDR perpetuated into the present that unhappy relationship between the intellectuals and political authority which had long since been pronounced dead."[48]

If, as Schirrmacher emphasizes, Christa Wolf (born in 1929) belonged to a generation of East German writers that, under National Socialism, was bereft of legitimate parental authority and found surrogate role models in the communist heroes of resistance and exile—namely, the founding generation of the GDR—then what happened to Wolf's generation in the Federal Republic? Was the authoritarian, petit bourgeois inheritance of the German Empire, the Weimar Republic, and the National Socialist years channeled exclusively into the German Democratic Republic? According to Schirrmacher, this inheritance was predominant in the Federal Republic chiefly among the critics of the dominant culture, who were focused obsessively on the Nazi past: they spent forty years catching up on the resistance to Hitler.[49] But what Schirrmacher makes out to be the prevailing—politically engaged—literary culture of the Federal Republic was by no means as ideologically homogeneous as he asserts.[50] Schirrmacher's essay, which promises in its subtitle to follow in the tradition of Theodor Adorno's or Erich Fromm's analyses of the "authoritarian character" and the "fear of freedom," fails to follow this tradition through to the 1960s and entirely passes over Alexander Mitscherlich's diagnosis of a "fatherless" society in the Federal Republic. In Mitscherlich's view, many West Germans clung to the infantile positions they had embraced during the time of National Socialism, and now they welcomed Adenauer, a latter-day representative of the old empire, as a kind of father figure.[51] This analysis, of course, would need to be buttressed with more solid sociohistorical foundations, but so would Schirrmacher's attempt to ascribe the authoritarian inheritance of Prussianism exclusively to the GDR. He places the "authoritarian personality" entirely in a premodern context and altogether ignores the question of industrial modernization and rationalization, as well as the mechanisms by which the social and economic causes of self-alienation are suppressed.

Schirrmacher's picture of a "premodern" GDR[52] does not take into account the avid endeavors of the GDR leadership to modernize and to surpass the Federal Republic economically. Schirrmacher conceives of the notion of "utopia" as elastically as his mentor Joachim Fest, to whom the critiques of modernity by members of the postwar generation of the Frankfurt School, such as Jürgen Habermas and Karl-Otto Apel, are anathema. "Today there exists in the West as in the East," Apel wrote in 1982, "a status quo thinking of the so-called pragmatists which sets up as an absolute value a notion of Progress that is dictated to us by the so-called 'imperatives' of technical and economic viability. This quasi-automatic and systemic notion of Progress in modern industrial societies has well and truly come to be acknowledged as the realm of pragmatism; and accordingly anyone is considered to be utopian who believes that it is possible to diverge from the generally agreed path and, for instance, to discuss in the public forum potential goals which are not considered to be inexorable in the process of industrialization."[53] From Schirrmacher's perspective, Wolf's criticism of all forms of instrumental rationality, be they capitalist or socialist, amounts to a flight from modernity. The critique of utopianism that is implicit in Schirrmacher's literary criticism not only tends to exclude from consideration the shared historical past of the two Germanies before 1945 but also sees the Federal Republic as having achieved a mature, sensible, efficient, and hardheaded political culture that renders self-criticism superfluous or, at best, confuses self-criticism with self-doubt and potential failure.

On 2 October 1990, the eve of unification, Schirrmacher's essay "Farewell to the Literature of the Federal Republic" alleged that writers such as Grass and Böll had retarded the Federal Republic at an infantile stage of development.[54] The major works dealing with National Socialism had been written from a childhood perspective: the eternal three-year-old Oskar Matzerath in Grass's *The Tin Drum*, for instance, represents a regressive political consciousness. This interpretation transgresses the first principles of textual analysis in that it makes no reference to the consciousness of the time before 1945 in the novel, which encompasses a good two-thirds of it, nor to the perspectives Grass offers on continuities from the Third Reich to the Federal Republic, nor to the "unreliable hero," who is anything but an object of identification for the reader but rather a catalyst for the independent orientation he allegedly impedes. Similar questions could be asked about the highly conscientious and self-reflective narrator in Wolf's *Kindheitsmuster* (Model Childhood). In his polemic against Wolf in the *Frankfurter Allgemeine Zeitung* on 2 June 1990, Schirrmacher bracketed out the self-critical dimensions of this novel and interpreted it simplistically as the author's "sympathetic representation of the petit bourgeois milieu at the time of the Third Reich." [55]

Schirrmacher, it appears, was set on resolving the contradictions of modernization in postwar West German society by constructing a simple dichotomy between a down-to-earth economic modernity and a dangerously infantile political utopianism, between a healthy psychological nonchalance and an abnormal attachment to ideology. The literary-historical dateline he and Greiner drew ruled out once and for all the nonsynchronous contradictions of modern German history highlighted by critical social historians since the early 1970s and again in the historians' dispute of 1986–87. In 1990, as in 1987, the "intimacy" between politics and culture (Habermas) had less to do with aesthetic evaluation than with political stabilization and ideological sanitization—that is, with enlisting German culture in the service of a new politics of integration. Greiner, and, in particular, Schirrmacher sought to do for the literary canon what Lübbe, Fest, Stürmer, and Nipperdey had set out to achieve for the German historical consciousness in the 1980s. In 1990, as in 1986–87, the critics of an alleged "moralization" of history and literature reinforced the ideological Right-Left schemata they claimed to oppose. For all their liberal-democratic self-understanding, their valorization of Western industrial modernity did not enhance but served to retard the self-critical and self-corrective impetus that liberal democracy claims for itself.

NOTES

1. Klaus Naumann, "Zwischen Normalität und Sonderweg," in *Deutsche Volkszeitung/die tat*, 13 February 1987. Cited in Wolfgang Fritz Haug, *Vom hilflosen Antifaschismus zur Gnade der späten Geburt*, Hamburg and Berlin, 1987, 228.
2. Karl Dietrich Bracher's contribution (untitled) to *Deutscher Sonderweg—Mythos oder Realität*, Kolloquien des Instituts für Zeitgeschichte, Munich and Vienna, 1982, 46 f.
3. Rudolf Vierhaus, "Die Ideologie eines deutschen Weges der politischen und sozialen Entwicklung," in Rudolf von Thadden (ed.), *Die Krise des Liberalismus zwischen den Weltkriegen*, Göttingen, 1978, 99.
4. K. D. Bracher, "Das Modewort Identität und die deutsche Frage. Exkurs über jüngere und jüngste Kontroversen," *Frankfurter Allgemeine Zeitung*, 9 August 1986.
5. Thomas Anz (ed.), *"Es geht nicht um Christa Wolf." Der Literaturstreit im vereinten Deutschland*, Munich, 1991, 16.
6. Helmut Dubiel, *Was ist Neokonservatismus?* Frankfurt, 1985, 55 f.
7. Hermann Lübbe, "Der Nationalsozialismus im deutschen Nachkriegsbewußtsein," *Historische Zeitschrift* 236 (1983): 585.

8. Ibid., 597.

9. Martin Broszat, "Eine Insel in der Geschichte? Der Historiker in der Spannung zwischen Verstehen und Bewerten der Hitler-Zeit," in M. Broszat, *Nach Hitler. Der schwierige Umgang mit unserer Geschichte*, Munich, 1988, 213 ff.

10. Martin Broszat, "Plädoyer für eine Historisierung des Nationalsozialismus," in Broszat, *Nach Hitler*, 280.

11. Ibid., 273.

12. Martin Broszat, "Resistenz und Widerstand: Eine Zwischenbilanz des Forschungsprojekts 'Widerstand und Verfolgung in Bayern 1933–1945,'" in Broszat, *Nach Hitler*, 137.

13. Martin Broszat, "Die Ambivalenz der Forderung nach mehr Geschichtsbewußtsein," in Broszat, *Nach Hitler*, 284.

14. Ernst Nolte, "Vergangenheit, die nicht vergehen will," in Reinhard Piper (ed.), *"Historikerstreit'" Die Dokumentation der Kontroverse um die Einzigartigkeit der nationalsozialistischen Judenvernichtung*, Munich and Zurich, 1987, 39. This appears in English in *Forever in the Shadow of Hitler? Original Documents of the "Historikerstreit," the Controversy Concerning the Singularity of the Holocaust*, trans. James Knowlton and Truett Cates, Atlantic Highlands, New Jersey, 1993, 18.

15. Ernst Nolte, "Zwischen Geschichtslegende und Revisionismus? Das Dritte Reich im Blickwinkel des Jahres 1980," in Piper (ed.), *Historikerstreit*, 13. Quoted in English in *Forever in the Shadow of Hitler?* 14.

16. Hans-Jürgen Puhle, "Die neue Ruhelosigkeit: Michael Stürmers nationalpolitischer Revisionismus," *Geschichte und Gesellschaft* 13 (1987): 387. An informative discussion of the historians' dispute in relation to the generational tensions of the late 1960s and early 1970s can be found in Geoff Eley, "Nazism, Politics and the Image of the Past: Thoughts on the West German *Historikerstreit* 1986–1987," *Past and Present* 121 (1988): especially 184 ff.

17. Ernst Nolte, "Vergangenheit, die nicht vergehen will," in Piper (ed.), *Historikerstreit*, 39, in English in *Forever in the Shadow of Hitler?* 18.

18. Jürgen Habermas, "A Kind of Settlement of Damages: The Apologetic Tendencies in German History Writing," in *Forever in the Shadow of Hitler?* 41.

19. J. Habermas, "Modernity versus Postmodernity," *New German Critique* 22 (Winter 1981): 8.

20. See Helmut Dubiel, *Was ist Neokonservatismus?* Frankfurt, 1985, 21.

21. Hans-Ulrich Wehler, *Das Deutsche Kaiserreich 1871–1918*, Göttingen, 1973 (English translation [by Kim Traynor], *The German Empire 1871–1918*, Leamington Spa and Dover, NH, 1985); Thomas Nipperdey, "Wehlers 'Kaiserreich.' Eine kritische Auseinandersetzung," *Geschichte und Gesellschaft* 1 (1975): 539–60; Hans-Ulrich Wehler, "Kritik und kritische Antikritik," *Historische Zeitschrift* 225 (1977): 347–84; *Modernisierungstheorie und Geschichte*, Göttingen, 1975; "'Deutscher Sonderweg' oder allgemeine Probleme des westlichen Kapitalismus?" *Merkur* 5 (1981): 478–87; "Zur Funktion und Struktur der nationalen Kampfverbände im Kaiserreich," in Werner Conze, Gottfried Schramm and Klaus Zernack (eds.), *Modernisierung und nationale Gesellschaft im ausgehenden 18. und im 19. Jahrhundert*, Berlin, 1979, 113–24; "Deutsches Bildungsbürgertum in vergleichender Perspektive—Elemente

eines 'Sonderweges'?" in Wehler, *Aus der Geschichte lernen? Essays*, Munich, 1988, 218–41; *Entsorgung der deutschen Vergangenheit? Ein polemischer Essay zum "Historikerstreit,"* Munich, 1988.

22. Thomas Nipperdey, "Under the Domination of Suspicion: Scholarly Statements Should Not Be Judged by Their Political Function," in *Forever in the Shadow of Hitler?* 144 f.

23. Cf. Bernd Faulenbach, "Das Besondere ist das Normale? Von der Idee eines besonderen deutschen Weges zur These deutscher Normalität," in Wieland Eschenhagen (ed.), *Die neue deutsche Ideologie. Einsprüche gegen die Entsorgung der deutschen Vergangenheit*, Darmstadt, 1988, 134.

24. Cf. Ulrich Beck, *Die Erfindung des Politischen. Zu einer Theorie reflexiver Modernisierung*, Frankfurt, 1993, 205.

25. M. Stürmer, "History in a Land without History," in *Forever in the Shadow of Hitler?* 16 f.

26. Thomas Nipperdey, "Probleme der Modernisierung in Deutschland," in Nipperdey, *Nachdenken über deutsche Geschichte. Essays*, Munich, 1986, 44–59.

27. Jürgen Habermas, "Die neue Intimität zwischen Kultur und Politik," in Habermas, *Die nachholende Revolution*, Frankfurt, 1990, 9–18.

28. T. Nipperdey, *Wie das Bürgertum die Moderne fand*, Berlin, 1988. Cf. my review in *Australian Journal of Politics and History* 37 (1991): 368 f. An integrative and "taming" role for culture not unlike that posited by Nipperdey also underlies Michael Stürmer's book *Scherben des Glücks. Klassizismus und Revolution* [Fragments of Happiness. Late Classicism and Revolution], Berlin, 1987, and Hermann Lübbe's *Politischer Moralismus. Der Triumph der Gesinnung über die Urteilskraft* [Political Moralism. The Triumph of Good Intentions Over the Power of Judgment], Berlin, 1987.

29. Peter Bürger, *Theorie der Avantgarde*, Frankfurt, 1974.

30. Jürgen Habermas, "Heinrich Heine und die Rolle des Intellektuellen in Deutschland," in Habermas, *Eine Art Schadensabwicklung*, Frankfurt a.M., 1987, 25–54.

31. Joachim Fest, "Postscript, April 21, 1987," in *Forever in the Shadow of Hitler?* 265.

32. Joachim Fest, "Encumbered Remembrance: The Controversy About the Incomparability of National-Socialist Mass Crimes," in *Forever in the Shadow of Hitler?* 66.

33. Ibid., 67.

34. See Wehler, *Entsorgung der deutschen Vergangenheit?*; Hans Mommsen, "Die Auflösung des Bürgertums seit dem späten 19. Jahrhundert," in J. Kocka (ed.), *Bürger und Bürgerlichkeit im 19. Jahrhundert*, Göttingen, 1987, 291.

35. Fest, "Encumbered Remembrance," 70.

36. Detlev K. Peukert, "Alltag und Barbarei. Zur Normalität des Dritten Reiches," in Dan Diner (ed.), *Ist der Nationalsozialismus Geschichte? Zu Historisierung und Historikerstreit*, Frankfurt, 1987, 53.

37. Hans-Ulrich Wehler, "Wider die falschen Apostel. Der Verfassungs- und Sozialstaat schafft Loyalität und Staatsbürgerstolz," *Die Zeit*, 9 November 1990.

38. Ian Kershaw, *The Nazi Dictatorship. Problems and Perspectives of Interpretation*, 3d ed., London, New York, Melbourne, and Auckland, 1993, 198–202.

39. Johanno Strasser, "Utopie und Freiheit," in Richard Saage (ed.), *Hat die politische Utopie eine Zukunft?* Darmstadt, 1992, 168 f.
40. Broszat, "Die Ambivalenz der Forderung nach mehr Geschichtsbewußtsein," 295.
41. Andreas Huyssen, "After the Wall: The Failure of German Intellectuals," *New German Critique* 52 (1991): 125. See also Stephen Brockmann: "The Politics of German Literature," *Monatshefte* 84 (1992): 46–58.
42. Heinrich August Winkler, "Mit Skepsis zur Einigung," *Die Zeit*, 28 September 1990.
43. See Habermas, "A Kind of Settlement of Damages," in *Forever in the Shadow of Hitler?* 42. Habermas is basing his argument on Wehler's essay "Wie bürgerlich war das Deutsche Kaiserreich?" which has been reprinted in Kocka (ed.), *Bürger und Bürgerlichkeit im 19. Jahrhundert*, 243–80.
44. Ulrich Greiner, "Die deutsche Gesinnungsästhetik. Noch einmal: Christa Wolf und der deutsche Literaturstreit. Eine Zwischenbilanz," in Anz, *"Es geht nicht um Christa Wolf,"* 213.
45. Ralph Giordano, *Die zweite Schuld oder Von der Last ein Deutscher zu sein*, Hamburg, 1987, 94.
46. Greiner's open letter to Günter Grass in *Die Zeit*, 25 February 1994.
47. Frank Schirrmacher, "'Dem Druck des härteren, strengeren Lebens standhalten.' Auch eine Studie über den autoritären Charakter: Christa Wolfs Aufsätze, Reden, und ihre jüngste Erzählung 'Was bleibt,'" in Anz, *"Es geht nicht um Christa Wolf,"* 77–89.
48. Ibid., 83.
49. Ibid.
50. Jochen Vogt, "Have the Intellectuals Failed? On the Sociopolitical Claims and the Influence of Literary Intellectuals in West Germany," *New German Critique* 58 (1993): 15 ff. Reinhard Baumgart sharply criticizes Schirrmacher for identifying the entire literature of the Federal Republic with the "Gruppe 47." R. Baumgart, "Der neudeutsche Literaturstreit. Anlaß-Verlauf-Folgen," *Text + Kritik* 113 (1992): 74.
51. Alexander Mitscherlich, *Massenpsychologie ohne Ressentiment*, Frankfurt, 1972, 124. See also Mitscherlich, *Auf dem Weg zur vaterlosen Gesellschaft*, Munich, 1963.
52. On the myth of a "premodern" GDR, see Sigrid Meuschel, "Überlegungen zu einer Herrschafts- und Gesellschaftsgeschichte der DDR," *Geschichte und Gesellschaft* 19 (1993): 5–14.
53. Karl-Otto Apel, "Ist die Ethik der idealen Kommunikationsgemeinschaft eine Utopie? Zum Verhältnis von Ethik, Utopie und Utopiekritik," in Wilhelm Voßkamp (ed.), *Utopieforschung*, vol. 1, Frankfurt, 1982, 334.
54. F. Schirrmacher, "Abschied von der Literatur der Bundesrepublik. Neue Pässe, neue Identitäten, neue Lebensläufe. Über die Kündigung einiger Mythen des westdeutschen Bewußtseins," *Frankfurter Allgemeine Zeitung*, 2 October 1990.
55. Schirrmacher, "'Dem Druck des härteren, strengeren Lebens standhalten,'" in Anz, *"Es geht nicht um Christa Wolf,"* 83.

8

Reckoning with the Past: Heroes, Victims, and Villains in the History of the German Democratic Republic

MARY FULBROOK

In the GDR, the following quip used to circulate among historians. Question: What is the hardest thing to predict under communism? Answer: The past. History is no longer subject to the blatant political instrumentalization characteristic of contemporary history in the GDR, but in more subtle, less explicit ways, interpretations of East German history remain highly politicized. Debates over interpretations of the recent past come into play in contemporary political battles; although historical interpretation is constrained by the empirical evidence, it is by no means completely determined by it.

Given the radical and rapid restructuring in eastern Germany after political unification with the west, interpretations of GDR history have not remained "purely academic." Explanations of power have become attributions of blame for sustaining a dictatorship, and interpretations have had major practical implications at a number of levels. At the most mundane but immediately important level, decisions on hiring and firing of individuals, and on support or closure of institutes, depend to a large extent on interpretations of complicity and collusion in the former GDR. At a political and juridical level, decisions have to be made about who should be made to account for their former actions, and what the consequences should be. Both the legal trials of prominent politicians such as Honecker and Krenz, *Stasi* chief Mielke, and others and the massive public controversies over the roles of intellectual and cultural luminaries such as Manfred Stolpe and Christa

Wolf illustrate the political relevance of all historical interpretation.

At a more ethereal level, the new Germany is seeking to perform a remarkable feat: to forge a common identity that can transcend the mutual hostilities of the Cold War era. In the united Germany of the 1990s, seeking once again to overcome a difficult, dictatorial past (shades of 1945 hover on the horizon of all debates), history plays a key role in attempts to construct a new national identity in a not completely unified nation. The discovery that *Ossis* and *Wessis* were, in fact, remarkably different from each other—that the societies of the two Germanies had diverged considerably over forty years of political separation—has led to a new concern with redefining the German nation, even among those left-liberal historians who used to proclaim the virtues of a postnational "constitutional patriotism."

In other words, there are attempts both to integrate a newly discovered history of the GDR into a now double history of the new Germany and to legitimate the ways in which East Germans in a variety of former positions have been dealt with after the *Wende*. Even among professional historians who have no practical axes to grind, political preconceptions have tended to color accounts. In many quarters, the old Weberian tenet of "value freedom," or adherence to professional objectivity in historical science, has been flung to the winds, as history is perceived as a means of "reckoning with the past."

The problem of history in united Germany is certainly not one of lack of sufficient empirical sources. The material basis for reinterpreting East German history is excellent. In a state without an official public sphere for the formation and consultation of popular opinion, the authorities developed remarkably extensive networks for tapping into what was really going on in the minds of the people. Records were collated and centralized in the GDR with extraordinary efficiency and thoroughness. That dedicated state information service, the state security police (more popularly known as the *Stasi*), collected kilometers of files on individuals and groups, now accessible through the Federal Office for the Documents of the State Security Police (the *Gauck-Behörde*). Substantial, detailed, and highly informative records were also kept by the various organs of the ruling communist party (the SED) and the affiliated bloc parties; by the official trade union organization (the Free German Federation of Trade Unions [FDGB]) and other mass organizations such as the youth organization Free German Youth (FDJ) and the League of Culture (*Kulturbund*); by sociological institutes such as the Leipzig Institute for Youth Research; and of course by the various state ministries and organizations. The records of the party and mass organizations are, along with the state archives, now open and available for historians to peruse, under the auspices of the federal archives (*Bundesarchiv*); there is no need to wait for decades of dust to accumulate before speculations and hypotheses can be checked against the evidence.

What is interesting about the development of approaches to GDR history, however, in the years since unification is that—despite the historians' paradise of virtually unlimited access to unbelievably extensive archival material—there is still a state of inchoateness about the more general interpretive framework to be applied. It is not so much that explicit political interests are biasing theoretical frameworks of analysis; rather, it is that implicit, often totally unexamined assumptions about the character of the East German dictatorship are tending to structure accounts of specific aspects, or to provide the general framework into which new materials are inserted, and that moral criteria of evaluation are being applied, often in ways that are hardly noticed.

In a sense, this is hardly surprising: for both practical and sound philosophical reasons, one could hardly expect a new form of "archive positivism" to compile a new, definitive *Gesamtinterpretation* of the East German dictatorship within a few years of its collapse, even if painstaking and wide-ranging empirical work could be expected to provide a firmer basis for valid generalizations in a few decades' time. Even when the empirical evidence on a specific question is remarkably clear, as in the case of establishing Manfred Stolpe's contacts with the *Stasi*, the issue of evaluating motives, intentions, and actual consequences remains highly contentious. New findings are always inserted into some form of metatheoretical framework or paradigm. This is especially the case when historical interpretation and moral-political evaluations are so closely linked.

The implicit historical picture that has been widely presented, from a variety of conflicting perspectives since the fall of the wall, has thus far done a remarkably good job of perpetuating the black and white imagery of the Cold War era and the associated mythology of German distinctiveness that has been widely prevalent in popular perceptions of Germans for generations. If anything, the new material has, in conjunction with the new political climate, sharpened this imagery. With the collapse of communism, concepts such as totalitarianism—which was out of favor for some time in the West—have come back into fashion as a means of denouncing a repressive dictatorship. What is perhaps more insidious is the increasing pervasiveness of the view that history should *not* be "value-free"—even in Max Weber's rather complex and highly qualified sense—but should have as part of its task a moral reckoning with the past and a celebration of a particular political standpoint.

The basic paradigm, or set of unexamined assumptions, into which many recent accounts of GDR history have been inserted presupposes what I call the "Checkpoint Charlie" theory of GDR history, resonating as it does with the tales of heroes and villains shown in the museum at the Checkpoint Charlie border crossing in Berlin. Individual contributions add detail and color to the depiction of the heroes and villains in an unjust dictatorship. I suggest that the real story of the East German dictatorship is a great deal more complex and that, even if we focus solely on the domestic anatomy of this state, leaving aside crucial questions about its international location (particularly the role of the Soviet Union), the reality is both more complex and to some extent more banal. I present some theses that run somewhat counter to the intuitive—and emotionally compelling—picture of the repressive dictatorship but provide more fruitful starting points for a serious reconstruction of GDR history than the Checkpoint Charlie approach that has informed much of recent writing. I conclude by reflecting more broadly on the issue of politics and value-freedom in contemporary history.

LEGACIES OF HISTORICAL MYTHOLOGY
IN POPULAR CONCEPTIONS

Popular Western (and particularly Anglo-American) interpretations of the GDR suffer to some extent from a surfeit of immediate experience and an imagination bolstered by a well-developed set of historical myths about "the Germans."

As far as Westerners are concerned, any unpleasant encounter with a blond, blue-eyed East German border guard at a crossing through the former Iron Curtain between the two Germanies, or any cursory glance at goose-stepping soldiers marching up and down East Berlin's majestic central avenue, Unter den Linden, might arouse uneasy memories of the Prussian military past. Any survey of the impassive crowds providing the fodder for official mass demonstrations, or the surly but quiescent faces queuing patiently for scarce goods in gloomy, ill-stocked East German shops, or waiting to be served in an unfriendly restaurant might easily provoke thoughts of the German tradition of obedience to secular authority—a tradition allegedly prevalent in German culture from Luther to Kant and reinforced mightily by the traditions of a strong Prussian state.

The word "dictatorship" lends itself to more immediate historical comparisons with the more recent, Nazi past. The totalitarian claims of the two states, the single political ideology imposed on the population, and the use of repression and force as the ultimate sanction for nonconformity are all too reminiscent of political patterns in the Third Reich. The political slogans and symbols, the mass parades of military formations and youth organizations, the suppression of freedom and diversity in favor of uniform support of "the cause"—however different in content in the two cases—are all too striking. Such superficially attractive comparisons are mightily bolstered by the Cold War denunciation of "totalitarian dictatorships," whether of Left or Right, which tended to equate the regimes of Hitler and Stalin. The GDR—communism with a German face—is doubly damned.

Any tendency among Germany's neighbors and erstwhile enemies to believe in the existence of a German national character was thus reinforced by superficial similarities between Nazi Germany and the GDR. And for triumphalist West Germans after 1989, who had so successfully shaken off the shackles of their own predemocratic past, the task of energetically "overcoming" the East German dictatorship was in some sense the measure of their own political maturity as seasoned democrats.

In the aftermath of the fall of the wall, impressions and assumptions along these lines have informed political actions, media discussions, and public debates and have left their sediments in the emerging academic literature on the GDR. The media have pursued a witch-hunt of former unofficial informers (IMs) for the *Stasi*. Western politicians and bureaucracts have entered the euphemistically termed "five new *Länder*" and ousted the old officials, administrators, and academics from their former positions, replacing them with *Besser-Wessis*—the Westerners who always know better. And despite a spate of political memoirs seeking to engage in self-justification, as well as a more muted but quite widespread sense of nostalgia, or *Ostalgie*, for the remembered security of the old days, the general thrust of recent literature on the GDR—whether Western or Eastern—has been to denounce the East German dictatorship, to describe it in the black-and-white terms of oppressor and oppressed.

In view of these impressions, the fact that the GDR appeared, for forty years, to be the most stable state in the Soviet bloc might scarcely seem surprising. Add to the indigenous Prussian traditions the presence of Soviet tanks and Warsaw Pact troops lurking at the edge of every forest, bristling along the sides of every through route, and displaying their fierce power at the watchtowers, fences, and no-man's-land of the inner-German border, and it would at first appear that there is really nothing left to explain. The Berlin Wall, symbol not only of the division of Berlin and Germany but also of Europe and indeed the world, appeared to summarize and encapsulate the essence of East German stability.

HEROES, VILLAINS, VICTIMS—AND TRABI-DRIVERS

What sort of a historical picture has been emerging in this general context? With the fall of the wall, there was an immediate and eager market for relatively instant publications on the GDR, feeding both a real hunger for knowledge and a whipped-up appetite for sensationalist revelations. The early spate of publications on the GDR might best be summarized as contributing to a tale of heroes, villains, victims—and Trabi-drivers.

The easiest history to narrate is one in which one can easily identify with the Goodies and the Baddies; moreover, the easiest history to sell is one that explores in loving detail the vicissitudes of the Baddies and their modes of undercover operation and depicts the heroic resistance of those who dared to rise up and challenge injustice. A slight complication in this particular story is the irritation and unease that persist between *Wessis* and *Ossis* in the post-*Wende* period; this is coped with by introducing the final category—the dumb, banana-eating, D-Mark-mad East Germans, or the "Trabi-drivers" (with reference to that endearing symbol of East German technological prowess and materialism, the two-stroke Trabant car), who simply benefited from the final outcome of the drama of oppression and resistance recounted in the tales of the heroes and villains.

In the months following the fall of the wall, there was a plethora of almost instantaneous literature on the heroes of the "gentle revolution" of 1989. Books appeared with titles taken from slogans of the revolution, such as *We Are the People!* and *Now or Never—Democracy!* They reproduced political pamphlets, programs, and eyewitness reports of demonstrations from the civic movements that had sprouted on all sides in the closing months of 1989.[1] These publications—essentially compendia of revolutionary documents and experiences—will prove to be an extremely valuable historical source. They contain records of many political ephemera of the heady weeks in late September to early November 1989, when "the people"—or at least the hundreds of thousands who dared, in those still dangerous circumstances, to come out and demonstrate—really appeared to be able to make history. They need, however, to be taken precisely as historical sources, to be subjected to an appropriately critical reading and evaluation, rather than as the digested and recounted "history" itself.

The compendia were rapidly followed by autobiographical contributions from would-be heroes: those who had participated in the unofficial environmentalist and peace movements under the wing of the church, those who had worked against the regime and had previously been unable to give their side of the story.[2] Again, these accounts are extremely valuable as inside stories that will have to be considered in conjunction with a range of other sources for the purposes of a comprehensive history. The experience of courageous individuals who risked their careers and the prospects of their partners, children, and friends in the struggle to achieve what they perceived as improvements in "actually existing socialism" should not be denigrated purely because it is one-sided. What is important here, however, is the somewhat more problematic reception of this literature.

From the point of view of national identity in the new Germany, such accounts at first played a major role in legitimizing and celebrating the initial moment of change. For the first time in their history, it appeared, the Germans had actually made a successful revolution; and as an added bonus, this had been a remarkably bloodless revolution. Moreover, it seemed as if the Germans themselves had actually brought about the fall of the wall. The role of the German people as a whole in achieving national unity in peace and freedom was to be celebrated.

But this vision of the heroes soon began to go sour for a number of reasons, not the least of which was the changing role—and the changing evaluation of that role—of the supposed heroes themselves. The sophisticated West German political machines drove in, steamrollering the East German democratic amateurs into oblivion; the international powers, and particularly the West German government, took the initiative in dictating the terms of unification; the visions of the early days became chimera on the horizons of idealistic daydreams.

Nevertheless, the days of the heroes began to be sedimented into the accounts of onlookers and the syntheses of more detached historians.[3] Here a problem began to arise: in some versions, the role of the heroes was projected backward into the whole of GDR history. This problem relates partly to the perception of the villains in the story: if, by definition, "my enemy's enemy is my friend," then anyone who was against the evil communist dictatorship must have been a hero. This is essentially a case of the black-and-white veracities of Cold War history being repeated after the demise of the Cold War itself. But, as we shall see, when the forty-year history of the GDR is recounted as one long battle of heroic resistance to unjust and repressive rule, and 1989 is represented as the simple continuation of 1953, then however emotionally arousing the tale, there is a serious distortion of the historical record.

As the tales of the heroes began to unfold, so too did the demonization of the villains. A few evil men at the top were to be held responsible for the miseries of the people.

Immediately after the unexpected opening of the wall, the East German Chamber of Deputies (*Volkskammer*), through a decision made on 13 November 1989, unleashed an investigation into corruption in the SED—an investigation that actually backfired, as people in the GDR were shocked by the revelations of (in fact, very modest) luxury and personal gain enjoyed by prominent politicians in their otherwise drab and miserable state.[4]

From the point of view of the members of the *Volkskammer*, this investigation served to deflect public attention away from the system as such and to concentrate anger on the abuses of power, the misuse of the system, by a few men at the top who were engaged in the pursuit of personal advantage rather than public good. By pointing the finger at a few individuals, it also effectively exonerated the vast mass of the people, in a manner comparable to the demonization of Hitler and his cronies in the aftermath of 1945.

The focus on a few men at the top also presupposed that the question of where power lay had already been answered: with precisely those few men who had, through the abuse of their positions, oppressed the miserable majority of people. This assumption remains implicitly embedded in a series of sensationalist accounts going back through a longer stretch of GDR history.[5]

The focus on the modest luxuries indulged in by a few top people in the party was not sufficient to engage public attention for long, however. Private hunting lodges and the alleged luxuries of "Volvograd"—the secluded compound of Wandlitz, north of Berlin, where Politburo members and their families had unlimited access to Western goods and rode around in that ultimate symbol of Western decadence and corruption, a chauffeur-driven Volvo—hardly amounted to a convincing depiction of serious villains. A new and more compelling candidate for the role of demon soon diverted attention from the party.

In the weeks after the fall of the wall, the *Stasi*, under its new guise as the Office for National Security, resisted serious disestablishment. But those who had opposed the *Stasi* under its old colors were not convinced by a mere change of name. On 15 January 1990, the *Stasi*'s forbidding East Berlin headquarters in the Normannenstrasse complex was stormed by citizens' groups, as were, at other times, regional and provincial *Stasi* headquarters.[6] With the revelations now emerging from the *Stasi* archives, public attention swung to this far more sinister and potentially more sensationalist candidate for the role of chief villain.

Daily revelations began to appear in the press about the former activities of particular individuals as *Stasi* informers. The so-called IMs began to be seen as the epitome of evil, the ultimate pillar of the police state. A mere hint that someone had served as an informer was often sufficient to destroy a career, a reputation.

A number of budding democratic politicians were the cause of acute embarrassment to their parties in the run-up to the elections of March 1990, as their activities in the service of the *Stasi* were revealed. Wolfgang Schnur, formerly a lawyer who allegedly defended dissidents and a founding member of one of the conservative party groups, was a casualty of this phase, as was Ibrahim Boehme, a founder of the East German Social Democratic Party. Lothar de Maizière, East German prime minister while the unification treaty with West Germany was being negotiated, was spared the embarrassment of any public questions until after his usefulness to Helmut Kohl's West German CDU had been served. Former church functionary and post-*Wende* prime minister of Brandenburg Manfred Stolpe was unique in holding out against massive criticisms of his self-confessed willing cooperation with the *Stasi*.[7]

Cultural figures such as Sascha Anderson (for the Prenzlauer Berg "alternative scene") and Hermann Kant (for the cultural Establishment in the form of the *Kulturbund*) saw their reputations demolished; Christa Wolf sustained an extraordinary onslaught for her critically positive and typically complex relationship with the state.

Revelations about the roles of particular individuals were soon accompanied by a growing body of more comprehensive monographs on the *Stasi* as an organization.[8] It was variously cast as a "state within a state" or—adopting the official phrase—as the "sword and shield of the Party," but whichever way it was interpreted, it was essentially represented as the epitome of evil, the ultimate powerhouse of the whole oppressive dictatorship.

In the shadow of public attention on the *Stasi*, the party itself was in danger of losing its place in the spotlight. But political and juridical proceedings soon refocused attention, and former prominent party officials—starting at the very top, with party leaders Erich Honecker and Egon Krenz—ensured, in their attempts at self-exoneration, that their role in the state was not unduly ignored. Here, of course, the memoir literature did not quite acquiesce in the role of villain, seeking to be cast perhaps in a new version of antihero. Just as, after 1945, it turned out that Hitler had apparently been the only Nazi in the Third Reich, after 1989, there seem to have been only anti-Stalinists and closet reformers in the East German Communist Party, the SED.[9]

Nevertheless, the focus of these accounts retained the "few men at the top" interpretation: the only question was which men at the top were really to blame. Many of those within a hair's breadth of the top—interpreted exceedingly narrowly as the triumvirate of party chief Erich Honecker, *Stasi* boss Erich Mielke, and Honecker's economics adviser and right-hand man Günter Mittag—now more or less claimed to have had nothing to do with the system of domination they were ostensibly so closely associated with. The apparent lack of power of the powerful was a remarkable feature of this phase of memoir literature.[10]

The problem with all these contributions on the villains— fascinating though they are—is that they presuppose a particular view of the overall structure of power. Whether castigating or seeking self-justification, the literature on the villains assumes that real power resided at the very top of the party and *Stasi* hierarchies. There is no analysis of the interplay between state and society. In some respects, this is comparable to the early postwar literature on the Third Reich (and much of the continuing popular literature on Nazism), which is characterized by a fascination with Adolf Hitler and his close associates. And, as with the literature on the heroes, the black-and-white, friend-foe mentalities of the Cold War era lived on almost unscathed by the collapse of the realities that had once sustained this one-dimensional approach.

At first, the great masses of the East German people were represented as the poor victims of dictatorship. They had been the unfortunates born or stranded on the wrong side of the wall. For those who did not have the courage to try to escape or to participate in public protests in the revolutionary autumn, there was nevertheless a degree of sympathy for fellow Germans, viewed as oppressed and disadvantaged but still essentially members of *ein Volk*.

The complexities of reality soon began to interfere with the clarity of this picture of innocent victims. As tensions began to grow between West and East Germans, the euphoria of November 1989 gave way to growing irritation and mutual criticism. The civic movements of the revolutionary fall, now castigated as hopelessly idealistic and irrelevant, faded into insignificance in comparison with the perceived problems of pressure on jobs and housing, the impact of mass population migration, and the mounting cost of reconstruction. Helmut Kohl's promised "blossoming landscapes" in the East German *Länder* appeared increasingly to entail some cost for the prosperous western brothers and sisters after all, and irritation began to grow with the alleged deficiencies in East German initiative and entrepreneurial abilities.[11]

Differences between *Ossis* and *Wessis* became more prominent in the public consciousness as the realization dawned that there had been more to the GDR than just the heroes and villains of the early stories. But these differences were not, as yet, inserted into any more comprehensive framework for understanding East German history. Nevertheless, this perhaps somewhat overstated caricature of current perceptions of the East German dictatorship is not without its traces in serious literature on the GDR, by both Eastern and Western authors.

The spirit of the broader paradigm that has up to now prevailed, the Checkpoint Charlie theory of the East German dictatorship, imbues not only much of popular debate but also more serious academic accounts. One weighty tome by two East German authors, *Untergang auf Raten* (which can be roughly translated as Decline and Fall), argues that the GDR was, in the last instance, based solely on the power of "Russian bayonets."[12] Its authors, Stefan Wolle and Armin Mitter, who were somewhat marginalized but not completely excluded from East German academic life before 1989, have plundered the documents at great length to produce work that is ultimately more a political reckoning with the past than a sober analysis of that past. From first to last, so their argument runs, the GDR was essentially in a state of incipient civil war, sometimes latent, sometimes more open. The dictatorship of the party, of the evil men at the top, was constantly opposed by the heroic people below, the innocent *Volk*. Thus 1989 was a direct continuation of 1953.

Untergang auf Raten, despite its length, is an easy and essentially enjoyable book to read. The authors write in a largely reader-friendly style, with a great deal of imaginative re-creation of mood and sense of time and place. The long quotations are highly compelling, often full of fascinating details. One has the impression, at first, of having here the final compendium, the total interpretation to pull it all together. But the edifice constructed in this book is in fact premised on preconceived ideas and assumptions: the scaffolding erected by the authors disguises rather than delineates the real structures of the East German dictatorship.

The authors implicitly make a number of erroneous assumptions: that "all outward appearances to the contrary notwithstanding," stability in the GDR was essentially and at all times based on the power of repression and coercion; that state and society stood in a constant, ongoing state of implicit civil war; that despite recounting a compelling historical narrative (often very revealing in its details), there was really no change between 1953 and 1989. For a history written by historians whose personal sympathy for the people and for history from below is so evident, there is remarkably little attention paid to the variety of patterns of popular opinion at different times in the GDR. There is virtually no attempt at explicit conceptualization of different forms of political culture among different groups and generations.

With much less by way of historical detail, such a picture has been produced in countless Western textbooks on the East German dictatorship. The pre-1989 Anglo-American and West German literature on the GDR was divided, of course, on a variety of fault lines.[13] But one major strand was that of a denunciation of the repressive dictatorship that was bolstered by liberal use of pictures of the repression of the June 1953 uprising by Soviet tanks, the erection of the wall, and the like. The static notions of oppressors and oppressed in this pre-*Wende* Western literature are reproduced, with far greater archival detail, in the post-*Wende* East German account of Mitter and Wolle.

Is this picture of a constant, if at times latent, civil war accurate? I suggest that the paradigm I have depicted here, however crudely, is essentially too simple, that we need a new, more complex paradigm for interpreting the history of the GDR. I would place at the center of that new paradigm a sense of periodization: the GDR was not static, it was not in a constant state of implicit civil war, but rather it had a more complex history.

TOWARD A NEW PARADIGM: THE "OCTOPUS THEORY" OF THE GDR

The complexities become apparent when one considers not only the flash points of GDR history selected for attention by Mitter and Wolle but also the longer, slower processes of change that can be captured only through the less sensationalist lenses of a social history approach. There are some extremely promising developments in this field, which seek to break out of the constraining assumptions inherited from the Cold War era and present new perspectives on what is still a largely unknown society.[14]

Once we accept that we know very little about the patterns of social change and popular historical and political consciousness in the GDR and start to subject these to a critical and open investigation, we begin to uncover some interesting features of GDR history. It becomes clear that force and repression were more important at some times than at others; dissent and resistance were quite different phenomena in the 1980s than in the 1950s. More is at stake in explaining the longevity and stability of the GDR than is implied in the simplistic, if immediately compelling, pictures of heroes and villains. Political history must be complemented by social history; history from above by history from below. And the shape of GDR history must be amended: the history of the GDR should be described not in terms of a "decline and fall" but rather as a "rise and fall."[15]

What, then, are the salient points for explaining the history of the GDR? First, the "victims" of history were not as passive as accounts that emphasize 1953 as the only moment of instability prior to 1989 suggest. The records of regime functionaries—party, trade union, mass organization, *Stasi*—are full of incidents of insubordination and expressions of opposition to the regime. In both 1956 and 1968, there was a lot more civil unrest in the GDR than was previously realized. Moreover, this unrest was not limited to the obvious "crisis years." Every year, there were scores of unofficial work stoppages or wildcat strikes, often comparable in origin to the early downing of tools by the Stalinallee building workers on 16 June 1953, but not turning into any mass strike as happened on that occasion. There were also numerous other expressions of disaffection: defacing the pictures of political dignitaries, emptying the fuel tanks of functionaries' cars, daubing swastikas and antiregime slogans on walls, and distributing subversive leaflets were infinitely more common than we previously supposed.

What is important about this type of discontent is that it was largely spontaneous, localized, and easily suppressed. The incidents of sabotage, graffiti, political jokes, and the like were also characterized by a degree of ideological confusion. Many of those expressing their feelings of hostility to the regime knew what they were *against* but were much less clear about any positive values: they lacked coherent aims or identifiable goals. The continued prevalence of Nazi slogans and symbols alongside appeals to Adenauer and Western democracy is quite striking. And fascinating though this material is, to say that a lot of people did not like the GDR very much for a lot of the time is not saying very much: by itself, it explains neither stability nor revolution.

The rise and fall of the GDR is perhaps best characterized not so much in terms of changing patterns of popular opinion but rather in terms of the changing shape of the regime and its effective penetration of society. The GDR enjoyed a "golden age" in the 1960s and 1970s, characterized by a relatively smoothly functioning political system with effective organs of coercion to back up the party and mass organizations. The reason, for example, that little was known of the popular unrest in the GDR in the late summer of 1968 is that its traces were so rapidly and effectively dealt with by the *Stasi* and the police, such that demonstrators were arrested, graffiti removed, and leaflets destroyed before such manifestations of opposition could become *öffentlichkeitswirksam* (achieve a public impact), something always dreaded by the party. Monolithic party discipline and the functionary system of rule, built up with some difficulty during the 1950s, were sustained through the late 1960s and 1970s until a degree of lability began to enter the system in the 1980s.

Moreover, the regime was most effective in establishing deep roots in society. There was a remarkable degree of intertwining of state and society, with large membership figures for the mass organizations, bloc parties, and SED. The statistics reveal, for example, that the FDGB officially had more members than the total number of those allegedly employed in the GDR; and in the 1980s, one in five adults was a member of the SED. The mushrooming *Stasi* intruded into every corner of East German life, observing, reporting, controlling, and interfering.

Furthermore, in the 1970s, there were a number of factors that allowed a degree of real popular accommodation with (if not exactly positive support for) the regime, in the expectation of better times to come: the proclaimed "unity of social and economic policy" under Honecker, which abandoned the notion of jam tomorrow in favor of housing and maternity benefits today; the proclamation of "no taboos" in socialist culture; the conclusion of *Ostpolitik* and the realization that the GDR was apparently here to stay and that people would have to come to terms with it; the signing of the Helsinki Declaration on Human Rights; and the signs of a possible incipient liberalization evident in phenomena such as the (often misinterpreted) church-state accord of 1978. All these phenomena served to raise expectations of the possibility of real change, particularly among generational groups that had lived their conscious lives under the GDR. These expectations were, however, increasingly frustrated by developments in the late 1970s and 1980s.

Changes began with the expulsion of Wolf Biermann in 1976 and the subsequent cultural clampdown, the worsening international climate as far as peace issues were concerned in the late 1970s, and the deterioration of the economic situation both within the GDR and on a wider scale. These changes in the domestic and international climate were accompanied by a key structural change in the space for dissent within the GDR. The church-state agreement of 6 March 1978 was seen by the regime as the final plank in its strategy of co-opting a compliant church as, essentially, the long arm of the state, a subordinate accomplice in the control of unruly spirits. It was viewed by the church leadership as a welcome affirmation of freedom of religious faith and practice in the GDR. It was interpreted by many within the church and in its broader environs, however, as an opening for the development of alternative views.

For all the criticisms that have been leveled against those who, like Manfred Stolpe, were prepared to sup with the devil in the shape of the *Stasi*, the co-option by the state of a relatively compliant church leadership was a precondition for the growth of a new phenomenon in the 1980s: what might be called "political activism." This differed in a number of respects from the spontaneous expressions of disaffection characterized above. In the course of the 1980s, new grassroots movements emerged: at first peace initiatives, followed by a degree of diversification in the spheres of the environment, human rights, and the rights of minorities. These groups focused on achieving realizable goals within actually existing socialism; they were characterized by new organizational features, networks across localities and regions, and the development of new strategies for demonstrating their views nonviolently. The groups that arose under the umbrella of the church in the 1980s were one of the key factors in ensuring the "gentle" character of the regime collapse in the fall of 1989. And they were a wholly new phenomenon: 1989 was not a continuation of 1953.

At the same time, circumstances were changing in at least two crucial respects. Starting with the oil crises of 1973 and 1979, and gathering pace in the early 1980s, the economic position of the GDR was deteriorating. Favorable loans and credit agreements with West Germany helped stave off the day of reckoning, but it was clear to individuals who had access to the true figures that this could not be postponed forever. In addition, the smoothly functioning political system was under increasing strain. A rising generation of middle-level functionaries, who were only too well aware of the real problems in their regions, were getting increasingly frustrated by the unwillingness of the ever-more-sclerotic gerontocracy around Honecker to face reality. (Question: What is the difference between a washing machine and the Politburo? Answer: You can decalcify the arteries of a washing machine.) This too was a crucial domestic precondition for at least the pattern, if not the initiation, of regime collapse in 1989.

Last, but by no means least, it almost goes without saying that, as part of a divided nation, the GDR was in a unique situation among eastern European states that affected every stage of its development and demise. However, it is important to add in this connection that Gorbachev was not simply a deus ex machina who came on stage and waved his magic wand, and the SED regime obliged by collapsing. The destabilization processes within the GDR had begun long before Gorbachev's accession to power provided the final impetus and crucial external precondition for the collapse of the communist regimes of eastern Europe.

The version of GDR history just presented can be characterized as the "octopus theory" of East German history. In contrast to the Checkpoint Charlie version, in which a few evil men at the top suppress the many below, this version emphasizes the ways in which an all-pervasive state extended its tentacles into nearly every corner of society. The few remaining niches of resistance and dissent that remained either lay dormant, or, under changing circumstances, slowly awoke to become the leaven fermenting the unrest that fed into the revolutionary upheavals of the fall of 1989. The accompanying sketch illustrates the contrast between the two paradigms.

HISTORY, POLITICS AND NATIONAL IDENTITY REVISITED

It has to be admitted that this interpretation of the East German dictatorship is both more complex and in some respects more mundane and banal than the Checkpoint Charlie version characterized in the first half of this essay. It does not, therefore, lend itself quite so easily to simplistic projects of building a new national identity as do the sensationalist tales of heroes and villains, the heroic overthrow of the unjust yoke of oppression, and the reunification in peace and freedom of the German people under their "unification chancellor," Helmut Kohl. Let us now turn to some broader reflections on the role of history in united Germany.

One could argue that it is not the task of historians to contribute to identity formation. But constructions of German history have been uniquely relevant to politics in recent decades in both East and West Germany, and the appropriation and politicization—if not the outright instrumentalization—of historical interpretations in projects of *Identitätsstiftung* (establishment of identity) can now scarcely be avoided.[16] In any event, current practices, such as the parliamentary investigative commission (*Enquetekommission*), or the raging debates in the press and elsewhere over the character of the institutional landscape and personnel of historical research in the new Germany, make any search for political irrelevance and the alleged purity of the ivory

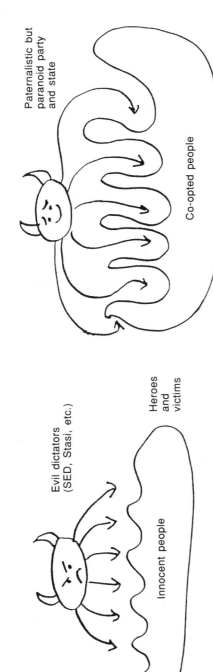

"OCTOPUS" THEORY*
of GDR history

Paternalistic but paranoid party and state

Co-opted people

Interpenetration of "state" and "society" = compliance; some bits not successfully co-opted (notably, church)

*As in M. Fulbrook, Anatomy of a Dictatorship: Inside the GDR, 1949–1989, Oxford: Oxford University Press, 1995.

"CHECKPOINT CHARLIE" OR "CIVIL WAR" THEORY*
of GDR history

Evil dictators (SED, Stasi, etc.)

Heroes and victims

Innocent people

Prevalent in media coverage, political debates, and many West and East German academic books tower doomed to failure. History in Germany is so closely intertwined with politics that the inescapable must be confronted.

What, then, should the relationship between history and the political construction of national identity be? Clearly not one of legitimation and myth-making. Historians have a crucial task to play in recounting a narrative that does not merely present a "worm's eye view" from a particular perspective but seeks to surmount individual perspectives and present a valid picture of the whole, into which each experience can be reinserted and reinterpreted. This picture of the whole must do justice to the views and aspirations of all the actors— whatever the feelings of sympathy or disdain aroused in the historian by particular actors' aims and practices.

Max Weber's conception of "interpretive sociology" is highly apposite in this connection: for all our moral indignation and dislike of the underhanded methods of cynical manipulation and destruction employed by the *Stasi* at the behest of and in conjunction with the SED, we must not blind ourselves to the fact that they were pursuing what they viewed as noble historical goals of human emancipation in conditions that were not, to revert to a phrase of Karl Marx, of their own choosing. The essential paternalism of the East German communists was quite realistically tempered with a paranoia doubly reinforced by the Nazi past and the divided present. In the view of many East German communists, the ends—to make a clean break with the utterly reprehensible Nazi past; to build a better, more equal, and humane society under extraordinarily difficult economic and political circumstances—fully justified what were often quite unpalatable means. To lose sight of these ambiguities in the interests of political and moral denunciation is to do an injustice to historical accuracy.

Similarly, to point out that not all "victims" were "heroes" is not to downplay the very real suffering of millions of people whose lives and prospects were truncated or distorted in myriad ways—whether through major political repression, the blocking of career prospects, or simply the battering of the soul, the suppression of the "upright gait," the physical choking on dust and pollution, and the moral compromises of everyday life.

Such ruminations also point up the difficulties of a view that proposes that "the facts should be left to speak for themselves." It is clear, for example, that for many years Manfred Stolpe participated in complicit discussions with the *Stasi*, thus breaking confidences and breaching trust within the church. How is this fact to be evaluated, and what should be done about it? Should one denounce Manfred Stolpe on moral grounds for having engaged in deceitful practices that served to sustain a dictatorship? Or should one applaud him for an ethics of responsibility that accepted the practical politics of the world in which he found himself and led him to do as much as he could to protect the church in whose best interests he claims he thought he was acting? Should one denounce him for betraying dissident pastors, such as Rainer Eppelmann, or applaud him for ensuring that their disciplining and punishment would be left to the church rather than being handed over to the infinitely worse procedures of the state? Or was this preference for mild discipline within the church in compliance with the state's own view that individuals such as Eppelmann should not be turned into publicly visible martyrs, potential rallying points for protest and international attention? Should Stolpe's *Stasi* connections render him unfit for public office in a democratic Germany, or does his clear understanding of the acute dilemmas faced by the GDR population render him particularly fit to represent their interests? The clear view of the majority of the electorate in Brandenburg was to reelect him as their minister-president, but this ran totally counter to the experience of virtually all other aspiring politicians with former *Stasi* connections.

As this single illustration demonstrates, neither the definitive demonstration of the "facts" of a case nor a serious engagement with the experiences and mentalities of the participants in the historical process is sufficient for establishing any incontrovertible evaluation. Even though, in principle, historical evidence can always "answer back"—historical interpretation is always open to empirical refutation—there are large areas of historical reconstruction that lie somewhere in between the clear shores of demonstrably false accounts and irrefutably true statements and hence remain open to a variety of interpretations.

When reevaluating the relationship among politics, morals, values, and historical interpretation, a number of levels or aspects may be differentiated. First, it is quite clear that history in united Germany is not characterized by the "blank spots" and distortions characteristic of some Marxist-Leninist versions of GDR history before 1989. However, historical writing remains politicized in a variety of other respects: the concepts used are themselves not value-free but are "emotionally drenched" and, to some extent, theory-driven; metatheoretical assumptions shape narratives and help structure accounts; and the role of empathy in interpretive understanding is often confused with identification or apologia.

If there is to be any role for history in constructing a national identity, it must be a subtle and complex one. It must be to raise awareness of the dilemmas and distortions inherent in all forms of social organization—whether capitalist or communist—and to raise the level of public and open debate, in which a variety of viewpoints may be represented and argued. It cannot be to present a one-sided picture, whether denunciatory or self-exonerating, seeking essentially to legitimate rather than to explain. The demise of the GDR can help address at least some of the public wounds (though never the personal tragedies) left by an inadequate "overcoming" of the infinitely more evil Nazi past, but only if it encourages people to engage in a direct confrontation with the problems of historical mythologizing and to examine explicitly the problems involved in living under, coming to terms with, or seeking to change a repressive dictatorship. The precondition for such an enterprise must be a sober attempt to understand both the peculiar structures and the informing mentalities of that dictatorship, without undue emotional investment in any particular point of view.

In the case of Germany, the quest for a national identity has been a remarkably dogged search for a remarkably elusive holy grail. It is perhaps time that Germans realized that their identity must be formed not from some notion of an ethnically and culturally homogeneous *Volk*, nor from a one-sided obsession with their past (whether to denounce or defend), but rather from accepting the plurality of debate on values and virtues—without necessarily a scapegoated other as the essential counterpoint. For historians, this means recognizing the ways in which concepts and theories are informed by presuppositions, but at the same time seeking to go beyond these presuppositions to evaluate, through both causal explanation and interpretive understanding, the realities of that past without emotional distortion or political evaluation.

NOTES

1. See, for example, Neues Forum Leipzig (ed.), *Jetzt oder Nie—Demokratie. Leipziger Herbst '89*, Munich, 1990; C. Schüddekopf (ed.), *"Wir sind das Volk!"* Hamburg, 1990.
2. For example, M. Beleites, *Untergrund. Ein Konflikt mit der Stasi in der Uran-Provinz*, Berlin, 1992; Erich Loest, *Die Stasi war mein Eckermann, oder: Mein Leben mit der Wanze*, Göttingen, 1991; Wolfgang Ruddenklaut, *Störenfried. ddr-Opposition 1986–89*, Berlin, 1992; Vera Wollenberger, *Virus der Heuchler: Innenansichten aus Stasi-Akten*, Berlin, 1992.

3. See, for example, Konrad Jarausch, *The Rush to German Unity*, New York and Oxford, 1994; Reiner Tetzel, *Leipziger Ring*, Darmstadt and Neuwied, 1990; Hartmut Zwahr, *Ende einer Selbstzerstörung. Leipzig und die Revolution in der DDR*, Göttingen, 1993.

4. See V. Klemm, *Korruption und Amtsmißbrauch in der DDR*, Stuttgart, 1991.

5. See, for example, Werner Filmer and Heribert Schwan, *Opfer der Mauer*, Munich, 1991; Peter Przybylski, *Tatort Politbüro*, 2 vols., Berlin, 1991–92.

6. See, for example, Stefan Wolle, "In the Labyrinth of the Documents: The Archival Legacy of the SED-State," *German History* 10 (1992): 352–65; Ulrich von Saß and Harriet von Suchodoletz (eds.), *"Feindlich-negativ." Zur politisch-operativen Arbeit einer Stasi-Zentrale*, Berlin, 1990.

7. On the Stolpe case, see Ralf Georg Reuth, *IM "Sekretär." Die "Gauck-Recherche" und die Dokumente zum "Fall Stolpe,"* Frankfurt and Berlin, 1992; Manfred Stolpe, *Schwieriger Aufbruch*, Munich, 1992.

8. See, for example, Bürgerkomitee Leipzig (ed.), *Stasi Intern. Macht und Banalität*, Leipzig, 1991; Karl Wilhelm Fricke, *MfS Intern*, Cologne, 1991; Joachim Gauck, *Die Stasi-Akten. Das unheimliche Erbe der DDR*, Hamburg, 1990; David Gill and Ulrich Schroeter, *Das Ministerium für Staatssicherheit. Anatomie des Mielke-Imperiums*, Berlin, 1991; Armin Mitter and Stefan Wolle, *"Ich liebe euch doch alle!" Befehle und Lageberichte des MfS, Jan.–Nov. 1989*, Berlin, 1990; Manfred Schell and Werner Kalinka, *Stasi und kein Ende: Die Personen und Fakten*, Frankfurt and Berlin, 1991; L. Wawrzyn, *Der Blaue. Das Spitzelsystem der DDR*, Berlin, 1990; Christine Wilkening, *Staat im Staate*, Berlin and Weimar, 1990.

9. See, for example, R. Andert and W. Herzberg, *Der Sturz: Erich Honecker im Kreuzverhör*, Berlin and Weimar, 1990; Manfred Gerlach, *Mitverantwortlich. Als Liberaler im SED-Staat*, Berlin, 1991; Erich Honecker, *Moabiter Notizen*, Berlin, 1994; Egon Krenz, *Wenn Mauern fallen*, Vienna, 1990; Günter Schabowski, *Der Absturz*, Berlin, 1990; Günter Schabowski, *Das Politbüro*, Hamburg, 1990; Markus Wolf, *Im eigenen Auftrag. Bekenntnisse und Einsichten*, Munich, 1991.

10. See, for example, B. Zimmermann and H.-D. Schutt (eds.), *ohnMacht. DDR-Funktionäre sagen aus*, Berlin, 1992.

11. For further details on popular identity and mutual perceptions, see M. Fulbrook, "Aspects of Society and Identity in the New Germany," *Daedalus* (special issue on "Germany in Transition") 123, no. 1 (Winter 1994): 211–34.

12. Armin Mitter and Stefan Wolle, *Untergang auf Raten*, Munich, 1993. I have reviewed this book, among others, in an article in *Geschichte und Gesellschaft* (forthcoming).

13. Cf. my analysis of the literature in *The Two Germanies 1945–1990: Problems of Interpretation*, Basingstoke, 1992.

14. For excellent early post-*Wende* contributions to such an approach, see, for example, Hartmut Kaelble, Jürgen Kocka, and Hartmut Zwahr (eds.), *Sozialgeschichte der DDR*, Stuttgart, 1994; Jürgen Kocka (ed.), *Historische DDR-Forschung: Aufsätze und Studien*, Berlin, 1993; Jürgen Kocka (ed.), *Die DDR als Geschichte*, Berlin, 1994; and the pre-1989 oral history project of Lutz Niethammer, Alexander von Plato, and Dorothee Wierling, *Die volkseigene Erfahrung. Eine Archäologie des Lebens in der Industrieprovinz der DDR*, Berlin, 1991.

15. See my analysis in *Anatomy of a Dictatorship: Inside the GDR. 1949–1989*, Oxford, 1995, from which parts of the following section are drawn.

16. On the political relevance, in different ways, of both East and West German historiography, see, for example, Richard J. Evans, *In Hitler's Shadow*, London, 1989; Alexander Fischer and Günther Heydemann (eds.), *Geschichtswissenschaft in der DDR*, Berlin, 1988; Jens Hacker, *Deutsche Irrtümer: Schönfärber und Helfershelfer der SED-Diktatur im Westen*, Frankfurt and Berlin, 1992; Georg Iggers (ed.), *Marxist Historiography in Transformation. New Orientations in Recent East German History*, Oxford, 1991; Konrad Jarausch (ed.), *Zwischen Parteilichkeit und Professionalität. Bilanz der Geschichtswissenschaft in der DDR*, Berlin, 1991; Charles Maier, *The Unmasterable Past*, Cambridge, MA, 1988.

Rewriting the History of the German Democratic Republic: The Work of the Commission of Inquiry

HERMANN WEBER

It is still early in our stocktaking of the history of the German Democratic Republic. The defensive posture being taken by many erstwhile functionaries in the former GDR and the taste for sensationalism in the west have contributed to a growing cynicism among the general populace. Deplorably, a denial of historical consciousness is once more erecting barriers against the darker chapters in our history. Into the bargain, the difficulties of everyday life in the former GDR have played their part in pushing the recent German past to the back of the individual and the collective consciousness.

There is much to be learned about the current circumstances from the course of events after 1945, when the Cold War and the economic miracle nearly succeeded in making the study of the National Socialist past taboo. The denial of historical memory after 1945 gave rise to distortions, in mind and in action, among individuals and in the public arena. To some extent, it is true, scholars soon began to concern themselves with the issue of National Socialism. But it fell largely to a younger generation to shoulder the burden of Germany's "brown inheritance" and to launch the long overdue debates about the crimes of National Socialism, about resistance to and compliance with the regime. There is a real danger that Germany could soon find itself in a similar situation, and no one can guarantee that the generation that is most immediately affected will have the time to explore its own history.

The task is all the more urgent because of the need to rid the east of its servile mentality. Decades of dictatorship by the SED (Socialist Unity Party) inevitably affected the attitudes and behavior of individuals in the former GDR. We thus need to analyze the system, its structures, and its consequences. The hierarchical structures of totalitarian Stalinism were based on the party elite's monopoly on power—and on the assumption of infallibility. In the final analysis, therefore, this elite group must be held responsible for the oppression and persecution that characterized the GDR.

Certainly, the rulers of the GDR and their minions were able to call upon a growing number of true believers to help prop up the system. Their understandable attempts at self-justification—one has the impression that it was frequently coupled with a bad conscience—cannot and must not stand in the way of the necessary confrontation with history. The capacity for a changed perspective, for democratic discourse, and for an "upright gait" cannot be achieved without critical scrutiny of political structures, as well as reflection on one's own activities during the forty-year SED regime. Historical experience has taught us once again that democratic attitudes and codetermination cannot prevail without democratic institutions—and that these need to be safeguarded. Our capacity to do so will be seriously reduced if we fail to come to terms with the history of the GDR.

Our understanding of the politics of the GDR, in other words, necessitates systematic historical research. Until 1989—thanks to the ideologically distorted perspective and the falsifications of historians in the GDR—the main burden of this task was inevitably borne by scholars of contemporary history in the Federal Republic. And the achievements of their research compare very well with those of the generously endowed (both materially and in terms of personnel) research institutes in the former GDR. The pluralist structures of research in the west produced numerous monographs over the years on the history of politics, culture, economics, education, and law and, since the 1960s, a large variety of general overviews of GDR history. All in all, these western studies left numerous questions about the history of the GDR. The reason for this was, above all, the lack of resources and personnel and, naturally, of source material.

Historians in the Federal Republic analyzed the history of the other German state critically, and their differentiated methodology and value judgments accorded with the spirit of academic pluralism. In contrast, historians in the GDR treated the history of their own state and that of its precursors apologetically, distorting the historical reality by creating myths and legends.

The so-called party-bound historiography of the GDR meant that the leaders of the SED expected their historians to justify the political direction of the party, both in the past and in the present. Because the SED claimed always to be acting in accordance with the "laws" of history, historiography was preordained. Historians were expected to mediate the pertinent facts so as to create a suitably functional interpretation of "tradition." The political and ideological instrumentalization of historiography meant that conformism to the interests of the party replaced diversity in historical representation and interpretation. Even more destructive than the constant hymns of praise to one's own "growth and development" was the fact that the official reading of history remained the only admissible one and that divergent views could not be expressed publicly. Thus the pluralism that is vital to all academic research was nonexistent. The party leaders demanded of the historians that they supply the "evidence" for the centerpiece of their ideology, namely, that the communists had always been "in the right"—from which one could deduce that this applied not only to the past but also to the present. Owing to this politicization, GDR historiography was constantly in danger of treating history as the retrospective projection of the present. After every change of political direction, it therefore became necessary to rewrite history.

Nevertheless, since the 1970s, historians were increasingly required, along with their ideological allegiance to the party, to pay due attention to historical accuracy. Historiography in the GDR had, for the most part, gradually overcome its primitive Stalinist misrepresentations of history. It is true that party-bound historiography prevailed, but tensions had developed between the demands of the party on the one hand and the claims by historical research to academic independence on the other: although almost all historians belonged to the SED and were subject to party discipline, they sought to create a degree of autonomy for themselves and to submit research that might enhance their international reputations. However, in the case of contemporary history and the history of the workers' movement, particularly histories of the GDR itself, ideologically distorted historical representations persisted. And it is here that we find blind spots that must be confronted.

The closer historiography was to the politics of the day and to the dogma of the SED leaders, the more it resembled the work of courtiers rather than that of historians. The more historians dealt with these contemporary themes, the more intimately connected they became with politics and the more they identified themselves with it. They internalized the prescribed interpretations of historical events and, through a process of self-censorship, sometimes even obeyed directives of the party leaders against their own better judgment. But just as the institutions were not all equally close to the party, so the quality of the work produced by individual historians was determined not only by their closeness to the party but also by their professional competence, or else by the extent of their dogmatism and ideological conviction.

After the revolutionary changes of 1989, many GDR historians adopted the concept of "Stalinism" in their work on the history of the GDR. This term, which hitherto had been considered taboo, became inflated and suffered from the lack of a clear definition; it became one of those empty formulas that obscure more than they explain. Historians from the former GDR now seldom use the concept and speak instead of "administrative socialism" or of the "failed experiment" of socialism. In this way, Stalinism, a dictatorial regime directed against the democratic workers' movement, is associated with the basic values of social democracy. But it was precisely due to the adoption of the concepts of the workers' movement, and the thesis of "real socialism," that the idea of socialism has been discredited in the GDR and in eastern Europe. The situation is similar to the claims made by historians in the former GDR that their historiography was a "Marxist discipline."

A Marxist interpretation of history is no less legitimate than other methodologies, and interesting insights can be expected of a perspective that strongly emphasizes economic development. But on closer examination, the claim of the SED to provide a Marxist interpretation of history does not hold water, particularly as far as the histories of the GDR are concerned. The notion that historiography in the GDR was a Marxist discipline must be corrected in at least three respects.

First of all, such interpretations were often Marxist merely in their terminology or in a few key dogmatic points. As far as the definition of past social structures or the "laws" of history were concerned, the GDR adhered in an orthodox manner to historical materialism. But in the evaluation of its own history, the GDR based itself on idealist rather than materialist assumptions. Explanatory models did not spring from a mix of economic, political, and organizational determinants but from ideological notions, which were then passed off as knowledge of allegedly "objective laws" of the historical process.

Second, it was by no means the case that Marxist critiques of ideology were applied. On the contrary, contradictions were covered up and differences reinterpreted. The subordination of historical repre-

sentation to the demands of contemporary politics did not permit
Marxist methodologies to serve the interests of empirical research. At
best, they were instrumentalized for politics; they served as stereotypes
to accommodate the actual events. To this extent, Marxism was an
ideology in the very sense that Marx criticized ideology: it justifies
the status quo and disguises its true nature.

Third, the official Marxist historiography of the GDR was determined by the SED alone. The ideological "engagement" that normally
prevailed in the GDR, thanks to the insistence of the SED, demonstrated not only a lack of objectivity (and objectivity never refers only
to the treatment of facts) but also a total lack of respect for historical
accuracy and the subordination of history to the exigencies of politics. History, in short, was to serve the political purposes of the SED,
based upon the axiom: since the party constantly follows the "wheel
of history," its course has a scientific foundation and is therefore correct.

Access to the sources is now the essential requirement for scholarly
historical inquiry. It is important to understand, however, that these
sources are not confined to the files held by the former Ministry of
State Security (*Stasi*). It has become clear that it is right and necessary to study these files, but it is disturbing that the discussions about
the *Stasi* files have threatened to degenerate into a media spectacle.
Morally, of course, the activities of the "unofficial collaborators" (IMs),
who informed against people who trusted them, are particularly contemptible. However, it is the full-time functionaries of the *Stasi* who
are politically responsible, and they should not be lost to view. But
first and foremost, the structures of authority should be clarified: dictatorship in the GDR was exercised by the SED leadership; the *Stasi*
acted—appallingly enough—as its "ancillary organ."

The study of the history of the GDR cannot restrict itself to the role
and function of the *Stasi*. There are numerous problem areas that need
to be worked through in detail. The swift publication of hitherto secret documents (first undertaken by erstwhile GDR historians) opened
the way to new insights, although initially a number of premature
conclusions were drawn, and this or that editor of archival material
did not display the necessary rigor, mastery of detail, or soundness
of judgment. Conspicuously, these "boom" times in GDR research have
lured people into the archives who—simply because they had never
occupied themselves with the GDR in their research—understand
nothing of the complexity of those forty years. Anomalies such as
this will gradually give way to a more normal situation.

For all that, the publications since about 1991 have broken some of
the old taboos of GDR history, for example, through studies of the

Soviet Union's "special camps" after 1945, illustration of the mechanisms used by the SED to maintain political control, and documentary evidence about the background to the uprising of 17 June 1953 and the building of the wall on 13 August 1961. These examples alone indicate just how important the archives are for research into the history of the GDR: the sources that have recently become available have helped explode the myths created by historians in the former GDR. Furthermore, the archives have made it possible to fill gaps in our knowledge about questions that, because the source materials were not made available to Western scholars, could hitherto not be explored comprehensively.

Nevertheless, German archives today present something of a predicament. Although it is possible to study the archives of the SED, the *Stasi*, the bloc parties, and the mass organizations, all materials in the national archives remain classified, in the usual way, for thirty years.

In eastern Germany, the archives, both central and regional, are in a tolerable state. Researchers now have access to the national archives of the GDR, and they can take advantage of useful and relevant information about the history of the German Empire that is contained in the Potsdam branch of the federal archives. Most notably, the scholarly foundation Archives of the Parties and Mass Organizations of the GDR holds crucial source material for the study of developments in the GDR. This foundation was instituted at the first gathering of its board of trustees on 14 September 1993. Its archives contain the 60,000 files of the Central Committee of the SED, as well as historical sources detailing the formation of workers' associations from the 1830s until the Second World War. These materials are supplemented by 270 collections of personal papers (among them, those of Wilhelm Pieck, Walter Ulbricht, and Otto Grotewohl), as well as 2,500 memoirs, photographs, and films.

In addition to all this, the foundation holds the archives of the Free German Council of Trade Unions (FDGB)—6,000 meters of files of the central and regional organizations of the FDGB, as well as forty-eight collections of personal papers. The foundation also gained possession of the library of the FDGB, and it now holds 1.5 million books. Furthermore, it possesses the papers of other mass organizations such as the Cultural Association (560 meters), the Democratic Women's League (100 meters), and the German-Soviet Friendship Society (450 meters). In March 1994, the foundation took over the archives of the FDJ (Free German Youth Organization), which contains over 30,000 files, only some of which have been utilized.

One of the most important steps in the reassessment of the GDR past has been the federal parliament's decision to establish a commission of inquiry. In operation from April 1992, the commission's goal was to investigate "the history and the consequences of the dictatorship of the SED in Germany" and to "improve the preconditions for scholarly inquiry into the SBZ/GDR past."[1] It was composed of sixteen members of parliament (ten of them from the eastern states), who were drawn from all parties represented in the federal parliament, called the *Bundestag* (the Christian Democrats [CDU/CSU], the Social Democratic Party [SPD], the Free Democrats [FDP], the Coalition 90/Green Party, and the Party of Democratic Socialism [PDS]). Each parliamentary member of the commission was allotted a stand-in member. There were eleven expert members on the commission (historians, political scientists, and so forth), several working parties were formed (on the *Stasi*, archives, and the economy), and there were six information groups. The latter inquired into the following:

1. Power structures and decision-making mechanisms in the GDR and the question of responsibility and guilt
2. Function and significance of ideology, integrative mechanisms, and disciplinary practices in state and society
3. The police and the legal system
4. The relationship between the two German states and the wider international framework of this relationship
5. The role of the church and how it interpreted this role in the various phases of the SED dictatorship
6. The possibility of nonconformist or oppositional conduct; the peaceful revolution in the fall of 1989; the reunification of Germany; the persistence of the structures and mechanisms of dictatorship

The Commission of Inquiry's frame of reference (remarkable though it may seem, it was ratified unanimously by the commission itself and accepted by the *Bundestag*) stated unequivocally: "The Commission of Inquiry shall neither anticipate nor displace the required historical research." It was the goal of the Commission of Inquiry, by entering into public debate, to help cement a democratic consciousness and to foster a common political culture for the whole of Germany. The commission's task was to proffer "contributions to political and historical analysis and to the moral evaluation of politics." The main practical outcomes that the Commission of Inquiry worked toward were:

- to contribute to the political and moral rehabilitation of the victims and to repair the damage wrought by the system of dictatorship in the GDR;
- to suggest possible remedies for the ongoing educational and vocational disadvantages suffered by people in the GDR;
- to help clarify the problem of corruption in government in the GDR;
- to secure, maintain, and make accessible the relevant archives;
- to improve the conditions for scholarly work on the history of the SBZ/GDR;
- to make recommendations to the *Bundestag* on legislative measures and on other political initiatives; and
- to make suggestions about the pedagogical and psychological assimilation of the GDR past.

The Commission of Inquiry's modus operandi included measures such as the following:

- discussions at the local level with individuals and groups, and dialogue with scholars about ways of reviewing the history of the GDR;
- hearings in an open forum; and
- gathering expert opinion and assigning research projects.

To each problem area, the commission assigned an information group that was made up of five to seven members from all parties and factions and was delegated to prepare drafts for submission to the *Bundestag*. The same procedure was followed by the working parties referred to earlier. The information groups first had to work out proposals for the two key sources of information for the Commission of Inquiry. They conferred about the delegation of experts' reports to scholars from outside the commission, and they determined the themes of the public hearings.

In the course of its two years, the Commission of Inquiry presided over a total of forty all-day hearings in Bonn, Berlin, and various places in the eastern part of Germany, and it heard 186 scholars and eyewitnesses. As well as the testimony of experts, the experiences of "Mr. and Mrs. Citizen" were taken into account. The minutes of these hearings, which were taken down in shorthand, have already been published by the *Bundestag*. They are a verbatim account of the entire proceedings, including all the individual addresses and all contributions to the discussions. These minutes, therefore, are an important source for the history of the GDR.

The open character of the hearings enabled interested members of the public to gain their own impressions of the *Bundestag*'s endeavor to examine the politics and history of the GDR. For instance, the Commission of Inquiry held hearings on matters such as criminal activity by governments (Leipzig, September 1992), changes in the party system in the GDR (Bonn, November 1992), the role played by the bloc parties (Bonn, December 1992), the *Stasi* (Berlin, January 1993), the hierarchy of power in the SED (Berlin, January 1993), Marxism-Leninism (Bonn, February 1993), education (Halle, 1993), the law (Bonn, 1993), art and culture (Berlin, May 1993), the uprising of 17 June 1953 (Berlin, June 1993), intra-German politics (Berlin, October 1993), the churches (Erfurt, December 1993), opposition to the regime (Jena, March 1994), the flight of GDR citizens to the west (Berlin, April 1994), and the issue of the two German dictatorships, that is, National Socialism and the GDR (Berlin, May 1993).

An important part of the process, finally, was to solicit expert academic opinion. Altogether, 148 reports were commissioned on 95 questions. The author of each report was asked to present the problematical dimensions of the issue on the basis of the latest research and the archival material that had recently become accessible. Special emphasis was placed on suggestions for further research.

The minutes of the public hearings, the experts' opinions, and other submissions, as well as the papers presented at the commission's conferences, formed the basis of the Commission of Inquiry's submission to the *Bundestag*. The reports on specific issues were drafted by the information groups and discussed and ratified by the commission.

In order to gain a clearer picture of the opening up of the Russian archives, the information group entrusted with archival matters went to Moscow from 5–7 July 1993, led by the chairman of the Commission of Inquiry and *Bundestag* deputy Rainer Eppelmann. Discussions were held with members of parliament in Moscow and with government authorities, academics, and directors of archives. In addition to the aforementioned hearings, the Commission of Inquiry held thirty-six nonpublic meetings—of the information groups, the working parties, and the project groups.

Although a parliamentary commission of inquiry is constantly in danger of succumbing to the dictates of politics and ideology, the returns from inquiries into the history of the GDR have generally been positive. Public debate about the SED dictatorship has been advanced. Former academics in the GDR have even formed an alternative commission of inquiry, headed by former dissident and proponent of a "third way" between Western liberal democracy and autocratic socialism Wolfgang Harich.

In the final stage of its work, the Commission of Inquiry found itself in the midst of campaigns for the federal elections of October 1994. In the spring of 1994, the discussions in the commission intensified. The majority, which consisted of Christian Democrats and Free Democrats, criticized the politics of the governments led by the SPD until 1982. The SPD minority in the commission pointed to the role of the "bloc parties" in the GDR: the eastern CDU, the Liberal Democrats, and, above all, the National Democrats and the Farmers' Party (both of which the SED had created in 1948) were pillars of the SED dictatorship. Nevertheless, after the demise of the GDR, the CDU and the FDP adopted the members of these parties and their functionaries, and they neglected to subject their history to critical scrutiny.

In June 1994, the commission submitted its report, which, due to the enormity and complexity of the problem, was in all likelihood little more than an interim report. Nevertheless, on 17 June, the *Bundestag* discussed the report of the Commission of Inquiry. Despite a number of weaknesses, the work of the commission was thoroughly presentable, and it was accepted. Only the PDS challenged the results of the commission's work. Accountability for large sections of the report submitted by the *Bundestag* (*Bundestag* publication 12/7820) was accepted by the entire commission. A number of chapters, however, resulted in a majority or a minority vote. This report was published, together with the minutes of the hearings and the experts' reports, in 1995.[2]

Some preliminary results of the work of the commission became available to the public even earlier. In September 1994, two expert members of the commission, Bernd Faulenbach and Hermann Weber, together with the chairman of the SPD group, Markus Meckel, published a 300-page collection of sixteen essays for the Klartext Verlag in Essen: *Die Partei hat immer recht—Aufarbeitung von Geschichte und Folgen der SED-Diktatur* (The Party Is Always Right—Confronting the History of the SED Dictatorship and Its Consequences).

In the meantime, the newly elected *Bundestag* has discussed whether a commission of inquiry should be formed to undertake further work on the history of the SED dictatorship. No doubt there were some weaknesses in the work of the commission that sat from 1992 until 1994. First of all, its program was too comprehensive to be managed in only two years. And then the commission found itself in the midst of an election campaign, which encouraged the politicization of its work. Not the least of the problems was that expert members were underrepresented on the commission: there were thirty-two parliamentarians (sixteen members and the same number of deputies) but only eleven expert members. Nevertheless, the positive results are more important: wide-ranging discussions about the SED dictatorship took place, and this could hardly have occurred without the Commission of Inquiry. After all, the commission was able to assemble comprehensive and important material and also make concrete suggestions to the *Bundestag*—for instance, about the harm suffered by those who were persecuted by the SED regime or about archival problems.

It would thus be desirable for the new *Bundestag* to establish a similar commission to continue the necessary and urgent work on the history of the GDR. And of course, academic research on the GDR will continue. A survey conducted by historians in the Centre for European Social Research at the University of Mannheim specializing in the history of the GDR showed that in research institutes and universities in Germany, over 570 research projects on the history of the GDR are already in progress, and the number of such projects will grow.

NOTES

This chapter was translated by Reinhard Alter.
1. SBZ is *Sowjetische Besatzungszone*, the Soviet Zone of Occupation from 1945 until the founding of the GDR in October 1949.
2. See Enquete-Kommission, *Aufarbeitung von Geschichte und Folgen der SED-Diktatur in Deutschland*, 9 vols., Frankfurt and Baden-Baden, 1995.

10

Historiography in the German Democratic Republic: Rereading the History of National Socialism

WOLFGANG RUGE

Not long before his untimely death, Leipzig historian Manfred Kossok wrote in his last (self-critical) essay on the theme of culpable immaturity: "To involve oneself with history does not mean to zero in on an imaginary or a prescribed target situated at some point in the future, and to establish guilt or innocence according to circumstances which prevailed at the point of departure. . . . Whoever takes history seriously will recognize that it is open not only to the future but also to events of the past, and that it cannot be tied down to some few common factors."[1]

These words hit precisely on the sore point of fascism research in the German Democratic Republic. First, this research, which was without question politically motivated, focused from the outset on a prescribed goal in history, namely, the inevitable (and thus predictable) fulfillment of the so-called revolutionary process of world history.[2] Second, the self-proclaimed mission of fascism research in the GDR was to hand down a guilty verdict on National Socialism. Third, fascism was reduced to a single common denominator—late capitalism (imperialism),[3] which had produced fascism and determined its criminal character.

These observations are value-free and are intended primarily to define the situation of historiography in the GDR, so that we are then in a position to interpret and explain it. I do not, however, endorse any facile condemnations of politicized academic research, nor do I seek to relativize the moral blame that attaches to National Socialism.

An academic discipline that is concerned with social processes and, consequently, with attempts to guide and direct these processes simply cannot be unpolitical. This applies to historians across the whole ideological spectrum—despite some claims to the contrary in the West. As I recently noted in an analysis of historiography in the GDR: "Only those historians apply themselves to social themes who, directly or indirectly, want to influence the current debate."[4] To this extent, the discipline of history will have to put up with the charge that it is the "handmaiden of politics." However, one must distinguish sharply between the unavoidable proximity of history to politics on the one hand and party-bound ideology on the other. Whereas the former can be defined as the committed search for historical truth, the latter assumes that the truth has already been discovered by the party, that it has been written into law, and that it is left to the historian to search for arguments to sustain and reinforce it.

There is no doubt that academics in the GDR were generally subservient to the party. Nevertheless, one should guard against accusing them of prostituting their research to politics. Fascism scholars in the GDR were no mere spectators viewing proceedings from an exterior vantage point, nor did they see themselves in this way. They considered themselves to be participants in the struggle against fascism, or at least they saw this struggle as their inheritance—the inheritance of a morally incontestable cause. They did not explore the past simply to vindicate their own actions and those of their comrades, but also to authenticate their current political commitment and to win support for it. But this accorded with official state doctrine, and for this reason, fascism scholars were willing to endorse it.

It is now being said—partly to divert attention from the "ordained anticommunism" in the Federal Republic—that antifascism in the GDR was "ordained" by the regime. This is a spurious claim. The overwhelming majority of the German people after 1945 had no need of any "ordinance" to help them reject fascism: they abominated the devastating war, and they recognized the connections between it and National Socialism. It is true that, subsequently, when the crimes of Nazism were suppressed from memory or attenuated in the Federal Republic, antifascism was bureaucratized in the GDR and frequently misused.[5] Nevertheless, a sizable proportion of the population remained convinced that the most immediate and pressing need was to prevent war, especially a war instigated by Germany. It was in no small measure thanks to the efforts of historians that this antifascist creed was kept alive through the constant remembrances in the GDR of the terrible reign of fascism.

In order to understand the antifascist foundations of the GDR, we must try (and this can be achieved only with the passage of time) to understand the GDR historically—and not only within the context of German history. It will then become apparent that, in contrast with almost all other modern forms of nationhood, the East German Republic, which came about as the consequence of a revolution—an exceedingly contradictory one—imposed upon it from outside, was not constituted as a nation-state but that its foundations were philosophical and ideological. It conceived of itself (and this was no mere rhetoric) as the representative of those social strata reckoned by all the progressive literature to be the victims of history: above all, the GDR saw itself as the advocate of the masses of people whose lives had been devastated by war.

This circumstance will come to play a greater role in future evaluations of the GDR, especially as a crucial realization about the nature of current and impending crises becomes increasingly evident—that nationalism is the true "curse of humanity," as Israeli writer Amos Oz puts it.[6] But nothing will come of this realization until humanity frees itself from the illusion that it can cultivate the idea of the "nation"—which is, after all, integral to the concept of the nation-state—and yet prevent it from spilling over into nationalism and chauvinism. Not only the collapse of socialism in the former Soviet Union and developments in the Balkans, but also the experience of a Germany that is increasingly hostile to asylum seekers and plagued by anti-Semitic excesses, have demonstrated once again that deference to the idea of the "nation" is by its very nature bellicose.

The fundamentally nonnational presuppositions of the GDR were not translated into reality with any degree of consistency[7] and, due to the influence of the Soviet Union,[8] were largely diluted. Nevertheless, the state's policy of outlawing intolerance toward other races and nations and its repudiation of war provided some ground rules for confronting the past and safeguarding the future. In the GDR, researchers into National Socialism saw themselves as committed antifascists faced with a twofold mission. First, they sought to expose and to criticize the economic, political, and ideological conditions that prevailed in the Weimar Republic, with the purpose of heading off the preconditions for the reemergence of fascism. Second, they were determined to expose fascism's behind-the-scenes benefactors, its financial sponsors, the advocates of militarism and war profiteers, and to act as a brake on those forces that were once again pressing for rearmament and, in the longer term, for an adventurist foreign policy.

The first of these research directions focused on the authoritarian traditions after 1918, revanchism, the undermining of parliamentary government, a judicial system blind in the right eye, and the lenient treatment of the National Socialist movement. The primary function of research was to expose a Federal Republic that saw itself as the legal heir to the Third Reich, evaded discussion and debate about the National Socialist period, was soft on Nazi "hanging judges," and frequently fostered antidemocratic tendencies—a Federal Republic that was (in many cases blatantly) loath to acknowledge the consequences of the Second World War. The second direction of research concentrated on the support given to the fascist movement by the large-scale capitalists, the military, and the landed aristocracy (*Junker*) and on the cooperation between these forces and the National Socialist state. On a number of salient points—destruction of Marxism, total revision of the Treaty of Versailles, colonization of eastern Europe—National Socialism had adopted many of the goals of the old elites.

In these two research areas, the achievements of historians in the GDR were appreciable, and some of their work was recognized internationally, although it also was subjected to hefty criticism. But all in all, the significance of their work has been widely acknowledged. Among the most important studies are those on the affiliations of industrial concerns and banks with National Socialism,[9] the history of the National Socialist German Workers Party (NSDAP)[10] and its rise to power,[11] its aggressive foreign policy,[12] the fascist war economy,[13] and National Socialism's policies in the occupied countries.[14]

All these and numerous other studies of fascism are intrinsically flawed by their being historical exposés. Apt as their conclusions might be, they disregard facts that run counter to their political terms of reference, and they reduce history, one-sidedly and selectively, to a single common denominator. But one must not forget that the predilection for particular research areas and the selection of historical facts (as well as the probability of blind spots) are by no means peculiar to Marxist historiography. Non-Marxist scholars, too, focus on those aspects of history that appear significant from their point of view, and they start from working hypotheses that one could easily mistake for preconceived opinions. Historians in the GDR, however, did not set out with merely preconceived opinions but with prescribed ones— that is, viewpoints determined by the party—and they adhered to these even if it became clear in the course of their research that they needed to be corrected. They were intolerant of premises and methodologies other than their own, and in many cases, they denounced as fraudulent or, at best, as erroneous research results with which they disagreed. Often they adopted a personal tone with their critics.

What precisely was exaggerated or concealed by historians in the GDR, and what were the distortions of the East German state? First of all, Bonn is not Weimar. The Federal Republic has been able to build relatively stable conditions for democracy. Today's extremism of the Right is no simple elongation of Hitler's fascism, and most people in the western part of Germany have developed a strong aversion to war. The portrayal of the Federal Republic as a state on the path to a new fascism and mobilizing for war tended to overlook concrete antidemocratic tendencies such as the denial, or even the whitewashing, of the National Socialist past and the general swing to the right in the Federal Republic. The critical perspective of GDR historians overlooked the fact that—precisely because of the experience of 1933–45—the ruling classes in the Federal Republic no longer resorted to open dictatorship or advocated a war of aggression. There were certainly parallels between Bonn and the final phase of Weimar,[15] but portraying the Federal Republic as a prefascist state was an exaggeration born of the Cold War, which it only served to exacerbate. Incidentally, we can now witness the mirror image of this exaggeration in claims being made by historians in the western part of Germany that the National Socialist regime and the GDR were essentially the same.

The role of monopoly capitalism, too, was partially distorted by historical research in the GDR. This is not to say that the influential bosses of the large industrial concerns were convinced democrats who rejected the notion of an authoritarian state and had no thought of translating their economic might into political power, both within Germany and beyond its borders. It is beyond dispute that they encouraged and supported—in many cases, financially—reactionary politicians, parties, and organizations. Nevertheless, most of them were highly skeptical about the socialist and revolutionary attitudes of Hitler and his fascists; in place of the swastika, they would have preferred a conservative government incorporating a body of "experts," as envisaged by Alfred Hugenberg. From the outset, a number of individual entrepreneurs (most commonly of the middle rank, a statistic that research in the GDR was loath to accept) and military personnel of the second rank did commit themselves to the Nazi movement. But initially, the most powerful captains of industry and finance employed National Socialism as a diversionary tactic against governments that, in their view, did not stand far enough to the right. They began to contemplate a "Hitler experiment" only after the Nazis had gained popular support,[16] thanks to an ingenious demagogy that was mindful of the mood prevailing among the masses. It was only after the so-called grab for power that the entire world of industry and banking in Germany accepted the fascist regime, aided and abetted it, profited from its crimes, and even instigated them.

This set of circumstances explains both the main thrust of fascism research in the GDR and the fact that it based itself on the "Dimitroff definition" of fascism, which, incidentally, does not even stem from Dimitroff.[17] This definition, which of course does not incorporate all the characteristics of its object (what definition can?), represents one of the main targets for Western historians in their criticisms of fascism research in the GDR. For this reason, we should examine it more closely. It needs to be confronted critically, but this can be done sensibly only if we take account of the historical circumstances that gave rise to it. The Dimitroff definition was formulated after the fascist dictatorship had been instituted in Germany, and it was conceived as an instrument in the struggle against fascism. It possessed no general validity, for it depicted fascism in power and was inapplicable to fascist or similar military regimes in less developed countries. It attacked financial capital as the main beneficiary of fascism, since National Socialism was still reaping the benefits of its "socialist" avowals and was heralding a "people's community." The Dimitroff definition also strongly emphasized the chauvinist and imperialist character of fascism, which at the time was still feigning peaceful objectives, and this was the definition of fascism that remained in force after the war. This can be explained largely by the wish to identify those who helped bring about the catastrophe—the world-renowned industrial concerns in the Federal Republic that were flourishing again as if "Aryanization" and Zyklon B, the pillaging of Europe, and the enslavement of foreign workers had never occurred.

Most fascism research in the GDR was well aware of the limitations of the Dimitroff definition. In discussions among themselves, historians were eager to refine and extend it, but ultimately they yielded to the dogmatic party hierarchy, which feared that the revision of generally accepted formulas would find no limits and eventually give way to the incursions of Western ideologues.

An important item in off-the-record discussions among historians in the GDR was the capacity of fascism to mobilize large sections of the population, especially the workers, against their own most vital interests. Attention was thus focused on a question of global significance, a question that has not altogether been resolved by non-Marxist historians either: the role played by the masses in the historical process, and the degree of influence they have on this process. The Dimitroff definition created the impression—and it evidently intended to do so—that a band of financially powerful individuals (admittedly only in specific circumstances) could contrive to engender mass movements and, with the help of hired professional demagogues, incite the populace to support the criminal designs of the Nazis. On this historical canvas, one side, the "seducer," is the active partner, and the other side, the "victim of seduction," does not warrant even a passive role in the historical process, that is, he or she does not even make an appearance. This is all the more astonishing when one considers that, in the Marxist view, it is the masses who "make" history.

Of course, fascism research in the GDR endeavored to portray the masses as active participants in the process of historical change and development. This is particularly evident in the studies of resistance to fascism, an issue in which the differences between Eastern and Western views of history were most marked. Each of the two German states had usurped half of the past for itself. In the West, "the men of 20 July 1944" were extolled as that which they were not— preceptors of a political order à la Federal Republic (as if there had been no other forms of resistance). In the East, historians depicted the communist resistance, which had never imagined the possibility of "debased" forms of socialism, as the vanguard of socialism in the GDR. Having corrected the disastrous "social fascism" thesis, they acknowledged (at best) the Social Democratic and, to some extent, the Christian resistance. From the indisputable fact that it was the Communist Party (criticism of its leaders was forbidden)[18] that made the greatest sacrifices in the struggle against fascism, it was concluded that only communist resistance represented bona fide antifascism.[19] Other opponents of Hitler, particularly those in the army, were judged to be politically inconsistent, and they were deprecated as advocates of an imperialist reorientation of fascist policy. Only in the GDR's final years, when the leaders of the party ventured onto the precarious terrain of the "nation," thus triggering debates about national heritage and tradition, was it possible to assess the liberal-bourgeois resistance with a greater degree of objectivity.[20]

Given that the struggle against the Hitler regime was not a struggle of the masses but was generally led by small groups, these studies of resistance were unable to verify the role of the masses in history. From the late 1970s, in order to make the resistance to National Socialism appear more significant than it really was, the Central Committee of the SED required all large-scale histories of the Nazi period to devote a set proportion of their text to the activities of antifascist resistance.[21]

Research in the GDR, of course, also examined the manipulation of the masses.[22] The publications on this question quite rightly observed that the prevailing social climate, shaped as it was in the Weimar Republic and more so in the Third Reich by official propaganda, mass media, schools, and the church, was conducive to the acceptance of nationalistic and fascist doctrines. Social and economic deprivation and poverty were rightly identified as factors that drove people to support the Nazi movement. It is symptomatic of these publications about the manipulation of the masses, however, that they focused on the manipulators and said little about the manipulated or their responses. Perhaps the most important factor in the analysis of fascism—namely, the psychological predisposition of the masses for nationalistic doctrines of salvation and skillfully disseminated enemy images—was disregarded. This can no doubt be attributed to historians' desire to arrive at a clear and unambiguous historical verdict, that is, to identify those responsible for contaminating education, the press, film, and so forth. There can be no question that such apportioning of guilt is fully justified, but it is also clear that the impossibility of identifying those responsible for the psychological motivations behind people's compliance with fascism made for the kind of one-sided verdicts characteristic of an academic discipline that was empowered to seek out the "guilty" parties.

It was detrimental to fascism research in the GDR that Marxist thinkers, starting with the masters themselves, were neglectful of psychology and, more particularly, mass psychology. Their analyses of the fascist mass movement failed to consider whether there is an apparently universal drive within people to raise themselves and their own kind above others, a temptation to seek advantage for themselves at the cost of these others (in extreme situations, with untold brutality), a need to subordinate themselves to a so-called authority figure, a hankering after secure moorings within hierarchical structures, and a herd instinct that prompts them to go along with the crowd, chime in with the chorus of the baying mob, and, ultimately, join in the killing. But this is not to say, as do various non-Marxist historians, that fascism can be explained exclusively by the character of the masses or—at the other extreme—simply by the distinctive attributes of the leaders, more specifically, the Führer.

Marxist historians of fascism also got themselves into considerable difficulty when they confronted the phenomenon of Hitler. They came no closer to answering the conundrum about the role of the individual personality in history and its relationship with historical determinants. In the eyes of GDR historians, Hitler basically remained a schematic figure, a faceless representative of abstract interests. His personal attributes and abilities (wildly overestimated by many Western historians), as well as the subconscious and sexual dimensions of his psyche, were simply pushed to one side because, in the opinion of the managers of ideology, they diverted attention from the substantive issues. On the insistence of these guardians of ideology, questions about the extent of Hitler's freedom to act on his personal initiative were mostly dispelled. It is no coincidence, therefore, that no biography of Hitler was published in the GDR.

Understandably, most historians of fascism in the GDR considered the publication of a Hitler biography to be essential. But it was not until the beginning of the 1980s that the party hierarchy agreed to such a project. Three volumes were planned, each by a different author. Only the first of these, covering the period until 1933, was completed. It met with strong opposition from doctrinaire functionaries, who criticized its alleged "personalization" of history and forced a number of changes in the text; they even saw to it that the volume did not appear under the fairly self-evident title *The Rise of Hitler* but rather as *The End of Weimar*.[23] The project was attacked primarily because political bureaucrats feared that readers could draw parallels between the cult of the leader in the Third Reich and that in contemporary socialist states and that they might also notice similarities in political structures, as well as in the measures taken to "persuade" and regiment the masses.[24]

There were a number of other aspects of the fascism complex that, thanks to rigid adherence to the Dimitroff definition, received scant attention in the GDR. Not until the early 1980s, for instance, did historians turn their attention to Nazi ideology,[25] which, despite its eclecticism, presented a relatively consistent picture, and to the exploitation of generational tensions by National Socialist demagogues.

The strong emphasis on the fascist instruments of oppression, the concentration camps, and the regime of terror was a corollary of the strict observance of antifascist traditions in the GDR. In this field, outstanding, even exemplary, work was done.[26] It is shameful, however, that relatively little attention was given to those victims who were most affected, namely, the Jews.[27] Although the suffering of the Jews was never in dispute among historians in the GDR, their condemnation of racist anti-Semitism fell far short of what was required, given the ongoing relevance of this question, and given that any declaration of faith in humanism is devoid of credibility if it does not contain an unequivocal condemnation of anti-Semitism as the most abhorrent of all ideological and political subterfuges.

The lack of detailed attention to the agonies of the Jews under the

Nazi regime is all the more puzzling given the fact that anti-Semitism had been all but eradicated from everyday life in the GDR. The neglect of the Jews by historians in the GDR cannot be excused, but perhaps it can be explained. There were a number of important reasons.

First, resorting to its official antifascism, the GDR disclaimed all responsibility for the crimes perpetrated upon the Jews and, shifting the burden of this responsibility and the attendant financial compensation onto the Federal Republic, denied the special status of the Jewish victims. Second, the critical focus on racism and anti-Semitism—the latter was, after all, directed against Jewish industrialists and bankers as well as against politically conservative Jews—was not helpful in drawing attention to the main issue: the imperialist, that is, the class character of fascism. Third, the portrayal of anti-Semitism as the most important and perhaps even the sole basis of National Socialism was to be avoided at any price. (In the West, anti-Semitism was often considered—wrongly—to be the personal obsession of the Führer.) To set so much store by Hitler's person would have been tantamount to announcing that any possible fascist developments in the future would be accidental. In other words, it would have depended upon someone giving birth to another demonic politician with an obsessive hatred of Jews. Fourth, fascism research in the GDR was less concerned with drawing attention to the suffering occasioned by the Nazis than with holding up those who were active in the resistance as role models of courage and heroism—particularly to young people in the GDR. Where it occurred, the resistance offered by German Jews (as distinct from the Jews of eastern Europe, for example, in the Warsaw uprising) was not seen as a specifically Jewish resistance but more generally as political opposition to Hitler: those who belonged to this resistance saw themselves as communists, social democrats, or pacifists, and historians in the GDR thought it appropriate to represent them as such. Fifth, the anti-Jewish feeling in the Soviet Union, and reluctance to contradict the Soviet version of history, may have played a part in understating the proportion of Jewish victims claimed by the Nazi regime.

Of the utmost importance was a sixth factor, which can likewise be attributed in some degree to the influence of the Soviet Union—namely, the political attitude toward the state of Israel that was adopted, for purely pragmatic reasons, by the party's leaders. Israel was not to be considered the Jews' historic answer to the Holocaust but as the spearhead of the United States in the Near East and thus as the declared enemy of the Arab world, with which the socialist countries were seeking friendly relations.

Seen in the light of the philosophy of history, interpretations of fascism in the GDR graphically illustrate the fundamental weaknesses afflicting Marxist interpretations of the past. The centerpiece of the Marxist understanding of history is formation theory, according to which presumed historical laws occasion a succession of social orders (formations). To be in a position, at last, to proclaim the inexorable approach of socialism/communism (after the slave society had been supplanted by feudalism, and feudalism had given way to capitalism), GDR historiography conceived of progress as self-evident and imagined that the world advances from an imperfect to a more perfect state, from a mean and contemptible to a blessed state. But since National Socialism would not fit into this scheme, it was proclaimed— according to the motto "it cannot be because it may not be"—that fascism fell outside the laws of history. And the ramifications of this were extraordinary. It is beyond dispute that the Hitler regime in Germany, the world war it unleashed, and the events of the postwar years decisively shaped the course of history in the twentieth century and will influence the course of events after the year 2000. If, therefore, we adhere to the notion that history is governed by laws, we also need to acknowledge that an event that does not adhere to these laws can determine the whole direction of the historical process. Or else—and this proposition seems dubious in the extreme—we will be forced to announce that regular and predictable processes are activated haphazardly.

This profound contradiction should have raised doubts about the existence of historical laws, at least as we know them, and it should have led to some basic reflections about the role of chance in history. But doubts and concerns such as these were categorically denied by GDR historians, not because of any rulings the party might have handed down, nor as a consequence of self-censorship, but because of a vague suspicion that the endeavor to incorporate fascism into the historical and philosophical system of Marxism could lead to the collapse of the entire edifice. Contemporary events offered a way out of this incertitude. Until well into the 1980s, the determination of the eastern bloc to hold its own in the arena of world politics, and the international recognition accorded to the GDR, seemed to reinforce the view that historical laws were guiding the progress of the GDR toward socialism and to vouch for the solidity of the theoretical foundations of Marxist research. Thus it was proclaimed, and generally accepted, that in fascism and World War II, progress had taken a detour—admittedly a major detour claiming a huge toll in victims, but a detour nonetheless.

The historical canvas that is now being unrolled by those historians in the former GDR who are willing to learn from history suggests that the terrible period from 1933 to 1945 was no deviation from the main path of German history. It is uncertain where this path is heading. In order to prepare ourselves for the surprises that are no doubt in store, we need to study its past course more thoroughly and with a more open mind than hitherto. In this process, obviously, the preconceptions and the fundamental errors of historiography in the GDR will need to be corrected, but it is just as necessary to preserve, maintain, and build upon many of the concrete and substantial outcomes of this research.

For now, unfortunately, one cannot help but notice that the discipline of history since the collapse of the GDR, dominated as it is by Western historians, is taking over (albeit transposed, as in a mirror image) some of the failings of GDR historiography, while discounting its positive achievements. Chief among these failings is an attitude of intolerance that not only refuses to concede the right of others to hold contrary points of view but also seeks to deprive them of this right—as evidenced by the purging of academe in the former GDR. Those who condone the "winding down" of GDR research institutions and the dismissal of their members, by likening the GDR to the wrongs of the Nazi regime, manifest only their boundless ignorance. The fascist state (its university teachers, incidentally, were with few exceptions accommodated by the Federal Republic) was constructed upon the basest of instincts; it ignited a global conflagration and left mountains of corpses. But the GDR, even if it failed by reason of its own ineptitude, was an experiment driven by humanist objectives. It saw itself as a leading advocate in the struggle against war, but its sole legacy—and this was bad enough—comprised mountains of files replete with the names of informants.

If scholars in the eastern and western parts of Germany are to grow together and achieve a cooperative, pluralist research environment, it is imperative that they learn from one another and that each side openly and fairly appraise the past work of the other. To do this, we must not only critically reassess research in the GDR but also review those Western arguments that stem from an ethnically and racially based nationalism and lay the sole burden of responsibility for fascism on individuals who have long since vanished into Hades. And we must reexamine a historiography that trivializes the crimes of the Nazis or was designed for use against communism in the Cold War.

NOTES

This chapter was translated by Reinhard Alter.

1. Manfred Kossok, "Im Gehäuse selbstverschuldeter Unmündigkeit oder Umgang mit Geschichte," *Beiträge zur Geschichte der Arbeiterbewegung* 2 (1993): 24–36.
2. The traditional parlance of the revolutionary workers' movement was "world revolutionary process." The term "revolutionary process of world history" indicates obliquely that the belief in a world revolution had begun to waver.
3. During the First World War, Lenin had already defined imperialism as the final stage of capitalism and declared that there were "no more intermediary stages" between capitalism and socialism. W. I. Lenin, *Werke*, vol. 25, Berlin, 1965, 370. The ensuing phases of imperialism were sometimes referred to as late capitalism in the GDR.
4. Wolfgang Ruge, "Nachdenken über die Geschichtswissenschaft in der DDR," *Zeitschrift für Geschichtswissenschaft* 7 (1993): 587.
5. It was symptomatic that, in GDR parlance, the wall that was built to prevent the exodus of the population was characterized as an "antifascist protective wall."
6. Amos Oz, *Im Lande Israel*, Frankfurt, 1984, 108.
7. During the last two decades of the GDR, the SED maintained an artificially constructed "two-nations" theory.
8. "Internationalism" had already been displaced in the Soviet Union on the eve of the Second World War by Russian nationalism, which was officially supported until the dissolution of the USSR and is currently having devastating effects on Russian society. It was evidently significant for the formation of a national identity in the GDR that, due to the fascist politics of occupation, the antifascism of the other eastern European countries was pervasively anti-German and prompted a return to national values. Consequently, a nonnational orientation no longer fitted into the framework of a "people's democracy."
9. Kurt Gossweiler, *Großbanken, Industriemonopole, Staat*, Berlin, 1971; Gossweiler, *Die Röhm Affäre*, Cologne, 1983; Lotte Zumpe, *Wirtschaft und Staat in Deutschland 1933 bis 1945*, Berlin, 1980. In view of the huge quantity of published works, only a small selection can be considered here. Comprehensive information about historical publications in the GDR can be found in the special issues (1960, 1970, 1980) of *Zeitschrift für Geschichtswissenschaft*.
10. Kurt Pätzold and Manfred Weißbecker, *Hakenkreuz und Totenkopf*, Berlin, 1981.
11. Kurt Gossweiler, *Kapital, Reichswehr und NSDAP 1919–1924*, Berlin, 1982; Helmut Beck, Wolfgang Ruge, and Marianne Thomas (eds.), *Sturz ins Dritte Reich*, Berlin, 1984.
12. Dietrich Eichholtz and Wolfgang Schumann (eds.), *Anatomie des Krieges*, Berlin, 1969; Gerhart Hass and Wolfgang Schumann (eds.), *Anatomie der Aggression*, Berlin, 1972; Wolfgang Schumann and Ludwig Nestler (eds.), *Weltherrschaft im Visier*, Berlin, 1975.
13. Wolfgang Bleyer, *Staat und Monopole im totalen Krieg*, Berlin, 1970; Dietrich

Eichholtz, *Geschichte der deutschen Kriegswirtschaft 1939–1945*, 2 vols., Berlin, 1984–85.

14. Wolfgang Schumann and Ludwig Nestler (eds.), *Europa unterm Hakenkreuz*, Berlin, 1988– (series in 8 vols., completed after the demise of the GDR).

15. Should the economic situation in Germany deteriorate further, there is a greater likelihood than in previous decades of the parliamentary democracy of the Federal Republic taking an authoritarian turn.

16. Indicative of this is the submission, discovered by Albert Schreiner (*Zeitschrift für Geschichtswissenschaft* 2 [1956]: 366 f.), from leaders of industry and commerce (Schacht, Schröder, Thyssen, et al., in consultation with Vögler, Reusch, Springorum) to President Hindenburg that demanded that Hitler be appointed chancellor (November 1932). In this submission, Hitler was described as "the leader of the largest national grouping," whose "weaknesses and faults, which are inevitable in all mass movements," could be eradicated. See also Dietrich Eichholtz and Kurt Gossweiler (eds.), *Faschismusforschung: Positionen—Probleme—Polemik*, Berlin, 1980.

17. The definition was: "Fascism is dictatorship by open terror of the most reactionary, chauvinist and imperialist sections of financial capital." The definition first turned up in the theses resolved at the 13th General Assembly of the Executive Committee of the Communist International in December 1933. See *Die Kommunistische Internationale. Auswahl von Dokumenten und Reden vom VI. Weltkongreß bis zur Auflösung der Kommunistischen Internationale*, Berlin, 1956, 266. This definition was reiterated by Dimitroff at the 7th Comintern Congress in 1935.

18. The party hierarchy emphatically demanded that the "leading role" of the Central Committee of the Communist Party, which was located outside Germany, be observed even where resistance groups were working independently and in isolation.

19. On the communist resistance, see *Geschichte der deutschen Arbeiterbewegung*, vol. 5, Berlin, 1966 (with bibliography); Heinz Kühnrich, *Die KPD im Kampf gegen die faschistische Diktatur 1933 bis 1945*, Berlin, 1983; Karl-Heinz Jahnke, *Jungkommunisten im Widerstandskampf gegen den Hitlerfaschismus*, Berlin, 1977.

20. Kurt Finker, *Graf Moltke und der Kreisauer Kreis*, Berlin, 1978; Finker, *Stauffenberg und der 20. Juli 1944*, Berlin, 1981.

21. This was the case, for example, with the *Geschichte Deutschlands im zweiten Weltkrieg*, written by a collective of authors under the direction of Wolfgang Schumann (6 vols., Berlin, 1982–).

22. Joachim Petzold, *Die Demagogie des Hitlerfaschismus*, Berlin, 1982.

23. Wolfgang Ruge, *Das Ende von Weimar*, Berlin, 1983.

24. The fate of the only Soviet Hitler biography (Daniil Melnikow, *Prestupnik nomer odin*, Moscow, 1982) is instructive. It remained unpublished for a long time because, according to a report by the chief editor of the journal *Nowi mir*, Twardowski, the Soviet leaders feared that readers could find too much "between the lines." Partly because of the numerous errors of fact it contained, this book was not translated into German.

25. Joachim Petzold, *Konservative Theoretiker des deutschen Faschismus*, Berlin, 1978.

26. Klaus Drobisch, *Widerstand in Buchenwald*, Berlin, 1977.

27. Kurt Pätzold, *Faschismus, Rassenwahn, Judenverfolgung*, Berlin, 1975; Pätzold (ed.), *Verfolgung, Vertreibung, Vernichtung*, Berlin, 1983.

11

Rewriting East German History: The Role of the Churches in the Collapse of the German Democratic Republic

JOHN MOSES and GREGORY MUNRO*

As part of the general need to evaluate the history of a regime that suddenly and dramatically imploded, it has become essential to examine the contributory role of the church. This is because Christians, especially Protestants, both clerical and lay, played a major part in the peaceful opposition to the regime and in its actual overthrow from October 1989 onward. For most of the forty-five years of its rule, the Socialist Unity Party (SED) regime had pursued a generally repressive policy toward organized religion and individual Christians that, superficially at least, appeared to rule them out as effective sources of opposition and resistance. But in the turbulent days leading up to the events of October–November 1989, the main resistance and initiative for reform of the system of real existing socialism (RES) appeared most emphatically to be coming from pastors and groups of dissidents who had allied themselves in a common cause of protest against what has become known as the "self-destruction" (Hartmut Zwahr) of the East German state being perpetrated by an increasingly incom-

* John Moses was responsible for the introductory paragraphs and for part 2 and Greg Munro for part 1. John Moses extends his gratitude to the German Academic Exchange Service (DAAD) for a grant during 1994 that allowed him to begin research on the role of the church in the overthrow of communism in the German Democratic Republic. He is also indebted to Professor Jürgen Kocka and Dr. Hannes Siegrist of the Arbeitsstelle fur vergleichende Gesellschaftsgeschichte, Freie Universität Berlin, for their hospitality and advice during his visit.

petent, ideologically ossified, and notoriously irreformable regime. So unsuspectedly widespread was the resistance coming from within and "under the roof" of the churches (even when some church people had allegedly collaborated with the regime) that any history of the collapse of communism in the former GDR that does not pay particular attention to the oppositional function of the churches must be considered totally inadequate.

Of course, the church did not perceive itself from the time of the establishment of the communist dictatorship in East Germany as a potential source of opposition. Neither had the new regime initially planned to oppress religion, because some churchmen had been outstanding "antifascists" in alliance with communists against the Nazi regime. But in the course of developments since 1945, the SED regime's official attitude toward organized religion hardened along doctrinaire lines. As a result, the church found itself in a similar position as under the Nazi dictatorship, namely, being forced to struggle for survival. And being the only organization in the GDR that could not be coordinated into the state administrative apparatus, it became both the center for ideological critique of the regime and the place where dissidents of all kinds, not necessarily Christian-inspired ones, could meet and organize. It had also become the target of infiltration efforts by the Ministry for State Security (*MfS* or *Stasi*), which came to see the church as an indigestible relic from the bourgeois past to be either eliminated or at least marginalized into social insignificance until it withered away.

The amount of literature generated by oppositional pastors and other dissidents, as well as social scientists and historians, since the "implosion" of 1989–90 is considerable. Some idea of its extent can be gauged from the 1993 survey carried out on behalf of the federal government, which registered 759 studies completed, currently in preparation, or in the planning stages on the former GDR, 10 percent of which had to do with churches, church groups, or religion.[1] It was to be expected that the collapse of the SED regime would be subjected to minute scrutiny from historians, sociologists, political scientists, and theologians. It has become a veritable industry that, from the church point of view, has taken on an apologetic dimension since the revelations that not a few prominent church personalities, lay and clerical, had been unofficial collaborators of the *Stasi*.[2] This latter episode in the history of the GDR has been most divisive, and there is a heated controversy as to whether the unofficial collaborators were guilty of betrayal of their coreligionists or were the hapless victims of circumstance, having been inveigled into being "discussion partners" of the *Stasi* through blackmail or naïveté. And there is the notorious example of Dr. Manfred Stolpe, now premier (SPD) of Brandenburg, who, as a leading lay official of the Evangelical Church, was engaged in protracted secret discussions with the *Stasi*. Although officially absolved by his ecclesiastical superiors of any ulterior motives, the discussion as to the prudence and justification of his negotiations is still on the public agenda.[3]

On the general interpretation of the church's role in the collapse of the GDR, one may already discern clearly emerging contours in the research that has appeared since 1989. There is scarcely unanimity on what the precise role of the church was, not even among oppositional pastors themselves. All this indicates that the role of the church in the history of the GDR, and during the *Wende* in particular, will be controversial for some time to come. Consequently, part one of this chapter outlines the oppositional role of the Protestant churches in particular to both the Nazi and the communist regimes in Germany as an essential prerequisite to understanding the present debate about the function of churches in the GDR. The second part discusses the discernible positions now being taken by scholars seeking to explain how the church survived under RES and came to be the center of oppositional activity. There are those who argue that the church simply adapted more or less to the oppressive regime, and there are those who champion the view of the church as the heroine—at times an unwilling one—who, in the hour of truth, rose up to lead the opposition against the "regime of lies" and monumental economic mismanagement.

1. CHURCH-STATE RELATIONS IN THE GDR

Theological and Historical Background

An effective understanding of the relationship between church and state in the GDR presumes some knowledge of the theological traditions of the German Evangelical churches. In the GDR, these were the product of the Lutheran and Calvinist heritages. The political significance of the Lutheran Reformation derives from Luther's doctrine of the two kingdoms (*Zwei Reiche Lehre*), according to which church and state occupied two entirely separate spheres of human life, neither having anything to do in practice with the other. In fact, in the divine plan for salvation, it was the task of the state simply to maintain order, by force if need be, without reference to the ethics of the New Testament. Indeed, the state was autonomous in every respect. The task of the church was to proclaim God's holy word for the spiritual edification of individual souls.[4] So the church-state relationship for Luther restricted the function of pastors simply to the care of souls. In matters of politics, the church had to remain passive, but the state had no right to interfere with the proclamation of the Gospel, hence the two separate realms, spiritual and temporal.

In contrast to Luther, Calvin insisted that the two realms overlapped. It was the duty of the church to sanctify the world by striving toward the realization of the Kingdom of God on earth.[5] This would be accomplished by demanding that politics conform to the ethics of the Gospel. If the state did not so conform, it was the duty of the church to admonish the state, which was intended to be a vehicle for the sanctification of the world in cooperation with the church.[6] For Luther, a corrupt state was really of no concern to the church; its mismanagement and injustices had to be accepted by essentially submissive subjects. However, for Calvin, there was the clear right of the individual subject to resist an unjust state, that is, one that did not rule in accordance with the ethics of the Gospel.

In Prussia, the Calvinist teaching increasingly gave way to a form of Erastianism, the subordination of the church to the state, which was the consequence of Luther's teaching. This process was accelerated after the merger of the Reformed and Lutheran churches in 1817.[7] Throughout the nineteenth century, the German Protestant churches not only conceded the state's exclusive right in the ordering of secular affairs but also regarded this process as a manifestation of divine providence in German history. In effect, the church became the handmaiden of the state, and German protestant theology accorded to the state a specific initiative in the realization of the Kingdom of God on earth.[8] Indeed, German theology implied that the state was the instrument of God's will on earth, and so it became the locus of German faith itself. This kind of theology of the state was precipitated in the work of Hegel, as well as in the dominant Prussian school of history in the nineteenth century, and reached its peak in the neo-Rankean school of the late nineteenth and early twentieth centuries.[9] Indeed, it became a major component of the mind-set of German cultural Protestantism (*Kulturprotestantismus*). The Kingdom of God and the state became virtually identical in the historical theology endorsed by most German Protestants up to the end of the First World War at the latest.

With the demise of the German monarchies in 1918–19 and the advent of the Weimar Republic, the churches experienced an acute identity crisis, because the democratic constitution expressly derived from the will of the people rather than from princes by divine right. At best, the churches' attitude to the Weimar Republic was ambivalent; it was not a state that could be fitted into their traditional theology.

This situation made the Nazi seizure of power in 1933 appear to be an acceptable, even welcome, solution to the churches' dilemma. Hitler could initially be apostrophized as a genuine *Obrigkeit* who could claim the allegiance of the churches as in the days of the Empire. The Führer was hailed by many Protestants as the savior of the Reich. However, Nazi church and racial policy soon drew vigorous protest in some church circles. It was at this point that the Calvinist heritage of the church reemerged through the work of the eminent Swiss theologian Karl Barth (1868–1968).[10]

Barth was the driving force behind the Barmen Declaration of 1934, which represented a sobering reappraisal of National Socialism on the part of a section of the Protestant church. It rejected the four centuries of Erastianism as practiced by the Lutheran churches since 1648 and marked the birth of the Confessing Church, which emerged as a significant dissident movement in the Third Reich. The pastors involved refused to countenance any longer the interference of the state in the realm of religion. Leading pastors such as Martin Niemöller had invoked the doctrine of the two kingdoms to affirm the church's independence from the dictatorial state.

Throughout the history of the Third Reich, the Confessing Church maintained its reputation as one of the most stubborn opponents of the Hitler regime, so much so that the exiled German Communist Party (KPD) began to seek the support of the church at its Brussels Party Conference of 1935, when it "recognized freedom of belief and conscience as a fundamental right."[11] In 1937, the KPD hailed the Confessing Church and the dissident elements within the Roman Church as "part of the great freedom fight of the German people."[12] By 1939, the KPD was pledging a "secure role in a socialist Germany for the Church which has been freed from inherited structures."[13]

The Church in the Soviet Occupation Zone, 1945–49

Until the formation of the Federation of Evangelical Churches (BEK) in the GDR in 1969, the East German provincial churches (*Landeskirchen*), together with the Protestant churches of West Germany, belonged to the Evangelical Church of Germany (*Evangelische Kirche Deutschlands*, or EKD). The East German churches' membership in the EKD posed an increasingly aggravating problem for the government of the GDR. As the prospects for reunification diminished in the 1950s, and as the West German government continued to maintain that it was the sole legitimate German government, the SED regime increasingly viewed the EKD as a threat to the GDR's claim to be a legitimate and sovereign German state.

In the early postwar years, the SED and the church had emphasized their common bonds as guardians of a reborn Germany freed from the scourge of Nazism, and indeed, the Evangelical bishop of Berlin, Otto Dibelius (1880–1967), was widely respected by both the church and the SED for his staunch opposition to the Nazi regime.[14] The Soviet occupation authorities were therefore initially benignly disposed toward Christians of antifascist reputation, and under these conditions, the Christian Democratic Union (CDU) was permitted to form itself into an independent bloc party, and the churches were allowed their own press. [15]

In 1946, the first congress of the SED reaffirmed the separation of church and state and also acknowledged the church as a legitimate institution in postwar Germany.[16] This policy was anchored in the 1949 constitution of the GDR, which guaranteed freedom of religion and conscience, as well as the church's status as a legal entity of the public law in the new East German state.[17] And it must be remembered that Christian Socialism had a distinguished pedigree in Germany, with many of Germany's more prominent publicists and clerics either openly or implicitly advocating some form of Christian Socialism.[18] So the foundation of the Christian Democratic Union in East Germany on 26 June 1945 was a supreme example of this initial mutual confidence between communism and Christianity. Under the leadership of Jakob Kaiser, the CDU initially followed an independent, critical policy toward a number of decisions by the Soviet and SED authorities. Then, in 1948, Otto Nuschke began to align the party with the SED regime. This policy was continued by Gerald Götting, who was general secretary of the CDU from 1949 to 1989.[19] Thus the party had lost most of its autonomy before the formation of the GDR in 1949.[20]

The first issue that caused a major rift in church-state relations in the GDR was the question of state control of education. In the constitution of 1949, the state declared that "the formal education of children is exclusively the competence of the state."[21] The church and the CDU sharply opposed the state's attempt to monopolize the education system and argued for a mixed school system, as provided for in the Weimar Church Law of 1919, which foresaw publicly funded state schools and privately funded church schools.[22] Here, the SED was not prepared to compromise, but apart from the education issue, the state did not initially intrude into any other traditional domains of the church.

The church tax was retained, and the state guaranteed its collection. In this way, state subsidies to the churches that dated from Imperial Germany were continued. In addition, church property was declared exempt from the land reform measures of the state.

Doubtless the SED pursued this course of action out of caution, given that a substantial proportion of the population of the GDR still declared their allegiance to the church.[23] However, one should recognize that there was undoubtedly a genuine measure of mutual respect between the SED and the Evangelical churches born out of solidarity during the struggle against the Nazi regime.

Stalinization and the Kirchenkampf, 1949–53

The relatively lenient treatment that the church had thus far received from the state ceased early in 1950. The SED became a centralized party enforcing the coordination of the noncommunist parties, including the CDU, which henceforth maintained only a token existence as a representative of the church's interests. The Stalinization of the GDR included an attack on the liberties of the church guaranteed in the 1949 constitution. Religious instruction in schools was severely curtailed. State subsidies to the churches were sharply reduced, and church meetings were constantly obstructed by the authorities. Church newspapers were only permitted to appear at irregular intervals.

At the Third SED *Parteitag*, Minister-President Otto Grotewohl announced the incorporation of dialectical materialism in the syllabus of all East German schools and institutes of higher learning.[24] Consequently, on 19 January 1951, the Central Committee of the SED proclaimed that all educational institutions had to be based on the foundations of Marxism and Leninism. The SED thus declared that the Marxist-Leninist worldview was now the only legitimate worldview of the GDR. Those members of the SED who retained their allegiance to the church were summarily expelled from the party.

This proclamation of the SED met with sharp criticism from the EKD in East Germany. On 11 December 1950, the Directory of the Church Province of Saxony had already warned the government that:

> For so long as the government attempts forcibly to impose the materialist World View upon the whole population and to mould the collective public life according to the foundations of this world view, the present difficulties in the relationship between Church and State will not cease and indeed will only become more pronounced if the Church remains true to its Confession and its mission.[25]

It was clear from the beginning of the conflict that the SED had no intention of compromising on this issue. Thus Hermann Scheler, a prominent academic at the Humboldt University of East Berlin, declared that if the SED ceased to fight against religion and superstition, it would betray its cause and destroy the very foundation of its existence. Reconciliation with religion would be tantamount to the voluntary destruction of the party.[26]

The alienation between church and state could not now be hindered. Political and economic policies combined to accelerate it. The early 1950s saw the continuation of the collectivization of agriculture and the nationalization of industry. Heavy industry was also built up on an ambitious scale, as a result of which the consumer goods sector was neglected. Serious shortages ensued, leading to considerable hardships for the population. By 1953, the situation had become critical, with widespread food shortages throughout the GDR.[27]

At this time, the government was also waging an intensive propaganda campaign against the church's youth associations. By 1953, it was clear that the thousands of families that continued both to worship in public and to observe the church's proclamations on the crucial questions of education and the integral role of the church in society were being penalized by the state. Career advancement and admission to institutes of higher learning for the children of church-committed families were made notoriously difficult.

Noteworthy is the fact that in contrast to the USSR and the eastern bloc countries of Czechoslovakia, Hungary, and Poland,[28] no prominent church leaders were ever detained, although some seventy-two pastors of the GDR had been arrested. Neither had any seminaries or churches been closed down by the state.[29]

Church and State 1953–1989

A new phase of church-state relations was initiated on 10 June 1953, when the government invited church leaders from all church provinces to meet government officials in East Berlin. Otto Grotewohl announced a complete cessation of all anticlerical measures of the government. Church youth organizations would henceforth be permitted to operate without government interference. Students who had been suspended from school because of their allegiance to the church would now be permitted to resume their education. The reason for this sudden change of policy is attributable to Stalin's death in March 1953. The successor government in the USSR was initially intent on opening a new era of peaceful coexistence with the West. Moscow also urged the Politburo of the SED's Central Committee to make extensive modifications to the socioeconomic program of 1949, which was still in force.[30] In addition, the GDR had been faced with a marked rise in the number of people fleeing to the West.[31] Then, one week after the government's meeting with the East German church leaders, the workers' uprising of 17 June commenced.

Although the church was not directly involved in the uprising, several pastors took part on their own initiative, and it was quite clear that the church's sympathies lay with the workers.[32] On 24 June, the East German bishops wrote to the Soviet High Commissioner Wladimir Semjonow, expressing their concern at the repressive measures adopted by the Soviet army and the East German government in the aftermath of the unrest. They argued that persecution would only exacerbate the already strained relationship between the workers and the government. The bishops explained:

> as Evangelical Christians we have a deep human understanding for the requests of the laboring men as they were brought to light on June 17 and, therefore, we do not believe that any real satisfaction can be achieved merely with soothing explanations and halfway measures.[33]

There can be little doubt that the sympathy and outrage expressed in the West over the brutal suppression of the workers' uprising, combined with the admonitions of the East German churches, contributed to the resumption of hostile church policy in 1954. In that year, the church was again requested publicly to support the National Front and again declined.[34] There was also a bitter conflict over the youth dedication ceremony (*Jugendweihe*), which was designed as a substitute for the traditional confirmation rite of the churches. As the ceremony was explicitly atheistic, in accordance with Marxist ideology, the church refused to accept any members of the state youth movement for confirmation.[35] The state retaliated by forbidding meetings of some church youth groups and withdrawing the church's constitutional right to consult state tax lists for the levying of church taxes.[36] The state also restricted the right of religious instruction in schools.[37] Finally, increased state pressure on families to leave the church was having an adverse effect on church adherence.[38] In 1956, the church also rejected a request by the government for a special declaration of the church's loyalty to the state.[39]

The irreconcilability of communism and Christianity was further documented when Soviet Party Secretary Khrushchev issued a directive to the Communist Party to engage in an ideological struggle that would finally lead to the disappearance of religion altogether.[40] The directive received enthusiastic affirmation by Kurt Hager, secretary of science and education in the Central Committee of the SED:

> It is imperative at the present time to accelerate the popular-scientific propaganda under the direction and control of the Party. This propaganda work must be carried out patiently without offending the feelings of believers. It is important to spread the teachings of dialectical materialism . . . which prove the validity of materialistic views concerning the development of nature and society.[41]

Clearly the SED was much more self-confident about the validity and credibility of Marxist-Leninist ideology and the long-term stability of the GDR, which it was believed would be enhanced by the gradual disappearance of institutionalized religion. This appeared to be confirmed by the GDR's admission to the Warsaw Pact in May 1955. West Germany was already a member of NATO. Then, after the failure of the four superpowers to resolve the question of a united Germany at the Geneva Conference in July 1955, the long-term existence of two German states appeared more likely to be an indefinite prospect in European and German politics.[42]

In February 1957, a new crisis in church-state relations began when the EKD concluded a military chaplaincy agreement with the West German government, which was now a member of NATO.[43] The East German Ministry for State Security was particularly critical of the church's participation in this agreement and saw the church as one of the leading ideological opponents of the regime.[44] Since February 1956, the Finance Department of the GDR government had ceased collecting church taxes, and from 1957, the annual state subsidy of 20 million marks was reduced to 10 million marks. The East German churches were forced to rely on grants from the West German EKD and the West German government. By its actions, the GDR government had in fact made the churches more dependent on the West. After some token face-saving trials for the illegal importation of foreign currency, the government gradually restored the church's funds.[45]

One of the most forthright critics of the SED regime at this time was Bishop Dibelius. In 1959, Dibelius argued that Luther's admonition to render obedience to state authority could not be applied to the GDR government, as there was no lawful authority. Dibelius asserted that the GDR government based its authority merely on arbitrary proclamations and regulations that were designed solely to preserve the regime in power.[46]

If the state had become a problem for the church, then the church was becoming increasingly one for the state. In February 1958, Erich Honecker had clarified the party's position on religion and the church as follows:

> In this matter it is apparent that there are comrades who are of the opinion that one's world-view, particularly one's religion, is a private matter. The strength of the Marxist-Leninist party of the working class, however, rests on the fact that the Party is actuated by a unified and closely guarded scientific world view which has no room for faith in a God, in supernatural powers, in superstition and reactionary ideas. It follows from this situation that the masses determine history, that the laws governing the development of nature, society, and ideas can be known and can be put to use for the realization of Socialism.
>
> In order that our Party may successfully fulfil its great historic task it is necessary that all members of the Party be made familiar with the world view of Marxism-Leninism and that those comrades who still hold to religious ideas be helped by patient enlightenment to free themselves from the same.[47]

From 1958, the GDR refused to deal directly with representatives of the EKD from West Germany and West Berlin, including the EKD's emissary to the GDR, Provost Heinrich Grüber. After the construction of the Berlin Wall in August 1961, the GDR also excluded Bishop Kurt Scharf (president of the EKD Synod).[48]

Evidence that the church would have been content to coexist peacefully with the state is provided in the 1958 declaration of the East German churches, intended to alleviate tensions with the SED. It acknowledged the church's "respect for the development of socialism and [its] contribution to the peaceful construction of the life of the people."[49] But such declarations were to no avail. From this time, the GDR's chief priority was to delineate its separate identity from West Germany even further. It was this policy that led to the strict isolation of the eastern provinces of the EKD from any further contact with their larger and more prosperous coreligionists in the west, the policy of *Abgrenzung*. This enforced separation eventually led to the establishment of the *Bund der Evangelischen Kirchen* (BEK) in 1969 and the East German churches' official withdrawal from the EKD.[50]

Under these circumstances, it was becoming increasingly necessary for the churches in the east to negotiate a viable basis for their continued existence in the GDR by themselves. There was no alternative but to reach a modus vivendi with the state. Party Secretary Walter Ulbricht had encouraged this through the oft-repeated phrase "Christianity and the humanistic goals of socialism are not contradictory."[51] The SED now proceeded upon a path of selective dialogue with individual provincial bishops in order to exploit perceived differences within the Church on the most efficacious means of dealing with the state.

The first successful episode in the SED's strategy was the resounding endorsement of the GDR by the highly regarded Leipzig theologian Emil Fuchs. In February 1961, Fuchs presented Ulbricht with a letter signed by 32,000 theologians and officers of the church.[52] It acknowledged certain differences in ideology but proclaimed "the basic consistency between socialism and Christianity's social and humanistic ideals and the ensuing need for cooperation in achieving these goals."[53]

Three years later, in August 1964, Ulbricht met with Bishop Moritz Mitzenheim (*Landeskirche* Thuringia) at the Wartburg (Eisenach). Mitzenheim had already established a controversial reputation for his preparedness to accommodate the state, and at this meeting, to the chagrin of many of his colleagues, Mitzenheim clearly endorsed Ulbricht's argument concerning the common humanistic responsibility of Christians and Marxists.[54]

It is important to note the very formidable opposition from within the church against these moves for a rapprochement with the GDR. The church, however, although desirous of avoiding an open confrontation with the state, was continually reminded of its past failures under the Nazi dictatorship and thus of the obligation to stand fast by Gospel principles. This could clearly be seen in the "Ten Articles on Freedom and Service of the Church," which was published by the GDR *Landeskirchen* on 8 March 1963. Obviously formulated after the Barmen Declaration of 1934, the "Ten Articles" set out to distance the church from the state. However, the articles stopped well short of Dibelius's position, which could be construed as a repudiation of a sinful state.[55] In this connection, it should be noted that in the late 1950s, Karl Barth had rejected the oft-repeated assertion that the GDR and the Nazi state were equally reprehensible regimes. Barth pointed to the foundations of the Nazi state in the social Darwinism of the late nineteenth century, which had found expression in the racism of the Nazi state. The Soviet system—and the GDR, which it had spawned—was at least derived from the French Revolution's demand for social justice.[56] Learning how to cope with the system of real existing socialism was a painful process for the Christians of the GDR.

As has been noted, throughout the 1960s, the state maintained pressure on the eastern regional synod of the EKD (that is, the churches of the GDR) to separate from the EKD of West Germany. In order to stave off this eventuality, in 1967, the eastern synod was convened at Fürstenwald and produced the so-called Fürstenwald Declaration, which held that the EKD should continue as a unified, all-German body because of the common suffering of the church under the Nazi dictatorship and the responsibility of the church as a whole to work against the currents of thought that had given rise to the Nazi dictatorship. (This responsibility had been explicitly affirmed in the Stuttgart Declaration of Guilt of October 1945.)[57] Furthermore, the church argued that separation in a time of ecumenical endeavor was nonsensical and destructive.[58] In a caveat, the church did, however, recognize that it bore a special responsibility for that part of Germany in which its members lived.[59] The force of the declaration was also compromised by Bishop Mitzenheim, who dissented from the synod's declaration and proposed a regionalization of the EKD in the GDR.[60] Concerted policy on the part of the various Landeskirchen in the GDR was not easy to achieve, but at least the majority wished at all costs to avoid Mitzenheim's proposal, whereby each province would be forced to deal separately with the state, thus rendering its objective of marginalizing Christianity so much easier.

In 1968, the SED announced a referendum for a new constitution to replace the 1949 constitution. In its final draft, the new constitution did not contain the specific guarantees accorded to the churches in 1949. The state proposed to provide the church with "the right to exercise its spiritual and community activity which concurred with the political interest and moral perception of the believing citizens."[61] The church noted with foreboding that the new constitution also provided for the possibility of individual agreements with the Landeskirchen. With this prospect in mind, the East German church formally separated from the EKD and formed itself into the Federation of Evangelical Churches in the GDR, the above-mentioned BEK. The BEK expressed the hope that it would strive to maintain contact and cooperation with the EKD. However, there can be little doubt that the formation of the BEK marked a victory—at least in the short term—for Honecker's Kirchenpolitik, namely, the creation of a separate Evangelical church within the GDR.

At the 1971 BEK Synod at Eisenach, the chairman of the BEK, Bishop Schönherr, used the phrase "church in socialism" to characterize the new position of the church in the GDR: "We want to be a Church not next to, not against but rather in Socialism."[62] It has to be understood that Schönherr's formulation was not intended to signal an accommodation with the SED regime. Schönherr wished to avoid a radical rejection of the GDR state, which would cast the church into a diaspora.

At the same time, the church had no intention of becoming a compliant mouthpiece for the government.[63] Nonetheless, the SED now believed that it had effectively domesticated the church. However, the experience of the laity at the parish level certainly did not reflect the apparent rapprochement at the highest levels of church and state.

Within the parishes of the GDR, the discrimination against the laity continued unabated. Active members of the church, particularly the children of pastors, were frequently excluded from university places. As in the 1950s, there was a renewal of pressure for children to leave the church youth groups and join the state youth organization, *Freie Deutsche Jugend*. The church workers charged with organizing parish meetings and youth gatherings were required to seek prior permission from the police for their meetings. Such meetings were not infrequently disrupted and even banned—often for the most petty reasons. A new regulation required theology students to undertake a course of study in Marxism-Leninism at the university. (This was the so-called *Grundlagenstudium*, which had been compulsory for all university students in the GDR.)[64] Against this background, there can be little doubt that a substantial proportion of the laity did not support Bishop Schönherr's efforts to accommodate the SED.

In order to focus German (and international) attention on the continuing persecution of the church in the GDR, Pastor Oskar Brüsewitz, in August 1976, committed an act of self-immolation in the public square of Zeitz in front of St. Michael's Church. Immediately before his suicide, Brüsewitz had displayed a banner critical of the state's treatment of the church and particularly of the state's demoralization of the youth who attempted to maintain their loyalty to the church.[65] Brüsewitz's martyrdom was as much a protest against the complacency of the upper echelons of the church hierarchy as it was against the SED regime. The Brüsewitz affair was also significant in that it focused attention on the emergence of a widespread sense of frustration with and alienation from both the state and the church on the part of young people. At this time, the SED was particularly stung by the caustic critique of intellectuals such as Rudolf Bahro, who described the SED as a hopelessly corrupt and petrified form of centralized Stalinist communism.[66] There was clearly a credibility risk for a church that was prepared to reach a modus vivendi with such a regime.

Commencing in May 1977, State Secretary Siegerwasser conducted a series of talks with the executive of the BEK on how to resolve the problems between the church and the state. These talks culminated in a meeting between Honecker and Bishop Schönherr on 6 March 1978. The results of this meeting showed that the SED finally realized that there was no prospect of the church being tamed, much less of its disappearing according to Marxist-Leninist theory. Schönherr was particularly emphatic that the church was determined to look to the welfare of its parishes. As he declared immediately after the meeting: "The relationship of Church and State is as good as the individual Christian citizen experiences it in his local social situation."[67]

The summit between Schönherr and Honecker resulted in a number of improvements for the church. The state recognized the independence of the church in the formulation and fulfillment of its pastoral and wider social responsibilities. The church was granted a modest but regular access to state radio and television, and its indispensable social work in prisons, hospitals, retirement homes, cemeteries, kindergartens, and schools was recognized.[68] In exchange, Schönherr reaffirmed the goal of the church in socialism as a "church which helps the Christian citizen and the individual congregation to find a way in socialist society with the freedom and responsibility of faith and to endeavour to seek the best for all and for the whole."[69]

It must be appreciated that this agreement was a modus vivendi between church and state. The state made no change in its ideological beliefs concerning religion. Both the church and the state wished to coexist, because the confrontations of the past were seen as mutually disadvantageous. The GDR quickly set out to extract as many political advantages as possible from this arrangement. The BEK's membership in the World Council of Churches helped promote the GDR's search for international recognition as a legitimate state. Likewise, official BEK contact with the EKD was seen as an avenue whereby East German interests could be voiced and even protected. This greater openness to international bodies would cause increasing difficulties for the SED in the 1980s, as it meant that international bodies were receiving information on GDR breaches of international covenants and could then publicly request the government to comply with such covenants.[70]

One other particularly interesting aspect of the summit of 1978 was the state's interest in assisting the church with preparations for the celebration of the 500th anniversary of the birth of Luther in 1983. Indeed, Honecker regarded the anniversary as of such importance that he personally chaired the committee in charge of preparations for the event.[71] Already, there had been interesting signs of revisionism in the SED's official interpretation of German history. Friedrich II and even Bismarck had begun to receive a more sympathetic treatment in the GDR universities in the late 1970s.[72] In the 1940s, and 1950s, Luther had been denounced as having betrayed Thomas Müntzer and the

German peasantry. He was now presented as an important and worthy part of Germany's history.[73] Clearly, the SED was attempting to reverse its earlier ideologically driven disavowal of so-called reactionary aspects of German history. By reclaiming such aspects of Germany's history, the SED could attempt to strengthen its claims to legitimacy in the GDR.[74]

Notwithstanding its decline in numbers, the church now appeared to be in a stronger position than at any other period in the history of the GDR. The state had been forced to make concessions in order to arrest its decreasing credibility as a protector of the welfare of the population and in the face of criticism by intellectuals in the GDR and by both the Right and Left in Europe (including the Eurocommunists).

Almost by default, in the 1980s, the BEK became the focal point for a number of pressure groups that continued to be thoroughly disenchanted with the SED. These included activists for the environment, the peace movement, conscientious objectors against military service, and human rights activists.[75] The church was the one institution that retained a measure of real independence from the state and thus attracted both Christian and non-Christian critics of the regime. The widespread sense of alienation from the SED regime of Honecker was accentuated by his refusal to initiate a reform program for the GDR similar to that introduced by Mikhail Gorbachev in the Soviet Union in 1985.

The new reformist momentum within and outside the church became noticeable in the early 1980s, when the church found itself protecting and supporting (initially somewhat hesitantly) various disparate groups meeting in support of the peace movement and human rights.[76] From 1986–87, when it became clear that the SED would make no attempt to emulate Gorbachev's reforms in the Soviet Union, there was an increasing degree of restlessness among these various groups, which were becoming more forthright in articulating their views. As the church was the one autonomous institution remaining in the GDR, these groups naturally looked to it for protection and support.[77] It was of particular significance that the church also gave its support at the parish level anywhere in the GDR where there was a demand for regular meetings and discussions on issues such as peace and disarmament, the environment, and human rights issues. The state, in turn, began to harass and arrest members of these dissident groups. This persecution merely strengthened the bonds between the church and these groups. Notwithstanding government protestations to the contrary, such attacks clearly violated the March 1978 accord.[78] The church attached particular weight to the right of all GDR citizens to travel in eastern and western Europe in accordance with existing covenants on civil and political rights.[79] At the BEK synods of 1987 and 1988, a number of speakers criticized the government for its inflexibility and insensitivity in the face of the overwhelming need for economic, social, and political reform.[80]

In May 1989, the Hungarian government began to open its border with Austria. This meant that GDR citizens could now reach the FRG via Hungary. By August 1989, approximately 55,000 East Germans had fled the GDR.[81]

Throughout 1989, a number of new pressure groups formed and were gathering public support at a dramatic rate, with increasingly active support from the church. These included *Neues Forum* (New Forum), *Demokratie jetzt* (Democracy Now), and *Demokratischer Aufbruch* (Democratic Awakening).[82] Within the church, a group called the Church in Solidarity had also been formed. Its demands included democratic elections, the formation of a *Rechtsstaat*, freedom of information, and economic reforms.[83] Beginning in October, there were regular demonstrations emanating from church buildings, most notably the St. Nikolai Church in Leipzig and the Gethsemane Church in East Berlin.[84]

On 6 and 7 October 1989, Gorbachev visited the GDR for the fortieth-anniversary celebration of the state's foundation. His speeches clearly showed that the USSR would not intervene to prop up the SED regime. This knowledge merely galvanized the demonstrators' determination to force the SED to relinquish power. At this time, members of the church frequently mediated between the demonstrators and the state and urged moderation on both sides. There can be little doubt that the church's mediation made a decisive contribution in ensuring that the "People's Revolution" of October–November 1989 did not degenerate into violence.

By way of recapitulation, it has to be appreciated that there was a considerable diversity of views within the church on the most appropriate foundation for the conduct of relations with the state. The traditional Lutheran understanding of the state (that is, the doctrine of the two kingdoms) was advocated by Bishop Ingo Braecklein of Thuringia. Braecklein urged the laity to render loyalty to the state. However, he would not endorse open church support for the socialist state, since it was not the province of the church to advocate one theory of government over another.[85] The idea of "church within socialism," first propounded by Bishop Schönherr in 1971, was widely supported by the hierarchy in the 1970s. Schönherr had urged the church to acknowledge that it had to carry out its mission within a socialist state without actively promoting it or opposing it. The third major school of thought, that of "critical solidarity," was an extension of the "church within socialism" view. This was advocated by Bishop Krusche of Magdeburg. Although he generally approved of the socialist system, Krusche maintained that the church must be free to criticize aspects of the state's conduct.[86] Finally, there was the idea of the church as an advocate for the weak and persecuted and as a critic of any abuse of power by the state. Here, the connection with the experience of the *Kirchenkampf* in the Nazi regime played an important role. This view was propounded by Bishops Rathke of Mecklenburg and Fränckel of Görlitz.[87]

The scholarly evaluation of the church's role in the history of the GDR and its indispensable function in the actual overthrow of the regime is proceeding at a breathtaking rate. Part two attempts to sketch the contours of this research.

2. SCHOLARLY RESEARCH

Precursors to Current Research

As Detlef Pollack notes, the theme of religion and the church in the GDR has always commanded considerable attention from the Western media.[88] Radio and television reported regularly on events relating to religion within RES. Indeed, the church was the one sphere in which the dissatisfaction of the GDR population with the regime could be observed. Journals in the West, such as the Roman Catholic *Herder-Korrespondenz*, the Protestant *Evangelische Kommentare*, and the *Lutherische Monatshefte*, devoted particular attention to religious developments in the GDR. And from the early 1970s, *Kirche im Sozialismus*, published in West Berlin but mostly featuring articles by church persons in the GDR, sought to report on church affairs there. Shortly before it ceased publication in 1990, it changed its name to *Übergänge* (Transitions), as "socialism" had collapsed.

Apart from these journals, there were the regular church information service publications, as well as the *Kirchliches Jahrbuch*, which appeared annually from 1949 to 1988 to cover events for the whole of the German Evangelical Church and always devoted a special section to events in the GDR. All these, of course, form essential published source material in themselves.

The voluminous writings of Reinhard Henkys (West Berlin) about the situation of the church in the GDR provided a continuous commentary throughout virtually the entire life of the regime. These were informative reports designed to keep Western church eyes focused on the predicament of coreligionists under the communist dictator-ship.[89] Church historians and secular social scientists in the West oc-casionally focused attention on the fate of the church in the East. The work of Otto Luchterhand, Horst Dähn, Martin Greschart, and the late Werner Jochmann testified to the strong but isolated concern of some Western scholars, in contrast to journalists, with the history of the church in the GDR.[90]

Apart from the numerous publications by Henkys, arguably the most impressive pre-1990 overall analysis was American Robert Goeckel's *The Lutheran Church and the East German State* (1990). Goeckel certainly communicates the idea that the church constituted a problem for the regime of RES and that a crisis was looming, given the extent of church involvement in the ecumenical movements for justice, peace, and the preservation of the environment. Goeckel also accurately portrayed how the church became a place where the defense policy of the GDR was increasingly coming under criticism. But historians are not prophets in the sense that they seek to foretell the course of events. Goeckel was content to register the seething discontent within the population that was gradually being ventilated "under the roof of the Church," but he could not predict that the situation would change, given the means of repression available to the government.

From authors based in the GDR itself prior to the *Wende*, there were numerous examples of research on individual themes, such as the work of the church among children and youth, conditions prevailing in country parishes, and the role of the pastor in the parish. By the mid-1980s, reports on political alternative groups by a number of the pastors and laypeople involved were appearing. One of the pastors, Erhart Neubert, managed to publish material critical of the regime under the pseudonym Joachim Christian in the West without coming to the attention of the *Stasi*.[91] Autobiographical material from GDR church leaders, both clerical and lay, that reported on the situation of the church under RES also began to appear in the 1980s in both GDR and West German publishing houses.

In the West, apart from the already-mentioned studies by Henkys, Dähn, and others that focused mainly on the church-state relation-ship, numerous studies appeared on the church's involvement in the peace movement, the social work of the church, and the question of the youth dedication service (*Jugendweihe*), which was instituted by the regime to compete with the confirmation ritual of both major denominations. However, most of this literature, according to Detlef Pollack, would not satisfy strict scholarly standards. It was only in the second half of the 1980s that really serious work on the sociology of religion in the GDR began, and pastors such as Erhart Neubert investigated the conditions for the reproduction of religion in RES.[92] Admittedly, conditions for scholarly investigation of church-oriented themes in the GDR were scarcely ideal, since there was the ever-present censorship, surveillance, and tutelage of the regime.

After the *Wende*, the historiography about the role of the church throughout the GDR, and especially during the final months, is really about establishing how, to what degree, and in what manner the churches were involved in the dissident movement. Did opposition emerge from the church milieu, or was it carried into the church by activists from outside who, in effect, forced the church to make available its resources as a base for opposition? What, too, was the real effect of the *Stasi* attempt to infiltrate and undermine the church? Revelations about these attempts illustrate just how incompatible with RES the presence of the Christian churches was in the mind of the SED regime. The fact that they could not be forced into a mere ghetto existence (*Nischendasein*) further indicates that at least some bishops and pastors were capable of standing up to the authorities.

Three Models of Explanation

To date, three representative models of explanation suggest themselves from the current literature, each with legitimate claims to scholarship on the subject of to what extent the church actually succeeded in frustrating the attempt to build a society in East Germany on the principles of Marxism-Leninism. They are the models of comparative totalitarianism, system theory, and milieu theory.[93]

The totalitarianism school attempts to analyze the dictatorship of RES in the GDR against the background of the "church struggle" in the Nazi dictatorship. On the surface, it seems to be a reasonable line to pursue, since the forty years of GDR dictatorship followed in virtually seamless continuity from the Nazi period. Under both regimes, the church had to struggle against the state's claims to omnipotence in all spheres of existence. The custodians of the Gospel were, in both instances, challenged to make a stand in order to survive. In both instances, the totalitarian regimes foundered on church resistance. Further, both regimes represented rival religions that sought to capture the hearts and minds of the population. The opposition of the Christian churches under these circumstances was inevitable, and in both instances, the individuals who wielded political power had clearly made false assessments of the ability of Christians to resist the official state ideology. The comparison, however, of the two German dictatorships and their respective church policies cannot be pressed too far. For example, the manner in which the Nazis persecuted the churches cannot be satisfactorily compared with the post-1945 communist "system of bureaucratic obstruction."[94] In addition, the nature of the communist dictatorship was different. Whereas the Nazis wielded power ruthlessly to enforce the leader's will, without reference to any restraints, communism, relying on the persuasive power of doctrines that most citizens inwardly rejected, shrank into a mere administrative "cartel for the maintenance of power." So the power structures of the two dictatorships were radically different, and this showed the asymmetry in the architecture of comparative dictatorship research. Can the history of the GDR be analyzed as a process of fading totalitarianism, that is, a system in which the "authorities" had increasingly forfeited their legitimacy, or their ability to command loyalty? An illustration of this is provided by the following popular saying from the 1980s, which reflects the humorous equanimity and resignation of the population with regard to the ridiculous contradictions in the system and, consequently, their immunity to its propaganda:

> Although there are no unemployed citizens, only half of them are working. Although only half actually work, all economic plans were over-fulfilled. Although all plans were over-fulfilled, there is nothing to buy in the shops. Although there is nothing to buy, the population have more than they need. Although they have more than they need, they still grumble and criticize the government. And although they criticize the government, they still give it 99.9% support at election time.[95]

Such a system had very little chance of "converting" the population to "new species beings," that is, citizens of a communist totalitarianism. This is a very different situation from that "enjoyed" by Germans in the "national community" (*Volksgemeinschaft*) under the Nazis. Indeed, there were many factors that rendered the comparative totalitarianism model for treating the history of the GDR virtually useless. The duration of the Nazi regime was only twelve years; that of the GDR some forty years. The degrees and nature of repression differed, as did the degree of social acceptance. Other major factors, such as differences in law, justice, constitution, economy, property and production relationships, and ideology, all make a meaningful comparison of the two dictatorships questionable. Nevertheless, there is clearly a case for regarding the history of the churches under both regimes as a useful tool of comparison.

Without doubt, the two main churches, Roman and Protestant, in both German dictatorships refused to bend to the states' claim to omnipotence. In doing so, they preserved their identity as custodians of a value system that had no choice but to resist systems that denied the fundamental tenets of Christianity. It is a historical fact that both National Socialism and communism wished to eliminate the churches for ideological reasons but failed to accomplish that goal. Indeed, only the churches possessed the inner resources to resist the totalitarian state doggedly and permanently. The churches represent a sphere of autonomy that not even dictatorships can successfully invade, although the preservation of this sphere has its price. To this extent, then, the totalitarianism model has its place in research.

The system theory model is strongly represented by Detlef Pollack, who is indebted to the sociological theories of Niklas Luhmann.[96] The system constructed by the SED regime in the GDR was designed to produce long-term stability, but paradoxically, it created an irresolvable state of instability. However, it cannot adequately be described as a politically manipulated system of oppression; it was also a "semi-modern industrial society," which inevitably reproduced individuals who were the indispensable technical experts, be they in the realm of science, education, the law, the arts, the economy, and even the political system itself.[97]

Naturally, the regime tried to suppress all striving for autonomy on behalf of these groups. But their very existence ensured that the GDR was not the "dead" society it may have appeared to be from the outside; rather, it was a society full of contradictions and tensions. Stability was secured under these circumstances by four factors. The first was the omnipresence of the Soviet Union, which guaranteed the continued existence of the SED regime. Second, the SED exercised a one-sided monopoly on power and on the distribution of resources. All decision making in the economic, legal, political, military, police, and cultural spheres was concentrated in one body. No social group could aspire to autonomy with any hope of realizing it. Also, numerous sources of potential opposition had been expelled. Pollack comments on the irony of this situation by pointing out that the regime could have used to advantage the initiatives and creativity of these groups, but through its doctrinaire shortsightedness, it robbed itself of their potentially valuable services and created vast areas of discontent.

The third factor of stabilization was the system of rewards and punishments that the SED regime set up to encourage the population to internalize the doctrines of Marxism-Leninism. All action in society was monitored to see that it conformed to the party program. If it did not, those thus accused had to reckon with political detention. This meant that society was divided according to a friend-enemy pattern that allowed no room for those who would prefer to remain neutral on ideological issues. Under these circumstances, the role of the *Stasi* loomed large in the GDR. The system would not have functioned without the all-encompassing and costly surveillance apparatus of this agency. However, its effect was ambivalent. Admittedly, the *Stasi* guaranteed outward conformity from the vast majority of the population, but inwardly, people withdrew into the private sphere and wished to have as little as possible to do with the state.

The fourth stabilizing factor was the closed nature of the system. GDR society was virtually hermetically sealed off from the outside world, especially the capitalist West. No one could leave it, so all had to come to terms with it. There was no way for the population (for example, via emigration) to express discontent with the system. This meant that the wishes of the population never had to be taken into account by the authorities, who, in doctrinaire and brutal naïveté, busied themselves with the implementation of their often irrational policies.

Pollack rightly observes that after the construction of the Berlin Wall, the GDR regime never had cause to "correct" its course, and this had serious results. It crippled the ability to learn by comparison and, consequently, the ability to engage in realistic negotiations with the West. The effect on the population was, on the one hand, to make them totally dependent on the regime, but on the other, to make the Western lifestyle the norm for the good life. The enforced isolation from the West actually strengthened the population's orientation toward it.

With these observations, Pollack underpins his thesis of the society "organized from above." However—and this is his central point—no industrial society can remain a closed organizational system manipulated from above. There will always be an "unorganized" remainder that demands institutionalization. In modern industrial societies based on the Western model, political parties, trade unions, and associations take care of the needs of professional groups within society. In the GDR, the "system" occupied these areas, with the result that society was split between a dictatorial leadership, omnipotent and omnipresent, and a population that was not permitted to articulate its interests.

This split, indeed gulf, in GDR society "led to a deficit in modernization" that affected all social groups.[98] Simultaneously, there developed a network of communication beyond the officially permitted channels that enabled the supply of certain goods and services, as well as places of retreat that were free from state interference, where a critical political-cultural discourse could take place. Naturally, one of the main places for this process was the church. In fact, churches were in a unique position, not having been entirely forced by the regime into a niche existence. Further, they had not closed their doors on dialogue, be it with government agencies or with dissident groups. By occupying this position, according to Pollack, they made manifest the basic social contradictions of GDR society that the regime had tried to paper over. They became, indeed, the locations where social conflicts were confronted, and articulate churchmen became the advocates of modernization and of social change.

By 1989, when the external stabilizing factors disappeared and the system began to break down, the regime's techniques for maintaining control became increasingly ineffective. This became overtly apparent when the fraudulent municipal elections of 1989 were openly criticized by churchmen in particular.[99] By then, the latent social differences were out in the open, and the dissident groups that met in churches began to demand reforms. Political initiative was wrenched from the discredited regime via the churches. This could happen because their position in the system enabled them to provide the space needed for mass protest and to mediate the transition.

Pollack stops short of describing these events as a "Protestant Revolution" but calls them "the collapse of an artificially sustained and consequently fragile social structure that had been kept viable through enforced isolation from external influences and internally repressive measures."[100] Admittedly, the churches played a decisive role at the time of the collapse, but afterward, they receded into the political background.

However, there are those who are equally emphatic that it is justified to label the events of 1989–90 in the GDR a "Protestant Revolution." Chief among these is Erhart Neubert.[101] He certainly shares Pollack's analysis of the GDR as an "organization society," but he sees a greater ideological-theological-cultural factor at work that was uniquely Protestant. That is to say, the enforced socialism of Marxism-Leninism had to provoke the opposition of East Germans, most of whom were Protestant, at least through their upbringing, and had internalized the Protestant social ethic. To them, the system was fundamentally alien. However, systematic ideological opposition to it was possible only through those pastors who had inherited the legacy of the great Lutheran theologian and opponent of National Socialism, Dietrich Bonhoeffer. Consequently, when one investigated the situation from parish to parish and from city to city in the GDR, one would find pastors and lay collaborators everywhere who became activist opponents of the regime. All other contributing factors notwithstanding, this Protestant-inspired activism was an essential prerequisite for the timing and nature of the revolution.

Through the appeal to Protestant theology, in particular Bonhoeffer's, as a determining factor in the behavior of pastors and their supporters, Neubert has introduced a complication into the explanation that not all scholars are willing to take into account.[102]

With Christoph Klessmann's milieu theory, we find an allied form of explanation that focuses sharply on the deeply entrenched tradition sustained in Protestant parsonages, church schools, and Protestant social (*Diakonie*) and youth work, all of which was existentially challenged by Marxism-Leninism. That it managed to survive, albeit in much reduced form, in spite of the best efforts of the regime to marginalize such traditional elements enabled the church to play the role described by Pollack and Neubert. By drawing attention to this factor, Klessmann has added a new explanatory dimension that goes beyond the restrictions of mere political history. In the church milieu, the durability and resistance of old structures and mentalities, modes of behavior, and values were preserved under the shell of so-called socialist progress.

Klessmann's work, though only in its infancy, constitutes a valuable methodological impulse for a range of detailed investigations that are bound to come. As if to provide a basis for this kind of research, an extensive and detailed study of the milieu of Protestant pastors in Prussia from 1850 to 1914 recently appeared from the pen of the West Berlin historian Oliver Janz. Called *Citizens of a Special Kind*, it is a pioneering social-historical examination of a group of people who exerted considerable influence directly and indirectly on the spiritual and political values of millions of their countrymen and -women.[103] This did not suddenly evaporate with the imposition of either the Nazi or the communist dictatorship.

Finally, no survey of the present topic can fail to mention the impressive, though controversial, work of West German (Heidelberg) church historian Gerhard Besier. He attracted angry attention with his collection of *Stasi* documents that revealed the extent of the secret "collaboration" of certain church people with the regime, and he has now compiled a massive narrative illustrating that the church in the GDR largely betrayed its Gospel calling in order to merely survive. It "adapted" to the Godless regime.[104]

Not unexpectedly, the work of Besier represents a massive reproach to many bishops, pastors, and laity in the former GDR, many of whom have felt obliged to state their side of the story in autobiographies and in published conference proceedings devoted to the issue.[105] In this way, the historiography of the church in the GDR has become highly politicized, as has the entire history of the SED regime. Nowhere has this fact been more in evidence than in the so-called *Enquete-Kommission* (Commission of Inquiry) report to the German parliament on the subject of assessing the history of the GDR.[106] Here, each element in GDR society has been subjected to the investigation of expert committees of historians, and their findings have been presented to the *Bundestag*. They consist of majority reports coupled with minority reports sponsored by the opposition. The reports on the role of the churches in the GDR and in the *Wende* illustrate once again that in Germany, history can be especially partisan. As none other than Jürgen Kocka recently observed, commenting specifically on the *Enquete-Kommission* report: "In the treatment of the GDR past at the present time, history and politics are unusually tightly intertwined. In the [report] the scientific establishment of truth and the process of the formation of political will are curiously linked."[107]

Indeed, the many parties involved in the emotion-charged history of the divided Germany since 1945 want to make certain that their specific roles will be shown in the best possible light. As the historiography of the role of the church illustrates, it is hard to conceive of it being otherwise.

NOTES

1. See *Forschungsprojekte zur DDR-Geschichte. Ergebnisse einer Umfrage des Arbeitsbereiches DDR-Geschichte im Mannheimer Zentrum für Europäische Sozialforschung (MZES) der Universität Mannheim*, compiled by Thomas Heimann with Ralf Eicher and Stefan Wortmann, Bonn, 1993.
2. The publication of a large selection of secret documents relating to dealings of church officials with the Ministry for State Security of the former GDR created a storm of indignation in church circles. See Gerhard Besier and Stefan Wolf, *Pfarrer, Christen und Katholiken*, (2d rev. and exp. ed.), Neukirchen-Vluyn, 1992. Many were and are deeply unhappy about Besier's interpretation of this material. Erhart Neubert addressed the problem in his *Vergebung oder Weisswäscherei—Zur Aufarbeitung des Stasiproblems in den Kirchen*, Freiburg im Breisgau, 1993. For a comprehensive and lucid English-language analysis of this question, see John S. Conway, "The *Stasi* and the Churches: Between Coercion and

Compromise in East German Protestantism, 1949–89," *Journal of Church and State* 36 (Fall 1994): 725–45. Most useful in this context is Arnim Kistenbrügge, "Wahrnehmungsfelder der Situation von Kirche und Theologie in den neuen Ländern der Bundesrepublik Deutschland," *Verkündigung und Forschung* 38, no. 2 (1993): 29–58, in which the reactions of theologians in the former GDR to the *Stasi* revelations are assessed.

3. See Erhart Neubert, *Untersuchungen zu den Vorwürfen gegen den Ministerpräsidenten des Landes Brandenburg Dr. Manfred Stolpe*, Potsdam, 1993.

4. Luther's theology was a powerful reaffirmation of Augustine's defense of the doctrine of original sin as expounded in *Civitas Dei*. Luther understood the world as being divided between the Kingdom of God, in which true Christians are nurtured by their faith and the grace of the Lord, and the temporal kingdom, which belonged to the state. The latter was a necessity, since the great majority of humankind was sinful and had to be cajoled or repressed by state authority. Cf. Timothy Lull (ed.), *Martin Luther's Basic Theological Writings*, Minneapolis, 1989, 655–703.

5. Robert F. Goeckel, *The Lutheran Church and the East German State—Political Conflict and Change Under Ulbricht and Honecker*, Ithaca and London, 1990, 17.

6. This conception of state and society gave rise to the Calvinist conception of the *Corpus Christianum*. Cf. Ernst Troeltsch, *The Social Teachings of the Christian Churches*, 2 vols., Louisville, 1992, 2: 617.

7. Robert M. Bigler, *The Politics of German Protestantism—The Rise of the Protestant Church Elite in Prussia, 1815–1848*, Berkeley, Los Angeles, and London, 1972, passim.

8. Cf. Fritz Fischer,"Der Deutsche Protestantismus und die Politik im 19. Jahrhundert," in Helmut Böhme (ed.), *Probleme der Reichsgründungszeit, 1848–1879*, Cologne and Berlin, 1968, 49–71.

9. Hans-Heinz Krill, *Die Rankerenaissance—Max Lenz und Erich Marcks. Ein Beitrag zum historisch politischen Denken in Deutschland, 1880–1935*, Berlin, 1962, passim.

10. On Barth, see John Bowden, *Karl Barth*, London, 1983.

11. Cited in Goeckel, *Lutheran Church*, 31

12. Ibid.

13. Ibid.

14. Cf. Otto Dibelius, *Ein Christ ist immer im Dienst*, Berlin, 1961. On Dibelius, see Klaus Scholder, "Otto Dibelius (1880–1980)," *Zeitschrift für Theologie und Kirche* 78, no. 1 (1981): 90–104.

15. Gregory W. Sandford, *From Hitler to Ulbricht—The Communist Reconstruction of East Germany, 1945–46*, Princeton, 1983, 48–50.

16. Goeckel, *Lutheran Church*, 42; cf. Lothar Kettenacker, "Church and Dictatorship: The German Churches under Nazi and SED Rule" (Conference Report), *German Historical Institute London—Bulletin* 15, no. 1 (1993): 40–6.

17. Ibid.

18. Cf. W. R. Ward, *Theology, Sociology and Politics—The German Protestant Social Conscience 1890–1933*, Bern, Frankfurt, and Las Vegas, 1979, passim; James Bentley, *Between Marx and Christ—The Dialogue in German Speaking Europe, 1870–1970*, London, 1972.

19. Cf. Gerald Götting, *Christians and Politics in the German Democratic Republic*, East Berlin, 1966, passim; Gerald Götting, *Der Christ beim Aufbau des Sozialismus*, East Berlin, 1963, passim.

20. Cf. Günter Erbe et al., *Politik, Wirtschaft und Gesellschaft in der DDR*, Opladen, 1978, 124–6.

21. Goeckel, *Lutheran Church*, 43.

22. Horst Dähn, *Konfrontation oder Kooperation? Das Verhältnis von Staat und Kirche in der SBZ/DDR, 1945–1980*, Opladen, 1982, 23.

23. For the confessional allegiance of the East German population, see Goeckel, *Lutheran Church*, 21.

24. Dähn, *Konfrontation*, 35

25. G. Heidtmann (ed.), *Hat die Kirche geschwiegen? Das öffentliche Wort der evangelischen Kirche aus den Jahren, 1945–1964*, 3d ed., Berlin, 1964, 122.

26. Kurt Gust, "East German Protestantism Under Communist Rule, 1945–1961," Ph.D. thesis, University of Kansas, 1966, 64.

27. Hermann Weber, *Geschichte der DDR*, 3rd ed., Munich, 1989, 232–4.

28. Cf. Patrick Michel, *Politics and Religion—Catholicism in Hungary, Poland and Czechoslovakia*, trans. Alan Braley, Cambridge, 1991, passim.

29. Goeckel, *Lutheran Church*, 73.

30. Cf. Weber, *Geschichte der DDR*, 234–6.

31. Alexander Fischer (ed.), *Die Deutsche Demokratische Republik—Daten, Fakten, Analysen*, Würzburg and Freiburg, 1987, 185.

32. Gust, "East German Protestantism," 77.

33. *Kirchliches Jahrbuch, 1953*, cited in Gust, "East German Protestantism," 78.

34. Gust, "East German Protestantism," 81.

35. Goeckel, *Lutheran Church*, 50. For the Catholic Church's view of the *Jugendweihe* see Klemens Richter, "Jugendweihe und Katholische Kirche," *Deutschland Archiv* 20 (1987): 168–80. The SED's attempt to frustrate the youth work of the churches in 1950–53 is examined in detail by Hermann Wentker, "'Kirchenkampf' in der DDR: Der Konflikt um die junge Gemeinde 1950–1953," *Vierteljahreshefte für Zeitgeschichte* 42, no. 1 (1994): 95–127.

36. Goeckel, *Lutheran Church*.

37. Ibid.

38. Ibid.

39. *Kirchliches Jahrbuch*, 17–8.

40. *Pravda*, 11 November 1954, cited in Gust, "East German Protestantism," 79.

41. Kurt Hager, "Über den wissenschaftlich-atheistischen Charakter unserer Weltanschauung," *Einheit* 4 (April 1955), cited in Gust, "East German Protestantism," 79.

42. Cf. Weber, *Geschichte der DDR*, 255–9.

43. Goeckel, *Lutheran Church*, 82. Besier and Wolf, *Pfarrer, Christen und Katholiken*, 11.

44. Besier and Wolf, *Pfarrer, Christen und Katholiken*, 11.

45. Ibid., 12–3.

46. Scholder, "Dibelius," 102–3.

47. "Die ideologische Entwicklung in der DDR," *Kirche in der Zeit* 6, 190, cited in Gust, "East German Protestantism," 64.

48. Goeckel, *Lutheran Church*, 54. For an account of these years, see Heinrich Grüber, *Erinnerungen aus sieben Jahrzehnten*, 2nd ed., Berlin and Cologne, 1968, 384–401.
49. Goeckel, *Lutheran Church*, 54.
50. Ibid., 56–85.
51. Ibid., 58
52. Ibid., 59–60; Otto Luchterhandt, *Die Gegenwartslage der Evangelischen Kirche in der DDR—Eine Einführung*, Tübingen, 1982, 16.
53. Goeckel, *Lutheran Church*, 59–60; cf. Franz Henrich (ed.), *Humanismus zwischen Christentum und Marxismus*, Munich, 1970, passim.
54. Goeckel, *Lutheran Church*, 60.
55. Cf. Scholder, "Dibelius."
56. Luchterhandt, *Gegenwartslage*, 20. See also Deutscher Bundestag (ed.), *Bericht der Enquete-Kommission "Aufarbeitung von Geschichte und Folgen der SED-Diktatur in Deutschland"* (Drucksache 12/7820, 31.05.94), 161.
57. Cf. Gerhard Besier and Gerhard Sauter, *Wie Christen ihre Schuld bekennen— Die Stuttgarter Erklärung 1945*, Göttingen, 1985, passim.
58. Luchterhandt, *Gegenwartslage*, 23–4.
59. Goeckel, *Lutheran Church*, 68
60. Ibid., 67.
61. Ibid., 73.
62. Lothar de Maizière, "Zwischen Anpassung und Verweigerung— Konsequenzen aus dem Leben in einem totalitären Staat," *Kirchliche Zeitgeschichte* 4, no. 1 (1991): 418.
63. Ibid.
64. Goeckel, *Lutheran Church*, 188.
65. Karl Wilhelm Fricke, *Opposition und Widerstand in der DDR—Ein politischer Report*, Cologne, 1984, 192–3.
66. Rudolf Bahro, *Die Alternative—Zur Kritik des real existierenden Sozialismus*, Frankfurt, 1977. Cf. Weber, *Geschichte der DDR*, 445–9, 490–1.
67. Luchterhandt, *Gegenwartslage*, 41.
68. J. K. A. Thomanek and James Melis (eds.), *Politics, Society and Government in the German Democratic Republic: Basic Documents*, Oxford, New York, and Munich, 1989, 160–1.
69. Ibid., 161.
70. Cf. Goeckel, *Lutheran Church*, 285–6.
71. *Martin Luther und unsere Zeit, Konstituierung des Martin-Luther-Komitees der DDR am 13. Juni 1980 in Berlin*, Berlin, 1980, passim.
72. Eckart Förtsch, "Revision des Preußenbildes—Ein neuer wissenschaftlicher Ansatz in der DDR," *Deutschland Archiv*, 12 (1979): 168 ff.
73. See Brent O. Peterson, "'Workers of the World Unite—For God's Sake!'" Recent Luther Scholarship in the German Democratic Republic," in James D. Tracy (ed.), *Luther and the Modern State in Germany*, Kirksville, 1986, 77–9.
74. Cf. Johannes Kuppe, "Die Geschichtsschreibung der SED im Umbruch," *Deutschland Archiv* 18 (1985): 278–94.
75. For a comparative study of the peace movement in the FRG and the GDR, see Helmut Zander, *Die Christen und die Friedensbewegung in beiden deutschen Staaten— Beiträge zu einem Vergleich für die Jahre 1978–1987*, Berlin, 1989.

76. See Fricke, *Opposition und Widerstand*, 189–204.
77. Cf. Gerhard Lehmbruch, "The Process of Regime Church in East Germany," in Christopher Anderson et al. (eds.), *The Domestic Politics of German Unification*, Boulder and London, 1993, 22.
78. Goeckel, *Lutheran Church*, 272.
79. For an account of the political and moral momentum built up by the agreements signed at the Conference on Security and Cooperation in Europe at Helsinki in 1975, see Uwe Thaysen, "The GDR on Its Way to Democracy," in Dieter Grosser (ed.), *German Unification—The Unexpected Challenge*, Oxford and Providence, 1992, 79.
80. Ibid., 272.
81. Dennis L. Bark and David R. Gress (eds.), *A History of West Germany—Democracy and Its Discontents, 1963–1991*, 2nd ed., Oxford, 1993, 594.
82. Ibid., 620.
83. Goeckel, *Lutheran Church*, 272.
84. For an account of the developments of October and November 1989, see Hannelore Horn, "Collapse from Internal Weakness—The GDR from October 1989 to Unification," in Grosser (ed.), *German Unification*, 55–71.
85. Goeckel, *Lutheran Church*, 174
86. Ibid., 174–5.
87. Ibid.
88. Detlef Pollack, *Kirche in der Organisationsgesellschaft—Zum Wandel der gesellschaftlichen Lage der evangelischen Kirchen in der DDR*, Stuttgart, 1994, 15.
89. See the list of contributions by Henkys to most aspects of church affairs in the GDR in *Christen, Staat und Gesellschaft*, edited by Gert Kaiser and compiled and commented on by Ewald Frie, Düsseldorf, 1993. Also see the bibliography in Pollack, *Kirche in der Organisationsgesellschaft*.
90. Pollack, *Kirche in der Organisationsgesellschaft*, 16.
91. Personal communication to the author by Dr. Neubert. See also the text of the inside back cover of his *Untersuchungen*.
92. Pollack, *Kirche in der Organisationsgesellschaft*, 18.
93. See Frie's introduction to *Christen, Staat und Gesellschaft*, 9, now also revised in article form as "Geschichte der Kirchen in der DDR. Neuerscheinungen im Jahre 1993," *Neue Politische Literatur*, November 1994.
94. The leading protagonists of the comparative totalitarianism school are Lothar Kettenacker, Günther Heydemann, and Hans Meier. Their research was ventilated, along with a variety of other contributions, at a conference organized by the German Historical Institute, London, and held in the Augustiner Kloster, Erfurt, 10–12 December 1992. The proceedings appeared as *Kirchen in der Diktatur*, Göttingen, 1993, edited by Heydemann and Kettenacker.
95. Cited after de Maizière, "Zwischen Anpassung und Verweigerung," 416–7.
96. See Frie's comment in his introduction to *Christen, Staat und Gesellschaft*, 10. For a comprehensive list of Luhmann's works, see the bibliography of Pollack's *Kirche in der Organisationsgesellschaft*, 485–6.
97. Detlef Pollack, "Der Umbruch in der DDR—eine protestantische

Revolution?" in Trutz Rendtdorff (ed.), *Protestantische Revolution?*, Göttingen, 1993, 43. There, he notes: "The GDR was not only a politically manipulated regime designed to suppress (*Unterdrückungsregime*) but also a semi-modern industrial society."

98. Ibid., 57–58, and Pollack, "Religion und gesellschaftlicher Wandel. Zur Rolle der evangelischen Kirchen im Prozess des gesellschaftlichen Umbruchs in der DDR," in Hans Joas and Martin Kohli (eds.), *Der Zusammenbruch der DDR. Soziologische Analysen*, Frankfurt, 1993, 253.

99. Ibid., 256. For example, the churches admonished the government after the blatantly rigged results of the municipal elections of 7 May 1989, stating that such obvious deceit on the part of the government would not be conducive to a just and peaceful society. On the contrary: "The authority and stability of the state required openness and honesty" (256).

100. Pollack, "Der Umbruch in der DDR," 71.

101. Neubert is the author of numerous books and articles that reflect his total commitment to his Lutheran upbringing. His contribution is thus of immeasurable value in that it, more than any other, highlights the religious-theological dimension in the formation of oppositional political will in the GDR. See his *Eine Protestantische Revolution*, Osnabrück, 1990.

102. It will be necessary for secular historians to make some effort to enter the world of ideas of committed Christians and to develop a methodology that enables them to take into account the undoubted effect that belief or faith can have on the social and political action of individuals. See Pollack's comment on this question in *Kirche in der Organisationsgesellschaft* (20), where he notes his concern with theologians who maintain that people motivated by their Christian commitment to political activism cannot be assessed by sociological method. This was so because matters of faith were sui generis, and motives were explicable only through faith. Pollack, a sociologist of religion, is clearly not at ease with this assertion by some theologians. On the legacy of Dietrich Bonhoeffer for the attitude of the churches in the former GDR to the regime, see Wolf Krötke, "Dietrich Bonhoeffer als Theologe der DDR. Ein kritischer Rückblick," in Rendtorff (ed.), *Protestantische Revolution*, 295–309.

103. Oliver Janz, *Bürger besonderer Art—Evangelische Pfarrer in Preussen 1850–1914*, Berlin and New York, 1994. For an introduction to Klessmann's contributions, see his "Zur Sozialgeschichte des protestantischen Milieus in der DDR," *Geschichte und Gesellschaft* 19 (1993): 29–53.

104. See note 2 above and Gerhard Besier, *Der SED-Staat und die Kirche. Der Weg in die Anpassung*, Munich, 1994.

105. See the discussion of this genre in Frie, *Christen, Staat und Gesellschaft*, 18–23.

106. *Bericht der Enquete-Kommission "Aufarbeitung von Geschichte und Folgen der SED-Diktatur in Deutschland"* (Drucksache 12/7820), 31 May 1994. The role and self-perception of the church in the various phases of the SED dictatorship are dealt with on pp. 158–88.

107. Jürgen Kocka, "Ein deutscher Sonderweg—Überlegungen zur Sozialgeschichte der DDR," *Aus Politik und Zeitgeschichte* 40 (October 1994): 34.

12

The Path to Academic Freedom: An East German Perspective

SIEGFRIED HOYER

One of the many statements on "coming to terms with the past in the German Democratic Republic" declares that it is the role of the historian "to rummage about in the past, to prevent things lapsing into oblivion, and to bring to light even unpleasant facts."[1] The words fail to convey how emotionally loaded the issue is. Only slowly are fundamental investigations into various areas of GDR society being undertaken; the universities are not one of the preferred topics. For the outside observer, it is difficult to comprehend how the GDR universities operated until 1989, vastly different as they were from the universities of the "old" Federal Republic and of most European countries in terms of the style of teaching and the place of the individual student within the university. The following report on the History Department at the Karl Marx University of Leipzig suffers from the fact that the author himself was personally involved; he not only experienced but also helped shape the course of events there. To reconsider critically one's own positions with the benefit of hindsight is a process fraught with difficulties.

The universities and technical colleges of the GDR in the second half of the 1980s were shaped by the Third University Reform Bill of 1968. It was not until this time that the highest institutions of learning were incorporated into the "unitary socialist education system." With it, an old dream of the workers' movement was realized—from the cradle to the university, education was to be imparted according to one plan and one goal, namely, the creation of the socialist human being. Tertiary education and research from that point were a component of a central economic plan. This prevented academic autonomy, which in any case, having been removed by the Nazis in 1933, had not been reestablished in the Soviet occupation zone after the war, and it also meant the loss of any kind of independence in university life. The administrative division between a Ministry of Education and a Ministry of Higher and Technical Education did nothing to conceal this.

In recent times, the year of the Third University Reform Bill, 1968, has been nostalgically linked with the left-wing revolts in Europe from Paris to Prague.[2] Was the GDR not responding to the pressures of modernization with "progressive" changes? Was not the removal of the old university structures (institutes and faculties) in favor of a structure comparable with the U.S. department system evidence of this? This interpretation is false in two respects. First, the precondition for reform, namely, the unitary socialist education system, had already become law on 25 February 1965 after being passed by the parliament.[3] Research quite correctly links the role of this law not only with the goal of uniformity of education in the GDR but also with a turning away from the brief period of de-Stalinization, with a broader choice of subjects and the adoption of reformist pedagogical ideas.[4] At that point, structural changes were imposed to ensure greater influence for the Socialist Unity Party (SED) in all disciplines, so that even small individual disciplines were more thoroughly permeated with Marxism-Leninism. One critical observer wisely viewed the university reform as a "time for changing or even removing the profiles of academic disciplines which appeared dispensable for the further development of socialist society."[5]

From the end of the 1960s, the selection of students for university study began with the switch to a two-year extended high school, because in principle, every student completing school was supposed to be allowed to study. This also applied to that section of the student population (25 percent) who, in addition to preparing for their school-leaving certificates, completed vocational training and accordingly took three years to follow this path. This training was to help prepare students to study technical and scientific subjects, although such students often became education or economics students. In these areas, the plan quotas had not been reached, and unfilled places were available.

One year after their entry into the extended high school program, or two years after beginning vocational training, students had to submit their applications for university study. Thereafter, a change in the chosen field of study was possible only in exceptional circumstances (for example, ill health) or if the prescribed enrollment numbers had been exceeded. At this point, an attempt was made to steer the applicant toward other subjects where places were still available, that is, to coax the applicant to agree to enroll in another area. This rigid planning mechanism led to a situation in which students barely identified with their subjects and were largely passive, because there was little place for their own initiative in shaping their future careers. The student was a planning unit; with incalculable intentions and barely controllable external influences of all kinds, the individual was the greatest disruptive factor.[6] Refusal to complete the by now obligatory military service or unwillingness to perform was dealt with much more severely than a failure in exams or an obvious incapacity to perform satisfactorily that might become evident in the course of study.

The ramifications of this process of schooling, of acquired conformity and of perfect control over the path of study in a manner that stressed attendance at the expense of creativity and critical thinking, were most evident in the education of future teachers. From the beginning of the 1980s, some fifty to sixty history teachers were enrolled at the Karl Marx University in Leipzig, for whom German was the prescribed second subject. The German Department took on roughly the same number of students for whom history was their second subject. All of them studied in preparation for employment at the polytechnic secondary schools. Despite the employment security and the salary, this was not considered particularly attractive employment, because, as became increasingly apparent in everyday life, teachers in the GDR did not have access to privileges and perquisites, even if they climbed the lower steps of the educational hierarchy. They remained in the iron grip of the orthodox leadership of the system. The educational authorities reserved for themselves the right to "delegate" teachers to another institution; outstanding academic achievement or a doctorate was not the primary requirement but rather proven practical performance and, of course, political devotion. In most cases, it was just possible to fill the annual figure for the enrollment of teachers with the applicants. More than half, and often more than 75 percent, of them were women. The most intelligent students had a chance to avoid the normal course of study by enrolling for a research degree course, which, after the first degree, would lead to a doctorate in three years. They would then be able to take up a position at a university or other academic institution.

The two other courses offered by the History Department trained teachers of Marxism-Leninism (history of the workers' movement) and diploma of history students. The latter were to work in publishing houses, museums, and other such institutions. In these two courses, the academic and political substance was different, although the need to apply early and to comply politically was the same; without completing these courses, an extended high school was inaccessible. Only students with outstanding academic records had a chance to enroll in the diploma of history course; every second year in Leipzig, the twenty places in that course were filled from among five to seven times that number of applicants.

In the 1980s, most of those who left school came from secondary school, only rarely via the so-called second path (*zweiter Bildungsweg*). For acceptance into the university, the student's grade average from all school subjects and the school's assessment of the student's personality and his or her social commitment played a large role. To enter the final round, very high grades in the chosen subject, in German, and in a foreign language were required. In many cases, though, the language competence suggested by the grade was at odds with actual performance. Most were in a position neither to converse in Russian nor to read anything more difficult than a basic text. Final decisions on entry were made by a commission at the university (for students training to become teachers) or within the department (for diploma of history students and teachers of Marxism-Leninism). It was possible to protest nonacceptance, and this was done successfully in some circumstances.

For future teachers of Marxism-Leninism, the ministry prescribed three years of work experience at a "social institution" such as a youth organization, a union, or some other "mass organization." Three years of military service was recognized as an adequate prerequisite. These students entered the university at the age of twenty-two at the earliest and brought with them their impressions of the political workings of "real socialism." From their ranks came critical minds that examined any discrepancy between reality and the claims made daily in the media. They reacted with sensitivity as the government's reports of success became increasingly shrill and when the gerontocracy at the helm of the GDR rejected the course of *perestroika* adopted by their "great friend and brother." But from the ranks of students of Marxism-Leninism also came rigid dogmatists for whom the world had come to an end.

The role of educating the students in history and providing intellectual stimulation fell to the professors and to the older assistants who were engaged in teaching. They taught according to a set plan that determined both the content and the number of students. At the same time, there was room for related topics, provided the student, much like the visitor to the land of the milk and honey (in the Grimms' fairy tale), could eat his way through the bland-tasting porridge.

In 1968, the History Departments (in the case of Leipzig, these included Departments of Pre-History, Ancient History, and Medieval History) had a staff of nine professors, two lecturers, and thirty-seven assistants. The areas of interest pursued by the staff covered every area adequately from the beginnings of history through to the contemporary period. Shortly before the end of the GDR, in 1988, the staff had more than doubled (with nineteen professors, eight lecturers, and forty-five assistants), whereas the number of students had barely risen. The reasons for this growth need not be discussed here. The disproportions became particularly severe because of the "official" areas of recruitment. Eleven of the nineteen professors worked in the area of the German and the international workers' movements. It is true that some of them read and researched in other areas without arousing official disapproval; most notable were the areas of social history of the nineteenth and twentieth centuries, regional history, and the history of the Weimar Republic and the Nazi era.

The course plan had been dominated by "survey lectures," a relic of the Second University Reform (1951), covering history from the medieval to the contemporary period and divided into German and general history.[7] In the 1980s, this became less rigid in the upper years. Talented students were able to gain some latitude through "individual promotion" by professors. This included, among other things, an exemption from tiresome obligatory classes. Discussion of the topic of "legacy and tradition" in German history steered interested students toward themes and areas that had hitherto been avoided.[8] More widespread diplomatic recognition of the GDR and associated cultural agreements led to a cautious raising of the curtain behind which large sections of the recent history of the world had remained hidden.

Now creativity was demanded from the students and was promoted among the future teachers, albeit warily. One can take as an example a student who enrolled in 1988 and declared from the beginning that Chinese history interested him above all else. Sinology had first of all been "siphoned off" from Leipzig to Berlin in 1968 and later wasted away as part of a Department of African and Near Eastern Studies. The student learned modern Chinese and, when the fall of the wall and the introduction of a single German currency opened the world to him, he hitchhiked for several weeks via Siberia to China. However, after unification, his desire to study at a Chinese university for several semesters had cold water poured over it by a professor from the old Federal Republic. Before the selection panel, the professor explained to the student that he had been in a socialist country long enough and did not need to go to another one immediately.

Looking back on the period before 1989, considerable deficiencies stand out. In ten years at the History Department in Leipzig, second in size only to that at the Humboldt University, there was not a single course on the history of the United States and nothing on constitutional or legal history. Only sporadically and through a guest from Berlin was the history of the neighboring Federal Republic offered; relevant specialist literature on this topic was available in the fortunately well-stocked *Deutsche Bücherei* but was accessible only with a special permit. The so-called classics seminars caused a major problem in the course structure. In them, a piece of writing by Marx and Engels or by Lenin would be taken apart and discussed, much in the manner of biblical exegesis. At the same time, the discussion of modern international methodologies was totally neglected. The "history of the GDR" proceeded from one party conference resolution to the next, and the crucial inner conflicts of 1953, 1956, 1961, and 1968 were presented as malicious attacks by the class enemy. It is true that the students who had not been pampered by the extended high school confirmed that this was an intellectually stimulating situation, but on a very modest level. It should be added that in ten years, the History Departments in Leipzig did not have a single guest professor for one semester or longer—not even from the other eastern bloc states.

After 1989, the universities generally and the historians specifically were accused of not involving themselves in the growing crisis in the GDR and ultimately in the demonstrations on the streets of Leipzig.[9] No doubt this is true, with only a few exceptions. However, it cannot be a matter of excusing the failure to take sides; what is required is an attempt at an explanation. Reflection on the crisis produced varied patterns of behavior. The inner, political situation in the History Department in Leipzig, as far as it can be reconstructed from personal observations, was complex. In contrast to the comparable department at the Humboldt University in Berlin, there had been no expulsions of student groups for political reasons. It is true that considerable pressure was brought to bear on some students to sign up as reserve officers or to participate in compulsory "deployment," but refusal to cooperate had no administrative consequences. When a small group of Marxism-Leninism education students were going to be sent to a factory on "probation" for having sent a critical letter to the Central Committee of the SED in 1987, the head of the department was able to negotiate the punishment down to a verbal warning. Certainly the state security police had informants among students and staff; to this day, we do not know who they were. In any case, I would not like to get to know them, because they caused no public nor any other recognizable damage to individuals.

As at other universities in the GDR, the banning of the Soviet magazine *Sputnik*, increasing attacks on perestroika by the GDR press and prominent public figures, the massacre on the "Place of Heavenly Peace," and the subsequent visit by Egon Krenz in Beijing led to heated discussion, but not to action. Students began to produce a photocopied critical magazine, which was presented to the head of the department and the party secretary before publication. Political life became less active, yet before November 1989, neither resignations from the SED nor decisions to leave the country are recorded. Some of the teaching staff, the assistants, and the students publicly committed themselves to a renewal of society on a socialist basis. Others, also from these groups, avoided any commitment to the decrepit state. When the regional SED leadership mobilized its members to occupy the pews in the Nikolai Church before the Monday mass, so that the civil rights campaigners could not enter the church and organize themselves for a demonstration march, a large proportion of the members stayed home. More than just a few of them, however, remained "hardliners" and waited for the moment when the security forces would "restore order."

Superficially, the winter semester began at the University of Leipzig as if nothing out of the ordinary were occurring in the country. Passages from the "Annual Plan of the History Department for 1990," written in the late summer of 1989, today read like a message from another world.[10] But the universities were drawn into the chaos of events. How many participated in the weekly peace prayers in the Nikolai Church? How many worked in action groups to record the environmental degradation that was particularly severe in the Leipzig area? Until that point, such problems had been taboo in the media and for the state. From which areas did these critical minds tend to come? The numbers remain just as big a mystery now as the number of those who left the country at the last moment via Hungary or Czechoslovakia.

An important element in the broader picture of what was happening in these weeks was the leadership's crisis management. Incriminated functionaries, who in many cases had fallen into disrepute because of their rigid style of rule, had to make way for younger people from the lower ranks. A good number of these people still shape the "Left scene" in Leipzig today, centered on the PDS (Party of Democratic Socialism, the successor to the SED). The university newspaper, an organ of the local leadership of the SED, was permitted to call into doubt the results of local elections in early 1989.[11] Just a few months earlier, civil rights campaigners had been incarcerated and persecuted for such actions. Critics cautiously grabbed the "holy cows," such as the compulsory course on Marxism-Leninism, by the horns. The course was to become more attractive, perhaps even optional, but of course, as one article put it, one could not do without the analysis of Lenin's views on imperialism.[12] At the executive meeting of the Historians' Society of the GDR on 29 November 1989—by which time the borders had been open almost three weeks—one Leipzig professor of the history of the workers' movement summed up: "We 'victors of history' have not learnt to live with defeats." He continued: "It is not a matter of randomly abandoning positions on a disordered retreat but of setting up defensive positions to be held."[13] He overlooked the fact that the army was not in retreat but in a state of full advance.

Events overtook timid attempts by the old cadres in government and in the universities to introduce greater openness and reform. The winter semester of 1989–90 had not yet ended when, in the first free elections since 1946, the population of the GDR provided a majority vote for the party (CDU-East) that stood for rapid unification with the Federal Republic. On 4 April 1990, during the break between the winter semester and the summer semester, the Leipzig university newspaper, which meanwhile had become an "organ of the rector," reported: "The compulsory course in Marxism-Leninism is dead, and that is just as well! Hardly anyone will shed a tear for it. Instead of it there will be a general studies course."[14] In the same issue, readers learned that the rector had granted the leading North Rhine Westphalian CDU politician, Dr. Kurt Biedenkopf, a certificate of appointment to a guest chair in the faculty of economics. The Interdisciplinary Center, once the university's expensive show pony, "bade farewell to the revolution," as one report put it. What had happened in the previous year (1989) could not be reconciled with the Marxist-Leninist theory of revolution: after 1789 and then 1917, how could the "popular democratic revolutions" of 1989 represent the beginning of humanity's path to greater heights?

It was with the fall of the wall that it became clear that the universities and colleges of the GDR would have to subject themselves to comparisons. Were they, in their organization and in their academic standards, really ahead of their time, as the SED's political propaganda had always proclaimed? Already in 1989 there began a campaign "for our country," initiated originally by Christa Wolf, Stefan Heym, and others.[15] Soon the leadership of the SED was joining the appeal. It was displayed in the corridor of the History Department—

many signed it, but not all. The contrary position was formulated by a member of the executive committtee of the Liberal Democratic Party and claimed that a state that had been rescued by Russian tanks in 1953 and practically epitomized an absence of independence could certainly not be called "our country." That display was torn down the following day.

With the exception of the abandonment of the compulsory course in Marxism-Leninism, teaching continued as usual in the History Department during the summer semester of 1990. At the same time, however, a number of science and medical staff, as well as some linguists, came together in a reform group that demanded radical changes. In the History Department, the first changes came from below, from the students. They demanded the replacement of the entirely redundant youth group (FDJ) with a student council and student participation at all levels. The representatives of the student body and the head of the department were to declare their positions open for election. On the newly elected council, professors, middle-ranking staff, and students were equally represented, which meant that professors could be outvoted. Critical questions were directed to the lecturers: What is your view of these developments? Did you not have an entirely different view on this issue a year ago? One distinguished colleague, whom students challenged to a debate on "terror in revolutions," backed out.

Most prominent among the students were the diploma of history students and some of the Marxism-Leninism education students. What were their motives? Having grown up within the constraints of the GDR's educational system, they saw the opportunity to determine their own course of study, perhaps even to obtain a degree that would be recognized across Europe. They pressed for critical discussion and demanded a role in student affairs, which had been denied them until that time by the FDJ. Only a limited number of them became involved in politics. Few of them joined the newly founded parties; more were interested in the goal of a reformed socialism. Existential needs and the disappearance of their subject forced those who had enrolled as Marxism-Leninism education students to battle for integration into historical studies, a battle that they eventually won.

In the summer of 1990, the universities in the GDR hit the headlines in the East and the West. Indeed, until that point, very little had changed. "The end of the gentle change" was signaled in Leipzig with a bang.[16] On 5 June, a group of scientists requested support from the education minister of the last GDR government, because all key positions at the Karl Marx University were still occupied by those who had assumed their positions before the fall of 1989.[17] A council initiated by these academics was to lend credibility to attempts at democratic reform. By telegram, the minister decreed the formation of a new rectoral college consisting of the pro-rector for medicine (representing the rector) and the deans of the medical and theological faculties. In doing so, he made it clear that the later election of the rector could occur only via a democratically elected council.[18]

"The spectrum" of reactions at the university, as it was appropriately noted at the time, "ranged from 'horror at what is being being done' to 'it was high time.'"[19] The situation during the break between semesters was highly contradictory. Within a few days, 250 members of the faculties of science, medicine, and linguistics supported the appeal for democratic renewal.[20] Other proponents of reform were disturbed by the harsh form of intervention. At the same time, no more "defensive positions" were built; rather, a strategy was developed that was to preserve the "socialist potential" in the soon-to-be-united Germany, especially in the humanities and the social sciences. The initiative for further action in the final phase of the GDR was passed on from the critical professors to middle-ranking academic staff, and, in particular, to the student council, dominated by leftist forces.

In the same issue of the university newspaper in which the declaration of the reform group had been printed after a three-week delay, and in which a brief item announced the resignation of the rector, the student council published a "program for renewal" directed at the senate. The student representatives pleaded above all for the renewal of the university through its own forces, that is, without any intervention from outside. To this end, commissions consisting of "democratically elected representatives of all member groups of the university," representatives from public life, and "emeriti of integrity" were to be formed. Their task would be to expose the university's employment practices and its Stalinist structures.[21] Following these principles, neither the abuse of a position of academic leadership for the purpose of political repression, nor service for the state security, nor academic incompetence would permit continued employment at the university. It was proposed that for the purpose of evaluating academic competence, foreign referees could be called upon. However the use of the word "foreign" in this suggestion proved problematical, because it excluded experts from the old Federal Republic, who, as a result of the treaty of unification, could no longer be regarded as foreign. The proposal brought back to mind the close contacts between some of the professors of history and philosophy and western European Marxists. In the end, the role of the "democrati-

cally elected representatives of all member groups of the university"
exemplified an appeal to grassroots democracy, which was promoted
vehemently in the History Department and elsewhere, not so much
by the students as by the representatives of middle-ranking academe
from the area of Marxism-Leninism studies. If they had had their way,
the faculty head would have had to justify every important decision
to council committees. In most cases, the demands for grassroots
democracy came from those who, as good comrades, had acquiesced
in the "democratic centralism" of the SED leadership. The university's
self-reformation proceeded from the dubious assumption that after
forty years of perverted development, when the university had been
a key component of the socialist system of education, especially in
the politicized humanities, there was enough democratic potential
available to create once more a pluralist and open-minded institution
of learning.

Because the initiative of the student council (behind which the mass
of middle-ranked academe in the humanities stood) was strongly rejected by the reform group,[22] the tone of the polemics in the following weeks became more heated and took on demagogic qualities. Now
it was the preservation of professorial interests, professorial domination of committees, or simply the professors as a group who were
accused of blocking reform. The changing of the old SED leadership
guard at the university was characterized by the student council president as the "invasion of the boss's armchair by the grey mice."[23] The
emphasis was shifted in a manner that was not immediately obvious.
The academic work group the Central Round Table in Berlin, supported by the civic movement, had demanded in early 1990 that "me-
diocrity in the universities" of the GDR be overcome. "The decisive
criteria for the selection" of new professors and lecturers should be
"academic competence and moral integrity."[24] The Leipzig student
council, in contrast, was of the view that, as its president put it, "in
only a few cases, namely those professors who had earlier shown some
capacity for conflict, was it recognized that a democratic understanding of academe was irreconcilable with professorial majorities on committees."[25] Academic competence had become irrelevant. This was clearly
directed at the group that, in the final phase of the GDR, had stood
for reform of the socialist university; otherwise, the student council
would have had to support the reemployment of all those who, as a
result of disagreements with the administration during GDR times,
had left for the Federal Republic. But nothing of the kind occurred.

It was only with the middle-ranking academics in the social science faculties, from whom one could expect an effort "to preserve

the psycho-sociologically authentic GDR-mentality,"[26] that the initiators of the student proposal saw a guarantee for the maintenance of educational institutions in the eastern part of a united Germany, which they understood as "places for the development of alternatives." Just who would be the beneficiaries and what would be the purpose of these alternatives were left unstated. That it was a matter of alternatives to the university system of the old Federal Republic and ultimately to the capitalist system along the lines of the 1968 revolution is apparent from the polemic against "the hierarchical structures in the academic realm [and] the dominance of the professors," features that were regarded as the "basic cause of the dilemma of the West German universities."[27]

A few weeks after the change of rectors in Leipzig, the minister for education in the last GDR government sent a letter to the electoral college, informing it that "the ministerial council had decided on immediate measures for the substantive reform of studies at the universities and colleges. . . . The decision aims . . . to achieve a comparability of studies in the universities of the GDR and the FRG. A precondition for this is the offering of courses leading to final examinations which will be regarded by employers as equivalent to those in the FRG."[28]

In the winter semester of 1990–91 the gap between those academics in the History Department who saw a fundamental reform of the teaching program as necessary and the proponents of a reform socialist position who wanted to preserve the program as much as possible became wider. The latter warned of "flawed discussions" that went too far and appealed to the "utopia" of a socialist future that one must not abandon. On the intellectual climate during these weeks, the spokesperson for middle-ranking academics observed: "The process of striking a necessary balance in the development of the Department, the discussion of restructuring and the formulation of new substantive ideas for teaching and research proved extremely complicated. . . . It required time. Psychological barriers had to be overcome. Hardly ever does it work at the first attempt."[29] Understandably, the barriers were highest where previously blatantly political considerations gave a distorted view of historical developments.

Some colleagues did not confine themselves to contemplating their role during the period of the GDR or the lack of substance in their academic work resulting from the political abuse of it. Rather, they attempted to maintain existing positions in the department ("plan positions") by making quick decisions. The rectoral college and the head of the History Department learned from the university newspaper of 5 May 1990 that on the previous day an "Institute for Universal and Cultural History" had been founded,[30] naturally as part of the university, and with the expectation that it would be financed by an ever-shrinking budget. The internationally recognized predecessor of this institution had been founded in 1909 by Karl Lamprecht under the name Cultural and Universal History but was razed in 1950–51 during a "storming of the academic fortress" and dissolved.[31] With a dusted-off and reformulated nameplate, the new founders of the institute intended to save their considerable staff, consisting of three professors with chairs, three other professors, and twelve other academics, whom they had been allocated partly as a result of cultivating good personal contacts with the Science Department of the Central Committee of the SED. When the rector's office and the minister rejected their proposal with reference to the forthcoming and necessary structural reform of the entire university, they mobilized international support, albeit in vain.

A few weeks after the unification on 3 October 1990, the states in the eastern part of Germany, abolished in 1952, were reestablished. As education and the universities had been the responsibility of the state governments until the Nazi-enforced coordination in 1933, and as the old Federal Republic had followed this federal tradition, the same principle was now to be applied on the territory of the former GDR. On 13 December 1990, the *Leipziger Volkszeitung* made it known that as a result of a cabinet decision in the state of Saxony, several tertiary institutions, including the Sport College in Leipzig, parts of the University of Leipzig, the city's Pedagogical College, and other establishments were to be dissolved. This affected some sections of the History Department, namely, the chairs in the history of the GDR/SED, history of the USSR/socialist countries of Europe, and methodology of Marxism-Leninism instruction. To be closed down also was the Franz Mehring Institute, which was controlled by the rector and served the further education of Marxism-Leninism teachers.[32] At the time, a number of staff members in the area of the history of the German and international workers' movements, as well as a section of the institute dominated by historians, were working on an edition of the complete writings of Marx and Engels.[33] Those working on the project were placed at first on a kind of reserve list (*Warteschleife*) but were dismissed later. They were allowed to apply for any of the professorial chairs to be created or for any assistant positions that would be advertised.

The legal basis for these measures adopted by the government in Dresden was Section 13, Article 1 of the unification treaty signed by the GDR and the FRG on 30 August 1990. It allocated to the state governments the power to "wind down" administrative bodies in such areas as justice, culture, education, and science if there would be no use for them in the united Germany.[34] In the areas of education and science, this affected, among other things, the party schools and the large, central institutes in Berlin with staffs of thousands whom no one could or would pay.

Unfortunately, not only was the relevant paragraph in the unification treaty broadly formulated, but the attached commentaries permitted vastly differing interpretations. Moreover, as the example of the history departments at the universities demonstrates, it was managed in different ways by the five state governments. Thus at the universities in Berlin, Halle, Jena, and Rostock, there was a closure of the entire department. This decision was reversed in Berlin as a result of a court decision. At the department in the Magdeburg Pedagogical College, nothing at all was "wound down"; meanwhile, in Leipzig, the decision of the cabinet in Dresden to close totally the History Department at the Pedagogical College was later reversed, and instead, only chairs in modern history were declared vacant. The issue of just which units were to be closed down—whether it was to be entire universities, faculties, or departments—remained controversial. Or was it up to the government in question to manage the problem as it saw fit? In the following weeks and months, this led to bitter protests, public controversies, and a series of court cases before the administrative courts. The consequences of this measure for personnel also remained the subject of controversy. Was it possible, for example, to terminate the employment of a professor or assistant who held tenure in the GDR? The court cases indicated that the judges' views on this issue differed from those of the cabinet in Dresden.

The government of Saxony was exposed to pressure from many sides as a result of its decision: the conditions of the unification treaty envisaged that closures cease by the end of December 1990. Radical reformers from within the ranks of the Saxon CDU and the civic movement, to whom some publications in the old Federal Republic had willingly given the opportunity to express their views, bemoaned the loss of the chance "to start everything anew."[35] When it was suggested that one could not simply close the universities and then open them some time later without damaging the interests of the students, they reacted aggressively. The decisive problem for the government remained that of finding a quick solution that would make the universities in the east attractive. There was not sufficient time for lengthy discussions.

Students in Leipzig demonstrated against closures, albeit in limited numbers. After their vigils on the Augustusplatz in front of the main building of the university in the cold of late December 1990, their president was told during a meeting with the Saxon minister of education that he could found a university wherever, whenever, and according to whichever principles he chose, but that he could expect no financial support for such experiments from a government that had been elected by the citizens of the state on the basis of, among other things, its education platform.

The closure brought a radical end to the discussions on necessary reforms that had been taking place since 1989. The solution that was finally reached corresponded to the available opportunities, but it was also a consequence of the inability of the universities in the former GDR to find a solution of their own before the end of 1990 that would have allowed them to survive in the education market. In the History Department, it was now a matter of ensuring adequate teaching arrangements in areas that had been closed down and formulating proposals for the structural reform of the entire department. At the same time, it was necessary to consider what profile the new chairs in the closed-down areas should have. In addition, the distortions caused by a large proportion of the staff being employed in the area of the history of the workers' movement, and treating it according to the party line, had to be removed. A convenient way of coming to terms with this problem was to gain support from colleagues in the old Federal Republic, who were given short-term teaching contracts and participated on the structural commissions that were to decide the new shape of the department.

In Leipzig, a mixture of academics from the old and the new federal states was preserved—possibly a feature peculiar to Leipzig. The range of subjects being offered became more lively thanks to a large number of guests. Problems stemmed from the drastically reduced number of positions, in particular, middle-ranking academics. The original forty-five assistant positions were ultimately reduced to a quarter of that number. More than a few talented academics drifted into other professions. It appears to be one luxury that modern society can afford—namely, that highly qualified specialists are educated with public money, only to find that there is no place for them in the marketplace.

The work of the structural commission, on which professors from east and west had been represented equally since the summer of 1991, made some level of conceptual thinking possible, after almost two years of acting and reacting in response to daily events. Above all, it was a matter of restoring a sense of proportion to the history curriculum, which, until 1989, had been distorted to the advantage of contemporary history. In doing this, local traditions could be preserved. This would mean that, apart from regional history, the study of eastern and southeastern European history, in collaboration with Slavic studies, would be fostered at the university. Also, a solution would be found for the former Lamprecht Institute, whose hurried reestablishment at the end of 1990 was unacceptable, not least because of the inability to find a place for it in the faculty's overall profile. In this matter, the current state of affairs remains unsatisfactory, because the young historian called to the position from within the university's own ranks had received a more attractive offer from another German university.

Apart from the financial situation, another crucial problem is the restriction on the decision-making powers of academic committees as a result of the adoption in the fall of 1993 of the Saxon University Law, which marked the path of future development. The oppressive burden of two authoritarian regimes on the universities in eastern Germany has created a particular sensitivity, especially among academics who grew up in the country, to harsh interventions by the bureaucracy. Whether and to what extent a modern mass university should be controlled and administered autonomously is certainly a subject of controversy in university politics. One can at least say that it is never the case that an increase in codetermination or self-determination stifles creativity.

The first step away from being a socialist university brought unlimited freedom, as there were no constraining legal guidelines. However, it was merely a provisional freedom, as that first step was necessarily followed by a second, the role of which was to reestablish a full capacity to function as a university. Clearly, this "double-step" was a process that was less than perfect. For all its problems, however, it will now enable Leipzig to establish its place alongside other German, European, and overseas universities.

NOTES

This chapter was translated by Peter Monteath
1. A. Mitter and S. Wolle, "Der Bielefelder Weg. Die Vergangenheitsbe-

wältigung der Historiker und die Vereinigung der Funktionäre," *Frankfurter Allgemeine Zeitung* 183 (1993): 23.

2. M. Middell, "Das Jahr 1968—ein europäisches Jahr?" *Leipziger Volkszeitung,* 15 September 1993.

3. "Gesetz über das einheitliche sozialistische Bildungssystem vom 25. 02. 1965," in *Gesetzblatt der DDR 1965*, vol. 1, pt. 6, sec. 4, 52 ff.

4. A. Fischer, *Das Bildungssystem der DDR*, Darmstadt, 1992, 39.

5. H. J. Meyer, "Zwischen Kaderschmiede und Hochschulrecht," *Hochschule-Ost* 6 (1992): 22.

6. M. Sieber and R. Freytag, *Kinder des Systems. DDR-Studenten vor, in und nach dem Herbst '89*, Berlin, 1993, 30.

7. "Die Verordnung über die Neuorganisation des Hochschulwesens vom 22.02.1957," *Gesetzblatt der DDR* 27 (1957).

8. H. Bartel, "Erbe und Tradition im Geschichtsbild der DDR," *Zeitschrift für Geschichtswissenschaft* 29, no. 5 (1981): 387–94; H. P. Harstik, *Nationales Geschichtsbild und nationale Tradition*, Hannover, 1988.

9. R. Eckert, "Entwicklungschancen und -barrieren für den geschichtswissenschaftlichen Nachwuchs in der DDR," *Aus Politik und Zeitgeschichte* 17/18 (1992): 28.

10. Every department at the universities and colleges in the GDR until 1989 had to prepare, on the basis of state directives in the context of the Five-Year Plan, an "Annual Plan for Teaching and Research" and report on its fulfillment at the end of the year.

11. *Universitätszeitung Leipzig* (hereafter *UZ*), 24 November 1989. The incensed mayor demanded a public apology from the author of the article in a following *UZ* (8 December 1989).

12. K. Kinner and M. Neuhaus, "Plädoyer für eine erneuerte marxistische Streit- und Denkkultur," *UZ*, 3 November 1989, 3.

13. Historikergesellschaft der DDR, *Wissenschaftliche Mitteilungen* 1 (1990): 5.

14. E. Blumenthal, "Gedanken zu einem studium generale," *UZ* 12 (1990): 5.

15. G. Wuttke, "Der Aufruf 'für unser Land' im Spannungsfeld von Anspruch und Wirklichkeit," *Utopie kreativ* 37/38 (1993): 109–19.

16. M. Schulze, "Das Ende der sanften Wende," *Sachsenspiegel. Unabhängige Wochenzeitung für Politik, Kultur und Wirtschaft*, 13 July 1990, 5.

17. "Leipziger Professoren vermissen geistige Erneuerung der Karl-Marx-Universität," *Frankfurter Allgemeine Zeitung*, 5 June 1990; see also K. Reumann, "Selbstreinigung an den Universitäten?" *Frankfurter Allgemeine Zeitung*, 29 June 1990; Cornelius Weiß in *UZ* 24 (1990): 1.

18. Ibid., 2.

19. Schulze, "Das Ende der sanften Wende," 5.

20. B. Heimrich, "Geschäftige Stille herrscht um die Talent-Sprungschanze," *Frankfurter Allgemeine Zeitung*, 25 August 1990.

21. "Die studentischen Konzilteilnehmer," *UZ* 24 (1990): 2.

22. *UZ* 25 (1990).

23. P. Pasternack, "Seit drei Jahren in diesem Theater: Hochschulerneuerung Ost oder Der libidinöse Opportunismus. Eine Farce," in H. Schramm (ed.), *Hochschule im Umbruch. Zwischenbilanz Ost*, Berlin, 1993, 16.

24. C. Dahme and H. Haberland, "Arbeitsgruppe Wissenschaft des Zentralen Runden Tisches," *Hochschule Ost* 5 (1992): 45.

25. Pasternack, "Seit drei Jahren in diesem Theater," 15.

26. W. Bialas, "Weiße Flecken auf weißen Westen. Zur Wissenschaftlichkeit und Parteilichkeit nach dem Ende der DDR-Historiographie," *Zeitschrift für Geschichtswissenschaft* 41, no. 8 (1993): 676.

27. P. Pasternack, "Perspektiven der Hochschulenentwicklung," *Hochschule-Ost* 1 (1992): 14 ff.

28. *UZ*, special issue, 13 August 1990, 2.

29. *UZ*, 22 October 1990, 3.

30. *UZ*, 5 November 1990, 1.

31. S. Hoyer, "Die Historischen Institute der Universität Leipzig von 1948 bis 1951," *Zeitschrift für Geschichtswissenschaft* 42, no. 9 (1994): 813 ff.

32. *Leipziger Volkszeitung*, 13 December 1990, 1, 18.

33. R. Dlubek, "Die Entstehung der zweiten Marx/Engels-Gesamtausgabe im Spannungsfeld von legitimem Auftrag und editorischer Sorgfalt," *MEGA-Studien* 1 (1994): 60–106, esp. 77.

34. *Einigungsvertrag. Sonderdruck aus der Sammlung das deutsche Bundesrecht,* Baden-Baden, 1990, chap. 5, art. 13.

35. See, for example, K. Reinschke, "Geist und Macht," *Die Union* 204 (1990); M. Rössler, "Hinter Befindlichkeiten stecken Besitzstände," *Frankfurter Allgemeine Zeitung*, 4 September 1992; M. Lesch, "Eine 'Genossenjagd' im Freistaat verhindern," *Die Welt* 56 (1992).

13

Jena and the End of History

PETER MONTEATH

In a controversial 1989 essay titled "The End of History?" former RAND Corporation analyst Francis Fukuyama announced the global triumph of liberal capitalism. Much in the spirit of his German equivalent Joachim Fest, Fukuyama claimed to have observed the demise of all utopian alternatives to a liberal capitalist world order. "The triumph of the West, of the Western *idea*," Fukuyama asserted, "is evident first of all in the total exhaustion of viable systematic alternatives to Western liberalism."[1] Thus the events of the late 1980s in Germany and elsewhere marked more than just the end of the Cold War; they were also "the end point of mankind's ideological evolution and the universalization of Western liberal democracy as the final form of human government."[2] This is not to suggest that the seeds of this triumph had not been planted much earlier. Indeed, citing both Hegel and his mid-twentieth-century Russian émigré acolyte Alexandre Kojève approvingly, Fukuyama looks to Napoleon's victory at Jena in 1806 as the event that ushered in the ineluctable ascendancy of liberal capitalism. To use Fukuyama's own words: "The Battle of Jena marked the end of history because it was at that point that the *vanguard* of humanity (a term quite familiar to Marxists) actualized the principles of the French Revolution. While there was considerable work to be done after 1806—abolishing slavery and the slave trade, extending the franchise to workers, women, blacks, and other racial minorities, etc.—the basic *principles* of the liberal democratic state could not be improved upon."[3]

Perhaps because of history's predisposition to quirks, or perhaps because Fukuyama is simply wrong, Napoleon's triumph in 1806 experienced a sequel in 1989–90. And because the modest town of Jena has experienced the end of history twice, it is an appropriate place to study the historical consequences of German unification. In particular,

271

the Historical Institute at Jena's university, which in 1934 received and still bears the name Friedrich Schiller University, offers itself as a prime example of the implications that the implosion of the GDR has had for the place of historical teaching and research in the new Germany.

A good part of the collection of oral and written material for this examination of the postrevolutionary fate of Jena's Historical Institute took place in the final weeks of 1992, just two years after German unification. Interviews were conducted with a wide range of those closely affected by the radical changes of the preceding years—university administrators, students, and, most important, present and former staff of the institute. Responses to the changes that had occurred in their midst varied enormously, ranging from bitter condemnation through passive acquiescence to active and enthusiastic support for the imposition of a new order. The historian is thus confronted with the awkward task of assessing competing narratives delivered by both the winners and the losers in the unification process, each having in common only the career-determining immediacy of the events they describe, and perhaps also (and this applies to the historians in particular) some bafflement at suddenly finding themselves the focus of a historical study.

The Historical Institute in Jena had much in common with equivalent institutes at East Germany's five other university history departments in Berlin, Leipzig, Halle, Rostock, and Greifswald. Given that all East German universities were controlled by the Ministry for Higher Education in Berlin, this is hardly surprising. Like other historical institutes in the GDR, where student-staff ratios in the universities before unification were seven to one, Jena's was vastly overstaffed by Western standards.[4] There were over forty teaching staff servicing a student population of around 350. Class sizes were correspondingly small, and teaching practices in some respects resembled those of schools. Unlike their West German counterparts, Jena's history students had a narrowly prescribed course of study, with long contact hours, often in excess of thirty a week. They tended to display a reverence for the words of their teachers, who were seen to impart historical truths that required recording rather than questioning. From 1951, all university students in the GDR had been required to complete a basic course of study in Marxism-Leninism; with rare exceptions, they were expected to endure the regimentation of membership in the *Freie Deutsche Jugend* (Free German Youth).

The rigors of long contact hours were balanced by a greater sense of group solidarity than their contemporaries in the Federal Republic could enjoy. Studying in essentially the same relatively small groups for many hours a week, for many weeks a year, and for many years, inevitably engendered close relationships that often continued beyond the working day. Collective working patterns fostered in this way appear to be an attractive alternative to the competitive individualism of Western institutions of higher education. The East German system thus avoided the alienation that plagued the Western system; this success, however, came at the price of failing to promote individual intellectual achievement that questioned the prescribed line. As one visiting Western academic put it, East German students had not gone through the experience of 1968; the questioning of academic authority was largely unknown to them.[5] Although this observation might not hold true for all sections of the student body through the course of GDR history, it is nevertheless evident that the East German student body was generally more passive and tractable than was its post-1968 West German counterpart.

This perceived reluctance to question authority can also be identified among the staff members. Over 90 percent of the staff were members of the ruling Socialist Unity Party (SED), a figure comparable to any other East German history department. In many cases, this membership stemmed from an initial and in some cases ongoing commitment to the doctrine of antifascism. Many of Jena's staff had been appointed as early as the 1950s, when revulsion against fascism was at its strongest, an awareness of the danger of the revival of fascism was intense, and many deliberately rejected working in the Federal Republic, which had permitted the continuing employment of university historians from Nazi times. The commitment to historical teaching and research in the GDR, at least initially, had been driven by a genuine sense of commitment to the construction of an antifascist society. For some, the passing of time brought with it a disillusionment with the development of the GDR, and an awareness of the failings of the doctine of antifascism as a basis from which to criticize East German society became more acute. Moreover, the increasing incursion of the state and party into the academic realm became more and more evident. These perceptions, however, were not accompanied by moves to overthrow or even reform the system. On the contrary, Jena's historians, with widely varying levels of devotion and enthusiasm, by and large continued to fulfill their appointed role of legitimating the East German state, creating for it a national history that distinguished it from its maligned neighbor. In general, the close links between the one-party state and the university were tolerated, and in some instances, they were even actively cultivated.

This is not to suggest that the research performance of Jena's historians can be dismissed as mere propaganda in the service of the state. Some of the historical research carried out in Jena has received international recognition. Like the students, staff in many cases worked collectively on large projects, rather than on a multiplicity of projects conducted by individuals or smaller teams. The outstanding result of this preference for large collective operations was the widely respected four-volume *Lexikon zur Parteiengeschichte* (Lexicon of Party History).[6] Dealing as it did with bourgeois political parties, this publication alone suggested that the interests of Jena's historians extended beyond the traditional realms of the working class and the Communist Party. They also widened their field of vision sufficiently to produce significant work on, for example, American history and the nineteenth-century German bourgeois democrat Robert Blum.[7] As was the case in other parts of the GDR in the 1980s, Jena, too, was touched by centrally directed moves toward a broadening of historical interests.[8] The government from this time sponsored a broader interpretation of the country's historical inheritance, a development that was symbolized in 1981 by the return to its old position in Unter den Linden of the statue of Frederick the Second and by the celebration of the "Luther year" in 1983. Moreover, this more generous view of the GDR's historical roots manifested itself in the publication of seminal biographies of "great" German statesmen such as Frederick himself, who could again receive the epithet "Frederick the Great," and Bismarck.[9] Further impetus for this broadening of historical attention was then provided by Mikhail Gorbachev's push for glasnost in the late 1980s, which was not without some, albeit vitiated, impact in Jena. In 1988, for example, one Jena historian organized a discussion in the main hall of the university dealing with the practice of anti-Semitism in the Third Reich, a topic that had not received widespread attention in East German historiography.

By the late 1980s, but clearly well before the fall of the Berlin Wall, the historians of Jena and of the other GDR universities were moving closer to the West. Theoretical and methodological differences certainly remained, but they had shrunk. East German historical works were being more readily received in the West, and often favorably; their authors were being invited to present their work at Western conferences, and such invitations were being accepted when possible. Georg Iggers, in reviewing the state of historical studies in East Germany over the previous decade, was able to observe in 1989:

> The last ten years have thus seen important changes in historical thinking and historical writing in the GDR as they have in the

rest of the world. Historical studies in the GDR continue to be much more explicitly Marxist than they do in Poland and Hungary, for example, where historical writing has freed itself much more from marxist terminology and conceptions. Yet the doctrinal gulf which existed between historians in the GDR and in the West has lessened. Dialogue and cooperation are today not only possible but are taking place.[10]

Although Jena historians showed some willingness to broaden the scope of historical research and to explore new areas of interest, it cannot be said that they or their students contributed to the collapse of the GDR. There were rumblings of discontent in the 1980s, when it was feared that the escalation of the Cold War could encourage the government to take preventive military action against the West. The SED's banning in November 1988 of *Sputnik*, a publication containing Soviet articles written in the spirit of glasnost and perestroika, also led to a tentative articulation of dissatisfaction. It is true that some students were involved in the formation of a group called *Reformhaus*, which, as the name suggests, actively supported the cause of reform, albeit quite later.[11] Similarly, some academics participated in a group that labeled itself *Aktionsgemeinschaft Demokratische Erneuerung der Hochschulen* (Action Group for the Democratic Renewal of the Universities), but this was not formed until December 1989, a month after the fall of the Berlin Wall.[12] In the so-called people's revolution of 1989, it must be said that the academics at the Friedrich Schiller University and their students had relatively little to say or do. Although many were later to chide themselves for a lack of civil courage at the crucial moment, the fact was that the historians had not managed to break with the German academic tradition of unquestioning loyalty to their employer, the state. As two of Jena's historians confess, "there is no avoiding the bitter recognition that, as in the GDR generally, so in Jena specifically, the historians . . . conformed to the system to the last moment, did not prepare the change of fall 1989, rather, if anything, partly hindered it."[13]

As was the case in other universities in the former GDR, the period since the fall of the Berlin Wall and the unification of Germany has been one of considerable turmoil and individual hardship. For a long time, there was a considerable lack of clarity over the future of the University of Jena generally and the Historical Institute specifically. In the end, the process undertaken at Jena was as harsh as if not harsher than that undertaken elsewhere; its end result bears little resemblance to the institute that had existed until 1989.

A key decision to be made early in the rebuilding of the university concerned which sections of the university were to shut down altogether, possibly to be rebuilt under the new political arrangements, and which were to survive and be adopted by the new government. Indeed, this choice between *Abwicklung* ("winding down," a euphemism for the abrupt closure of departments or faculties) and *Überführung* (adoption) was required by the unification treaty. In December 1990, the decision was made by the responsible Ministry of Art and Science in Thuringia's capital, Erfurt, that, along with the faculties of law, education, economics, and philosophy, history would be "wound down." Jena's was the only former East German historical institute to be subjected to total closure. The argument was that to attain any level of credibilty, to distance the department fully from its former function as a pillar of the communist East German state, to become once again internationally competitive and respected, a fresh start with new personnel would have to be made. Only in this way would Jena be able to rebuild a reputation for academic excellence and independence and, in so doing, avoid losing its students to the universities of the "old federal states."

The decision to wind down Jena's Historical Institute did not mean that all of its staff would automatically lose their jobs. As in all other universities of the former GDR and in other departments within the Friedrich Schiller University, all staff were subjected to a process of evaluation to determine whether they were fit to retain their posts. In Jena, it should be noted, this process of evaluation began before unification rendered it compulsory. As pressure for reform built up even before the GDR's implosion, a university senate committee had been established to evaluate all professors. With unification, however, the process was taken over by the state government of Thuringia, which applied it more thoroughly to all members of staff.

The process was twofold and was carried out by two separate commissions appointed by the state Ministry of Art and Science: a so-called *Personalkommission* (Personnel Commission) and a *Fachkommission* (Academic Commission). The Personnel Commission consisted entirely of East German citizens, some of them from the university, others from various areas of public life. Its role was to examine the personal integrity of the staff members. Membership in the SED in itself was not sufficient to bring about dismissal, but active involvement in infringements against basic human rights was. As the official regulations of the state of Thuringia put it, personal suitability would be considered to be lacking

> if the person concerned has violated the basic principles of humanity or the rule of law, in particular those human rights guar-

anteed by the International Agreement on civil and political rights of 19 December 1966, or the basic principles contained in the General Declaration on Human Rights from 10 December 1948, for example by

—compromising freedom of conscience and religion

—the violation of the freedom of research and teaching

—promoting or impeding academic staff for non-academic, political or ideological reasons.[14]

Proven activity on behalf of the *Stasi* was also grounds for dismissal, and for this reason, access was gained to material provided by the Gauck authority, the body charged with investigating *Stasi* files. Finally, staff members were considered inappropriate for continued employment if they had held high office in a party or other mass organization in the former GDR, if they had occupied a prominent position at the university with a particularly ideological mandate, or if they had belonged to the privileged political elite, the so-called *Nomenklaturkader*.[15]

The second part of the evaluation process applied purely academic criteria. The committees carrying out this stage of the evaluation consisted of a mixture of East and West German academics. Their goal was to evaluate solely the academic achievements of those concerned. It was apparent long before the demise of the state that university positions in the GDR had been made available to some members of staff according to political rather than academic criteria. Consequently, the publishing record of some academics was abysmal, and they were unlikely to be retained. Nevertheless, some care needed to be exercised in the application of this criterion. The GDR system facilitated publication and overseas travel for those with close links to the party and reputations for political reliability; for others, such possibilities were strictly limited. Quantity of publications was therefore an unreliable guide to academic competence and had to be treated with some circumspection.

Apart from the work of these evaluation commissions, the role of another commission was crucial in the refounding of Jena's Historical Institute. This was the *Strukturkommission* (Structural Commission), which was entrusted with the task of determining the structure of the postunification university. As with the evaluation commissions, the establishment of the Structural Commission was the responsibility of Thuringia's conservative-liberal state government. A subcommittee of this commission, consisting almost entirely of West Germans (there was just one East German representative), was allocated the task of deciding on a structure for the new Historical Institute. In so doing, it chose not to consult with the remaining staff of the institute. It was decided that the new institute, like the old, would have five chairs. They would be in the areas of medieval history, history of the early modern period, regional history and medieval history, history of the nineteenth and twentieth centuries, and contemporary history.

The outcome of these developments for the Historical Institute was radical change. Many staff members opted not to submit themselves to the rigors of the evaluation process. Some were in the relatively fortunate position of being able to take early retirement. Of those who chose to submit themselves to evaluation, all received short-term contracts at the beginning of 1991 to support them until the expected completion of the evaluation eight months later. None of these people was found to be compromised by contacts with the *Stasi*; nevertheless, a number were judged to have compromised their professional integrity through their political activities to such an extent as to forbid the renewal of their contracts. This was the case with two of the five former holders of chairs, including the director of the institute at the time of unification. Unfortunately, the full details of these particular cases cannot be known, but it can be said that the grounds for dismissal are not entirely convincing in terms of the official criteria. Given that two other holders of chairs had chosen retirement and another had received a negative academic evaluation, this left Jena without a single Ordinarius (full professor) from GDR times. The Structural Commission, which was transformed into a selection committee, eventually appointed five former West Germans to the five vacant chairs. Just two of the former staff were eventually offered professorships at lower levels (C3 as opposed to the C4 category of the Ordinarius); one of them, Herbert Gottwald, was elected director of the institute in August 1991 and was permitted to remain in that position with the tacit disapproval of the state government beyond the official reestablishment of the institute in October of that year.

In the middle and lower ranks of the institute, things were not much better. Indeed, in all the formerly East German universities, this so-called *Mittelbau* has been hardest hit by developments.[16] After a prolonged period of uncertainty, in Jena only nine academics from the former GDR have regained employment in the new Historical Institute.

Students, too, were adversely affected by the harshness and thoroughness of the changes in Jena. The few postgraduate students were permitted to continue their studies, but no additional postgraduates were admitted in the lengthy transitional period. Undergraduate students suffered considerably from the shortage and uncertainty of course offerings. They could not count on the continuing availability of staff members. This unpredictability applied, of course, to the existing East German staff, whose careers were at stake, but also to a number of West German historians, who had been brought to Jena on short-term contracts to fill some of the gaping holes in the teaching program. Those students who were caught in the middle of their degrees by the political transformation were required to complete bridging courses after the reconstitution of the institute.

Given the harshness of the measures accompanying the winding down of the Historical Institute, it is not surprising that they were greeted in some quarters with bitterness and resentment. There was, however, no collective rear-guard action against the changes. Most of the historians acquiesced in what they saw as the inevitable. Some were appeased by the opportunity to take early retirement; others were mollified by offers of short-term research positions and by the groundlessly optimistic intimations that they would be able to secure employment in Jena or elsewhere in the not too distant future. There were many threats of seeking redress through the court system, but these were rarely carried out, and then only in the form of individual action. Legal circumstances in the state of Thuringia militated against the kind of collective action that had been pursued with some limited success by the staff of the History Department at the Humboldt University in Berlin. Indeed, many of those who had lost their positions complained of a lack of solidarity at the University of Jena in the face of what they perceived as the wholesale takeover of the university by the West. Some members of the university were accused of pure opportunism, acting vigorously to please their new masters, and with little regard for the well-being of their erstwhile colleagues.

The measures imposed on Jena's historians were replicated in the other historical institutes of the former GDR, that is, those in Berlin, Leipzig, Halle, Greifswald, and Rostock. Although only Jena's historians were subjected to the sudden and dramatic process of winding down, the medium-term results were the same everywhere. In all cases, the original staff was decimated, and only a handful survived to practice their profession in the united Germany. Similar circumstances prevailed among the many historians who were located in the Academy of the Sciences in Berlin. The closing down of the academy was accompanied by promises that its employees would be absorbed by new positions opening up in the universities. Not surprisingly, this occurred only in the rarest instances.

Those few historians who survived the radical changes have identified the reasons for this lack of solidarity elsewhere. The East German university system was not exactly characterized by selfless equality.

As one critic put it: "The conservatism of the historical profession in the East is even more marked than in the West. The privileges, the links with the government, the selection process, the academic regulations—all of these things had led to a markedly hierarchical occupational structure."[17] Given that the system was one that blatantly favored established academics who cultivated close links with the party, the absence of solidarity was arguably an inevitable outcome of the collapse of an iniquitous system. In this respect, the reaction of some Jena historians is comparable with that of the young Berlin historians who eagerly distanced themselves from their older and more privileged colleagues in forming the *Unabhängiger Historiker-Verband* (Independent Association of Historians) in early 1990. The criticism leveled at their older and more established colleagues by the members of this association was more vehement than anything ever offered from the West. As its two founding members put it in their call for the formation of an independent association:

> For decades any free intellectual movement choked on an inedible mush of lies and half-truths. Scholarly foolishness and hackneyed commonplaces were presented as "the only scientific ideology." Pseudo-scholars jumped onto the bench of Marxist omniscience and defamed in their stupid arrogance entire epochs of modern intellectual history. While one was morally indignant about the book burnings of the Nazis, for forty years in the GDR under the dictatorship of the SED a "cold book-burning" on a much bigger scale took place.[18]

The only solution to this state of affairs, the young historians argued, was

> a clear identification of those historians who resisted that and are prepared to follow new directions. Because everywhere—at the head of all institutes, among the editors of all journals, in all the publishing companies—the old people are still there. Everywhere the old power structures and mentalities are still in place.[19]

Whether greater solidarity could have rescued Jena's history from its harsh fate is a moot point. The truth of the matter is that both within Jena and outside it, there was widespread recognition of the need for radical transformation. Financial contingencies alone militated against preserving a department of its former size. There is also something to be said for the argument that the swiftness of the "surgical intervention," as the institute head described it,[20] enabled a fresh beginning free from the burdens of the past. Commendable also in Jena were the albeit limited efforts to ensure that the exchange of ideas between West and East was not a one-way process. Jena played host to many Western academics on short-term contracts during its period of turmoil, but it also received and exploited the opportunity to send some of its own academics west. Thus the two reappointed professors have been able to spend some time teaching at formerly West German universities.

These positive points aside, there is also room for criticism of the process of winding down as it was applied to Jena's History Department. Given unavoidable gaps in information, it would be improper to be critical of individual cases of dismissal (though clearly, in at least a couple of instances, grounds for objection exist). However, it is appropriate to be critical of the general processes and principles involved.

The winding down of the Historical Institute in Jena was indicative of a reluctance to acknowledge the capacity of East German historiography to reform itself from within. To develop new methodologies and new areas of interest was no easy matter under an oppressive regime; nevertheless, East German historians in the 1980s had considerably broadened their interest in the German past, and in adopting a keener interest in social history, like their West German counterparts, they helped reorient German historiography away from its preoccupation with a nation-state–centered "view from above." This is not to suggest that all of Jena's historians had adapted to the greater openness and pluralism of the 1980s, nor that all were capable of adapting to the changed intellectual environment after the events of 1989–90. Clearly, the line between intellectual flexibility or adaptability on the one hand and self-serving opportunism on the other is a thin and problematical one. Only time, however, could have demonstrated genuine adaptability, and this time was denied Jena's historians. The granting of longer periods of adaptation would have had the added advantage of easing the awkward and stressful transitional measures endured by students. For both the historians and the students, greater time would have enabled a more considered appraisal of the East German system and their own particular roles within it.

In this matter, it is difficult to avoid a comparison between the current fate of the East German historical profession and the fate of German historians in the immediate aftermath of the Second World War. Indeed, Georg Iggers has identified interesting parallels between these events. As he points out, the pressure to be a party member was much greater in the GDR than in Nazi Germany, as was the level of regimentation of the history profession, but under Hitler's rule, the physical dangers of nonconformism were more intimidating.[21] Arguments that

Nazi indoctrination lasted merely twelve years in comparison with the forty-year rule of the SED are disingenuous. It is widely acknowledged that right-wing antidemocratic tendencies were widespread in the German historical profession both before and after 1933, and arguably, Nazi ideology had gained a more secure foothold among the German population than socialist ideology was ever able to achieve in the GDR. The inescapable conclusion stemming from such a comparison is that East German historians have been dealt with much more uncompromisingly than the German historians of 1945.[22] In the wake of the Second World War, the treatment of academics and their institutions was characterized by a high level of tolerance concerning their Nazi pasts. Such restraint, as has been pointed out by Hermann Lübbe, was a function of the efforts to integrate those concerned into a new, democratic order.[23] The blatant discrepancy between the treatment of the historians in 1945 and 1990 leads to well-founded accusations of West German hypocrisy, even if the periods in question are separated by some four decades.

The process by which members of staff lost their positions was less than auspicious. Confronting the possibility of imminent unemployment and the loss of self-esteem likely to accompany it is a circumstance to which East Germans, provided they had been willing to conform to the system, were unaccustomed. Even in the West, where job insecurity was much more widespread, it is a daunting and emotionally damaging experience. For this reason, it should have been a matter of the highest priority to establish with the greatest possible clarity the criteria by which the noncontinuation of employment would be determined. This does not appear to have always been the case. In particular, it was an affront to members of staff to receive in their notifications of noncontinuation references to a newspaper article by a West German historian who had worked in Jena and had argued that West German historians should not be required to continue working with those East German colleagues nominated for dismissal.[24] This is not intended as a criticism of the West German historian concerned; rather, it is a criticism of the Jena authorities who unwisely displayed inappropriately servile respect for Western opinion.

The opportunity to reform the historical institutes and the universities of the former GDR was not grasped as an opportunity to deal with inequalities and deficiencies within the German university system as a whole. The reforming zeal of those committed to transforming the East German universities was limited strictly to the territory of the former GDR. With the wholesale adoption of a Western model of university administration in the East, there are limits to the level of democratization taking place. It is true that West Germany had experienced the revolts and reforms of 1968; East Germany had not. But the West German system remains a strictly hierarchical one in which chairs bring with them enormous privileges and powers, and staff at lower levels often wander from one form of insecurity to the next. With greater foresight and imagination, it is conceivable that the revamped formerly East German universities could have provided a model for the entire united Germany to follow, one that might even have attempted to salvage some of the desirable features of the communist system.

In Jena, decisions concerning the future teaching and research interests of the Historical Institute were made with a minimum—in some cases, an absence—of consultation with Jena's historians. In the appointment of new staff, local involvement was also limited. As with the question of structural reform, here too the opportunity for creative thinking, perhaps in this instance in collaboration with Jena's own historians, was not exploited. True, there is one significant change that reflects an interesting development in recent West and East German historiography, namely, the allocation of a chair and a lectureship to the area of regional history. Viewed more cynically, perhaps this development is designed to militate against fears of a revived obsession with national history. Significant though this step is, it hardly represents a radical break with the past. If Jena is any indication, German historiography remains doggedly inward looking; the tradition of historical navel-gazing looks set to continue. The choice of chairs in Jena does nothing to shift the focus of teaching and research away from Germany and toward an understanding of the wider world in which, like it or not, Germany has a significant role to play and that is represented increasingly within Germany's multicultural society itself. Such a narrowness of historical interests appears particularly inappropriate at the Friedrich Schiller University, where Schiller himself, in his inaugural lecture in Jena 200 years before the fall of the Berlin Wall, spoke in praise of "universal history."[25]

The four decades in which the Friedrich Schiller University served the needs of a communist regime have now become part of history, just as the GDR itself fast recedes into the past and becomes a popular topic of historical inquiry. This invites and even demands a reconsideration of those years from the perspective of the present, in which a new order has been established and consolidated. Indeed, as early as June 1992, the university staged a colloquium with the aim of reviewing the impact of communist rule on the history of the university. Perhaps not surprisingly, there was much to be condemned, as numerous cases of persecution and corruption were recalled. Official regret was proclaimed, and the victims of persecution within the university were offered apologies for their maltreatment, which had ranged from ex-matriculation to lengthy incarceration. Without doubt, communist rule destroyed the careers and, even more tragically, the potential careers of many.

In this process of reviewing the GDR past, however, it appears that an appealing and convenient division into perpetrators and victims has occurred. The perpetrators, absent from the colloquium, were those who had sustained a system of oppression and whose active complicity had been exposed and justly punished through evaluation or winding down. The victims were those who had offered varying forms of active and passive resistance to the regime, often at the cost of their livelihood. From the perspective of 1992, it was possible to construct a glorious tradition of resistance, one worthy of mention alongside some of the great names of German history. Thus one participant argued: "Even in these years [of the GDR] the special liberal tradition of this teaching institution shone through, the spirit of German classicism, the spirit of the fraternities, the spirit of the '48ers and that of the Scholls. The idea of the genuine university was alive, the idea of independent, autonomous research and teaching, of calling into question and having one's own opinion."[26] Clearly it is with this tradition of resistance that the representatives of the new order at the university prefer to identify.

It remains to be seen whether history will remember that group of people who neither engaged in persecution nor offered resistance, but simply conformed to the daily pressures of life in the GDR, living unheroically within the restrictions imposed by an authoritarian regime. At the Jena colloquium, the only exception to this tendency to write this (majority?) group out of history was a student who began his contribution with the question: "How do we enter a dialogue with those who were neither the obvious victims nor the obvious perpetrators?" He went on to draw the grim conclusion that "the truth at this university has not appeared yet."[27]

Subtle changes to the physical environment of the Friedrich Schiller University in Jena complement the arrival of a new order. Inside the main building of the university, a plaque honoring the memory of Rudolf Breitscheid and Theodor Neubauer[28] has been removed and replaced with one that reads: "Truth will liberate you. To the victims of political persecution at the Friedrich-Schiller-University. 1933–1945; 1945–1989." Thus the evils of the Nazi and the German communist regimes are commemorated indiscriminately; the totalitarianism thesis makes its comeback to rewrite the history of the university. In the courtyard of the main building, a portrait of Bismarck, removed in 1970 to make way for a communist-inspired plaque commemorating the reopening of the university after the Second World War, has now been put back in its old place. Obviously, the celebration of the unified German nation-state is back in vogue. Finally, the bust of Karl Marx, who received his doctorate from Jena in 1841, has been removed from the row of busts commemorating the university's most famous teachers and graduates. Marx, it was argued, had never actually been to Jena; he had merely enrolled there for the purpose of having his thesis examined, thus circumventing the hostility to his work that had expressed itself in Berlin. It seems that Jena also had the added attraction to the impecunious student of lower enrollment fees.

These changes need not give rise to despairing pessimism. The bust of Marx has not been replaced by one of Hegel, who taught in Jena from 1801 to 1806, fitting though this might seem. The refounding of the Historical Institute at the Friedrich Schiller University is being accompanied by the transfer to Jena of the methodological and interpretive pluralism of historical practice in the old Federal Republic. No longer will the findings of historical research and the goals of history teaching be predetermined by the narrow interests of a political elite. And no longer will teachers, researchers, and students alike be denied exposure to the work of dissenting colleagues abroad or in Germany. Nevertheless, it is appropriate to voice concerns about the nature and function of German history since unification, concerns that are of great significance both within and beyond Germany. If the historical experiences of 1989–90 in Germany and eastern Europe confirm the triumph of liberal capitalism, if we are inevitably approaching the final stage of history characterized, as Fukuyama put it, by "liberal democracy in the political sphere combined with easy access to VCRs and stereos in the economic,"[29] then the question has to be asked whether we need history anymore. Do the recent developments in Jena and elsewhere signify the end of history as a discipline? Is there any point in studying and researching history if its function is merely to teach us that it is inevitable that we have arrived where we already are? If Fukuyama and his many German kindred spirits are right, are we really any better off than Jena's East German historians and students, whose commitment to the teleology of Marxism has been so harshly judged and punished? Perhaps we, as historians, should be following the example of Fukuyama's hero Kojève, who, secure in the belief that the end of history had rendered art and philosophy redundant, abandoned teaching to become a European Economic Community bureaucrat. Or perhaps we can find some solace in the fact that Kojève died in 1968, the year that challenged the self-satisfied materialism and paternalism of the 1950s and 1960s.

NOTES

1. Francis Fukuyama, "The End of History?" *The National Interest* 16 (Summer 1989): 3.
2. Ibid., 4.
3. Ibid., 5.
4. The corresponding figure for the Federal Republic in 1988 was twenty-three to one. These statistics are from Dieter E. Zimmer, "Wunder im Osten. Wurden die ostdeutschen Hochschulen 'plattgemacht'? Eine erste umfassende Analyse widerlegt viele Vorurteile," *Die Zeit*, 20 May 1994, 46.
5. Interview with Professor Othmar Nikola Haberl, 30 November 1993.
6. Dieter Fricke (ed.), *Lexikon zur Parteiengeschichte: die bürgerlichen und kleinbürgerlichen Parteien in Deutschland (1789–1945)*, 4 vols. Leipzig, 1983, 1984, 1985, 1986.
7. Siegfried Schmidt, *Robert Blum. Vom Leipziger Liberalen zum Märtyrer der deutschen Demokratie*, Weimar, 1971. These three areas—the history of political parties, the biography of Robert Blum, and U.S. history—are those that a member of the institute, Herbert Gottwald, identifies in retrospect as the main achievements. See H. Gottwald, "Ansprache anläßlich der Wiederbegründung des Historischen Instituts der Friedrich-Schiller-Universität Jena am 25. Oktober 1990 in der Aula der Universität," in Rainer Eckert, Wolfgang Küttler, and Gustav Seeber (eds.), *Krise— Umbruch—Neubeginn. Eine kritische und selbstkritische Dokumentation der DDR-Geschichtswissenschaft 1989/90*, Stuttgart, 1992, 250.
8. For a discussion of this broadening of interests, see especially Helmut Meiner and Walter Schmidt (eds.), *Erbe und Tradition in der DDR. Die Diskussion der Historiker*, Berlin (GDR), 1988; Walter Schmidt, "Zur Entwicklung des Erbe- und Traditionsverständnisses in der Geschichtsschreibung der DDR," *Zeitschrift für Geschichtswissenschaft* 33 (1985): 208; Günther Heydemann, "Geschichtswissenschaft und Geschichtsverständnis in der DDR seit 1945," *Aus Politik und Zeitgeschichte* 13 (1987): 15–26.
9. Ingrid Mittenzwei, *Friedrich II. von Preußen. Eine Biographie*, Berlin, 1979; Ernst Engelberg, *Bismarck. Urpreuße und Reichsgründer*, Berlin, 1985.
10. Georg G. Iggers, "New Directions in Historical Studies in the German Democratic Republic," *History and Theory* 28 (1989): 76–7.
11. For a report on the activities of this group, see Christoph Axhelm, "Die Beteiligung der Studenten am politischen Umbruch 1989 in Jena," in Rektor der Friedrich-Schiller-Universität (ed.), *Vergangenheitsklärung an der Friedrich-*

Schiller-Universität Jena. Beiträge zur Tagung "Unrecht und Aufarbeitung" am 19. und 20. 6. 1992, Leipzig, 1994, 212–9.

12. On this group, see Dietfried Jorke, "Die 'Aktionsgemeinschaft Demokratische Erneuerung der Hochschulen' in Jena," ibid., 219–25.

13. Herbert Gottwald and Peter Schäfer, "Zwischen Rigorismus und Behutsamkeit. Vergangenheitsbewältigung—eine Meinung aus dem Historischen Institut," *Alma Mater Jenensis. Universitätszeitung* 3, no. 5 (10 January 1992): 3.

14. Ulrich Fickel, *Endgültige Fassung der Evaluationsordnung des Thüringer Ministers für Wissenschaft und Kunst*, Erfurt, 29 May 1991, 2.

15. Ibid., 2–3.

16. Zimmer, "Wunder im Osten," 46.

17. Norman Naimark, "Politik und Geschichtswissenschaft im osteuropäischen Kontext," in Konrad Jarausch (ed.), *Zwischen Parteilichkeit und Professionalität. Bilanz der Geschichtswissenschaft der DDR*, Berlin, 1991, 125–38, 132.

18. Armin Mitter and Stefan Wolle, "Aufruf zur Bildung einer Arbeitsgruppe Unabhängiger Historiker in der DDR," in Eckert, Küttler, and Seeber (eds.), *Krise—Umbruch—Neubeginn*, 160.

19. Ibid., 161.

20. Interview with Professor Herbert Gottwald, 1 December 1992.

21. Georg G. Iggers, "Geschichtswissenschaft und autoritärer Staat. Ein deutsch-deutscher Vergleich (1933–1990)," *Berliner Debatte Initial* 2 (1991): 125.

22. For an indication of the survival of Nazi academics in the postwar university system in the Federal Republic, see especially Ludwig Elm, *Nach Hitler. Nach Honecker. Zum Streit der Deutschen um die eigene Vergangenheit*, Berlin, 1991, 131–9.

23. Hermann Lübbe, "Der Nationalsozialismus im deutschen Nachkriegsbewußtsein," *Historische Zeitschrift* 236 (1983): 587.

24. Reiner Pommerin, "Wenn ehemalige SED-Professoren 'Demokratie' lehren-Erfahrungsbericht," *Die Welt am Sonntag*, 14 July 1991, 43. Attention was drawn to this article in a letter from Rector Schmutzer dated 19 July 1991 to the dismissed Professor Manfred Weißbecker.

25. Friedrich Schiller, "Was heißt und zu welchem Zweck studiert man Universal-Geschichte? 1789. Eine akademische Antrittsrede," in *Schillers Werke in zwei Bänden. Band II*, Salzburg, n.d.

26. Günter Zehm, "Repression und Widerstand an der Friedrich-Schiller-Universität 1945–1989," in *Vergangenheitsklärung an der Friedrich-Schiller-Universität Jena*, 32–3.

27. Tilo Schieck, "Aufarbeitung aus studentischer Sicht," ibid., 225, 229.

28. The historian Theodor Neubauer (1890–1945) played a leading role in antifascist resistance in Thuringia. He was executed by the Nazis in 1945.

29. Fukuyama, "The End of History?" 28.

CONTRIBUTORS

Reinhard Alter was associate professor in the Department of German at the University of Western Australia. He was head of the department in 1986–90 and 1992–94. His research was in the area of continuity and change in modern German history and culture. Publications include books on Gottfried Benn (*Gottfried Benn. The Artist and Politics 1910–1934*, Bern, Frankfurt, and Munich, 1976) and Heinrich Mann (*Die bereinigte Moderne. Utopie und Wirklichkeit in Heinrich Manns "Untertan" und politischer Publizistik zwischen Kaiserreich und Drittem Reich*, Tübingen, 1995). He died in 1996.

Hans-Georg Betz is assistant professor of European studies in the Paul Nitze School of Advanced International Studies, Johns Hopkins University, Washington, DC. His publications are on new social movements in the Federal Republic, including *Postmodern Politics in Germany: The Politics of Resentment*, New York, 1991, and *Radical Right-Wing Populism in Western Europe*, London, 1994.

Mary Fulbrook, a graduate of Cambridge and Harvard, is professor of German history at University College, London. Her books include *Piety and Politics: Religion and the Rise of Absolutism in England, Wuerttemberg and Prussia; A Concise History of Germany; Germany 1918–1990: The Divided Nation; The Two Germanies, 1945–1990: Problems of Interpretation; Anatomy of a Dictatorship: Inside the GDR, 1949–89; National Histories and European History* (editor); and *Citizenship, Nationality and Migration in Europe* (editor with David Cesarani).

Siegfried Hoyer was a student and then a staff member (from 1966) and finally a professor (from 1977) at the University of Leipzig in the GDR. He became head of the History Department there in 1990. His main fields of research are religious movements in the later Middle Ages, the Reformation period, and university history. His books include *Der deutsche Bauernkrieg 1524/26*, 5th ed., Berlin, 1987; *Thomas*

289

Müntzer, Schriften, liturgische Texte und Briefe, Leipzig, 1989; and *Alma Mater Lipsiensis. Die Geschichte der Karl-Marx-Universität Leipzig 1409–1983*, Leipzig, 1984 (coauthor).

Konrad Jarausch is Lurcy Professor of History at the University of North Carolina at Chapel Hill. Trained as a diplomatic and political historian, his interests have turned to social history, quantitative methods, and historiography. His books include *Students, Society and Politics in Imperial Germany: The Rise of Academic Illiberalism*, Princeton, 1983; *The Unfree Professions: German Lawyers, Teachers, and Engineers, 1900–1950*, New York, 1990; and *The Rush to German Unity*, New York, 1994.

Reinhard Kühnl is professor of political science at the University of Marburg. He is the author of many publications on the history of the Weimar Republic, National Socialism, theories of fascism, and neofascism in the Federal Republic. His books include *Deutschland zwischen Demokratie und Faschismus*, Hamburg, 1969; *Faschismustheorien*, Hamburg, 1979; and *Der Historikerstreit*, Cologne, 1987.

Hermann Kurthen received his PhD from the Freie Universität Berlin, was German Academic Exchange Service (DAAD) associate professor at the University of North Carolina at Chapel Hill, and is presently a research fellow of the German Marshall Fund of the United States. He published *Ausländerbeschäftigung in der Krise?* Berlin, 1989, and has coauthored books and contributed papers to several edited volumes, refereed journals, and other publications in Germany, Italy, the United States, and Canada about international comparative labor migration, ethnicity, welfare and stratification, antidiscrimination policies, political correctness, and multiculturalism. Currently he is completing a book titled *Antisemitism and Xenophobia in Germany After Unification*.

Claus Leggewie is professor of political science at the University of Gießen, and he currently holds the Max Weber Chair in the Center for European Studies at New York University. He has published numerous works on the New Right in Germany, including *Die Republikaner*, Berlin, 1989, and *Druck von rechts*, Beck, 1993. His latest book, which appeared in 1995, is titled *Die 89er*.

Peter Monteath is senior lecturer in the Department of German Studies at the University of Adelaide. His main research interests are in the areas of Holocaust history and the Spanish Civil War. Books include *Zur Spanienkriegsliteratur. Die Literatur des Dritten Reiches zum Spanischen Bürgerkrieg*, Frankfurt, 1986; *Writing the Good Fight: Political Commitment in the International Literature of the Spanish Civil War*, Westport, 1994.

John Moses is associate professor of history at the University of Queensland. He was educated in Munich and Erlangen, and his publications span a wide range of interests, including German labor history, German historiography (in particular, the Fischer controversy), German colonialism in the Pacific, and, in more recent years, *Deutschtumspolitik* in Australia. He is currently working on the nexus between religion and nationalism in modern Germany and the rise and fall of German communism.

Greg Munro lectures in European history at the Australian Catholic University in Brisbane. His principal area of research is German church history, 1914 to 1945.

Lutz Niethammer was professor of history at Hagen until 1991, when he accepted a chair at the University of Jena. His publications are on continuities and discontinuities from the Third Reich to the Federal Republic of Germany, social history, and oral history. Books include *Bürgerliche Gesellschaft in Deutschland*, Frankfurt, 1990, and *Posthistoire: Has History Come to an End?* London, 1992.

Wolfang Ruge, emeritus professor, was born in Berlin in 1917, immigrated to the Soviet Union, and studied history in Moscow and Sverdlovsk. From 1956 to 1983, he worked at the Historical Institute in the Academy of Sciences in the GDR and became director of the research team working on the Weimar Republic. He is the author of a number of large-scale works on the Weimar Republic and of biographies of Erzberger, Stresemann, and Hindenburg. He has published on the November 1918 revolution in Germany, the history of the German Communist Party, and German foreign policy between the wars. His latest book is titled *Stalinismus—eine Sackgasse im Labyrinth der Geschichte*.

Hermann Weber, emeritus professor at the University of Mannheim and coeditor of the *Jahrbuch für Historische Kommunismusforschung*, is a leading authority on the history of the German Democratic Republic. His books include *DDR. Grundriß der Geschichte 1945–1976*, Hannover, 1976; *Kleine Geschichte der DDR*, Cologne, 1980; and *Die SED nach Ulbricht*, Cologne, 1974. He was appointed a member of the Commission of Inquiry established by the German *Bundestag* to investigate the history of the Socialist Unity Party in the GDR.

INDEX